CW01238360

WHITEHALL HISTORIES: NAVAL STAFF HISTORIES
Series Editor: Capt. Christopher Page
ISSN: 1471-0757

NAVAL OPERATIONS OF THE CAMPAIGN IN NORWAY

NAVAL STAFF HISTORIES
Series Editor: Capt. Christopher Page
ISSN: 1471-0757

Naval Staff Histories were produced after the Second World War in order to provide as full an account of the various actions and operations as was possible at the time. In some cases the Histories were based on earlier Battle Summaries written much sooner after the event, and designed to provide more immediate assessments. The target audience for these Naval Staff Histories was largely serving officers; some of the volumes were originally classified, not to restrict their distribution but to allow the writers to be as candid as possible. These histories have been in the Public Record Office for some time, and are here published for the first time.

The Evacuation from Dunkirk: 'Operation Dynamo', 26 May–4 June 1940
Edited and with a preface by W. J. R. Gardner

Naval Operations of the Campaign in Norway, April–June 1940
Edited and with a preface by David Brown

NAVAL OPERATIONS OF THE CAMPAIGN IN NORWAY
April–June 1940

Edited and with a Preface by
DAVID BROWN
Naval Historical Branch, Ministry of Defence, London

FRANK CASS
LONDON · PORTLAND, OR

First published in 2000 in Great Britain by
FRANK CASS PUBLISHERS
Newbury House, 900 Eastern Avenue
London, IG2 7HH

and in the United States of America by
FRANK CASS PUBLISHERS
c/o ISBS, 5804 N.E. Hassalo Street
Portland, Oregon, 97213-3644

Website: www.frankcass.com

© Crown Copyright 2000

British Library Cataloguing in Publication Data

Naval operations of the campaign in Norway, April–June
　　1940. – (Naval staff histories)
　　1. Great Britain. Royal Navy – History – World War,
　　1939–1945　2. World War, 1939–1945 – Campaigns – Norway
　　3. World War, 1939–1945 – Naval operations, British
　　I. Brown, David, 1938 Sept. 13–
　　940.5'45941

ISBN 0-7146-5119-2 (cloth)
ISSN 1471-0757

Library of Congress Cataloging-in-Publication Data

Naval operations of the campaign in Norway, April–June 1940 / edited and with a preface by David Brown.
　　p. cm. – (Whitehall histories, Naval Staff histories)
　Originally published in 1951 as Confidential book number 3305 and deposited in the Public Record Office. With new introd.
　Includes bibliographical references and index.
　ISBN 0-7146-5119-2.
　　1. World War, 1939–1945–Campaigns–Norway. 2. World War, 1939–1945 – Naval operations, British. I. Brown, David, 1938– II. Great Britain. Naval Staff. III. Series.

D763.N6 N38 2000
940.54'2181–dc21   00-031708

*Published on behalf of the Whitehall History Publishing Consortium.
Applications to reproduce Crown copyright protected material in this publication should be submitted in writing to: HMSO, Copyright Unit, St Clements House, 2–16 Colegate, Norwich NR3 1BQ. Fax: 01603 723000.
E-mail: copyright@hmso.gov.uk*

Typeset by Regent Typesetting, London
Printed in Great Britain by
Bookcraft (Bath) Ltd, Midsomer Norton, Somerset

CONTENTS

List of Illustrations	vii
Foreword by Admiral Sir Michael Boyce, the First Sea Lord	ix
Preface to the New Edition by David Brown	xi
Addendum to Sources	xvii
Naval Operations of the Campaign in Norway:	[i]
Foreword	[iii]
Contents	[iv]
Appendices	[vii]
Plans	[viii]
Sources	[ix]
Abbreviations	[x]
Introduction	1
Chapter I: Preliminary Events	5
Chapter II: German Invasion of Norway	18
Chapter III: The Allied Counter Offensive and General Employment of Naval Forces	51
Chapter IV: The Landings at Namsos	70
Chapter V: The Landings at Aandalsnes, Aalesund and Molde	78
Chapter VI: The Withdrawal from Central Norway	88
Chapter VII: The Expedition to Narvik: Phase I (14 April–7 May)	98
Chapter VIII: Operations at Bodo, Mo and Mosjoen	104
Chapter IX: The Expedition to Narvik: Phase II (7–28 May)	110
Chapter X: The Retreat from Northern Norway	120
Chapter XI: Comment and Reflections	134

CONTENTS

Appendix A: Allied Warships Employed in Connection with Operations in Norway, April–June 1940, with Main Armament and Commanding Officers	143
Appendix B: German Warships Mentioned in Narrative, with Main Armament, Etc.	151
Appendix C(1): Disposition of the Home Fleet, Noon, 9 April	154
Appendix C(2): Dispositions during the Retreat from Central Norway, 30 April–3 May	155
Appendix C(3): Dispositions, 8 June	156
Appendix C(4): Dispositions of Allied Submarines during British Minelaying and German Invasion of Norway, 8–9 April	157
Appendix D: Similarity of German Silhouettes	158
Appendix E: Summary of Air Attacks on HMS *Suffolk* – 17 April 1940	159
Appendix F: HMS *Furious*	161
Appendix G: Some Extracts of General Auchinleck's Dispatch, Dated 19 June 1940	162
Appendix H: Naval Losses and Damage (Allied and German)	164
Index	169

LIST OF ILLUSTRATIONS

Between pages 4 and 5.

1. The sloop HMS *Bittern*, damaged aft by a bomb off Namos. She had to be sunk by the British on 30 April 1940.
2. HMS *Suffolk* at Scapa Flow, 18 April, having limped home with severe bomb damage.
3. Royal Navy *Skuas*. Photo taken August 1940.
4. German Destroyer *Erich Giese* burning in Ofot fjord, 2nd Battle of Narvik, 13 April 1940.
5. Troops of the 61st Division at boat stations on board *Oronsay*, prior to departure for Norway, 20 or 21 April 1940; HMS *Fury* passing.
6. With the evacuation convoy off Namsos, 3 May 1940. The smoke on the horizon is from the destroyer HMS *Afridi*, sunk by bombs.
7. HMS *Escort* seen from a troopship, probably Gourock, late May 1940.
8. Troops man an anti-aircraft gun at Harstad fjord, end of May 1940. *Effingham* is the vessel above the gun barrel.
9. Herjangs fjord bombed, probably 9 May, *Aurora* under attack; see also Figure 12.
10. Troopship *Mashobra*, bombed 25 May at Harstad, subsequently sunk by the Royal Navy prior to the evacuation. Note hole in side and troops being taken off. The *Vindictive* is in the background. See also Figure 16.
11. Flag Officer Narvik, Admiral of the Fleet Lord Cork and Orrery, and General Auchinleck on the bridge of HMS *Cairo* during the bombardment before the landings at Narvik, 28 May 1940.
12. Damaged petrol tanker being towed by trawlers in Herjangs fjord. Again, probably 9 May; see also Figure 9.
13. The destroyer HMS *Eskimo*, torpedoed 13 April 1940. She got home and was rebuilt. Finally disposed of in 1949.
14. The cruiser HMS *Effingham* in a Norwegian fjord, shortly before her loss by grounding on 17 May 1940.
15. Bomb damage, HMS *Cairo*, sustained 27 May 1940.
16. HMS *Vindictive* under attack, probably 25 May 1940. HMT *Mashobra* in foreground. Eight bombs fell close to *Vindictive* but no damage resulted. See also Figure 10.
17. Troopship *Chobry* escorted by a Tribal-class destroyer, possibly 16 or 17 April 1940.
18. Bren-gun carriers on board *Effingham*, prior to the assault on Bodo, 17 May 1940.

All prints reproduced by permission of the Imperial War Museum, London.

Foreword by Admiral Sir Michael Boyce GCB OBE ADC
First Sea Lord and Chief of Naval Staff

Sixty years on since Germany's momentous invasion of Norway and the abortive attempt by the Allies to prevent it, this is a fitting anniversary for re-publication of the Naval Staff History to be made available to a wider audience. This campaign took place early in the War, and it is fair to say that many lessons were learned during its conduct. Perhaps chief among them was the demonstrated need for a fully-integrated command system to cope with joint and combined operations on this scale, backed up by clear political direction. Even today, we find that the achievement of these vital aims cannot be taken for granted, a fact recognized in the recent Strategic Defence Review in which a high priority was placed on improving our ability to conduct joint operations – operations in which the maritime contribution is likely to be every bit as crucial as it was in the past.

This History concerns itself mainly with the naval aspects of the events and, notwithstanding the widely held view that the Norwegian Campaign was a ramshackle disaster, the Royal Navy has much to be proud of: transporting and then evacuating the ground troops; the provision of anti-aircraft defences in critical areas; the delivery of fighter aircraft into theatre; and the serious damage inflicted on the German Navy in Norwegian waters which left them with no major unit fit for sea, and virtually halved their destroyer force.

Based on a Battle Summary produced very soon after the events had occurred, for internal use within the Admiralty, I whole-heartedly commend this account which is endowed with an immediacy and candour that the casual reader and serious researcher alike will find to be of excellent value.

Ministry of Defence
March 2000

PREFACE TO THE NEW EDITION

The Norwegian campaign of 1940 is often held up as an example of how to get most things wrong when planning and conducting a military operation, and in many ways this perception is valid: all of Germany's strategic aims were fulfilled, and the British were forced to conduct an ignominious evacuation. Notwithstanding the many mistakes and misconceptions, there was much from a naval perspective that was well done. This Naval Staff History, formerly Confidential Book number 3305(2) and published in 1951, was based on a Battle Summary written soon after the events, and provides a dispassionate Royal Navy view of the campaign. Later evidence has provided a more complete account of the high-level decision-making, both political and military, which had such a major bearing on the operations. However, is not the purpose of this preface to provide a detailed modern reappraisal of the work, but rather to set out a few ideas which may interest the new reader.

The Implications of Sea Control and Inshore Operations

Having decided on the invasion of Norway, to achieve their operational aim, the swift seizure of key ports and centres of communication, the Germans needed temporary local sea control, which could only be guaranteed by surprise. They lost the latter, but, against all odds and logic, retained just enough of the former to succeed, owing to a combination of the misuse of intelligence in the Admiralty, and disbelief about German intentions in the Norwegian Störting, many of whose members were unwilling to accept the many ominous indications. British naval intelligence was never as complete again in this campaign as it had been on the eve of the landings, and maritime supremacy was such that sea control was rapidly gained in the areas in which the Allied navies had to operate.

In addition, the Allied navies' sea-denial operations outside the area of sea control were effective, hastening the departure of the surviving German Navy units and preventing the use of ships larger than coasters and fishing vessels for reinforcement and resupply of the west coast. This was achieved almost entirely by submarines and surface forces – the only sizeable enemy ships to be sunk by air attack were victims of Royal Navy dive bombers.

Fjords can be traps or havens. On the basis of German experience during the Norwegian Campaign, they are more likely to be the latter. In the first five days of the campaign, two cruisers and 11 destroyers were lost to naval action inshore, ambushed by coastal defences and, at Narvik, penned in by damage, lack of fuel and loss of sea control. Mines later added to the losses.

The Allied ships were never trapped by enemy action – they were free to come and go, but not as they pleased, for they were trapped by the task. Ships designed to operate on the high seas were employed in narrow waters, with navigational hazards and variable, sometimes freakish, weather presenting sufficient hazard even without the enemy. None of the ports or anchorages provided a natural haven for long. German tactical common sense indicated which fjords were most likely to be in use, and confirmation was just a matter of time. Thereafter, and too often, Allied ships had neither the sea-room nor the warning time to deploy into an optimal air-defence formation or to take evasive action.

Readiness and Availability

There is an age-old naval formula on sailing – 'Ready in all respects for sea and war'. The Royal Navy and the other services have been brought up on the philosophy that the next war will have to be fought with existing equipment, at least in the early stages. This was certainly the case in Norway, where the Navy fought a new type of war under the old rules. In doing so, under traditional circumstances, there is no doubt that the Royal Navy lived up to its traditions.

But where tradition failed, the Navy had to adapt. The ships of the Fleet had not been designed to operate close inshore against a heavy scale of air opposition, but such was the need of the Army, and the lack of anti-aircraft artillery ashore, they were obliged to stand their ground, specialist ships sacrificing their mobility by acting as stationary anti-aircraft (AA) guard ships off otherwise unguarded harbours. Repeatedly, the AA cruisers and sloops expended all their AA ammunition in a single day, and had to be withdrawn to replenish, but in every case they were replaced and no major supply port was left undefended. These sitting ducks gave a good account of themselves, but at the cost of two of them sunk and three badly damaged in the process.

Stretch was a serious difficulty during the Narvik campaign. By 15 May, no fewer than seven separate locations in the immediate area were being served by the Navy, in the sense that men and materials were being delivered or defended, besides two naval anchorages. Close by, Bodo and Mo, blocking the overland advance of the German relieving forces, also required resupply by sea.

Even when the full strength of the Home Fleet's cruisers and destroyers had been available to draw on, the Navy was feeling the strain. This became even more marked as the North Sea and Channel became active naval theatres in the wake of the simultaneous collapse of the Dutch Army and the German breakthrough on the Meuse; and the warlike noises from Italy obliged the government to despatch 20 destroyers and AA ships to the Mediterranean. Narvik was left with no more than the bare naval essentials and the capital ships of the Home Fleet were unable to proceed to sea for lack of escorts until the end of the month.

PREFACE TO THE NEW EDITION

Leadership

Given units that are ready in all respects, the key to success becomes leadership – not merely the sustenance of morale, or even the ability to take decisions which any officer worth his salt should exercise, but the knack of taking the right decision under pressure and of adapting rapidly to the situation. War, particularly at sea, does not spare those who make mistakes, and the Captain of *Glorious* paid for his with his life, and those of nearly all his ship's company. Ironically, the loss of *Glorious* and her escorts, and the damage inflicted by *Acasta* on *Scharnhorst,* probably averted an even more serious disaster that would have ensued had the German battlecruisers found the returning troop-laden convoys.

Single-Service Attitudes

One lesson from this campaign is that navies, armies, air forces and allies need to be aware of each other's problems and not take one another for granted. For example, there must be a recognition of the relationship between the length and intensity of a land campaign, and the consequent attrition in the supporting services, in this case the Royal Navy and Royal Air Force. The solutions are, of course, improved communications, joint and combined training and headquarters, and whatever seminars, conferences and symposia are necessary to establish mutual comprehension. It is too easy to forget that in spring 1940, an Admiral's staff afloat seldom comprised more than a flag lieutenant and a secretary; the specialists were provided from the officers of his flagship, who could not be spared from their routine duties for extended liaison visits. The ideal joint-force headquarters for an amphibious operation was soon recognized in the Second World War to be a ship specially fitted out for (and dedicated to), the purpose, where military, naval and air staffs could plan side by side, undistracted by actual fighting.

Air Power in the Campaign

The importance of air power was well understood by the Royal Navy long before April 1940. Indeed, the first offensive counter-air options undertaken by British air forces were the Naval Air Service attacks on the Zeppelin assembly sheds and bases. The offensive potential of aircraft was fully appreciated and recognized by the inclusion of a carrier in the first Home Fleet response to the German invasion of Norway, by the recall of two carriers from the Mediterranean, and by the active presence offshore of an aircraft carrier on 37 out of the 62 days the campaign lasted. The offensive potential of these ships was seldom realised, but it was certainly understood by the Germans, who targeted the carriers above all others (although they never sank one by air attack). The effectiveness of the Fleet's own air power off Norway was in defence. It is of interest that, in the days when carriers equipped with fighter aircraft were in the area six Allied vessels were sunk or damaged. During their absences for refuelling and collecting more aircraft and stores, the total was 11.

The crucial element in the importance of air power during this campaign, however, is in the use the Germans made of it. British ships were operating against a modern air force outside the umbrella of the Royal Air Force, and no one was yet familiar with the flexibility of the Luftwaffe's tactical units, with their system of 'commando-servicing' and massive airborne logistic support, which could make a recently captured airfield fully operational within a couple of days. The importance of air power, as with any other military power, lies in the way that it is used, and for the campaign in Norway, as in the Low Countries and France, the Luftwaffe had not just the numbers, but the vision as well.

Command and Control

Command and Control by its very nature involves personal relationships, and, no matter how obvious the various lines of demarcation may be between the parties, the frequent use of the intuition which comes from long acquaintance.

The Ministerial Committee on Military Coordination appointed Admiral of the Fleet the Earl of Cork and Orrery as combined Commander-in-Chief for 'Operation Rupert', and he was dispatched with verbal instructions from the Chairman of the Committee, the First Lord of the Admiralty, Winston Churchill. The Admiral's original remit was to seize Narvik as quickly as possible, but on arrival he was told by the Admiralty not to act except in concert with his two-star military deputy; the latter's written orders from the Chief of the Imperial General Staff (CIGS) stated that he was not to land in the face of serious opposition until sufficient troops had arrived, but with the rider that 'boldness is required'. As a consequence, whatever their personal relations and differences of background, character and rank, Cork and Orrery and Major-General Mackesy had little chance of succeeding with such contradictory and confusing instructions.

Churchill subsequently commented on the reluctance of naval officers to give orders to subordinate commanders of other services, but he was ill-placed to do so, for his framing of the signal restraining Cork and Orrery left the Admiral little scope for exercising broad command authority: 'we think it imperative that you and the General [i.e. Mackesy] should be together and act together and that no attack should be made except in concert'.

By the time he made his criticisms of the perceived naval command style, of course, Churchill was Prime Minister and had wider concerns, which perhaps led him to forget his mishandling of intelligence and misunderstanding of priorities at the beginning of the campaign and the fact that British forces had thereby been worsted by the Germans.

Reputations and Misconceptions

Individually, most of the commanding officers of the ships involved in the campaign did well thereafter. At the time, the naval establishment did not consider that the Royal Navy had under-performed off Norway. In any case, within a fortnight of the end of the campaign, national survival was at stake; British fortunes continued to decline, then, just when there was a glimmer of light in the autumn of 1941, they

PREFACE TO THE NEW EDITION

started another slide when the Japanese joined in the war. There was a need to absorb and recognize the lessons of Norway, rich and plentiful, before the amphibious return could begin, but there was not the leisure in wartime for lengthy recriminations. These came after the peace, with the inevitable hunt for scapegoats, and when politicians started to compile their self-exculpatory memoirs, and returned citizen-warriors wrote theirs from a relatively narrow, and sometimes very subjective, viewpoint. From these emerged the myth of 'the disastrous Norwegian campaign'. It is hoped that the publication of this Naval Staff History will provide a more contemporary perspective, and that new readers will come to the same conclusion, that, notwithstanding the mistakes inherent in war, the 'Royal Navy in particular can be proud of its share in the venture'.

DAVID BROWN
Former Head of Naval Historical Branch, Ministry of Defence
March 2000

ADDENDUM TO SOURCES

The original list of sources uses the old numbering system. As a guide to further research, the existing PRO references set out below embrace the documents from the original list, where they still exist.

War Diaries:

Home Fleet	ADM 199/361
Battle Cruiser Squadron	ADM 199/379
1st Cruiser Squadron	ADM 199/388
2nd Cruiser Squadron	ADM 199/379
18th Cruiser Squadron	ADM 199/385
20th Cruiser Squadron (AA Ships)	ADM 199/378

Dispatches

Home Fleet	ADM 199/393
Flag Officer, Narvik	ADM 199/485
Lt-Gen Auchinleck & Maj-Gen Mackesy Lt-Gen Massy	ADM 199/485

Reports of Proceedings

VA Cunningham	ADM 199/477
VA Edward-Collins	ADM 199/476, /475, /477
VA Wells	ADM 199/479, /480
VA Whitworth	ADM 199/473, /474
RA Vivian	ADM 199/475, /476
Captain Denny	ADM 199/477
Lt-Col Simpson, RM	ADM 199/482
Black Swan	ADM 199/475, /476
Cairo	ADM 199/478
Furious	ADM 199/479
Glasgow	ADM 199/474, /477
Hotspur	ADM 199/473
Janus	ADM 199/477
Nubian	ADM 199/475
Suffolk	ADM 199/475

ADDENDUM TO SOURCES

Logs of various ships   Class ADM 53

Pink Lists, April 1940	ADM 187/7
Report of BoI: Loss of HMS *Glorious*	ADM 178/201
BR 1738: The War at Sea, Vol 1	ADM 199/2377
BR 1840: (1): The German Campaign in Norway	ADM 234/427
BR 642G. Summary of German Warships: January 1942 (silhouettes)	ADM 234/136
Staff History, Submarines (draft)	ADM 234/380

Published Works

Navy Lists, April–June 1940
House of Commons Debates, Vol 360
The Second World War – The Rt Hon W S Churchill, OM, CH, PC, MP
Assault from the Sea – RAdm L E H Maund, CBE
I Saw it Happen in Norway – Carl J Hambro

RESTRICTED

~~CONFIDENTIAL~~ *Attention is called to the penalties attaching to any infraction of the Official Secrets Acts*

B.R. 1736 (46)
~~C.B. 3305 (2)~~

NAVAL STAFF HISTORY
SECOND WORLD WAR

Battle Summary No. 17

NAVAL OPERATIONS OF THE CAMPAIGN IN NORWAY

APRIL — JUNE 1940

B.R. 1736 (10) dated 1943 and B.R. 1736 (10) (1) dated 1947 are hereby superseded and all copies are to be destroyed in accordance with B.R. 1

This book is based on information available up to and including March 1950

T.S.D. 57/50

HISTORICAL SECTION
NAVAL STAFF
ADMIRALTY

Foreword

BATTLE SUMMARY No. 17, 'The Conjunct Expeditions to Norway', was originally written in 1942. It was then, as its title implies, mainly concerned with the landings and inshore operations, with the result that the interesting and instructive Fleet operations of the campaign were not adequately dealt with. Much information about enemy plans and movements, too, has become available from the documents captured at the end of the war.

In the present edition, re-named 'Naval Operations of the Campaign in Norway', emphasis has been laid on the deep sea operations rather than on the amphibious operations on the Norwegian coast. Chapters I and II, dealing with the operations of the Home Fleet from the time of the initial German landings to the arrival in Norway of the Allied expeditionary forces, and Chapter III, dealing with the Allied plans and the general employment of naval forces during the campaign, have been entirely re-written.

In Chapters IV to X, tracing the individual fortunes of the various landings and withdrawals, the original version has been adhered to as closely as possible, but it has been amplified, and where necessary amended in the light of information derived from German and other sources which have now become available; and the subject matter has been re-arranged, in order to conform with chronology.

Chapter XI—Comment and Reflections—is entirely new.

Plans have been produced illustrating initial submarine and U-boat dispositions, and the approximate movements of surface forces during the opening phase of the campaign and the final withdrawal from Narvik.

March, 1950

Contents

		Page
Foreword		iii
Introduction		1

CHAPTER I
Preliminary Events

1.	German plan of invasion	5
2.	The British Minefield and Plan R.4	8
3.	Preparations and movements, 4th–7th April 1940	9
4.	German Fleet reported at sea, 7th April	9
5.	First enemy contact : Loss of H.M.S. *Glowworm*, 8th April	12
6.	The sinking of S.S. *Rio de Janeiro*	13
7.	Vice-Admiral Whitworth's movements, 8th April	13
8.	Movements of Commander-in-Chief, H.F., 8th April	14

CHAPTER II
German Invasion of Norway

9.	The German landings, 9th April, 1940	18
10.	Admiral Whitworth's encounter with the *Gneisenau* and *Scharnhorst*, 9th April	19
11.	British dispositions, Vest Fjord area, 9th April	21
12.	Movements of Commander-in-Chief, H.F., 9th April	22
13.	First Battle of Narvik, 10th April	26
14.	Operations in Vest Fjord area, 10th–12th April	29
15.	Movements of Commander-in-Chief, H.F., 10th–12th April	32
16.	Movements of German naval forces, 9th–13th April	34
17.	*Furious* aircraft attack at Narvik, 12th April	35
18.	Second Battle of Narvik, 13th April	36
19.	Cruiser operations, 10th–14th April	42
20.	Submarine activities, 4th–14th April	45
21.	General situation, 15th April	47

CHAPTER III
The Allied Counter Offensive and General Employment of Naval Forces

22.	Plans and policy	51
23.	Question of direct attack on Trondheim	53
24.	General employment of Home Fleet, April–June, 1940	57
25.	Carrier and F.A.A. operations	59
26.	Employment of A.A. cruisers and sloops	62
27.	A/S trawlers on Norwegian coast	63
28.	The southern area : surface operations	64
29.	The southern area ; submarine activities	67
30.	The conjunct expeditions	68

CONTENTS

CHAPTER IV
The Landings at Namsos

		Page
31.	Operation Henry	70
32.	Operation Maurice : first landings, 16th–17th April	71
33.	Naval movements and landing of French, 17th–20th April	74
34.	German air attacks on Namsos	75
35.	Final reinforcements, Namsos	76

CHAPTER V
The Landings at Aandalsnes, Aalesund and Molde

36.	Operation Primrose	78
37.	Operation Sickle : first landings, 18th–19th April	81
38.	Sickle reinforcements	83
39.	Situation on shore, 27th–28th April	86

CHAPTER VI
The Withdrawal from Central Norway

40.	Decision to withdraw, 28th April	88
41.	Plan of evacuation	88
42.	Retreat from Aandalsnes, Molde and Aalesund	90
43.	Retreat from Namsos	93

CHAPTER VII
The Expedition to Narvik : Phase I
14th April–7th May

44.	Inception of Operation Rupert	98
45.	Opening moves : conflicting instructions	98
46.	Operations in Ofot Fjord, 16th–26th April	101
47.	Changes in Squadron : Army reinforcements	102

CHAPTER VIII
Operations at Bodo, Mo and Mosjoen

48.	Object of operations	104
49.	The first landings	104
50.	Area placed under the Narvik Command	105
51.	German landing at Hemnes	106
52.	Mo and Bodo reinforced	107
53.	Loss of the *Chrobry* and H.M.S. *Effingham*	108

CHAPTER IX
The Expedition to Narvik : Phase II
7th–28th May

54.	Development of Base	110
55.	Landing at Bjerkvik	112
56.	Preparations for assault on Narvik	115
57.	Plan of operations	116
58.	The capture of Narvik	118

CONTENTS

CHAPTER X
The Retreat from Northern Norway

		Page
59.	The decision to withdraw	120
60.	Withdrawal from Mo and Bodo	121
61.	Plan of general withdrawal	122
62.	The withdrawal	124
63.	The German naval sortie (Operation Juno)	127
64.	The sinking of H.M.S. *Glorious*, *Ardent* and *Acasta*, 8th June	128
65.	British reactions, 9th June	129
66.	Movements of Commander-in-Chief, Home Fleet, 9th–15th June	131

CHAPTER XI
Comment and Reflections

		Page
67.	The Commander-in-Chief, Home Fleet's remarks	134
68.	System of Command	135
69.	The importance of wireless silence	136
70.	Tactical loading of expeditionary forces	138
71.	Risks and chances	138
72.	The principles of war as applied in the campaign	139
73.	Conclusion	141

Index .. 169

APPENDICES

A. Allied warships employed in connection with operations in Norway, with main armament and Commanding Officers
A (1) A/S trawlers employed on Norwegian coast
A (2) Naval Commands in Norway
B. German warships, with main armament
C (1) Disposition of Home Fleet, Noon 9th April 1940
C (2) Dispositions during retreat from Central Norway
C (3) Dispositions during retreat from Northern Norway, 8th June 1940
C (4) Dispositions of Allied submarines, 8th–9th April 1940
D. Similarity of German ship silhouettes
E. Summary of air attacks on H.M.S. *Suffolk*, 17th April 1940
F. H.M.S. *Furious* : statistics of operations, 11th–24th April 1940
G. Some extracts from General Auchinleck's despatch, dated 19th June 1940
H. Naval losses and damage (Allied and German)

PLANS

1. Theatre of Operations: Principal Naval events of campaign
2. Theatre of Operations: Naval operations, 7th–Noon 9th April 1940
3. Theatre of Operations: Naval operations, Noon 9th–Noon 11th April
4. Theatre of Operations: Naval operations, Noon 11th–Noon 13th April
5. Theatre of Operations: Naval operations, Noon 13th–Noon 15th April
6. Theatre of Operations: Situation, 15th April 1940
7. Allied submarine dispositions
8. German submarine dispositions, 9th April 1940
9. Harstad to Narvik: 1st Battle of Narvik
10. Harstad to Narvik: 2nd Battle of Narvik
11. Reference chart: The Trondheim area, Kongsmo to Stadtlandet
12. Reference chart: The Narvik Area, Tromso to Mosjoen
13. Reference chart: Oslo Fjord
14. Reference chart: Harstad to Narvik (Rupert operations)
15. Theatre of Operations: Withdrawal from Narvik and loss of the *Glorious*, 8th–9th June 1940.
16. Theatre of Operations: Naval operations, 10th–13th June 1940

SOURCES

War Diaries

Home Fleet	T.S.D.4144, 4586–4589/40
Battle Cruiser Squadron	T.S.D.4286/40
1st Cruiser Squadron	T.S.D.4111, 4386–4389/40
2nd Cruiser Squadron	T.S.D.4140, 4411/40
18th Cruiser Squadron	T.S.D.4113, 4137/40
20th Cruiser Squadron (A.A. Ships).	T.S.D.5261–5263/40

Dispatches

Home Fleet	M.0166/41
Flag Officer, Narvik	M.014100/40
Lt.-General Auchinleck and Maj.-General Mackesy.	017624/40
Lt.-General Massy	

Reports of Proceedings

Vice-Adm. Cunningham	M.012225/40
Vice-Adm. Edward-Collins	M.08137, 08161, 08953/40
Vice-Adm. Wells	M.011871, 015561/40 and A.0486/40
Vice-Adm. Whitworth	M.08336, 010710/40
Rear-Adm. Vivian	M.08104, 010531/40
Captain Denny	M.08602, 08753, 08837/40
Lieut.-Col. Simpson, R.M.	M.010909, 011169/40
Black Swan	M.09020, 010850/40
Cairo	010964A/40
Furious	08952/40
Glasgow	07744, 08807/40
Hotspur	08362/40
Janus	M.09349/40
Nubian	M.08110/40
Suffolk	M.07169, 08361/40

Logs of various ships
Historical Section, T.S.D./H.S., War Diary (signals)
" Pink " Lists, April 1940
Navy Lists, April–June 1940
Report of Board of Enquiry : Loss of H.M.S. *Glorious*
Home Fleet Narrative
B.R. 1738.   The War at Sea, Vol. I
B.R. 1806 (47).   Naval War Manual, 1947
B.R. 1840 (1).   The German Campaign in Norway
G.H.S.4.   German Surface Ships : Policy and Operations
U-Boat Operations, Vol. I, 1939–45
German Naval Staff War Diary
B.R. 642G.   Summary of German Warships, January 1942 (silhouettes)
Naval Air Warfare Development (draft)
Staff History, Submarines (draft)
House of Commons Debates, Vol. 360.
' The Second World War '—The Rt. Hon. Winston S. Churchill, O.M., C.H., P.C., M.P.
' Assault from the Sea '—Rear-Admiral L. E. H. Maund, C.B.E.
' I Saw it Happen in Norway '—Carl J. Hambro.

ABBREVIATIONS

A.A.	Anti-aircraft.
A/S	Anti-submarine.
A.S.I.S.	Ammunition Store Issuing Ship.
A.T.	Admiralty telegram.
A.C.N.S.	Assistant Chief of Naval Staff.
C.O.	Commanding Officer.
C.S.	Cruiser Squadron.
D.C.N.S.	Deputy Chief of Naval Staff.
M.N.B.D.O.	Mobile Naval Base Defence Organisation.
O.R.P.	Polish Ship.
S.N.O.	Senior Naval Officer.
T.S.D.S.	Two-speed destroyer sweep.

TIME

Zone minus 1 (B.S.T.) is used throughout.

Introduction

ON THE 9th April 1940 Germany invaded Denmark and Norway. Denmark fell in a day and within 48 hours all the airfields and the principal seaports in Norway were in the hands of the invaders. No warning had been given to her victims, though rumours and various pieces of intelligence had pointed to some such development; still less did a *casus belli* exist, especially with Norway, with whom, indeed, there was a traditional friendship of many years standing. The treachery of the proceeding was only equalled by its success.

From the start it was apparent that little could be done by the Allies in the face of German air superiority in the south; but expeditions were hastily organised in an attempt to dislodge them from central and northern Norway. The former speedily failed; but the northern expedition had more success and eventually re-took Narvik. By that time, however, events elsewhere had moved too swiftly; the Low Countries had been overrun, France, beaten to her knees, was about to sue for armistice, and to many invasion seemed to stare the United Kingdom in the face.[1] The decision was taken to abandon Norway.

This battle summary deals with the naval side of the operations of the campaign in Norway. The services of the land and air forces are only touched on in it so far as is necessary to explain the naval movements and operations.

The campaign fell into two well-defined phases, viz.:—

Phase 1

From 7th April, when German invasion forces were first reported at sea, to 14th April, when the Allied counter-offensive in Norway was about to develop. During this period the Allied naval effort was chiefly concentrated on bringing to action the enemy naval forces employed on the operation. These efforts met with varying success, but the German heavy units, with the exception of the 8-in. cruiser *Blücher*, which was sunk by the Norwegian coastal defences, were all back in German ports by the 14th.

Phase 2

The Allied counter-offensive, from 14th April when the first flights of the expeditionary forces were reaching the coasts of Norway, to 14th June, when the last return convoys reached United Kingdom ports. Throughout this phase the Navy's part was chiefly the business of carrying troops and stores to Norway and home again, with some service inshore in support of the advance on Narvik, and the anti-aircraft protection of the temporary bases at Namsos and Aandalsnes.

In studying the story of what Mr. Winston Churchill describes as this 'ramshackle campaign', it must be remembered that the events recorded took place under circumstances very different from those obtaining at the end of the war.

---

[1] The Commander-in-Chief, Home Fleet, never considered invasion possible under the conditions existing at any time in 1940.

The campaign was the first major clash in history in which all three arms—'sea, land and air'—were involved. Such knowledge as existed of the potentialities of air attacks on ships and the most effective counter-measures was largely theoretical; radar was still in its infancy; and the experience derived from the remarkable series of amphibious operations which characterised the Allied strategy from the landings at Diego Suarez in 1942 to the end of the war was as yet undreamed of.

The British, too, in those early days, were still paying the penalty of the pre-war policy of 'appeasement' and the consequent unreadiness for war when it came; many months were to elapse before deficiencies both in trained personnel and material of all kinds could be made good. In a word, measures which could, and probably would have been readily undertaken five years later, could not be contemplated at the time the campaign was fought.

The events which led up to the campaign in Norway centred on the great importance, both economic and strategic, of Scandinavia to Germany.

The 1938 statistics showed an annual consumption by Germany of seventeen million tons of pure iron, six and a half million tons of which came from sources which the Allied blockade had already cut off, and six million tons from Sweden. If this latter supply could be denied to her or seriously impaired, it seemed she could not long continue the war. In summer most of it was shipped from the Swedish port of Lulea, in the Gulf of Bothnia; but in winter this port was ice-bound, and the route then taken was from Narvik and Kirkenes down the coast of Norway. Here, it appeared to the Allies, was a golden opportunity for their superior sea power to strike a serious blow at a vital war commodity;[1] but the whole 1,000-mile passage could be made in Norwegian territorial waters and interference with the traffic would involve the technical infringement of Norwegian neutrality.

It was an intolerable situation that the Allies should be thus shackled by their own scrupulous observance of the letter of that International Law which the Germans notoriously set at nought and outraged whenever it suited them; and as early as 19th September 1939 the First Lord of the Admiralty[2] had called the attention of the Cabinet to the matter.[3] From then on throughout the winter he strove to obtain approval to force the traffic outside territorial waters, by laying minefields—which would be duly declared—in suitable positions off the Norwegian coast.

The Germans were of course fully aware of the importance of the iron ore to them, but they were confident that arrangements could be made with Sweden, such as a given winter storage at Lulea and, if necessary, transport of the ore by rail to the south, whereby all their needs could be supplied.[4] Meanwhile they were content to rely on Allied respect for international law to protect the traffic on its normal winter route, and decided that at the outset a neutral Norway would be to their advantage. Before many weeks, however, Grand Admiral Raeder, the commander-in-chief of the German Navy and probably the ablest strategist of all the German war leaders, was casting covetous eyes

---

[1] Actually, this view under-estimated the importance of scrap iron to the German war economy, and it exaggerated the difference which the stoppage of the Narvik route alone would make to the overall importation from Sweden.

[2] The Right Hon. Winston S. Churchill, C.H., M.P.

[3] Churchill, THE SECOND WORLD WAR, Vol. I, p. 421 (English Edition).

[4] In January 1940 the Swedish Foreign Minister informed the Norwegians privately that it was 'technically possible' to export 90 per cent of the iron via the Baltic.

on the Norwegian coast,[1] and on 3rd October 1939 he called the attention of the Führer to the desirability of gaining bases there; this he followed up a week later with definite suggestions for the occupation of that country.

At about the same time, there were indications of increased cordiality between Great Britain and Norway. An Allied footing there[2] would not only menace the iron ore, but might, under certain contingencies, open the 'back door' to the Baltic, with its relatively undefended German seaboard.

The Russian invasion of Finland (30th November) and the proposal of the Allies to send aid to the hard pressed Finns, who could only be reached through Scandinavian ports, seemed to present an opportunity for them to obtain just such a foothold as the Germans most wished to avoid. This caused serious alarm in Berlin. Contact was established with the Norwegian traitor Quisling and on 14th December Hitler ordered the Supreme Command to prepare plans for the invasion of Norway and Denmark.

Planning continued throughout the winter, and on 16th March 1940—though the Russo-Finnish peace treaty just concluded (12th March) had removed the immediate cause of anxiety—Hitler decided that the operation, which was known as 'Weserübung', should take place about a month before his projected invasion of France and the Low Countries, and fixed 9th April as D-day.[3]

It so happened that towards the end of March Mr. Churchill's representations at last bore fruit and the Allied Governments decided to lay mines off the coast of Norway, in order to 'force traffic outside Norwegian territorial waters'. All possible consideration was to be shown for Norwegian susceptibilities, but it was realised that this step was not unlikely to provoke the Germans to violate Norwegian neutrality and it was therefore decided to hold troops in readiness to land at Stavanger, Bergen, Trondheim and Narvik, should there be clear evidence of their intention to do so. The date chosen for laying the first minefield was 5th April; this was subsequently altered to the 8th.[4]

Thus it came about that each of the belligerents independently was initiating operations scheduled to take place in neutral Norway within the same 24 hours, a sufficiently intriguing situation, though the scope and method of their plans were very different.

---

[1] The German Admiral Wegener, in his book published in 1929, SEA STRATEGY OF THE WORLD WAR, had stressed the strategic advantages that would accrue to the German Navy from the possession of the coast of Norway. No doubt Admiral Raeder was familiar with this work.

[2] This was precisely what the Allies were most desirous of obtaining by diplomatic methods, which, however, received scant encouragement from the Scandinavian Governments.

[3] It is probable that the *Altmark* incident, when on 16th February Captain Vian in the *Cossack* demonstrated that there was a limit to Great Britain's patience and that under certain circumstances she was prepared to violate Norwegian neutrality, played its part in producing this decision.

[4] Had the original date been adhered to, it is probable that the Norwegians would have been more on the *qui vive* on 9th April.

1. The sloop HMS *Bittern*, damaged aft by a bomb off Namos. She had to be sunk by the British on 30 April 1940.

2. HMS *Suffolk* at Scapa Flow, 18 April, having limped home with severe bomb damage.

3. Royal Navy *Skuas*. Photo taken August 1940.

4. German Destroyer *Erich Giese* burning in Ofot fjord, 2nd Battle of Narvik, 13 April 1940.

5. Troops of the 61st Division at boat stations on board *Oronsay*, prior to departure for Norway, 20 or 21 April 1940; HMS *Fury* passing.

6. With the evacuation convoy off Namsos, 3 May 1940. The smoke on the horizon is from the destroyer HMS *Afridi*, sunk by bombs.

7. HMS *Escort* seen from a troopship, probably Gourock, late May 1940.

8. Troops man an anti-aircraft gun at Harstad fjord, end of May 1940. *Effingham* is the vessel above the gun barrel.

9. Herjangs fjord bombed, probably 9 May, *Aurora* under attack; see also Figure 12.

10. Troopship *Mashobra*, bombed 25 May at Harstad, subsequently sunk by the Royal Navy prior to the evacuation. Note hole in side and troops being taken off. The *Vindictive* is in the background. See also Figure 16.

11. Flag Officer Narvik, Admiral of the Fleet Lord Cork and Orrery, and General Auchinleck on the bridge of HMS *Cairo* during the bombardment before the landings at Narvik, 28 May 1940.

12. Damaged petrol tanker being towed by trawlers in Herjangs fjord. Again, probably 9 May; see also Figure 9.

13. The destroyer HMS *Eskimo*, torpedoed 13 April 1940. She got home and was rebuilt. Finally disposed of in 1949.

14. The cruiser HMS *Effingham* in a Norwegian fjord, shortly before her loss by grounding on 17 May 1940.

15. Bomb damage, HMS *Cairo*, sustained 27 May 1940.

16. HMS *Vindictive* under attack, probably 25 May 1940. HMT *Mashobra* in foreground. Eight bombs fell close to *Vindictive* but no damage resulted. See also Figure 10.

17. Troopship *Chobry* escorted by a Tribal-class destroyer, possibly 16 or 17 April 1940.

18. Bren-gun carriers on board *Effingham*, prior to the assault on Bodo, 17 May 1940.

CHAPTER I

PRELIMINARY EVENTS

1. German plan of invasion [PLAN 2

The German plan of invasion hinged on surprise and was characterised by admirable staff work. Seven army divisions under the command of General von Falkenhorst were employed,[1] three in the assault phase, and four in the follow-up. Some eight hundred operational aircraft and between two and three hundred transport planes supplemented the initial seaborne landings, which were planned to take place simultaneously at Oslo, Arendal, Kristiansand (south) and Egersund, Bergen, Trondheim and Narvik.

The whole available German naval strength was to be used in support of this bold operation, undertaken without command of the sea (except as regards the Kattegat and Skagerrak) in the face of very superior Allied naval forces;[2] the latter, it was rightly judged, could be largely neutralised by surprise in the first place and later by air forces operating from captured Norwegian airports. So far as the naval side of the operation was concerned, it was considered that the greatest difficulty and risk would lie in the return of the naval units to Germany after the landings were completed.

On 6th March 1940 Grand Admiral Raeder issued the directive outlining the naval part in the invasion. The forces allocated to Norway were organised in six groups, Groups 1 and 2 operating in the north and the remaining four groups in the south, as shown in the following table:—

GROUP	TASK
GROUP 1. Commanded by Vice-Admiral Lütjens[3]	
BATTLECRUISERS *Gneisenau* (Flag) *Scharnhorst*	To act as covering force for the whole operation, sailing with main landing forces. Having reached the line Shetlands–Bergen, to create a diversion in company with Group 2 in the North Sea; then to patrol in the southern part of the Arctic and after completion of the landings to cover the return of the other naval units to Germany.

---

[1] One for Denmark, six for Norway.

[2] The risks were soberly assessed and accepted by Grand Admiral Raeder. ". . . The operation in itself is contrary to all principles in the theory of naval warfare. According to this theory it could be carried out by us only if we had naval supremacy. We do not have this; on the contrary we are carrying out the operation in face of the vastly superior British Fleet. In spite of this, the Commander-in-Chief, Navy, believes that, provided surprise is complete, our troops can and will successfully be transported to Norway.

On many occasions in the history of war those very operations have been successful which went against all the principles of warfare, provided they were carried out by surprise. . . ."—Report of Commander-in-Chief, Navy, to Führer dated 9th March 1940.

Actually, no principle was contravened, since the plan involved no invasion *by sea*, except across the Skagerrak, where they exercised local command. North of Bergen the operation was of the nature of synchronised raids. No seaborne follow-up was contemplated, reliance for this being placed on the air, of which they had full control, and the advance of the army overland from Oslo.

[3] Deputy Commander-in-Chief. The Commander-in-Chief, Admiral Marschall, was sick.

Sec. 1   PRELIMINARY EVENTS

Group	Task
Destroyers *Wilhelm Heidkamp* (S.O.) *Anton Schmitt* *Diether von Roeder* *Hans Lüdemann* *Hermann Künne* *Georg Thiele* *Bernd Von Arnim* *Wolfgang Zenker* *Erich Giese* *Erich Koellner*	Under Commodore Bonte, to effect occupation of Narvik, involving the landing of 2000 men under General Dietl, and then to rejoin the battlecruisers.

GROUP 2. Commanded by Captain Heye, C.O. *Hipper*

8-in. Cruiser *Hipper* **Destroyers** *Friedrich Eckholdt* *Theodor Riedel* *Bruno Heinemann* *Paul Jacobi*	Occupation of Trondheim, involving the landing of about 1700 men, after which to rejoin the battlecruisers.

GROUP 3. Commanded by F.O. Scouting Forces, Rear-Admiral Schmundt

(a) **Light Cruisers** *Köln* *Königsberg* *Bremse* 1st E-boat Flotilla (7)	Occupation of Bergen, involving the landing of 1,900 men.

(b) Commanded by S.O. 6th T.B. Flotilla

Torpedo Boats
Leopard
Wolf

Depot Ship
Karl Peters

GROUP 4. Commanded by Captain Rieve, C.O. *Karlsruhe*

Light Cruiser *Karlsruhe* **Depot Ship** *Tsingtau* **Torpedo Boats** *Luchs* *Seeadler* *Greif* 2nd E-boat Flotilla (7)	Occupation of Kristiansand and Arendal, involving the landing of about 1100 men.

GROUP 5. Commanded by Rear-Admiral Kummetz

8-in. Cruiser *Blücher* (Flag) **Pocket Battleship** *Lützow* **Light Cruiser** *Emden*	Occupation of Oslo, involving the landing of about 2000 men.

GROUP	TASK
TORPEDO BOATS	
Möwe	
Albatros	
Kondor	
1st R-boat Flotilla (8)	
2 Whale Boats	

GROUP 6. Commanded by S.O., 2nd Minesweeping Flotilla
    4 Minesweepers   Occupation of cable station at Ekersund, involving the landing of 150 men.

The following measures were ordered as protection for the operation :—

  (1) The battlecruisers *Scharnhorst* and *Gneisenau*, later to be joined by the *Hipper*, were to patrol the southern part of the Arctic.

  (2) Twenty-eight U-boats to be disposed in suitable areas, stretching from Narvik and the Shetlands down to the Skagerrak and Eastern Approaches to the English Channel.

  (3) A minefield to be laid in the Skagerrak on the day of the initial landings, and other fields to be declared off the west coast of Norway.[1]

  (4) Air reconnaissance and protection during daylight.

  (5) Anti-submarine patrols in the Kattegat, Skagerrak and further westward.

The invasion of Denmark, which was to take place simultaneously, was also provided for in the naval plan. A group which included the old battleship *Schleswig-Holstein* was to land a force to occupy Korsör (1840 men) and Nyborg (150 men) in the Great Belt ; and four other groups, consisting of small craft, were charged with the occupation of Copenhagen (1000 men), the Little Belt bridge, by Middelfart (400 men), and other key points on the Danish coast.

The immediate follow-up for Bergen and the ports to the southward (including Copenhagen) was to be embarked in transports,[2] disguised as ordinary merchant ships, and sailed singly so as to arrive at their destinations shortly after the assault forces. Troops were not to be sent to Narvik and Trondheim by transports owing to the risk of interception on the Shetlands–Stadlandet line ; but six steamers camouflaged as ordinary merchant ships and loaded with military stores were to be despatched to these northern ports (three to each) timed to arrive before the warships,[3] and arrangements were made for two tankers to arrive at Narvik and one at Trondheim to fuel the naval units.[4]

Further reinforcement and the build-up was to be carried out by the 2nd Sea Transport Division (11 ships totalling 52,500 G.R.T.) and the 3rd Sea Transport Division (12 ships totalling 74,550 G.R.T.) working back and forth between Oslo and German ports.

---

[1] It had been intended that aircraft should lay mines in Scapa Flow, to hamper the movements of the Home Fleet, and this operation had been arranged to start on 28th March, when it was cancelled on the 27th by Reichs Marshal Goering without reference to the Naval Authorities, much to Admiral Raeder's annoyance.

[2] The 1st Sea Transport Division consisting of 15 ships with a total of 72,000 G.R.T., carrying 3761 troops, 672 horses, 1377 vehicles and 5935 tons of Army stores.

[3] For Narvik, the *Rauenfels*, *Alster* and *Barenfels* ; for Trondheim, the *Sao Paulo*, *Main* and *Levante*. As things turned out, of these ships the *Levante* alone reached her destination and she was three days late. (*See* Sec. 21 *postea*.)

[4] The *Jan Wellem* and *Kattegat* for Narvik and the *Skagerrak* for Trondheim. Only the *Jan Wellem* (from Murmansk) reached her destination. (*See* Sec. 21 *postea*.)

2. The British Minefield and Plan R.4 [PLAN 1

During the first week of April 1940, while the final German preparations were taking place, the Allies were going forward with their plans for interrupting the ore traffic. The operations, naturally, would be covered by the Home Fleet,[1] based on Scapa Flow and commanded by Admiral Sir Charles Forbes.

It was decided that three areas should be declared dangerous, one off the eastern shore of Vest Fjord, in about 67° 30′ N., 14° E.; another off Bud, about 63° N., 7° E., and a third off Stadtlandet, about 62° N., 5° E. Destroyers of the 20th (Minelaying) Flotilla under Captain Bickford were to lay the field in Vest Fjord and the minelayer *Teviot Bank* (Commander King-Harman) that off Stadtlandet, the date for laying being 8th April. No mines were to be actually laid off Bud. All three areas however were to be declared dangerous as soon as the first mines were laid, but not before, in order to reduce the chance of meeting Norwegian ships of war whilst laying; for it was known that Norway would use force to prevent the violation of her neutrality. Indeed, although the Allies considered it essential to lay one minefield, they decided that 'the laying of a second one should be given up rather than have an incident with a Norwegian patrol vessel'.

As already mentioned, the Allies had decided to hold troops ready to occupy the ports of Stavanger, Bergen and Trondheim, and ready to land at Narvik, but they did not intend to land troops in Norway 'until the Germans have violated Norwegian neutrality, or there is clear evidence that they intend to do so'. These measures were known as Plan 'R.4'.

The troops for Stavanger and Bergen, two battalions each, were to sail in cruisers, while a single battalion for Trondheim sailed in a transport, arriving two days later than the others. For Narvik the expedition was planned on a larger scale. There the initial landing was to be carried out by one battalion, which was to sail in a transport accompanied by two cruisers, all under Admiral Sir Edward Evans; these were to be followed by an oiler, by the rest of a British Brigade, and later by some French troops—a total strength of about 18,000 men. The port was then to become a regular base with its local defence forces and fuel supplies.

A striking force consisting of two cruisers and three destroyers under Vice-Admiral Sir George Edward-Collins, 2nd Cruiser Squadron, was to be held in readiness at Rosyth 'to deal with any seaborne expedition the Germans may send against Norway'; and the Commander-in-Chief, Home Fleet, earmarked three ships of the 18th Cruiser Squadron, under Vice-Admiral Layton, as a striking force from Scapa, though these ships were to continue the service they were employed on in support of the Norwegian convoys until required.

Big ship cover was to be provided by the *Rodney*, *Valiant*, *Renown* and *Repulse*, screened by 10 destroyers. It is to be noted that these operations would have to be undertaken without an aircraft carrier, since the Home Fleet did not possess one, though Germany was at that time the only Power with which we were at war.[2]

---

[1] *See* Appendix A.
[2] The *Ark Royal* and *Glorious* were in the Mediterranean in order to carry out essential training. The *Furious*, though belonging to the Home Fleet, had been refitting at Devonport, and was then at the Clyde, but was not yet fully operationally fit.

3. Preparations and movements, 4th–7th April 1940 [Plan 2

On 3rd April the Cabinet took the final decision to proceed with the minelaying and on the following day Admiral Evans hoisted his flag in the cruiser *Aurora* at the Clyde, where the force for Narvik was to start its voyage, with orders to be ready to sail on the 8th. The other cruiser for Narvik, the *Penelope*, left a Norwegian convoy she was protecting and arrived at Scapa on the 6th.

The ships for Stavanger and Bergen assembled in the Forth under Vice-Admiral John Cunningham, 1st Cruiser Squadron, and the troops and stores were embarked in the *Devonshire, Berwick, York* and *Glasgow* on the 7th.

The *Teviot Bank* escorted by four destroyers[1] of the 3rd Flotilla under Captain Todd (Capt. (D) 3) left Scapa on 5th April to lay the minefield off Stadtlandet. Since reports indicated that the four heaviest ships of the Norwegian Navy—vessels of some 4000 tons, 40 years old, each mounting two 8-in. guns—might all be in a position to interrupt the laying of mines in Vest Fjord, the Commander-in-Chief decided to send Vice-Admiral Whitworth in the *Renown* with a screen of destroyers[2] to support the northern minelayers; the *Birmingham* and a couple of destroyers,[3] then cruising to the northward against a German fishing fleet, were to join his flag off the coast of Norway. Admiral Whitworth sailed from Scapa in the evening of 5th April, and next morning was joined by Captain Bickford with four minelayers[4] of the 20th Destroyer Flotilla and Captain Warburton-Lee with four[5] of the 2nd Flotilla, which were to escort the minelayers and subsequently to patrol off the minefield. One of the *Renown's* screen, the *Glowworm*, soon parted company; she stopped to pick up a man fallen overboard. In the thick and blowing weather she lost the squadron, and two days later, meeting a superior force of the enemy she was overwhelmed. Two other destroyers, the *Hyperion* and *Hero*, were sent back for oil, after which they were to pretend to lay the minefield off Bud. With his screen thus depleted, Admiral Whitworth continued his passage intending to meet the *Birmingham* and her destroyers off Vest Fjord in the evening of the 7th.

Meanwhile, the Germans had started embarking troops on the 6th and the first of their groups—those bound for Narvik and Trondheim—left their home waters late that night.

4. German Fleet reported at sea, 7th April [Plan 2

At 0848, 7th April, a reconnaissance aircraft reported a cruiser and two destroyers in 55° 30′ N., 6° 37′ E. (about 150 miles south of the Naze), steering to the northward. This message reached the Commander-in-Chief, Home Fleet —then at Scapa Flow—at 1120; half an hour later he received a message from the Commander-in-Chief, Rosyth (timed 1120), stating that the cruiser was probably *Nürnberg* Class, with *six* destroyers,[6] and that 23 Wellingtons and 12 Blenheims were leaving at 1115 and 1150 to bomb the enemy.

---

[1] *Inglefield, Ilex, Isis, Imogen.*

[2] *Greyhound, Glowworm, Hyperion, Hero.*

[3] *Hostile, Fearless.*

[4] *Esk, Impulsive, Icarus, Ivanhoe.*

[5] *Hardy, Hotspur, Havock, Hunter.*

[6] They were escorted by eight aircraft which drove away the British shadower.

A further signal from the Commander-in-Chief, Rosyth (timed 1352) arrived at 1400 : aircraft had reported three enemy destroyers in 56° 06′ N., 6° 08′ E. at 1315. Their course was given as 190°, 12 knots ; it looked as though they were homeward bound.

Twenty minutes later (1420) a message from the Admiralty (A.T. 1259/7) came in :—

> "Recent reports suggest a German expedition is being prepared. Hitler is reported from Copenhagen to have ordered unostentatious movement of one division in ten ships by night to land at Narvik, with simultaneous occupation of Jutland. Sweden to be left alone. Moderates said to be opposing the plan. Date given for arrival at Narvik was 8th April."
>
> All these reports are of doubtful value and may well be only a further move in the war of nerves. Great Belt opened for traffic 5th April.[1]

On receipt of this message, Sir Charles Forbes ordered the fleet to go to one hour's notice for steam. Three hours elapsed.

Then, at 1727, arrived another message from the Admiralty (A.T. 1720) : at 1325 an aircraft had sighted two cruisers, one large ship (possibly *Scharnhorst* Class) and 10 destroyers in 56° 48′ N., 6° 10′ E., steering 320°.[2] This was the first indication of enemy heavy ships being at sea to reach the Commander-in-Chief. He had already ordered certain cruiser and destroyer movements[3] on the strength of the earlier reports, and on receipt of this latter signal[4] he at once ordered all ships at Scapa to raise steam. At 2015, 7th April, the heavy ships of the Home Fleet sailed from Scapa ; the Rosyth striking force sailed an hour later.

The report of the enemy fleet being at sea decided the Admiralty to give up the minefield off Stadtlandet, and the *Teviot Bank* was recalled ; no change was made in the plan for laying the mines in Vest Fjord.

---

[1] The Commander-in-Chief subsequently remarked that in the light of later events 'it was unfortunate that the last paragraph was included'.

There had been various indications that some large scale naval operation was afoot ; after the second week in March, all U-boat activities against the trade routes had abruptly ceased, pointing to their employment elsewhere ; U-boat and destroyer minelaying was also suspended ; Germany's two capital ships, the *Scharnhorst* and *Gneisenau*, had been seen in Wilhelmshavn roads on the 4th April, and German wireless from that port had been unusually active since the evening of the 6th. Several aircraft reported intense activity during the night 6th/7th April in Kiel and Eckenforde, Hamburg and Lubeck, with wharves brilliantly lighted by arc lamps, and much motor traffic with unshaded headlights. Cumulatively, this intelligence pointed in one direction, as can be clearly seen now ; but unfortunately at the time it was wrongly assessed.

[2] The two German forces reported at 0848 and 1325 were almost certainly the same force, consisting of the *Gneisenau*, *Scharnhorst*, *Hipper* and 12 destroyers. They had left port in two groups shortly before midnight 6th April and joined up at 0300, 7th. The positions in which the British aircraft reported them correspond closely to their own reckoning at the time, though the German ships sighted no hostile aircraft till 1330.

[3] At 1546, four destroyers nearing Rosyth with Convoy H.N.24 were ordered to complete with fuel on arrival and to keep steam. At 1558, the *Sheffield* and four destroyers were ordered to raise steam ; and at 1607, Vice-Admiral Edward-Collins was ordered to proceed, as soon as the four destroyers with H.N.24 had fuelled, in the *Galatea*, with the *Arethusa* and eight destroyers to arrive in position 58° 30′ N., 3° 30′ E. at 1700 (if possible) 8th April, and then sweep to the northward.

[4] The important enemy report contained in this signal was brought back by the R.A.F. bombers after their attack on the enemy ships, which had taken place west of Jutland in approximately 57° N., 6° E. between 1322 and 1327. The projected force of 35 bombers had been reduced to 18 Blenheims ; of these, 12 succeeded in attacking, but they could claim no hits. They did not get back till between 1612 and 1652, which accounts for the delay between time of sighting (1325) and the receipt of the report by the Commander-in-Chief (1727). An attack report made on the way home was not received.

Having received from Rosyth a more exact account of the enemy, based on photographs, the Commander-in-Chief signalled to the fleet after leaving harbour, ' We are endeavouring to intercept enemy ships reported by aircraft at 1325 in 56° 50′ N., 6° 10′ E., course 320°, 17 knots ; one battlecruiser, one pocket battleship, three cruisers and about 12 destroyers '. With this end in view he steered for a position in 61° 00′ N., 1° 00′ E. at 19 knots, increasing to 20 knots at midnight, 7th/8th.

He then had in company three capital ships (*Rodney*, *Valiant* and *Repulse*), three cruisers (*Sheffield*, *Penelope* and the French *Emile Bertin*[1] which had arrived at Scapa that afternoon) and 10 destroyers.[2] Vice-Admiral Edward-Collins, with the *Galatea*, *Arethusa* and 11 destroyers[3] was steering from the Forth for the position in 58° 30′ N., 3° 30′ E., after which he was to sweep to the northward. He was joined next morning by four more destroyers,[4] which had brought a convoy to the Forth.

The *Renown* was already approaching the coast of Norway in support of the Vest Fjord minelayers, and the *Birmingham* was on her way to join her.

Two other cruisers were also at sea, under Vice-Admiral Layton, the *Manchester* (flag) and *Southampton*. They had sailed from Scapa that morning (7th) to cover two Norwegian convoys ; O.N.25 which had left Methil on the 5th escorted by the anti-aircraft cruiser *Calcutta* and four destroyers,[5] and H.N.25 which was about to sail from Bergen.[6] Admiral Layton met O.N.25 some 15 miles north-east of Muckle Flugga during the afternoon, but in consequence of the report of the enemy fleet at sea it was turned back in the evening for British waters, by order of the Commander-in-Chief.[7] Admiral Layton had received a signal from the Commander-in-Chief timed 1934, 7th, saying that the fleet would be in position 61° N., 1° E. at 0700, 8th ; but the situation at midnight he described as obscure. ' Nothing definite was known of the larger enemy force since 1342 ', says his diary. ' There was no precise information as to the whereabouts, and no information as to the intentions of the Commander-in-Chief '. He therefore remained with the convoy while it ' continued its slow progress into a north-westerly gale '.

As for destroyers, apart from the ten with his flag, the Commander-in-Chief had nearly 50 under his orders ready for service, with a score refitting, some of which would soon be completed ; and six French destroyers had arrived at Scapa that day.[8]

---

[1] The *Emile Bertin* lost contact soon after putting to sea and returned to Scapa.

[2] *Codrington* (D.1), *Griffin*, *Jupiter*, *Electra*, *Escapade*, *Brazen*, *Bedouin*, *Punjabi*, *Eskimo*, *Kimberley*.

[3] *Afridi* (D.4), *Gurkha*, *Sikh*, *Mohawk*, *Zulu*, *Cossack*, *Kashmir*, *Kelvin* ; O.R.P. *Grom*, *Blyskawica*, *Burza*.

[4] *Somali* (D.6), *Matabele*, *Mashona*, *Tartar*.

[5] *Javelin*, *Janus*, *Juno*, *Grenade*.

[6] The Commander-in-Chief, Rosyth, asked the Admiralty to stop the convoy at Bergen ; but it ' fortunately weighed anchor contrary to instructions ', says the Rosyth diary, and proceeded to a rendezvous outside on the 8th April, thus escaping from the invading Germans. About noon on the 9th, Captain J. S. Pinkney, Master of s.s. *Flyingdale*, who had been appointed ' guide of the convoy ', fell in with the German tanker *Skagerrak*, then on her way to Trondheim. Her conduct aroused his suspicions, and hearing soon afterwards from a Swedish ship that the Germans had landed at Bergen, he took charge of the convoy and put to sea, falling in with a destroyer escort sent by the Commander-in-Chief, Home Fleet, a couple of hours later. Captain Pinkney was subsequently awarded the O.B.E. for his initiative on this occasion.

[7] Twenty-four ships, however, lost touch and continued their voyage. Of these, 13 were sunk or captured by the enemy.

[8] *See* Appendix A. Appendix C (1) gives the disposition at noon, 9th April.

During the night of 7th/8th April, the fleet maintained its north-north-easterly course at 20 knots, and at 0530, 8th—the time at which the minelaying was completed—was in 60° 28′ N., 0° 28′ E.

5. First enemy contact : loss of the *Glowworm*, 8th April [PLAN 2

Meanwhile Admiral Whitworth had arrived off the mouth of Vest Fjord in the evening of 7th April, expecting to meet the *Birmingham* and her two destroyers ; but on reaching the rendezvous he had neither sight nor news of them. The minelayers with their escort were detached and laid their mines between 0430 and 0530, 8th, while the *Renown* with the *Greyhound*—the only remaining destroyer of her screen—patrolled in roughly 67° 30′ N., 10° 30′ E., 30 miles to the westward of the entrance to Vest Fjord and 100 miles from the minefield.

At about 0830, Admiral Whitworth received a signal timed 0759, 8th, from the *Glowworm* (Lieut.-Commander Roope) which had lost the squadron the day before[1] (*see* Sec. 3 *ante*) reporting two enemy destroyers in about 65° 04′ N., 6° 04′ E., 140 miles distant from the *Renown*, which with the *Greyhound* turned to the southward at their best speed and steered to intercept the enemy.[2]

Further signals from the *Glowworm* showed that she was engaging a superior force, the last signal being timed 0855 ; it was not till the war was over that the details of her fate became known.

The two enemy destroyers reported by the *Glowworm* at 0759 were part of the main German force which had been sighted by British aircraft on the previous day, 7th April; in the bad weather and heavy sea, they had lost contact with their heavier consorts. The first of them to be sighted by the *Glowworm*, soon after 0710, was the *Hans Lüdemann* : the British destroyer fired recognition signals, but on orders from the S.O., 3rd German Destroyer Flotilla, the enemy ship made off to the N.W. at 35 knots, followed by two salvos from the *Glowworm* which appear to have fallen short.[3] Shortly afterwards the *Glowworm* sighted the second German destroyer, the *Bernd von Arnim*, on her starboard bow, heading in the other direction. The enemy ship opened fire at 0802 in 64° 05′ N., 06° 18′ E., and a running fight ensued ; in spite of accurate fire on the part of the *Glowworm*, the German destroyer was not hit, though she suffered some damage to her superstructure from the heavy seas, which nearly capsized her. The wireless message sent by the *Bernd von Arnim* on being attacked was picked up by the main German force which was not far off, and the *Hipper* was at once ordered to the destroyer's assistance. Owing to the bad weather it was not until 0857 that she was able to identify which was the hostile destroyer and to open fire. The *Glowworm* fired a salvo of two or three torpedoes which the *Hipper* avoided ; then, considerably damaged by enemy gunfire, the destroyer laid a smoke screen and momentarily

---

[1] The *Glowworm* after losing touch had proceeded back towards Scapa, as she had no rendezvous, until ordered by the Commander-in-Chief to proceed north once more to a position 67° 00′ N., 10° 00′ E. to meet the V.A., B.C.S.

[2] At about the same time the Commander-in-Chief, then some 300 miles to the south-west of the *Glowworm*'s position, detached the *Repulse*, *Penelope* and four destroyers to proceed at their best speed to her assistance. The Commander-in-Chief remarked that if this was the same German force as that reported by aircraft on 7th, it would have had to have made good 27 knots, which, though possible, he deemed improbable. The explanation seems to be that the *Glowworm*'s signalled position was in error nearly 60 miles to the northward. The Germans placed the encounter in 64° 05′ N., 6° 18′ E.

[3] The German ships had orders to avoid action until their missions in Norway had been completed.

disappeared from view. The *Hipper* entered the *Glowworm*'s smoke screen and, failing to answer her helm owing to the high seas, found herself in the path of the British ship. The destroyer rammed her just abaft the starboard anchor wrecking her own bows, then crashing down her side tore away 130 ft. of the *Hipper*'s armoured belt and her starboard torpedo tubes. She herself was fatally damaged: listing heavily with her torpedo tubes under water she lay wrecked and blazing and blew up a few minutes later, sinking in 64° 27′ N., 6° 28′ E.

The *Hipper* picked up 40 survivors, including one officer, a Sub-Lieutenant; the captain of the *Glowworm* was being hauled aboard and had just reached the cruiser's deck when he let go exhausted and was drowned.[1]

6. The sinking of S.S. *Rio de Janeiro* (1200, 8th April)   [PLAN 2

Less than three hours after the loss of the *Glowworm*, there occurred some 500 miles to the southward an incident which might well have compromised the German invasion scheme, had the correct inference been drawn. The Polish submarine *Orzel*, on patrol in the Skagerrak, intercepted the German S.S. *Rio de Janeiro* (bound for Bergen) just outside territorial waters off Kristiansand. After her crew had been given the opportunity to abandon ship, she was torpedoed, sinking at about noon. A Norwegian destroyer and local fishing folk rescued some hundreds of German soldiers in uniform, who stated that they were on their way to Bergen, to protect it against the Allies. This report reached the Norwegian parliament (the Storting) that evening, but it was not credited and no special steps were taken to warn the Navy and coast defences—the only part of the Norwegian forces mobilised at the time—or to take any other precautionary measures.[2]

The report also reached the British Admiralty, where it seems to have been recognised as evidence that the invasion of Norway was in fact under way; but Admiral Raeder's diversion was having its effect and there the chief interest centred on bringing to action the enemy heavy ships reported at sea the day before. Apart from a hint to the Allied submarines on patrol, which were being re-disposed to intercept the heavy ships, no special action was taken; nor was the report of the *Rio de Janeiro* incident passed to the Commander-in-Chief till 2255 that evening (8th).[3]

7. Vice-Admiral Whitworth's movements, 8th April   [PLAN 2

Meanwhile, Admiral Whitworth had continued to the southward making 20 knots for the first hour, but easing down later, because the flagship showed signs of damage through steaming into the heavy sea. Further signals from the *Glowworm* showed that she was engaging a superior force, the last signal being timed 0855; not long afterwards, it had to be assumed that she was sunk.

At 1045 a signal came from the Admiralty, directing the eight destroyers of the Vest Fjord mining force to join him, and at 1114 a message that the report

---

[1] When the details of the *Glowworm*'s gallant action became known, H.M. The King approved the posthumous award of the Victoria Cross to her Commanding Officer Lieut.-Commander G. B. Roope.

[2] Carl J. Hambro, President of the Storting, I SAW IT HAPPEN IN NORWAY.

[3] The episode considerably perturbed the German Naval War Staff, who noted in the War Diary that it 'must result in disclosing the German operation and alarming the Norwegians so that surprise is no longer possible. Reuter reported at 2030 from Oslo " that the ship had been torpedoed near Kristiansand with 300 men on board." Thus the enemy has been warned and action by him must be expected at any moment.'

about a German expedition to Narvik in A.T.1259/7 might be true and that German ships might be then on their way. 'On the presumption that the enemy would proceed to Narvik,' he writes in his diary, 'and giving their force a maximum speed of 25 knots, I found I could reach the line of advance ahead of them at 1330. I steered for this point. In the visibility, which was now reduced to 2 or 3 miles, there was, however, little chance of intercepting an enemy force with only one destroyer in company; and I decided to turn to the north-eastward, at 1330 and rendezvous with the minelaying force.' The destroyers joined at 1715, some 20 miles west by south from Skomvaer Light; and the squadron stood away to the westward to fulfil a plan formed on receiving an aircraft report of the enemy, timed 1400 and received 1516, which put a battlecruiser, two cruisers, and two destroyers in 64° 12′ N., 6° 25′ E., steering west.

'This force,' says Admiral Whitworth, 'might well have been that which had sunk *Glowworm*, whose last report had given the enemy course as 180°. I appreciated the situation as follows. The German force reported by *Glowworm* might (*a*) return to their base at once, (*b*) make for Iceland, (*c*) make for Murmansk, where it was possible a German tanker was waiting to refuel them, (*d*) be part of a force proceeding to Narvik. Our own forces were at sea to the southward; and I therefore determined to dispose my force to deal with the situation, if the enemy chose the alternative of proceeding to the northward. Accordingly, I prepared a plan which provided for a line-ahead patrol by destroyers to the westward of Skomvaer Light, with *Renown* in a position some 50 miles to the northward. It was my further intention to form an extended screen at dawn, and sweep to the southward.'

Two hours later (1915) came A.T.1850/8: 'Most immediate. The force under your orders is to concentrate on preventing any German force proceeding to Narvik.' But, 'the weather was such as to make it advisable to keep my ships concentrated, and I conceived it my first duty to maintain them in a condition of sea-going and fighting efficiency.' The Admiral therefore told his squadron, 'Our object is to prevent German forces reaching Narvik: my present intention is to alter course at 2100 to 280°, and to turn 180° in succession at midnight: enemy heavy ships and light forces have been reported off Norwegian coast; position of *Birmingham* force is not known.' The squadron duly turned to the new course, but the destroyers found themselves unmanageable in the seaway, so the Admiral altered more to the northward. In the meantime he had heard from the Commander-in-Chief that more ships were coming to him, the *Repulse, Penelope, Bedouin, Eskimo, Punjabi* and *Kimberley*, which had parted from Sir Charles Forbes that morning to go to help the *Glowworm*. Accordingly at 2200 Admiral Whitworth signalled his position to the *Birmingham* and *Repulse*: ' 67° 9′ N., 10° 10′ E., course 310°, speed 8 knots, wind N.W., force 10; nine destroyers in company; intend to patrol entrance to Vest Fjord when weather moderates.' The *Birmingham* never joined him. Soon after making his signal he received her 8 o'clock position: she was 80 miles away in 66° 12′ N., 7° 52′ E., hove to with one destroyer in company and running short of oil, so Admiral Whitworth ordered her to Scapa. The *Repulse* and her consorts joined him in the afternoon of the 9th.

8. Movements of Commander-in-Chief, 8th April [PLAN 2

As already mentioned the Commander-in-Chief on receipt of the *Glowworm*'s enemy report had detached the *Repulse* with reinforcements to close her position; at the same time, the speed of the fleet was increased to 22 knots.

During the forenoon the Admiralty signal ordering the minelaying destroyers and their screen to join Admiral Whitworth was received (1045). The Commander-in-Chief subsequently remarked that this message, which led to the Vest Fjord being left without any of our forces on patrol in it, had a very far-reaching effect. The situation was not clear to him at the time, but he assumed that the Admiralty would not have withdrawn the destroyers patrolling the minefield without good reason, and he did not wish to break wireless silence as the enemy was between the *Renown* and the battle fleet and the *Repulse*.

In the early afternoon the Admiralty informed the Commander-in-Chief[1] that the cruisers for Plan R.4 had been ordered to disembark troops and would leave Rosyth at 1400 to proceed northwards ; that the *Aurora*[2] and destroyers in the Clyde were leaving at 1300 for Scapa, and that the *Emile Bertin* and French destroyers were preparing for sea. The *Manchester, Southampton*, the four destroyers then with the *Teviot Bank* and the two destroyers off Bud were also put at his disposal.

The abandonment of Plan R.4 greatly surprised Sir Charles Forbes, in whose mind the reports of the day before had left no doubt that the operation which Plan R.4 had been designed to counter was actually under way.[3] He already had sufficient cruisers at his disposal, and the troops embarked in Vice-Admiral Cunningham's ships might have been very useful. Had they been sailed, for example, as soon as the report of the *Rio de Janeiro* incident reached the Admiralty, they could have got to Stavanger—which with its airfield was to prove the key to the whole campaign on the west coast of Norway—ahead of the Germans.[4] (The *Rodney* and *Valiant* could have been far enough south to provide big ship cover.)

At 1400 a flying boat scouting ahead of the fleet sighted a German squadron of one battlecruiser, two cruisers and two destroyers in 64° 12′ N., 6° 25′ E. steering west. This was the Trondheim group—*Hipper* and four destroyers—which was cruising in this area till the time arrived to make for the fjord. The westerly course they were reported on thus had no real significance, but was very misleading to the British Commander-in-Chief. The full version of the aircraft's report reached him a little after 1500 ; and he altered course to north at 1530 to intercept this squadron, altering again to 340° at 1615 because he 'considered on course 000°, allowing enemy speed 18 knots, he might slip past if he steered south of west'—the flagship's position being 63° 21′ N., 4° 28′ E. at 1600. He also sent off his second flying boat to search at that time and the *Rodney*'s aircraft at 1843,[5] but neither gave him further news of the enemy. By this time it was blowing hard from the N.N.W., and speed had been reduced to 14 knots at about 1800 to ease the destroyers' suffering in the head sea.

---

[1] A.T.1216/8 received 1300 and A.T.1317/8 received 1400.

[2] Admiral Sir Edward Evans was ordered to haul down his flag, but to remain in the *Aurora* if he so desired. This the Admiral decided to do, and he accompanied her to sea.

[3] It is not known why Plan R.4 was thus easily given up at this particular juncture. It must have been envisaged from the first that any German expedition would be covered by their fleet, and the Commander-in-Chief Home Fleet had at his disposal forces superior to the whole German naval strength, without counting the cruisers used as troop carriers in Plan R.4.

[4] Rosyth to Stavanger, 350 miles, *i.e.* 18 hours at 20 knots or 14 hours at 25 knots. The Germans landed only 150 men at Egersund and 1100 men at Kristiansand (south). Rail communication from Stavanger ran through Egersund only as far as Lister Fjord, *i.e.* about half-way between Stavanger and Kristiansand.

[5] The Commander-in-Chief was by this time so certain that the Germans were about to invade Norway that he personally told the pilot of this Walrus that he was to allow himself enough fuel to land in Norwegian waters and then give himself up ; that he would be free next day, since Germany was going to war with Norway, when he was to get hold of enough fuel to take him back to the Shetlands. All of this he did.

In the meanwhile, several messages had been received indicating a large enemy movement in the Kattegat and Skagerrak. At 1512, A.T. 1435 informed the Admiral:—'Naval Attaché, Copenhagen, reports *Gneisenau* or German warship *Blücher* with two cruisers, three destroyers, passed Langeland Belt, northbound, daylight today, 8th April. Similar force now passing northward of Moen through Sound at 1100. Large concentration of trawlers north Kattegat. Report A.1.' Some hours later a report from the submarine *Triton* stated that the *Gneisenau* and a heavy cruiser, with the *Emden* and some destroyers, passed the Skaw, going westward, at 1800. This force was almost certainly that which had left Kiel at 0200, 8th, on its way to occupy Oslo. It actually consisted of the *Blücher*, *Lützow*, *Emden* and some torpedo boats and light craft. According to the Germans, after passing the Skaw at 1800 it was subjected to constant submarine alarms. Two torpedo tracks were sighted and avoiding action taken, but no damage was suffered.[1] A '*Blücher*' with two other cruisers and a destroyer was also reported by the *Sunfish* at 1815 in 57° 57′ N., 11° 07′ E. (20 miles north-east of the Skaw) steering north-west.

At about 1930, 8th April, by which time the battle fleet should have intercepted the enemy and the *Repulse* should have been well to the north of him, if the flying boat's estimate of his course was anything like correct, the Commander-in-Chief reviewed the situation. There appeared to be one enemy battlecruiser to the north, but this was by no means certain; if so, whither was she bound? Probably Narvik, as the iron ore trade was the natural objective. There appeared to be a battlecruiser and perhaps two pocket battleships in the Kattegat or Skagerrak. Our own cruiser forces were sweeping up north from the latitude of Rosyth with no big ship covering force in their vicinity. The *Warspite* and *Furious*[2] were proceeding up the west coast of Scotland. The Admiralty had just ordered Admiral Whitworth to concentrate on preventing any German force proceeding to Narvik (A.T. 1850/8).

Under these circumstances the Commander-in-Chief decided to order the *Repulse*, *Penelope* and screen to continue to the northward and to reinforce Admiral Whitworth, while himself would turn to the southward with the *Rodney*, *Valiant*, *Sheffield* and screen, to try to bring the large enemy vessels in the south to action with the help of the cruiser screen.

At 2000 the battle fleet's position was 64° 22′ N., 3° 40′ E. and ten minutes later course was altered to 195° and speed increased to 18 knots. Just then A.T. 1842/8 arrived, which is digested as follows in the Commander-in-Chief's diary:—

  (*a*) Two objectives—
     (i) to prevent German northern force returning;
     (ii) to deal with possible German forces reported passing Great Belt at 1400/8, if they are going to Stavanger or Bergen.
  (*b*) The Commander-in-Chief's force to sweep to south with light forces spread to northward, keeping east of 2° 35′ E.
  (*c*) Admiral Cunningham's force to sweep to northward, keeping west of 1° 50′ E.
  (*d*) Admiral Edward-Collins to act as striking force by night, keeping between 1° 50′ E. and 2° 35′ E.

---

[1] The *Triton* had unsuccessfully attacked the *Gneisenau* before making her enemy report.

The *Furious* had been ordered north from the Clyde on 8th April. Her two T.S.R. Squadrons were embarked, but unfortunately her Fighter Squadron (801) was at Evanton and therefore too far off to comply with what was obviously an urgent order. She was therefore unable to provide any fighter protection in the ensuing days.

Two further signals from the Admiralty were received that evening: A.T. 2018/8, to the effect that Admiral Layton was to patrol during the night in 62° 10′ N. between 1° 50′ E. and 2° 35′ E., unless he should receive other orders from Sir Charles Forbes, and A.T. 2102/8, which referring to the *Triton*'s signal and presumably also to the flying boat's report in the North Sea that afternoon, said it was 'possible the two German forces intend to make a junction, which we calculate they could do about 0500 in about 60° N.; not intended to alter instructions in A.T. 1842'.

Accordingly, the Commander-in-Chief ordered the following dispositions (summary of Commander-in-Chief's 2252/8):—

> His position at midnight would be 63° 15′ N., 3° E., course 180°, speed 18 knots. He estimates that the enemy reported by the flying boat in the afternoon ' may have passed south and east of me '.
>
> Admiral Layton to rendezvous at 0700 in 61° 9′ N., 3° E. The cruisers with Admirals Edward-Collins and Cunningham to be stationed in pairs along the parallel of 59° 30′ N., by 0500, four stations 20 miles apart, stretching westwards from 4° 30′ E., and at that hour they should steer 355° at 16 knots until they meet the fleet, when they should turn to 180°.

These arrangements were annulled by the Admiralty ' because patrol line placed dispersed and weaker forces in position where they might be caught between two enemy forces with our battle fleet 135 miles away '; instead, the cruisers were to rendezvous in 59° 30′ N., 2° 30′ E. at 0500 on the 9th and thence steer to meet the fleet (A.T. 0210 and 0235/9).

The cruiser admirals could not carry out these instructions exactly. Admiral Edward-Collins, with the *Galatea*, *Arethusa* and 15 destroyers, had reached the position 58° 30′ N., 3° 50′ E. at 1445, 8th, and then turned north to sweep.[1] Soon afterwards he received the enemy report from the flying boat, but he considered that the Commander-in-Chief ' knew my position and movements with reasonable accuracy '; he therefore kept wireless silence, and decided to steer 000° throughout the night.

He did not long maintain this course, however; first there came the Admiralty orders to act as a striking force between 1° 50′ E. and 2° 35′ E., then the Commander-in-Chief's order for a cruiser patrol line, and finally the Admiralty order for the cruisers to concentrate and steer to meet the fleet. The first order meant turning to the westward and reducing speed in a head sea, and when the signal to concentrate came it was not possible to reach the new rendezvous without a large increase of speed, so he altered course to meet Admiral Cunningham, who he was aware, ' would steer northward from the position ordered '. Admiral Cunningham had sailed from Rosyth that afternoon (8th) with the *Devonshire*, *Berwick*, *York* and *Glasgow*, and after meeting Admiral Derrien in the *Emile Bertin* with two French destroyers[2] in 58° N., 2° W. (off Kinnaird Head) stood to the north-eastward to carry out the sweep ordered in A.T. 1842/8.

Events were now moving swiftly, and from 0100, 9th April, numerous reports, mostly from the Admiralty, but also from the submarines *Truant* and *Seal* stationed in the Skagerrak, showed that the Germans were invading Norway.

---

[1] The *Glowworm*'s signals were received in the forenoon, but the Admiral thought her too far north ' to warrant my departing from the Commander-in-Chief's ordered plan '.

[2] *Tartu*, *Maillé Brézé*.

CHAPTER II

GERMAN INVASION OF NORWAY

9. The German Landings, 9th April 1940 [PLANS 1, 11, 13

The invasion of Norway was indeed in full swing during the early hours of this eventful day. So far as the Norwegians were concerned, complete surprise was achieved. On the evening of the 8th April, the relations between the two countries, between whom a longstanding traditional friendship had hitherto existed, appeared entirely normal; before this night was out, a murderous assault was let loose on all the Norwegian strategic centres. Their Army was not mobilised; no serious opposition could be offered to the landings, once the weak naval forces and coast defences were passed. It is greatly to the credit of the Commanders of these forces that despite the shock of suddenly being confronted by foreign warships arriving out of the darkness, almost without exception they made the instant decision to offer what resistance they could.

But it was of little avail.

At Trondheim and Bergen the landings took place practically unopposed, though at the latter place the *Königsberg*[1] and *Bremse* were damaged by shore batteries; at Kristiansand four separate attempts to enter the fiord were foiled by gunfire from Odderöy Island, and a German steamer ahead of the groups was hit and set on fire; there and at Arendal further delay was caused by mist, but both places were occupied before noon. Only at Oslo was the landing seriously checked.

Oslo lies at the head of Oslo Fjord, some 60 miles from the sea.[2] The German Force (Group 5)[3] reached the entrance to the fjord about midnight, 8th/9th, and passing the outer defences—a battery at Rauöy, ten miles up the fjord, which opened fire—at high speed, reached the narrows at Dröbak (about 18 miles short of Oslo) at about 0340, 9th. So far they had only encountered a Norwegian whaleboat armed with one gun, which had opened fire and had been promptly overwhelmed. Just above Dröbak the channel narrows to three cables in width; here were the inner defences, situated on islets, Oscarsborg and Kaholm. At 0420, as Admiral Kummetz leading the force in the *Blücher* approached, the Norwegian batteries on Oscarsborg suddenly opened fire at a range of only 500 yards; the ship was hit repeatedly and the fire control equipment of her main armament was put of out action. Though crippled, she replied on both sides with her heavy and light A.A. guns, and increasing to full speed had reached Kaholm, when she was struck by several torpedoes fired by the torpedo battery there. With all her engines out of action, the *Blücher* dropped anchor east of Askholmene, a mile and a half further up the fjord; fierce fires on board could not be got under control and at 0623 she heeled over to port and sank in deep water. Most of the life-boats and floats had been destroyed by the fires, and the crew and troops were forced to swim ashore, which caused considerable losses.

At 0450, after the *Blücher* had been heavily hit, Admiral Kummetz handed over the command of the group to the Captain of the *Lützow*, Captain Thiele.

---

[1] The *Königsberg* received three hits by 8-in. shells fired by the Kvarven battery, which inflicted such damage that her Captain decided he could not take her to sea that evening to return to Germany, as had been intended. She was consequently still at Bergen next morning, when the F.A.A. carried out an attack which sank her.

[2] *See* Plan 13.

[3] *See* Sec. 1 *ante*.

He, having observed the fate of the *Blücher*, withdrew the force and subsequently landed its troops at Sonsbukten some ten miles to the southward, intending to carry out an attack on the defences guarding the Dröbak Narrows from both land and sea. After heavy attacks by the Luftwaffe, however, the Norwegian resistance gradually gave way; but not before the minelayer *Olav Tryggvason*,[1] stationed at the undefended naval base at Horten, had fought a spirited action with the German torpedo boat *Albatros* and two minesweepers, in which she sank one of the latter (R.17) and forced the *Albatros* to withdraw.

By midday, Oslo was virtually in the hands of the enemy, owing to his overwhelming air superiority; but thanks to the check at Dröbak, the operation had not gone 'according to plan,' and there had been time for the Norwegian Royal Family, Government and Parliament to escape from the capital, taking with them all the gold in the Bank of Norway.

In the north the landing at Narvik had gone exactly as planned. Arriving off the entrance to Vest Fjord in the evening of 8th April, Commodore Bonte's ten destroyers parted company with the battlecruisers and proceeded up the fiord. Avoiding the British minefield, from which, it will be remembered, the patrolling destroyers had been withdrawn by order of the Admiralty some ten hours previously, they suddenly appeared out of a snow squall off Narvik at early dawn.[2] A gallant, but ineffectual resistance was offered by two Norwegian coast defence vessels, the *Eidsvold* and *Norge*.[3] Outnumbered and taken by surprise[4] there was little they could do. The *Eidsvold*, which was lying outside the harbour, had only time to return a peremptory refusal to a demand for surrender before she was sunk by torpedo and gunfire with the loss of nearly all her crew. The *Norge*, at anchor inside the harbour, opened fire on the *Bernd von Arnim* as she went alongside to land her troops a few minutes later, but was soon hit by two torpedoes and sunk, with heavy loss of life.[5] The disembarkation of General Dietl's troops then proceeded unopposed.[6]

10. Admiral Whitworth's encounter with the *Gneisenau* and *Scharnhorst*, 9th April
[PLAN 2

While this was going on at Narvik, a sharp engagement was taking place to seaward of Vest Fjord between Admiral Whitworth's force and the German battlecruisers. After detaching the destroyers to Narvik (2000, 8th April) the

---

[1] *Olav Tryggvason*, built 1934, 1,747 tons, 4 4·7-in., 1 3-in. H.A. guns, 2 17·7-in. torpedo tubes.

[2] Sunrise at Narvik, 9th April, 0425; Civil twilight (sun 6° below horizon) commenced 0323.

[3] *Norge* and *Eidsvold*, 2 8·2-in.; 6 5·9-in.; 8 3-in., 2 3-pdr. H.A.

[4] Actually, the surprise was not complete. The Naval Authorities at Oslo had warned the '3rd District' (which included Narvik) at 1925, 8th April, that a German attack was imminent. Two lookout boats sighted and reported the Germans at 0310, 9th, by wireless, as British. The receipt of this signal just before the arrival of the Germans raised doubts as to their identity in the coast defence vessels.

[5] About half the crew of the *Norge* was lost. Among the survivors was the Norwegian Senior Naval Officer, Commodore Askim, who, having gone down with his ship, was rescued in an unconscious state. When the final Allied evacuation took place (June, 1940) Commodore Askim succeeded in escaping from Norway and was subsequently Naval Attaché in the U.S.A. On the night of the 8th/9th May 1945, as Naval member of the Allied Supreme Commission representing General Eisenhower, he had the pleasure of handing to the German General Böhme at Lillehammer the written order for the surrender of the German Naval units then in Norway.

[6] Major Sundlo, the Norwegian officer commanding in Narvik, was one of the few Norwegian traitors working in touch with Quisling. His action was speedily disavowed by the Norwegian officers in the area, but not in time for any resistance to be made in Narvik.

Gneisenau and *Scharnhorst* had steered to the north-westward in order to take up their patrolling position in the Arctic. This course brought them into contact with Admiral Whitworth in the *Renown*, who, with his nine destroyers, was then returning to the south-eastward after spending the night to the west of the Lofoten Islands, waiting for the weather to moderate before establishing a patrol off Vest Fjord.

'From midnight onwards,' runs Admiral Whitworth's diary, ' the weather improved ; but knowing that the destroyers would be widely strung out on account of the weather I decided to wait until the first sign of dawn and sufficient light to make the turn to the south-eastward without losing touch with them or any part of them.' The squadron turned at 0230, the 9th, snow squalls making ' the visibility variable ' ; but ' dawn twilight[1] strengthened to the eastward, and conditions improved '. An hour or so later, roughly in 67° 20′ N., 9° 40′ E., some 50 miles to the westward of Skomvaer Light, they sighted a darkened ship coming out of a snow-squall with apparently a second ship astern of her. The presence of two ships was soon confirmed ; they were thought to be a ' Scharnhorst ' and a ' Hipper ', though later evidence has shown that they were the battlecruisers *Scharnhorst* and *Gneisenau*.[2] They joined battle just under half an hour from the first sighting.

When she first sighted the German ships, at 0337, the *Renown* was steering 130°, at 12 knots, with her destroyers stationed astern. The enemy lay broad on the port bow, 10 miles distant or rather more, steering to the north-west, on a course approximately opposite to that of the British force. The *Renown* maintained her course for ten minutes, then altered to 080° increasing speed to 15 knots and soon after to 20 knots ; at 0359 she hauled right round to 305°, roughly parallel to the enemy, with her " A " arcs just open ; at 0405, when just abaft the beam of the leading German ship, she opened fire at 18,600 yards. It was not till 0411 that the *Gneisenau* returned the fire ; she had sighted the British force at 0350, but in the poor light to the westward had not recognised it as such until 0400, when the alert was sounded for action. The *Scharnhorst* on the other hand did not sight the *Renown* until the latter opened fire at 0405. A fierce engagement ensued during the next ten minutes or so, both the *Gneisenau* and the *Scharnhorst* firing at the *Renown*, which was engaging the *Gneisenau* with her heavy armament, and the *Scharnhorst* with her 4·5 in., all the destroyers joining in with their 4·7 in., though at such range their fire could ' hardly have been effective '. The *Renown* was hit twice, without serious damage ; the *Gneisenau* received a hit at 0417 on the foretop at a range of 14,600 yards, destroying the main fire control equipment, and temporarily disabling her main armament. At 0418, with only her secondary armament in action, the *Gneisenau* altered course to 030°, ' with the obvious intention of breaking off the action '. To cover the *Gneisenau's* retirement, the *Scharnhorst* crossed her stern, making a screen of smoke, whereupon the *Renown*, turning northward, brought all her guns to bear on the *Scharnhorst*.

There followed a chase to windward that lasted an hour and a half, until about 0600. The wind was rising and had shifted from north-north-west to

---

[1] Sunrise at Narvik, 9th April, 0425 ; civil twilight (sun 6° below horizon) commenced 0323.

[2] The strong similarity of the silhouettes of the modern German ships of various classes frequently rendered their identification very difficult. This difficulty was emphasised in the conditions of light and storm under which this action was fought. The Germans, too, were in doubt as to what they were fighting, the identification in the *Scharnhorst* being a *Renown* class and in the *Gneisenau* the *Nelson*. In the latter the opinion was held that two enemy heavy ships were present, though only one was seen at a time.

north-north-east, with a heavy swell and a great sea. The destroyers soon fell astern out of the battle. The *Renown* continued to engage the *Scharnhorst* but did not succeed in hitting her; both German ships were firing at the *Renown*, the *Gneisenau* with her after turret, and the *Scharnhorst* yawing occasionally to fire a broadside. At 0434 the *Gneisenau* received a second hit which struck 'A' turret by the left hood of the rangefinder. It wrecked the watertight hood which resulted in the flooding of the turret, putting it out of action. A third hit struck the after A.A. gun on the port side of the platform, doing little damage. Just before 0500, the German ships disappeared in a rain-squall. Admiral Whitworth had increased to full speed early in the fight, before the turn to the north, but had soon to ease to 23 knots and afterwards to 20, at which speed he barely held the range: when the enemy disappeared in the rain, he 'decided to alter course to bring the sea on the other bow and endeavour to make more speed,' and accordingly turned to the eastward and increased to 25 knots. When the weather cleared, however, some 20 minutes later, the German ships were still heading northwards and were farther off than before. The *Renown* turned again to bring the enemy fine on her bow, and opened fire; but the 'fire continued to be ineffective, both sides altering course to avoid the fall of shot'. There were further squalls of rain or sleet hiding the target; the *Renown* strained herself 'to the maximum' in trying to overhaul her opponent (for a few minutes she went 29 knots) but at last the enemy ran out of sight.

The last brief sight of the German ships came at 0615—'far ahead and out of range'. Admiral Whitworth stood on to the northward in the *Renown* until a few minutes after 0800; then he turned westward, hoping to cut off the enemy 'should they have broken back to southward', but no further contact occurred.

11. British dispositions, Vest Fjord area, 9th April [PLAN 2]

Vice-Admiral Whitworth had already ordered his destroyers to patrol the mouth of Vest Fjord and the *Repulse* detachment ' to prevent German forces entering Narvik '. Then, soon after 0900, he received A.T. 0820/9, which told the Commander-in-Chief to make plans for attacking the enemy in Bergen and Trondheim, adding ' Narvik must be watched to prevent Germans landing, as we shall probably want to land a force there.' At that, Admiral Whitworth decided to concentrate his force off the fjord: he gave the *Repulse* a rendezvous for 1300 in 67° N., 10° E.—some 60 miles south of his own position when making the signal—and told Captain Warburton-Lee to join at 1800 in 67° N., 10° 30′ E.

The Admiralty and the Commander-in-Chief changed these dispositions. In a signal timed 0952/9, Sir Charles Forbes ordered Captain Warburton-Lee to ' send some destroyers up to Narvik to make certain that no enemy troops land '. The Admiralty made A.T. 1200/9, also addressed direct to Captain Warburton-Lee[1]:—

> ' Press reports state one German ship has arrived Narvik and landed a small force. Proceed Narvik and sink or capture enemy ship. It is at your discretion to land forces, if you think you can recapture Narvik from number of enemy present. Try to get possession of battery, if not already in enemy hands: details of battery follow.'

They had already told Admiral Whitworth that Germans had arrived, and that he must ' ensure that no reinforcements reach them ' (A.T. 1138/9), but this signal did not come to him until next day. Captain Warburton-Lee decided

---

[1] Repeated to Admiral Whitworth.

to go to Narvik with the four ships of his proper flotilla, the 2nd, leaving Captain Bickford with the rest to patrol the minefield he had laid the day before near the mouth of Vest Fjord. One ship, the *Impulsive*, had gone home in the morning with a damaged paravane boom, which left Captain Bickford the *Esk*, *Icarus* and *Ivanhoe*, minelayers, with no torpedoes and mounting but two guns, and the *Greyhound*, late of the *Renown's* anti-submarine screen. For Narvik there were the *Hardy*, flotilla leader, the *Hotspur* (Commander Layman), *Havock* (Lieut.-Commander Courage) and *Hunter* (Lieut.-Commander de Villiers); and the *Hostile* (Commander Wright) arrived unexpectedly after the flotilla had started on its mission.[1]

Captain Warburton-Lee meant originally to reach Narvik by 2000 that night, and made his plan as the flotilla steamed up Vest Fjord, passing it by signal to his consorts. But having nothing to go by beyond the press report in the Admiralty's signal he bethought him of the pilots' station at Tranoy, where he arrived about 1600, and sent on shore there for what they could tell him. The pilots had seen six ships 'larger than the *Hardy*' going to Narvik, besides a submarine; the entrance to the harbour was mined; and the Germans held the place very strongly. The English, thought the pilots, would need twice as many ships. Captain Warburton-Lee signalled this intelligence to the Admiralty, the Commander-in-Chief, and Admiral Whitworth, and added: 'Intend attacking at dawn high water'.

This signal, timed 1751, reached Admiral Whitworth a little after 1800. The Admiralty's order to attack had been repeated to him, and he now considered whether he might improve the power of the attack. When the *Repulse* and the ships with her joined, about 1400, he had disposed his force thus: the *Penelope* to patrol a line running south from Skomvaer Light, rather more than 50 miles outside the minefield and about 150 miles from Narvik; the *Renown* and *Repulse* to cruise north and south on a line 30 miles farther west, with the *Bedouin*, *Punjabi*, *Eskimo* and *Kimberley* as a screen. The *Penelope* might go in, and so might the four destroyers, though that would deprive the capital ships of their screen; he had already ordered Captain Bickford to continue the patrol by the minefield, cancelling the signal in the morning that those four destroyers should join his flag at 1800. But the time of high water being 0140 on the 10th, Captain Warburton-Lee's signal implied an attack in the morning twilight, for which it was too late to send reinforcements in the thick weather prevailing. Moreover, so Admiral Whitworth reasoned, the plan had been made 'with the forces ordered by the Admiralty'; and 'the addition of other forces, involving delay and revision of the plan, was liable to cause confusion'. He decided, therefore, to leave things as they stood.

12. Movements of Commander-in-Chief, Home Fleet, 9th April

[PLANS 2 AND 3

While these developments had been taking place in the north, the Commander-in-Chief had been operating in the Bergen–Trondheim area. Throughout the night of 8th/9th April, while the various first reports of the invasion were coming in, he held his southerly course, being joined by Vice-Admiral Layton with the *Manchester* and *Southampton* at 0630, 9th, and by Vice-Admirals Edward-Collins, Cunningham and Derrien with their seven

---

[1] The *Hostile* had been with the *Birmingham*, cruising against the German fishing fleet. Being detached with a prize, and intercepting signals about the enemy and the British concentration off Vest Fjord on the 8th, she went north to find Admiral Whitworth, and eventually joined Captain Warburton-Lee instead, p.m. 9th.

cruisers and 13 destroyers (eight British, three Polish, two French)[1] some three hours later. The *Tartar* and the three Polish destroyers were detached to the northward to join Convoy HN.25[2]—at least 37 ships—then waiting off Hovden (61° 40′ N., 4° 45′ E.) and escort it to the United Kingdom, the remainder of the fleet continuing to the southward.

By this time it was clear that Germany was carrying out a full scale invasion of Norway, seizing (among other places) all the ports that the Allies had hoped to save from her control by occupying themselves, but the strength of his forces in the various areas was naturally in doubt. At 0630, 9th, the Commander-in-Chief asked the Admiralty for news of the German strength in Bergen, as he wished to send there Admiral Layton's two cruisers—then just arriving in the fleet. This signal reached the Admiralty about the time A.T. 0820/9 to the Commander-in-Chief was being framed :—

> ' Prepare plans for attacking German warships and transports in Bergen and for controlling the approaches to the port on the supposition that defences are still in hands of Norwegians.
>
> Similar plans as regards Trondheim should also be prepared, if you have sufficient forces for both.
>
> Narvik must be watched to prevent Germans landing, as we shall probably want to land a force there.
>
> At what time would forces be ready to cross the 3-mile limit in operations against Bergen and Trondheim ? '

A first report from reconnoitring aircraft put ' at least one *Köln* class cruiser in Bergen ' (A.T. 0935) ; and at 1015, the Admiralty sanctioned the Commander-in-Chief's proposal to attack there, though warning him later in A.T. 1211, that he must no longer count on the defences being friendly. The attack on the ships in Trondheim was annulled until the German battlecruisers should be found, ' as it would entail dispersion of forces ' (A.T. 1132).

Sir Charles Forbes said, in answer to A.T. 0820, that the ships could go in by the fjords north and south of Bergen ' in three hours from the order, Go ' (1032/9). By then the Rosyth ships had joined, so he could strengthen the attacking force. Admiral Layton left the fleet accordingly about 1130, an hour after A.T. 1015 came, with the *Manchester* and *Southampton*, *Glasgow* and *Sheffield* and the seven destroyers of the 4th and 6th Flotillas. He had orders :—

> ' . . . . to attack enemy forces reported in Bergen : these include one *Köln* class cruiser.
>
> Defences may be in hands of enemy.
>
> Three or four destroyers are to enter by Fejeosen Fjord, 60° 44′ N., remainder by Kors Fjord, 60° 8′ N. Object, to destroy enemy forces and report situation.
>
> Cruisers are to be in support at both entrances, which U-boats may be patrolling.'

He was south of Bergen, with Fejeosen Fjord nearly 80 miles to the north-east and Kors Fjord, bearing about east-north-east, a dozen miles nearer ; it was blowing hard from north-west with a rough sea ; the destroyers could keep up only 16 knots. ' Owing to the movement southward of the fleet during the forenoon ', writes Admiral Layton, ' it was unfortunately necessary to retrace a lot of ground to windward to get to Bergen. At 1408, aircraft reported that there were two cruisers in Bergen instead of one. With only seven destroyers available, the prospects of a successful attack now appeared

---

[1] Admiral Edward-Collins originally had 15 destroyers with him. But an accident robbed him of four in the early morning of the 9th, when the *Kelvin* ran on board the *Kashmir*, both ships being so severely damaged that they had to return to harbour escorted by the *Zulu* and *Cossack*.

[2] See Sec. 4 *ante*.

distinctly less, though there was some hope that the enemy could not yet have got the shore guns effectively manned'. However, soon afterwards there came orders from the Admiralty annulling the attack (A.T. 1357/9) and the squadron turned to rejoin the fleet.[1]

The Commander-in-Chief had turned north at noon, being then in 59° 44′ N., 2° 57′ E. The weather was clear, and German aircraft had been shadowing the fleet since about eight in the morning. In the afternoon their bombers came ; between 1430 and 1800 or thereabouts, some part of the fleet was constantly engaged. The Germans came from the eastward and made their first and apparently their principal attack on Admiral Layton's ships, returning from the coast. Near misses slightly damaged the *Southampton* and *Glasgow* ; and the *Gurkha*, which had got separated from the remainder, was so badly damaged that she subsequently sank. Providentially the *Aurora*, in joining the fleet from the Clyde, made contact with her some hours later and in time to save most of her company, a task on which she was still employed at 2130.

As for the main body of the fleet, the business began about 1530, when a diving aircraft hit the flagship *Rodney* with a bomb. After a lull between 1600 and 1700, the attack freshened for about half an hour, both diving and at high level. Several bombs fell near the ships, especially the *Rodney* again, and the *Valiant*, *Devonshire*, *Berwick*, and the destroyers, but there were no more hits. The British fire seems to have brought down one enemy machine,[2] reported by the *York* as falling in flames between the *Devonshire* and the *Berwick* ; yet the ships with Admiral Layton spent some 40 per cent of their 4-in. ammunition.

During these attacks from the air, fresh orders came for attempting Bergen. The *Furious* was on her way to the fleet, and the Commander-in-Chief had already suggested in his signal 1032/9 that torpedo attack by her aircraft would give the ' best chance of success ', if the Germans had the coast defences in their power : he proposed an attack at dusk on the 10th. The Admiralty agreed, at the same time arranging with the Royal Air Force to send bombers in the evening of the 9th and for the naval air station at Hatston to send some in the morning of the 10th. In the meantime, cruisers and destroyers must patrol the approaches to prevent the enemy from reinforcing Bergen and Stavanger, and to pin down their ships already there : Sir Charles was ' to consider a sweep with light forces off the south-west corner of Norway '. But the afternoon's experience made him change his mind about the *Furious*. She ' could not work in latitude of air attack to-day ', so he proposed her attacking the enemy in Trondheim, farther north, ' leaving Bergen to the Royal Air Force ' : indeed he gave the Admiralty his ' general ideas ' in the same signal 2231/9, to ' attack enemy in north with surface forces and military assistance, leaving southern area mostly to submarines, due to German air superiority in south '.

The enemy force which had been sent to occupy Bergen consisted of the cruisers *Köln*, *Königsberg* and *Bremse*, two torpedo boats, and the M.T.B. depot ship *Karl Peters*. At 1800, 9th, Royal Air Force bombers attacked them, but in spite of near misses, little damage was caused. An hour later, the *Köln*, accompanied by the torpedo boats, put to sea on the return journey to Germany; the *Königsberg* was not considered seaworthy owing to injuries received from the Norwegian batteries, and she remained with the *Bremse* and *Karl Peters* to supplement the harbour defences.

---

[1] ' Looking back on this affair, I consider that the Admiralty kept too close a control upon the Commander-in-Chief, and after learning his original intention to force the passage into Bergen, we should have confined ourselves to sending him information.' Churchill, THE SECOND WORLD WAR, Vol. I, p. 470.

[2] It is now known that two Ju.88s failed to return to their base : cause of loss is unknown to the Germans.

MOVEMENTS OF THE COMMANDER-IN-CHIEF, HOME FLEET, 9TH APRIL

The *Köln* and her consorts did not get far that night. Enemy wireless signals indicated the presence of the British forces which soon afterwards established patrols to seaward of the approaches to Bergen, so Rear-Admiral Schmundt decided to postpone the attempt and anchored at the head of Mauranger Fjord (60° 08′ N., 6° 16′ E.) till the following evening, 10th April, when he resumed his passage, arriving home without incident on the 11th.

Meanwhile, the Commander-in-Chief, Home Fleet, had sent back Admiral Layton to the coast the evening before, as soon as the Admiralty orders for watching Bergen and Stavanger had been deciphered. Admiral Edward-Collins followed with the *Galatea* and *Arethusa*, the *Émile Bertin*, and the two French destroyers. Sir Charles' 1837/9 thus disposed them : two of Admiral Layton's cruisers with destroyers ' to sweep down Norwegian coast ' from Fejeosen Fjord south of Kors Fjord, and the other half of his force to sweep from Kors Fjord to Obrestad, 20 miles south of Stavanger, while Admiral Edward-Collins patrolled off Fejeosen. The object given was ' to stop reinforcements for Stavanger and Bergen '. They were to cruise until 0400, the 10th, and then to steer for a rendezvous in 61° N., 1° E. It is not clear from his diary how far Admiral Layton acted on these orders, for he says merely that he had instructions (under Sir Charles' 1614/9 and A.T. 1451/9, when he turned back) to ' maintain a patrol off the entrance to Bergen to prevent enemy forces escaping ' and that ' this patrol was maintained during the night ' ; yet he altered course for the rendezvous at four in the morning, as Sir Charles' 1837/9 prescribed. Captain Pegram of the *Glasgow*, commanding the southern patrol, had this latter signal from a consort, the *Sheffield*, but only at 0145, the 10th. When approaching the coast the evening before, he had come upon the *Aurora* rescuing the survivors of the *Gurkha*, and she asked to join the *Glasgow*, as she had no other orders. Thereupon, Captain Pegram sent her with one destroyer to stop the gap at Bommel Fjord, 30 miles to the southward, while he patrolled north and south of Kors Fjord, 7 miles off-shore, with the rest of his group. When the *Sheffield* passed on Sir Charles' later signal, it was too late to reach Obrestad in the time, but Captain Pegram stretched south as far as Utsire, 25 miles short of Stavanger, before turning away to seaward for the rendezvous.

No surface contact with the enemy occurred during the night, with the exception of an attempt by the *Manchester* to ram a U-boat. But in the south the submarine *Truant* scored a success, torpedoing the cruiser *Karlsruhe* at 1858, 9th, an hour after she had left Kristiansand on her homeward passage. She sank at 2150, her end expedited by torpedoes from German torpedo boats, which had taken off her crew.

The various groups of ships off Bergen (with the exception of the *Aurora*, which proceeded direct to Scapa with the *Gurkha's* survivors) made their way to the rendezvous in the morning and found there the *Codrington* and other destroyers sent by Sir Charles Forbes with orders for them all to proceed to harbour for fuel—the British destroyers to Sullom Voe, the cruisers and the French ships to Scapa—where they arrived that evening, without incident except for an ineffective bombing attack on the 2nd Cruiser Squadron. On arrival, ammunitioning and fuelling was commenced without delay—an operation interrupted by an air raid on Scapa which lasted from 2100 to 2220. About 60 bombers were employed, but warning of their approach had been received by radar ; they achieved no damage, but lost six of their number.

The Commander-in-Chief himself, in the meanwhile, had held on to the northward after the air attacks in the afternoon of the 9th till 2000, then steering west at 16 knots from 61° 40′ N., 2° 47′ E. for the night, and turning to the eastward again at 0500, 10th April. About an hour later, the first news of the destroyer attack on Narvik arrived—an intercepted signal from Captain D (2) to Captain D (20) timed 0551 :—' One cruiser and three destroyers off Narvik, am withdrawing to westward '.

At 0730 in 61° 24′ N., 1° W. the *Warspite* and *Furious* joined the fleet, as did several fresh destroyers (at any rate, replenished ones) after which the original destroyer screen went home for oil. The strength of the fleet then stood at three capital ships, *Rodney*, *Valiant* and *Warspite*; three cruisers, *Devonshire*, *Berwick* and *York*; the *Furious* aircraft carrier and 18 destroyers.

With this force the Commander-in-Chief steered to the north and east, making for a suitable position from which to attack the enemy ships in Trondheim with aircraft at dawn next morning. This course also provided cover for Convoy HN.25, which after its fortunate escape from Bergen[1] was making its way to the United Kingdom escorted by the four destroyers detached from the fleet the day before.

Soon after steadying on the north-easterly course came the pleasing tidings that at 0700 sixteen Skuas led by Lieutenant W. P. Lucy, R.N., and Captain R. T. Partridge, R.M., of the Fleet Air Arm from Hatston had attacked the *Königsberg* at Bergen and sank her with three direct hits with 500 lb. S.A.P.C. bombs;[2] and at 1132 the Commander-in-Chief received news of Captain Warburton-Lee's dawn attack on the enemy in Narvik, which is described in the next section.

13. First Battle of Narvik, 10th April [PLAN 9

To return to the northern area.

As a result of the intelligence received from the pilots at Tranoy in the afternoon of 9th April, Captain Warburton-Lee took his flotilla down the fjord again,[3] turning back half an hour before midnight to arrive off Narvik at dawn. A.T. 2059/9 told them to patrol during the night east of 16° 33′ E., in the narrow stretch of Ofot Fjord some 20 miles west of Narvik, lest the enemy should run through Tjeldsundet into Vaags Fjord, thus escaping to the northward; and the signal ended, ' Attack at dawn : all good luck '. Captain Warburton-Lee ignored this signal, if he received it : very likely he feared giving away his presence to the enemy, for the Admiralty had warned him before that there might be batteries either side of the narrows, near Ramnes and Hamnes Holm, which the Germans might have seized and manned.[4] If so, they could perhaps report him to friends at Narvik before the time came for his attack, and surprise must have seemed all-important for the little flotilla.

---

[1] See Sec. 4 *ante*, footnote

[2] Of this fine attack, the Vice-Admiral, Orkneys and Shetlands (Vice-Admiral Sir Hugh Binney) remarked : ' This was, I think, the first occasion on which Skuas had been used in action for the real purpose for which they were designed, viz., a dive-bombing attack on an enemy warship. The ship was sunk, the attack was a complete success and I consider it was brilliantly executed ... the distance to Bergen and back is 560 miles, not greatly inside the maximum endurance of the Skua '.

[3] The flotilla was reported on a south-westerly course in Vest Fjord by *U.51* at 2100, 9th April. (Admiral Doenitz, War Diary.)

[4] Actually these batteries (according to the Germans) were non-existent.

A.T. 0104/10 said the Germans were supposed to have come to Narvik 'in apparently empty ore ships', which might have stores still on board and must be sunk, if possible; and Captain Warburton-Lee was to try to find out how the enemy did land and in what strength, and whether they had seized the Norwegian batteries. Lastly, A.T. 0136 said: 'Norwegian coast-defence ships *Eidsvold* and *Norge* may be in German hands: you alone can judge whether, in these circumstances, attack should be made. We shall support whatever decision you take'. Perhaps this last message added to Admiral Whitworth's misgivings, though he could now do nothing; it could make no difference to Captain Warburton-Lee, whose mind was made up. The flotilla passed Tranoy again on the way in at 1 o'clock in the morning, 10th. They had then 'continuous snowstorms with visibility seldom greater than two cables... on the one occasion that land was seen the whole flotilla almost ran aground'. Ships lost touch at intervals, twice through merchant vessels crossing the line. But all arrived off Narvik a little after 0400, when the sky cleared and they could see for nearly a mile.

The plan of attack appears in the signals Captain Warburton-Lee made to the flotilla the day before. Apart from the pilots' information and the Admiralty messages described already, A.T. 1307/9 had told him of a three-gun battery, 18- or 12-pounders, on a hill north of the ore quay in the harbour and west of the town, facing north-west; that is to say across the mouths of Herjangs and Rombaks Fjords. It was this signal that gave the warning, too, of possible batteries at the narrows in Ofot Fjord. He proposed the *Hardy*, *Hunter* and *Havock* should attack the shipping inside the harbour. The *Hotspur* and *Hostile* would stay outside to engage the fort if it opened fire; to keep watch for German ships he expected to find patrolling, or coming in from the sea or from the two fjords north of Narvik; to be ready to cover a retreat of the main body with smoke and to take disabled ships in tow. If the business prospered, and 'opposition is silenced' the *Hardy*'s first lieutenant would lead a party to land at ore quay.

The German destroyers had put their troops ashore as planned, during the 9th, and by midnight, three of them, the *Zenker*, *Giese*, *Koellner*, were lying in Herjangs Fjord, off Elvegaard; four more, the *Heidkamp*, *Schmitt*, *Lüdemann* and *Künne*, had made fast alongside the pier in Narvik harbour, and two others, the *Thiele* and *Von Arnim*, were at anchor off Ballangen about 15 miles to the west of Narvik. The *Roeder* had been ordered to patrol the outer reaches of the fjord as a protection against submarines, but at dawn, on the 10th, she entered Narvik Harbour, anchoring at 0420 off the eastern shore. Ten minutes later, at 0430, the British flotilla made the first of its three attacks. The *Hardy*, *Hunter* and *Havock* went in and engaged the German destroyers alongside the pier with guns and torpedoes; a torpedo from the *Hardy* hit the *Heidkamp* aft, blowing off its stern and killing the German Captain (D), Commodore Bonte.

The *Anton Schmitt* was hit by one torpedo in the forward engine room, and by a second in the after boiler room, which sealed her fate; she broke in two and sank.

The *Roeder* was hit by two shells which set her on fire and destroyed the fire control equipment. The other two destroyers (*Lüdemann* and *Künne*) in the harbour tried to cast off when the alarm was first given, but both received hits which temporarily disabled them.

In the harbour at anchor were some 23 merchant ships,[1] and heavy explosions marked the end of six of the German ships. One, the *Neuenfels*, had been run ashore on 9th April, and one, the *Jan Wellem*, 11,776 tons (a whale depot ship in service as submarine supply ship) remained undamaged.

Meanwhile, in the mist and snow, the *Hotspur* and *Hostile*, outside the harbour, did not discover the three destroyers in Herjangs Fjord. They joined the *Hardy* in the second attack and the *Hotspur* torpedoed two merchantmen. Captain Warburton-Lee then drew off for a short consultation. The German ships had returned the fire, but had done no harm with either guns or torpedoes and their guns were apparently silenced. After an hour's fighting, no ships had appeared outside. Accordingly the flotilla went in again, this time keeping a mile outside the harbour, except the *Hostile*, which stood in to the entrance to fire her torpedoes.

So far, things had gone well. They had, without loss to themselves, sunk two destroyers, the *Schmitt* and the *Heidkamp*, and put out of action three more inside the harbour, besides sinking half a dozen merchant ships. Their good fortune was now to change; as the flotilla drew off after the last attack, to proceed down Ofot Fjord, they sighted, just before 0600, fresh ships coming from Herjangs Fjord. Captain Warburton-Lee reported them as a cruiser and three destroyers, adding ' am withdrawing to westward '. In actual fact they were the three destroyers, *Wolfgang Zenker*, *Erich Giese* and *Erich Koellner*, which after disembarking their troops had anchored off Elvegaard. It was not until about 0520 that they received the message sent out by the *Lüdemann* : ' Alarm : attack on Narvik '. Weighing anchor immediately, they made at full speed in the direction of Narvik, sighting the British force at 0540. The *Hardy* and her accompanying destroyers increased speed from 15 knots to 30 knots, engaging the new enemy at a range of some 7,000 yards. Then out of the mist ahead appeared two more ships three or four miles off, apparently coming in from the sea. At first it was hoped in the *Hardy* that the newcomers might be British cruisers; they were in fact the German destroyers *Bernd von Arnim* and *Georg Thiele*, which had been lying at anchor to the west of Narvik in Ballangen Fjord. It was not long before the heavier German guns[2] began to take their toll; they disabled the *Hardy*, which beached herself on the south shore of Ofot Fjord, 7 miles from Narvik.[3] They sank the *Hunter* and disabled the *Hotspur* which drifted on to her sinking consort, exposed to the fire of four enemies, before she managed to get clear. The *Hostile* and *Havock*, 2 miles ahead and practically untouched, turned round to help. The Germans, says Commander Wright of the *Hostile*, were ' zigzagging across the *Hotspur*'s rear, doing target practice at her at a range of about 8,000 yards, surrounding her with splashes '; but the German ships had not escaped damage, and at 0625 the *Thiele* and *Arnim* retired with some of their guns out of action; the remaining destroyers also soon fell back and the three British ships withdrew unhindered. Thus the fight ended at 0630. Half an hour later, as they were on their way out some 25 miles west of Narvik, a large ship appeared out of the snow and mist. This was the German ammunition ship *Rauenfels*. The

---

[1] British 5, Swedish 5, Norwegian 4, Dutch 1, German 8. (B.R. 1337, Merchant Ship Losses, 1946). The German ships were apparently the *Aachen, Altona, Bockenheim, Frielinghaus, Hein Hoyer, Jan Wellem* (undamaged), *Martha Hendrik Fisser, Neuenfels* (beached). (War Diary, April 1940, p. 288.)

[2] The German destroyers all had five 5-in. guns. The British destroyers had four 4.7-in. guns except the *Hardy*, which had five 4.7-in.

[3] The *Hardy* floated off next high water, and drifted ashore 2½ miles to the eastward, near Skjomnes, where she remained a wreck.

Havock opened fire; she ran herself ashore on the south side of the fjord and blew up when a benzine tank was hit. The loss of her supplies was severely felt by the Germans.

Of the British force, two ships had been sunk, one disabled and its gallant leader killed.[1] German casualties[2] were two destroyers sunk and five damaged; the flotilla had also destroyed half a dozen merchantmen, in addition to the *Rauenfels*, but unfortunately not the large supply ship *Jan Wellem*, which had been lying by the pier and provided stores for many a day.

14. Operations in Vest Fjord area, 10th-12th April [PLANS 9, 12

Admiral Whitworth received Captain Warburton-Lee's signal, that a cruiser was chasing the flotilla, soon after 0600, the 10th. He sent in the *Penelope* to help, at the same time ordering the four destroyers of his screen to join her, and he told Captain Yates of the *Penelope* ' support retirement of 2nd Destroyer Flotilla, counter-attacking enemy force as necessary. Then establish a patrol off the minefield with the object of preventing further enemy forces reaching Narvik'. Captain Bickford, already by the minefield, sent in his only fully-armed ship, the *Greyhound*, on his own account at 0800, and she met Commander Layman's three ships near Tranoy about an hour and a half later. Commander Layman then decided to go in the *Hotspur* to Skjel Fjord, 50 miles away to the westward in the Lofoten Islands, taking also the *Hostile* to look after the cripple. Captain Yates agreeing when he came up about 1100, the two ships made their way to that haven, which was soon to shelter other cripples.

Admiral Whitworth elaborated his arrangements in the following signal to Captain Yates, timed 1116/10 :—

> ' Present situation. Enemy forces in Narvik consist of one cruiser, five destroyers and one submarine. Troop transports may be expected to arrive through Vest Fjord or through Inner Leads, disregarding minefield.
>
> Your object is to prevent reinforcements reaching Narvik. Establish a destroyer patrol between positions 67° 47′ N., 14° 20′ E., and 68° 2′ N., 13° 40′ E., one destroyer also to patrol north-east of minefield during daylight.
>
> Enemy submarine may operate in Vest Fjord. Enemy may debouch in force to attempt to drive you off prior to his reinforcements arriving. Establish warning and A/S patrol 30 miles north-eastward of your patrol line.
>
> *Renown* and *Repulse*, unescorted, will operate in vicinity of 67° N., 10° E.
>
> Report your dispositions.
>
> Oiler *British Lady*, escorted by *Grenade*, *Encounter*, are due Skjel Fjord, 68° N., 13° 15′ E., p.m. 12th April. This fjord may be used for *Hotspur* if required.'

---

[1] H.M. The King approved the posthumous award of the Victoria Cross to Captain Warburton-Lee.

[2] Losses and damage inflicted by the 2nd Destroyer Flotilla at Narvik on 10th April 1940.
    Wilhelm Heidkamp out of action, Captain (D), Commodore Bonte, killed: sunk on the morning of the 11th April, 81 dead.
    Anton Schmitt sunk, 50 dead.
    Diether Von Roeder, hit five times by gunfire; boiler room 2 out of action; severe damage to the ship's side; no longer seaworthy, 13 dead.
    Hans Lüdemann, hits on No. 1 Gun and Compartment III. No. 1 Gun out of action; fire in Compartment III, magazine flooded, 2 dead.
    Hermann Kunne, damaged by splinters; so badly shaken by the torpedo explosion on *Anton Schmitt*, which lay alongside her, that the main and auxiliary engines and electrical equipment were rendered useless until after the battle, 9 dead.
    Georg Thiele, seven hits by gunfire; fire control apparatus and No. 1 gun disabled; magazine flooded, fires in both the forward and after parts of the ship, 13 dead.
    Bernd Von Arnim, five hits by gunfire; boilers, 3, 2 out of action; seaworthiness reduced by hits on the ship's side and forecastle, 2 dead.
    Wolfgang Zenker, *Erich Giese*, *Erich Koellner* } No damage or losses. Roughly 50 per cent of their ammunition used.

The destroyer patrol line was 20 miles long, right across Vest Fjord, roughly 10 miles above Skjel Fjord on the north and the minefield on the south side. As it turned out, the *Greyhound* and *Havock* attacked a submarine during the afternoon near the mouth of Vest Fjord, Captain Yates having sent them down the fjord before receiving the above signal ; whereupon Admiral Whitworth ordered them to hunt ' for at least 24 hours—submarine must on no account be allowed to escape '. This left the four big destroyers and the three minelayers at Captain Yates's disposal.

At 1254, however, Admiral Whitworth received a signal (timed 0808/10) from the Commander-in-Chief, ordering him to ' concentrate on allowing no force from Narvik to escape '. As this changed the object, so Admiral Whitworth changed his dispositions (1511/10 to *Penelope*) :—

> 'Your object is now to prevent escape of enemy forces from Narvik through Vest Fjord or possibly through Tjeldsundet. Endeavour to maintain a warning destroyer patrol south of Tjeldoy with your main force north-west of Tranoy. If this position is untenable in dark hours, withdraw to south-westward of Tranoy.
> You have freedom to alter these dispositions according to weather, local conditions, and enemy counter moves.'

That evening the Admiralty informed the Commander-in-Chief of the policy for the immediate future in A.T. 1904/10, of which the following is an extract :—

> ' As enemy is now established at Narvik, recapture of that place takes priority over operations against Bergen and Trondheim. Expedition is being prepared as quickly as possible, and you will be further informed when plan and time table are completed. In the meantime it is of primary importance to prevent Narvik's being reinforced by sea. Possibility of seizing and holding a temporary base near Narvik with small military force is under urgent examination : in the meantime, you will presumably arrange for a temporary refuelling anchorage in the north. As Narvik must also be of primary importance to the Germans, it seems possible that battlecruisers may turn up there.'

But the Admiralty was anxious to try another naval attack without delay on the enemy ships (believed to consist of two cruisers and half a dozen destroyers) at Narvik, and had already ordered Admiral Layton to send three ships of the 18th Cruiser Squadron—then on their way to Scapa—with eight destroyers, as soon as they had completed with fuel. These orders were countermanded, as Admiral Layton's ships would be needed to conduct the expedition mentioned in A.T. 1904/10 (above), and the *Penelope* was told off instead (A.T. 2012/10) :—

> ' If, in light of experience this morning, you consider it a justifiable operation, take available destroyers in Narvik area and attack enemy tonight or tomorrow morning.'

And Captain Yates answered (*Penelope* to Admiralty, 2310/10) :—

> 'Consider attack is justifiable, although element of surprise has been lost. Navigation dangerous from wrecks of ships sunk today, eliminating chance of successful night attack. Propose attacking at dawn on Friday (12th), since operation orders cannot be got out and issued for tomorrow in view of present disposition of destroyers on patrol.'

These signals came to Admiral Whitworth for information only. Still, he felt bound to point out that the ships under his orders had been given three different things to do : to prevent the Germans from escaping from Narvik, to prevent fresh forces from joining them, and to attack them there. ' In my view ', he says, ' the situation required clarifying ', so he made this signal to the Admiralty, timed 2219 :—

> ' Your 2012/10th April to *Penelope* appears to conflict with the policy outlined in your 1904/10th April, not to *Penelope*, which, in my view, is the correct one under the circumstances.
> Further casualties to ships now under my command will jeopardize the prevention of reinforcements reaching Narvik.'

The Admiralty stood by their plan, telling Captain Yates they should 'back whatever decision you make' and approving his attack at dawn on the 12th. But certain occurrences during the night 10th/11th April, reported by the *Bedouin*, Senior Officer in Ofot Fjord, raised misgivings, and at 0930, 11th, Captain Yates signalled to the Admiralty :—

> 'Senior Officer, Destroyers, reports, while on patrol last night south of Tjeldoy, he approached Baroy Island Light. Several loud explosions took place in his vicinity. The explosions were of a different character and appeared to indicate controlled minefield and shore-fired magnetic torpedoes. Activity was also observed ashore at Baroy Island. The indications were that shore defences were fully prepared. He withdrew his patrol to south-west. He is of opinion that the operation on the lines of yesterday's attack could not be carried out effectively.
> In light of this report, I concur, and regret I must reverse decision given in my 2310/10.'

Nevertheless, the Admiralty still hoped to bring off this attack. They told Captain Yates to 'have all preliminary preparations made in case carrying out of attack on enemy forces in Narvik is ordered'. Unhappily, the *Penelope* ran on shore that afternoon on her way to Bodo, and was out of action in consequence for a long time to come. Next day the Admiralty ordered an attack on a different scale.

Rumours of German reinforcements had reached Admiral Whitworth in the meantime through Commander Wright at Skjel Fjord. The Norwegian police there told him that a man-of-war had been seen in the evening of the 10th in Tennholm Fjord, some 50 miles south of the minefield; that a large German tanker was lying there, hoping for a pilot to take her to Narvik; and that several big German merchantmen 'believed to be transports' had arrived at Bodo, at the mouth of Vest Fjord. The Admiral 'considered the first duty of the force under my command remained the prevention of reinforcements reaching Narvik, of which these were apparently some. It also seemed possible that the ships were unloading at Bodo'. Accordingly, he told Captain Yates to 'get a pilot at Tranoy. Take two destroyers and firstly attack enemy transports reported at Bodo . . . and secondly, try and capture tanker at Tennholm . . . Warship reported at Tennholm must be considered. You should endeavour to be back on your patrol by dark today', the 11th—this last, presumably, that the *Penelope* should be in time to attack Narvik next morning. Then, 'lest there should be doubt as to his first object' Admiral Whitworth added, 'attack on enemy transports must take precedence over attack on Narvik'. The *Penelope* took the *Eskimo* and *Kimberley* with her; but failed to find a pilot at Tranoy, Captain Yates went on to try at Fleinvaer, a few miles from Bodo at the mouth of the outer fjords, meaning to go in without a pilot should he fail again in finding one. There, however, about 1500, the 11th, the *Penelope* struck a rock. She soon floated off, but had injured herself seriously, and made her way to Skjel Fjord in tow of the *Eskimo* with considerable difficulty. Meanwhile, Captain Yates sent the *Kimberley* up to Bodo, where she learnt that one German merchant ship only had been to the port since the invasion, and that was the *Alster*, which the *Icarus* had captured early that morning while patrolling near the minefield in Vest Fjord with the other minelayers.[1]

---

[1] The *Alster* had sailed from Brunsbüttel with the motor transport for Narvik on 3rd April. She left Bodo p.m. 10th, and the *Icarus* turned her over to a guard from the *Penelope* at Skjel Fjord before that ship sailed for Bodo on the 11th. The mechanical transport was turned over to the Norwegians; the *Alster* was used to hoist out the *Eskimo*'s mountings after the second Battle of Narvik, and subsequently to load and bring down a cargo of iron ore from Kirkenes. The Norwegians sank the tanker (the *Kattegat*) reported in Tennholm Fjord (*see* Secs. 1 and 21 *postea*).

The remaining destroyers continued to cruise that day 'to prevent reinforcements reaching Narvik'. Admiral Whitworth gave orders to Captain Bickford ' to control Vest Fjord ' north-eastward of the patrol line he had prescribed in his orders to Captain Yates the day before, and to station a warning patrol between Tranoy and Tjeldoy. The Admiral himself continued off the Lofoten Islands with the two capital ships, stretching some 80 miles to the westward of Skomvaer. An Admiralty report of a possible German rendezvous in 67° N. between 4° 30′ E. and 6° E. sent him further west to patrol to the northward of this position during the night (11th/12th) ; next morning he joined the Commander-in-Chief, who had been moving north from the Trondheim area.[1]

15. Movements of Commander-in-Chief, Home Fleet, 10th-12th April

[PLANS 3, 4

Meanwhile the Commander-in-Chief held his north-easterly course throughout the 10th April, altering to the eastward at 2000 that evening for a position some 90 miles north-west of Trondheim, whence the *Furious* was to fly off her aircraft to carry out the attack arranged between the Commander-in-Chief and the Admiralty, on the enemy ships there. These, according to R.A.F. reports consisted of two cruisers, besides destroyers and merchantmen. The last report received before the attack, timed 1645, 10th, placed a ' Hipper ' class ship at anchor off the town, and a ' Nürnberg ' at the head of the narrows in Trondheim Fjord, 10 miles to the westward.

In fact, when this report was made, the German units in Trondheim consisted of the *Hipper* and four destroyers, the *Paul Jacobi, Theodor Riedel, Friedrich Eckholdt* and *Bruno Heineman*. They had entered the fjord in the early hours of the 9th and by midnight had put all their troops ashore. On the 10th at 1500 the *Hipper* and three of the destroyers were ordered to leave that night and return to Germany, but shortage of fuel prevented this, and eventually at 2100, 10th, the *Hipper* got under way, accompanied only by the *Eckholdt*. There was some delay owing to a submarine alarm in the fjord, and it was not till 0200, 11th, that she passed through Ramsöy Fjord (63° 30′ N., 8° 12′ E.)— which had been chosen as being less likely to be patrolled by the enemy, owing to its navigational difficulties—and shaped a north-westerly course at high speed to get clear of the land. The *Eckholdt* was ordered back to Trondheim, as she was unable to keep up in the heavy sea. It is interesting to note that had the *Hipper* been a couple of hours earlier her diversionary course would have taken her straight into Admiral Forbes' fleet on its easterly course at about 0200 ; as it was she passed unseen some 25 to 30 miles to the westward, while the *Furious* was flying off, and, passing through the waters lately traversed by the fleet, turned to the southward for Germany at 0740.

Accordingly when the 18 machines with torpedoes left the *Furious* at about 0400, in 64° 30′ N., 8° E., some 90 miles from the town, to attack the German units reported in Trondheim they found the enemy cruiser—or as they believed, the two enemy cruisers—gone. While the fleet cruised north and south of the carrier, with a few destroyers watching the entrance to Fro Havet, the northern approach to Trondheim, the *Furious*'s airmen could see below them in the fjord only two destroyers and a submarine, besides merchantmen. The third destroyer seems to have escaped detection, and the other, the *Eckholdt* which had set out with the *Hipper* on the previous night, did not return until 0530

---

[1] See Sec. 15 *postea*.

MOVEMENTS OF COMMANDER-IN-CHIEF, HOME FLEET, 10th–12th

that morning. The British aircraft attacked both the destroyers they had sighted, but several torpedoes grounded in shallow water, exploding before they reached their targets and the attack was without success.

The 'disappointing result' caused Admiral Forbes to order a 'proper reconnaissance' of Trondheim by two machines, armed with bombs to attack the men-of-war after they had reported what they found in the fjords: they sighted two destroyers, one of which they attacked unsuccessfully, some seaplanes, and a few merchant vessels.

The result was disappointing indeed; yet it was not the airmen's fault, as Captain Troubridge of the *Furious* pointed out in his letter of proceedings. At the end of the month, when the *Furious* went home, he wrote of these young officers and men; 'All were firing their first shot, whether torpedo, bomb, or machinegun, in action; many made their first night landing on 11th April (sc. 12th—after their first attack at Narvik), and, undeterred by the loss of several of their shipmates, their honour and courage remained throughout as dazzling as the snow-covered mountains over which they so triumphantly flew'—a tribute reminiscent of Lord St. Vincent's saying of an earlier Thomas Troubridge that 'his honour was bright as his sword'.

While the fleet was cruising in the offing during these air operations a report of a merchant ship near Mausundvaer (63° 51' N., 8° 45' E.) in the north-west approaches to Trondheim was received. The *Isis* (Commander Clouston, S.O.) and *Ilex* were ordered to proceed through Fröy Fjord to investigate. Having searched in the reported vicinity and the southern part of Fro Havet without success, Commander Clouston decided to carry out a reconnaissance up Inner Trondheim Lead and Skjorn Fjord, to investigate the outer limit of the defences in Trondheim approach.[1] Several German aircraft were sighted, but no opposition from shore defences was encountered till shortly after entering Trondheim Fjord at 1320, when fire was opened from Brettingsnes, then abaft the port beam, at a range of about 3000 yards. Commander Clouston at once altered course to seaward and a smart engagement ensued, the destroyers engaging the battery with H.E. as they retired under smoke, up to a range of 10,000 yards. Though narrowly missed, neither ship was hit, and Commander Clouston gained the impression that the battery lacked modern fire control equipment. Course was then shaped through Fro Havet to rejoin the Commander-in-Chief.

On the return of the reconnoitring aircraft, the Commander-in-Chief shaped course to the northward towards Narvik, intending to launch an air attack on the enemy Captain Warburton-Lee had fought the morning before. At 1500, 11th April, Vice-Admiral Cunningham with the *Devonshire*, *Berwick*, *Inglefield* and *Imogen*, was detached to search the Inner Lead from Trondheim to Vest Fjord, with instructions to mop up any enemy ships found there. The *Isis* and *Ilex*, then on their way back from Trondheim, were ordered to join this force. The search was carried up to lat. 66° 17' N., by the next day and later on north of Narvik as far as Tromsö, but no enemy was encountered.

Half an hour after Admiral Cunningham parted company, enemy air attacks on the fleet started and continued till 1700. The destroyer *Eclipse* was hit and her engine room flooded. The *York*, *Escort* and *Hyperion* were detailed to stand by her and escort her to Lerwick, where she eventually arrived in tow of the *Escort* on the 17th.

While these attacks were in progress, the Admiralty informed the Commander-in-Chief (A.T. 1607/11) of a possible enemy rendezvous in the coming

---
[1] *See* Plan 11.

twenty-four hours in 67° N., between 4° 30′ E., and 6° E. This position was about 150 miles to the north-westward of the Commander-in-Chief, and about half that distance to the south-westward of Vice-Admiral Whitworth, who reported that he was in 67° 50′ N., 8° 11′ E., at 1741, steering 235° at 24 knots. That night (11th/12th) the Vice-Admiral patrolled to the northward of the possible rendezvous, while the Commander-in-Chief having reached 65° 43′ N., 8° 50′ E., at 2000, steered 290° (taking him about 45 miles to the southward of it) till 0445, 12th, when he altered course to the northward to join the battle cruisers. The junction was effected at 0730 in about 67° N., 6° E. Nothing was seen of any enemy ships; on the contrary, Air Force reports which soon began to come in placed both German battlecruisers and one cruiser in 57° 31′ N., 4° 52′ E. (off the south-west corner of Norway) at 0857, 12th, steering 142° at 15 knots. The battlecruisers ' had thus managed to pass all the way from north of the Lofoten Islands to the Skagerrak without being sighted by any of our air or surface vessels ',[1] and were then beyond our reach, almost back in their home waters. A brief account of their movements during the invasion period will be found in the following section.

16. Movements of German naval forces, 9th–13th April [PLANS 3, 4

After outdistancing the *Renown* in the morning of the 9th April, Admiral Lütjens with the *Gneisenau* and *Scharnhorst* had stood to the northward till 1200, when course was altered to west along the parallel 70° N. The general situation as he knew it decided Admiral Lütjens to make the return journey to Germany independently of the Narvik and Trondheim groups, keeping well to the westward and after turning homeward passing close to the Shetlands. Owing to a technical defect in the *Gneisenau* the signal which he sent giving this intention failed to reach the Naval Group Command, West, and at 0800, 10th April, the latter asked him to report his position and intentions. Admiral Lütjens was then in position 69° N., 5° 30′ W. (to the north-east of Iceland); he did not wish to give away his position, so at noon sent the *Scharnhorst's* aircraft to Trondheim with orders to make the report called for three hours after leaving him. This report crossed a signal sent by Group Command, West, at 1500:—

> ' All available cruisers, destroyers and torpedo boats are to proceed to sea tonight. Narvik destroyers are to concentrate with the Commander-in-Chief. It is left to your discretion whether *Hipper* with three destroyers join you or break through and proceed direct to Home port.'

The Narvik destroyers were unable to put to sea, partly owing to damage inflicted by the 2nd Flotilla, but mainly owing to shortage of fuel; they consequently remained in Narvik, with disastrous results to themselves (*see* Sec. 18 *postea*).

Admiral Lütjens anticipated an alteration to these orders as a result of his signal by the aircraft, but he altered course at 1630 to 105° and steered for the rendezvous between Vest Fjord and Trondheim. When at 2238, 10th, he received the expected approval of his intentions, he altered course to the south-west, and at 0400, 11th—just as the *Hipper* was clearing the Home Fleet 300 miles to the eastward, and the *Furious* was flying off for the abortive attack on Trondheim—he hauled round to the southward. Admiral Lütjens was aware from enemy reports that the main British naval concentration

---

[1] Commander-in-Chief, Home Fleet's report. The Commander-in-Chief was of course working on the identification of the two German battle cruisers by Admiral Whitworth's force on 9th April as one battlecruiser and one cruiser.

was off the Norwegian coast, in the Trondheim and Lofoten areas ; this, combined with the weather—rain and short visibility—facilitated the passage of the battlecruisers, and at 1200, 11th, being then some 75 miles to the northward of the Faeroes, they altered course for home, and passing 40 miles to the eastward of the Shetlands during the night of the 11th/12th, effected a rendezvous with the *Hipper* at 0830, 12th. It was at this moment that the British reconnaissance aircraft appeared, and shortly afterwards intercepted messages warned the Germans that bombers were on their way to attack them, but the weather seriously deteriorated, visibility fell to under a mile and no contact occurred. That evening the formation reached the Jade without incident.

Mention has been made of how the cruisers at Bergen, Kristiansand and Oslo fared ; the only other important unit—the *Lützow*—after the check at Drøbak on the 9th April, had anchored off Oslo in the forenoon of the 10th. That afternoon she left for the return journey to Kiel ; owing to the danger of enemy submarines, she proceeded southwards at high speed through the western waters of the Skagerrak. On 11th April, at 0029, a torpedo, fired by the British submarine *Spearfish*, struck the *Lützow* aft, seriously damaging and putting out of action her rudder and propellers, tearing a considerable hole in the ship's side and flooding the after part. The ship drifted before the wind in a south-westerly direction, towards the Skaw, heavily down by the stern. At 0400 she was met by boats of the 17th A/S Flotilla, and the 19th Minesweeper Flotilla, which formed an A/S escort, took her in tow, and kept her head round, for it was feared that the heavy sea then running would break her stern right off. Most of the crew were taken off by patrol boats ; the *Lützow* eventually reached Kiel on the evening of the 13th, and was out of action for twelve months.

17. *Furious* aircraft attack at Narvik, 12th April [PLANS 4, 12

After meeting Vice-Admiral Whitworth in the morning of 12th April, the Commander-in-Chief steered to the northward for the Lofoten area. Detachments were again reducing the strength with the flag. The *York* and two destroyers escorting the damaged *Eclipse* had left the fleet the previous afternoon, as had two other destroyers sent in to fuel. Vice-Admiral Cunningham's force was still searching the fjords. And from this time another commitment was influencing the Commander-in-Chief's dispositions—the hastily organised Allied expeditions to Norway. These will be dealt with separately,[1] but the first convoy (N.P.1) consisting of the s.s. *Empress of Australia*, *Monarch of Bermuda*, and *Reina del Pacifico* had sailed from the Clyde on 11th April, being joined next day off Cape Wrath by the s.s. *Batory* and *Chrobry* from Scapa, and was steering for Narvik accompanied by Vice-Admiral Layton in the *Manchester*, with the *Birmingham*, *Cairo*, five destroyers and the *Protector*.[2] On the same day (12th) General Mackesy, commanding the land forces, with an advance party consisting of half a battalion of the Scots Guards, sailed from Scapa in the *Southampton*, and Admiral of the Fleet the Earl of Cork and Orrery hoisted his flag in the *Aurora*[3] and sailed from Rosyth to take charge of the naval side of

---

[1] *See* Chapter III *postea*.

[2] The convoy was joined by the repair ship *Vindictive* with six destroyers on the 13th April.

[3] Admiral Sir Edward Evans had left the *Aurora* on her arrival at Scapa in the evening of the 10th April and proceeded by air to Stockholm with an Allied Anglo-French Mission to establish contact with the Norwegian Authorities. On the conclusion of the work of the Mission he was again sent to Scandinavia on a special mission from the British Government to the King of Norway.

the combined operations at Narvik,[1] though news of this appointment did not reach the Commander-in-Chief, Home Fleet, till the early hours of the 14th (A.T. 2314/13).

In order to ensure the safe passage of Convoy N.P.1, the Commander-in-Chief detached the *Valiant, Repulse,* and three destroyers in the afternoon of 12th April, with orders to meet it, after which the *Valiant* was to provide cover to Vaags Fjord, while the *Repulse* and destroyers proceeded to the base for fuel.

Thus in the afternoon of 12th April, the Commander-in-Chief had with him only the *Rodney, Warspite, Renown, Furious* and six destroyers, while twelve destroyers were working in the southern approaches to Narvik.[2]

With this force the Commander-in-Chief arrived off the Lofoten Islands to support the *Furious*, whose aircraft were to attack Narvik. The aircraft were to make a dive-bombing attack on the shipping that evening, the 12th, and to photograph the port and its approaches, leaving their ship in roughly 68° N., 11° E., with a flight of 150 miles or so each way; and the Commander-in-Chief told the *Furious*, 'Attack on ships in Narvik to be pressed home and hope to hear all ships, including merchant ships which are either transports or storeships, have been sunk; no shore A.A. batteries so far as known, and most of enemy destroyers badly mauled'. The *Renown* and three destroyers stood by the *Furious* during the attack, while the Commander-in-Chief stretched 40 to 50 miles to seaward and back with the *Rodney* and *Warspite*, screened by the other three destroyers in the fleet. The leading squadron of aircraft left the ship soon after 1600, dropped their bombs at heights between 1,200 and 400 ft., claiming four hits on German destroyers,[3] and arrived on board again a little after 2000, just four hours from their setting out. They lost two out of the eight machines through the enemy's fire, but saved both crews. Lieut.-Commander Sydney-Turner remarked that his attack 'was carried out in conditions of which the squadron had had no previous experience and without a reconnaissance, which would have been extremely valuable in deciding tactics of approach. The only maps available were photographic reproductions of Admiralty charts, which showed no contours'. The other squadron, starting forty minutes later, had the worst of the weather and turned back near Baroy Island. 'Ceiling now 100 ft., visibility 250 yards, very heavy snowstorms', said their commander. They got back in the dark at 2030.

18. Second Battle of Narvik, 13th April 1940 [PLAN 10

Soon after he gave his instructions for the air attack, the Commander-in-Chief had a signal from the Admiralty to attempt Narvik again by sea:—' Orders for cleaning up enemy naval forces and batteries in Narvik by using a battleship heavily escorted by destroyers, with synchronized dive-bombing attacks from *Furious*'. Accordingly, he planned an attack for the following day by the *Warspite* and nine destroyers under Admiral Whitworth. The squadron would

---

[1] The following force came under Lord Cork's command when within 100 miles of Vaags Fjord: *Effingham, Enterprise, Cairo, Vindictive, Protector* and auxiliary craft, and the convoy destroyers; also the *Aurora* and *Southampton* until the troops in Convoy N.P.1 had landed, when these two ships rejoined the Commander-in-Chief, Home Fleet. The *Protector* was to return to Rosyth after net laying.

[2] The number of Narvik destroyers includes the *Grenade* and *Encounter*, which arrived at Skjel Fjord with the oiler *British Lady* p.m. 12th.

[3] According to the Germans, no hits were obtained on the destroyers; some casualties, mostly on land, were caused by splinters.

SECOND BATTLE OF NARVIK, 13TH APRIL 1940

assemble at 0730, the 13th, in 67° 44′ N., 13° 22′ E. inside Vest Fjord, a hundred miles from Narvik, and go in with some destroyers ahead sweeping and the others forming an anti-submarine screen for the *Warspite*—the sweeps to be hauled in when within 10 miles of Narvik. The *Warspite* would go ' to a position 5 miles from Narvik, depending on circumstances, and from there cover the advance of the destroyers into the harbour and adjacent waters where enemy ships may be located '. The *Furious*, cruising outside with the Commander-in-Chief, had orders to send aircraft to attack shore defences supposed to be on Baroy Island and by Ramnes and the opposite shore in the narrows of Ofot Fjord, and others to attack the ships and batteries in and near Narvik. These attacks would ' synchronize with *Warspite*'s approach ' and had stated times in the orders, which Admiral Whitworth was to alter should there be need ; but he managed to keep them unchanged. The Commander-in-Chief with the *Rodney*, *Renown*, *Furious* and five destroyers would cruise outside the Lofoten Islands some 30 miles off shore, in the vicinity of 68° N., 11° 30′ E. There were also four destroyers at or near Skjel Fjord.[1]

Admiral Whitworth shifted his flag to the *Warspite* in the night, 12th/13th, after the *Renown* and *Furious* returned to the fleet, and sailed for the rendezvous inside Vest Fjord with the *Cossack*, *Hero*, *Foxhound* and *Forester*. There the *Bedouin* and *Punjabi*, *Kimberley* and *Icarus* joined, while the ninth destroyer, the *Eskimo*, remained patrolling near Tranoy Light, some 60 miles farther in. This was fortunate, for shortly before 1100, the 13th, she sighted a submarine between her and the squadron, then just coming in sight. The submarine dived, and the *Eskimo* and some destroyers of the screen drove it down with depth charges over the area from which it could threaten the *Warspite*. A bomber from the *Furious* duly met the squadron off Baroy soon after 1200, but neither the aircraft nor the *Warspite* could see anything to attack there. Soon afterwards the blackened bow of the *Rauenfels* was passed, a grim reminder of what lay before them. Meanwhile the *Warspite* had sent up her own aircraft to scout, a service it did to perfection. ' I doubt ', says the Vice-Admiral, ' if ever a shipborne aircraft has been used to such good purpose '. It first reported a German destroyer off Hamnesholm in the narrows, a dozen miles above the squadron, then another beyond the narrows : these were the *Hermann Künne*, and the *Erich Koellner*. The *Koellner*, although undamaged in the engagement on the 10th, had run aground in Ballangen Fjord shortly before midnight on the 11th ; the damage sustained was severe and the ship was no longer seaworthy. Accordingly, it was decided to anchor her off Taarstad where she was to be used as a barrage-battery ; she was on the way thither, escorted by the *Künne*, when sighted by the *Warspite*'s aircraft. The *Künne* immediately retired before the British ships, exchanging fire at 12,000 yards, the limit of visibility ; the captain of the *Koellner*, realising that he could not accept action, headed for Djupvik Bay, on the south shore of the fjord (68° 24′ N., 16° 47′ E.), hoping from this position, at a range of 3,000 to 4,000 yards, to be able to use his torpedoes against the approaching squadron, before it could sight him and open fire. The *Warspite*'s aircraft had meanwhile flown to the head of Herjangs Fjord, 20 miles off, where it bombed and sank a submarine, the *U.64*, which fired at and hit the aircraft. On its way back, it sighted the *Koellner* putting into Djupvik Bay, and its signals enabled the leading British ships to train guns and tubes to starboard, ready to engage the

---

[1] Admiral Whitworth's force was as follows : *Warspite* (Captain Crutchley), *Bedouin* (Commander McCoy), *Cossack* (Commander Sherbrooke), *Eskimo* (Commander Micklethwait), *Punjabi* (Commander Lean), *Hero* (Commander Biggs), *Icarus* (Lieut.-Commander Maud), *Kimberley* (Lieut.-Commander Knowling), *Forester* (Lieut.-Commander Tancock), *Foxhound* (Lieut.-Commander Peters).

enemy the moment they passed the mouth of the bay. The *Koellner* fired her torpedoes and one salvo from her guns and was then smothered by the British fire ; in addition, both the *Bedouin* and the *Eskimo* hit her with torpedoes, while her own torpedoes missed.[1]

It was then nearly 1330. The British ships were a dozen miles from Narvik, looking for the German destroyers in the haze ahead. When the *Künne* first sighted the British at the entrance to Ofot Fjord, she had signalled a warning to the other six destroyers, which were all at anchor in Narvik harbour. The S.O. of the 4th German Destroyer Flotilla, Captain Bey, who had taken over command of the group when Commodore Bonte was killed on the 10th, immediately ordered them to put out to meet the enemy. The *Hans Lüdemann* was the first to leave, followed by the *Wolfgang Zenker*, and shortly afterwards by the *Bernd von Arnim* ; the *Thiele* and the *Giese* had not got sufficient steam to leave and the *Diether von Roeder* was too badly damaged to move. *U.51*, in harbour at the time, submerged, under the impression that it was an air-raid, but evidently put out into Vest Fjord later on.

As the three German destroyers left the harbour they met the *Künne*, and all four turned so as to fire their torpedoes. Commander Biggs of the *Hero* describes the action outside Narvik harbour in the following words :—

> ' From 1300 to 1355, *Hero* engaged three separate enemy destroyers with her two foremost guns at ranges between 10,000 and 15,000 yards. During this period it is estimated that only six hits were obtained on enemy ships. This was largely due to the large number of ships firing at a few enemy destroyers from practically the same bearing, which made the picking out of own fall of shot extremely difficult. It was also due to the fact that only the two foremost guns could be brought into action, owing to the restriction imposed by the *Hero*'s being guide of the fleet and also employed on sweeping duties.
>
> Owing to her duties as guide of the fleet, which necessitated long periods on a steady course at a steady speed, *Hero* appeared to be practically continuously under fire, but the ship was not hit except for one small splinter.'

The German destroyers outside the harbour, which were later joined by the *Thiele*, were gradually forced back ; German reports claim, however, that up to this point, after an engagement lasting 1½ hours, with the exception of the *Koellner*, sunk in Djupvik Bay, none of their destroyers had been hit. If this was the case, their end came all very suddenly ; at 1350 they received the order : ' Retire up Rombaks Fjord '.[2] The *Künne* apparently failed to pick up this message, for she made for Herjangs Fjord ; there she beached herself off Troldvik, and her crew were sent to reinforce the 139th German Mountain Regiment, which was defending the area north of Narvik. The *Eskimo*, following hard in her track, came up and torpedoed her, while the other British units were attacking the *Giese*, which had just raised enough steam to leave harbour : her guns were silenced and she was set on fire in a few minutes, close inshore, north of the harbour, where her captain gave the order to abandon ship at 1330. The *Punjabi* was badly hit at this time and withdrew with main steampipe and guns out of action, but reported herself fit for service an hour later. The *Warspite* was engaging the enemy whenever a target presented itself but, owing to the smoke of the destroyer engagement, fire was intermittent. Speed was adjusted to maintain support of the destroyers, and to keep the flagship clear of the torpedo danger as far as possible.

---

[1] The *Warspite*'s aircraft thus played its part in carrying out the following clause in the orders : ' It is specially important that destroyers sighted should be engaged before they can fire torpedoes at *Warspite* '. The *Penelope*, lying disabled at Skjel Fjord, also signalled reports she received of the enemy's leaving Narvik (*Penelope* to *Eskimo*, 1155/13).

[2] By this time the German destroyers were practically out of ammunition, having expended a good deal in the action of 10th April.

According to the plan of attack, aircraft from the *Furious* should have joined the battle at this stage. Her aircraft had come punctually over Baroy Island, but the one for Ramnes and Hamnesholm had failed to get beyond Baroy, the weather being very thick when it arrived there. The striking force over Narvik, ten Swordfish under Captain Burch, R.M., ' fought their way ', as Captain Troubridge has it, ' through the narrows into Ofot Fjord with a ceiling of 500 ft. and snow squalls that occasionally reduced visibility to a few yards '. As they came to the open fjord, the weather improved, and they arrived at exactly the proper moment. They dived from 2,000 ft. to drop their bombs at 900 ft.—about 100 bombs, of which one in three were 250-pounders, and the rest 20-pounders. They claimed two hits with the large bombs on German destroyers outside Narvik at the cost of two aircraft.[1]

The British destroyers then divided, some going into Narvik harbour, while others chased the enemy up Rombaks Fjord. The *Cossack*, followed later by the *Foxhound* and *Kimberley*, went inside the harbour, where there remained only the crippled *Diether von Roeder*, which they sank after a short but fierce exchange of fire, but not before she had obtained four hits on the *Cossack*, one in No. 2 boiler room cutting the main steam pipe and severing the telemotor leads. Unable to manœuvre, the *Cossack* went aground 50 yards south of the lighthouse at the entrance ; there she remained till 0315 next morning.[2]

The *Foxhound* stopped to rescue survivors from the *Erich Giese*, which lay burning outside the harbour, and the *Kimberley* then joined the other part of the flotilla. The *Eskimo* had seen the Germans make off into Rombaks Fjord, so went after them with the *Forester* and *Hero*, followed by the *Bedouin* and *Icarus*. Five miles in, the fjord narrows to a neck only a quarter of a mile across, opening beyond the neck, but still in places only half a mile wide. The British ships went up the fjord through a smoke cloud laid by the retreating enemy, the *Warspite*'s aircraft keeping them posted about the German destroyers' movements. The leading ships entered the inner fjord, where they sighted and engaged two of the last four German warships afloat in the area ; one of them, the *Georg Thiele*, turned to fire her remaining torpedoes, and in doing so ran on shore, disabled, at Sildvika, three miles or so beyond the neck of the fjord ; but one of her torpedoes struck the *Eskimo* right forward, blowing off her forecastle as far as abaft ' A ' gun. Her ' B ' gun's crew, though badly shaken by the explosion, ' magnificently continued firing as if nothing had happened. It looked as if the *Eskimo* would sink immediately '.[3] The *Eskimo* fired her last torpedo, which missed, and then steamed stern first back through the narrows till the wreckage of her bow struck the bottom and brought the ship up. The *Forester* stayed by her, while the *Hero* and *Icarus*, joined by the *Kimberley*, which had come round from Narvik, went on to the head of the fjord.

There, a mile or two beyond Sildvika, they found the last three German destroyers. All seemed deserted, and after a few rounds had been fired to make sure, the survivors of their crews were seen wending their way up the valley. One destroyer, which proved to be the *Hans Lüdemann*, was on an even keel, and the *Hero* and *Icarus* sent armed whalers to examine her. As they approached, another slowly turned over and sank, revealing the third scuttled and aground inshore of her. The whalers took possession of the *Lüdemann* and the white

---
[1] The German narrative states that none of the destroyers received a direct hit ; bombs fell very near the *Hermann Künne*, and the *Bernd Von Arnim*, but did very little damage.

[2] Vice-Admiral Whitworth's report stated that the *Cossack* drifted on to a submerged wreck, but there is no mention of this in the *Cossack*'s detailed report of the incident.

[3] Report of Commanding Officer, H.M.S. *Forester*.

ensign was hoisted above the Nazi flag; she was 'resting on the bottom, upright, with the engine room flooded. There was a fierce fire burning in the tiller flat and it appeared the depth charges might explode any moment'.[1] A swift search for secret matter proved fruitless; all that was found was a mass of charred papers, still burning, on the bridge.

When these last two actions began, the *Warspite* was about 5 miles west of Narvik, slowly following the destroyers, and firing at what seemed at first to be a battery on shore, but proved to be the destroyer alongside in the harbour. The Admiral ceased fire when the *Cossack* and her consorts went inside, and lay off the entrance until that fight was finished. Then he went into the outer part of Rombaks Fjord and ordered all the destroyers available to concentrate in the fjord. This was about the time of the *Eskimo*'s torpedoing and her retreat stern first through the narrows, leaving little room for other ships. The *Hero* and *Icarus* went on through, as we have seen; so did the *Bedouin*, which then reported, at 1520, ' one aground out of action, two more round the corner out of sight (there were actually three). If they have torpedoes, they are in a position of great advantage. *Hero* and *Bedouin*, ammunition almost exhausted. *Bedouin*, ' A ' mounting out of action '. On this the Admiral ordered the *Bedouin* out to close him, and when she came in sight he told her to arrange a fresh attack, ' sending most serviceable destroyer first: ram or board if necessary '. Accordingly, the *Bedouin* went in again, stern first this time, as she had four guns aft, but only two fit for action forward. She joined the *Hero*, *Icarus* and *Kimberley* at the head of the fjord about 1630, and ordered the torpedoing of the *Hans Lüdemann* which, although on shore, still remained upright. As soon as the Prize Crew had been taken off and the White Ensign hauled down, a torpedo was fired at her which broke her back and set her on fire forward. ' Had these four enemy destroyers ', remarks Commander Biggs of the *Hero*, ' been determined to make one last stand in the farthest end of the inner Rombaks Fjord, and had they been resolutely commanded, it might well have been an expensive business to destroy them, as not more than two of our ships under way could have operated against them at any time '.[2]

Thus ended the second Battle of Narvik. The risks of running the enemy to earth in the confined waters of the fjords had been correctly assessed and boldly accepted, and the result proved an outstanding success. The Germans lost their eight remaining destroyers and the U-boat (*U.64*) sunk by the *Warspite*'s aircraft; their garrison at Narvik was for the time being virtually isolated, and, moreover, the British squadron had found no sign of serious defences established on shore.

The *Warspite* then returned off Narvik. Finding it quiet there at 1730, except for a mild exchange of fire between the grounded *Cossack* and a small gun or two on shore, Admiral Whitworth ' considered the landing of a party to occupy the town, as the opposition had apparently been silenced '. But, his report goes on, ' with the force available only a small party could be landed, and to guard against the inevitable counter-attack, it would be necessary to keep the force concentrated, close to the water front, and to provide strong covering gunfire: in fact, I considered it would be necessary to keep *Warspite* off Narvik '. Then a German officer taken prisoner by the *Foxhound* spoke of submarines in the fjords, and German aircraft appeared, a dozen coming in sight at 1800. ' Apart from the above conditions, I felt that to place, at the end of a long and strenuous day, a party of less than 200 tired seamen and

---

[1] Report of Commanding Officer, H.M.S. *Hero*.

[2] According to German sources their destroyers had by that time expended all their ammunition.

marines in the midst of a force of not less than 2,000 professional German soldiers would be to court disaster, even allowing for the moral effect which the day's engagement must have had on the enemy. The cumulative effect of the roar of *Warspite*'s 15-in. guns reverberating down and around the high mountains of the fjord, the bursts and splashes of these great shells, the sight of their ships sinking and burning around them must have been terrifying . . . '

That moral effect would not last. To take full advantage of it ' would have required a trained organised military force, ready to land directly the naval engagement had ceased. If such a force had been present, I believe that they would have succeeded in establishing themselves so strongly in Narvik that its eventual capture would only be a matter of time and reinforcements. I thereupon decided against keeping *Warspite* stopped in the fjord off Narvik, subject to submarine and air attack '. Admiral Whitworth started down the fjord accordingly with the *Warspite* and most of his destroyers about 1830, leaving one or two ships to stand by the injured *Eskimo* in Rombaks Fjord and *Cossack* in Narvik ; but hearing there were wounded men in the ships left behind, he soon turned back that they might come on board the *Warspite*, and this took up the rest of the night.[1]

Meanwhile, A.T. 2115/13 had urged on Sir Charles Forbes the ' occupation of town of Narvik to ensure unopposed landing later '. Whether this signal reached Admiral Whitworth does not appear in his report. However, knowing that a regular expedition was on its way to Vaags Fjord, the outer approach to Narvik from the northward, and thinking this expedition might be diverted direct to Narvik, he made this signal to the Commander-in-Chief and the Admiralty (2210/13) :—

> ' My impression is that enemy forces in Narvik were thoroughly frightened as a result of today's action, and that the presence of *Warspite* was the chief cause of this. I recommend that the town be occupied without delay by the main landing force.
>
> I intend to visit Narvik again tomorrow, Sunday (14th), in order to maintain the moral effect of the presence of *Warspite*, and to accept the air and submarine menace involved by this course of action.'

Next day the Admiralty asked for an account of the German strength at Narvik, to which Admiral Whitworth answered (1027/14) :—

> ' Your 0913. Information from Norwegian sources estimates 1,500 to 2,000 troops in Narvik. German naval officer prisoner states that there are many more than this, but I think this statement was made with intent to deceive. He also states that guns on shore are being positioned with the main object of opposing a landing, but *Cossack*, aground in Narvik Bay for 12 hours yesterday, was not seriously molested.
>
> My 2210/13. I am convinced that Narvik can be taken by direct assault without fear of meeting serious opposition on landing. I consider that the main landing force need only be small, but it must have the support of Force B (his present squadron) or one of similar composition : a special requirement being ships and destroyers with the best available A.A. armaments.'

That morning, the 14th, the squadron went out into Vest Fjord, leaving the *Ivanhoe* (which had joined from Skjel Fjord the evening before) and the *Kimberley* for the time being at Narvik, with orders to prevent the discharge of cargo, which might include stores and munitions for the German garrison, from several merchantmen, some of them German, which had been left afloat

---

[1] German aircraft attacked the *Ivanhoe*, which was patrolling near Baroy Island after a search by the Skjel Fjord destroyers for the submarine sighted in the morning by the *Eskimo*, but they did not molest the *Warspite* and ships in her company. The *Foxhound* encountered a submarine off Hamnesholm as the squadron steered westward down the fjord in the evening.

there in the hope of our being able soon to carry them off as prizes. If necessary they were to be sunk; but both destroyers had to leave the port that day, the *Ivanhoe* going to hunt a submarine reported in Vaags Fjord, and there the matter stood.[1]

The *Cossack*, *Eskimo* and *Punjabi* went to Skjel Fjord for repairs before going home; the rest of the squadron stayed in Vest Fjord to meet Lord Cork and to be ' ready to operate against Narvik when required ' says Admiral Whitworth. However, the time for that was not yet come, and on the 15th he took the *Warspite* out, and met the Commander-in-Chief in the evening when a redistribution of destroyers was effected; he then cruised to the westward of Skomvaer Light, having orders from Sir Charles Forbes to keep outside Vest Fjord, ' unless required for an operation '. He had three destroyers[2] with the *Warspite* and six working in Vest Fjord, while by this time others had arrived with the expedition.

The Commander-in-Chief himself departed for Scapa the same evening (15th) with the *Rodney*, *Renown* and six destroyers,[3] the *Furious* having gone north the day before to oil at Tromsö, carrying out an air reconnaissance of the northern approaches to Narvik on the way.

19. Cruiser operations, 10th–14th April [PLANS 3, 4, 5

While the operations off the coast of Norway described in the foregoing sections were taking place, the ships of the 2nd and 18th[4] cruiser squadrons which had returned to Scapa on 10th April had not been idle.

At 0134, 11th April, Vice-Admiral Layton received orders to detail a cruiser to take General Mackesy and an advance party to the Narvik area. He had already been warned by telephone from the Admiralty that his force would probably be required to cover an expedition to Narvik, and at 1032 (11th) orders arrived from the Commander-in-Chief, Home Fleet, requesting him to organise a force of two cruisers and six destroyers[5] to operate in the south part of the Indreled, sweeping northward along the coast from Aalesund.

Various conferences with General Mackesy, the Commanding Officers and others concerned, were held by Admiral Layton on the 11th and 12th while the ships completed fuelling, ammunitioning and making good defects. The *Glasgow* (Captain Pegram, Senior Officer) and *Sheffield*, with the *Somali*, *Mashona*, *Afridi*, *Sikh*, *Matabele* and *Mohawk* sailed for the inshore operation at 2000, 11th; and next day, as already mentioned (*see* Sec. 17), Admiral Layton sailed with the *Manchester* and *Birmingham* to meet convoy N.P.I, the *Southampton*, screened by the *Electra* and *Escapade*, with General Mackesy and the advance party having left a few hours previously for Vaagsfjord, where she arrived without incident on the 14th.

---

[1] The *Ivanhoe* and *Kimberley* went home with the Commander-in-Chief the following day.

[2] *Hostile*, *Havock*, *Foxhound*.

[3] *Esk*, *Ivanhoe*, *Forester*, *Icarus*, *Kimberley*.

[4] *Galatea* (Flag, Vice-Admiral Edward-Collins), *Arethusa*, *Aurora*; *Manchester* (Flag, Vice-Admiral Layton), *Birmingham*, *Southampton*, *Glasgow*, *Sheffield*.

[5] This latter order caused considerable embarrassment to Rear-Admiral (D), who found it quite impossible to provide another force of six destroyers in addition to those already earmarked for Admiral Layton's force and a relief screen for the battleships which would be required shortly. Verbal approval was obtained by telephone from the Admiralty to use some of the former, as extra destroyers from the Western Approaches Command were accompanying the troop convoy.

Admiral Layton fell in with the troop convoy[1] off Cape Wrath at 1900, 13th April, and shaped course for Vest Fjord at 14 knots, being joined by the *Valiant* sent by the Commander-in-Chief, the *Vindictive* and three destroyers[2] from Scapa and three destroyers[3] from Sollum Voe next afternoon. The passage was uneventful, but at 1907/14th orders were received from the Admiralty diverting the troops in the *Chrobry* and *Empress of Australia* to Namsos. They were then in position 68° 10′ N., 10° 20′ E. (approximately 130 miles from Vaagsfjord). The convoy therefore divided, Admiral Layton with *Manchester*, *Birmingham*, *Cairo*, *Vanoc*, *Whirlwind*, *Highlander*, taking the Namsos detachment, and the remainder, with the *Valiant*, and 10 destroyers continuing for Vaagsfjord. Their further proceedings will be dealt with later.

At just about the time the convoy split, the first British landing on Norwegian soil was taking place. This was by an advance party from the *Glasgow* and *Sheffield* at Namsos (Operation Henry). Captain Pegram's force had arrived off Stadtlandet in the afternoon of the 12th and swept to the northward along the coast of Aalesund. Further north, Vice-Admiral Cunningham's force[4] had reported Namsos and the neighbouring fjords clear on the 12th and then proceeded to rejoin the Commander-in-Chief off the Lofoten Islands. Meanwhile enemy reports from aircraft on the 12th had reported a pocket battleship, a cruiser and many merchant ships on Captain Pegram's station: these he was searching for early on the 13th when he intercepted a signal from the Admiralty to the Commander-in-Chief (A.T.0216/13) proposing a landing from his two cruisers at Namsos in order to forestall the Germans.[5] Later that day he received orders to carry out this plan. His destroyers, however, which he had sent to Aalesund after the 'many large merchant vessels' (which turned out to be Norwegian) were delayed there, and the parties could not be landed till the evening of the 14th, after which the *Glasgow*, *Sheffield* and three destroyers cruised in the offing off Kya Light, subsequently joining Admiral Layton. Captain Nicholson (Captain D.6) with three destroyers remained at Namsos to arrange for the landing of the expedition on its way there and to meet General Carton de Wiart, V.C., the Military Commander, who was arriving by air.

Meanwhile Vice-Admiral Edward-Collins had received orders from the Admiralty at 1355, 11th April, to send one ship to Rosyth to hoist the flag of Admiral of the Fleet Lord Cork.[6] He chose the *Aurora*; she left Scapa at 1700 that day, embarked Lord Cork the next forenoon and sailed again at 1200, arriving, after an uneventful passage, at Skjel Fjord on the 14th. Admiral Edward-Collins left Scapa with the *Galatea* and *Arethusa* at 1300, 13th April, for Rosyth, to embark troops for a landing at Namsos (Operation Maurice). Brigadier Morgan and the battalions of the first flights embarked in the two cruisers and the transport *Orion* on the 14th, but delays in embarking a battery of A.A. guns in the latter delayed their sailing. That evening the instructions were given to divert part of Admiral Layton's convoy to Namsos, and Admiral Edward-Collins' force remained at Rosyth till the 17th when it sailed for Aandalsnes[7] (Operation Sickle).

---

[1] S.S. *Empress of Australia, Monarch of Bermuda, Reina del Pacifico, Batory, Chrobry, Protector*, escorted by the *Cairo, Witherington, Volunteer, Vanoc, Whirlwind, Highlander*.

[2] *Codrington* (Captain D.1), S.O., Escort, *Acasta, Ardent*.

[3] *Fearless, Griffin, Brazen*.

[4] See Sec. 15 ante.

[5] See Sec. 31 postea.

[6] The *Effingham* and *Enterprise* were to be sailed from Portsmouth to Narvik as soon as possible when Lord Cork was to transfer his flag to the *Effingham*, and the *Aurora* was to rejoin the 2nd C.S. Actually the *Aurora* remained with Lord Cork for some time longer.

[7] See Sec. 37 postea.

While these steps were being taken in the effort to retrieve the situation in Norway, possible repercussions from the occupation of Denmark had to be considered, and it was decided to lose no time in making sure of the Faeroes. H.M.S. *Suffolk* (Captain Durnford) had just completed repairs at Govan when the invasion occurred. She accordingly embarked a force of 250 Royal Marines with two 3·7-in. howitzers at Greenock on 12th April, and sailed that night at high speed for Thorshavn, arriving there next afternoon whither she had been preceded by the destroyers *Hesperus* and *Havant*, which had carried out an anti-submarine search in the vicinity. With the assistance of a couple of trawlers, the *Northern Sky* and *Northern Foam*, all personnel and stores were landed by 2130 on the 13th and the *Suffolk* then sailed for Vest Fjord to join Vice-Admiral Cunningham. Next forenoon, being then in 64° 5′ N., 2° E., she fell in with the German tanker *Skagerrak*, which was scuttled by her crew to avoid capture. The *Suffolk* then continued on her way to the Lofotens, but that evening she was recalled by the Admiralty (A.T. 1935/14) to Scapa to prepare for a bombarding operation (Operation Duck) in support of the projected landing at Aandalsnes.

Meanwhile Vice-Admiral Cunningham, with the *Devonshire* and *Berwick* had been covering his four destroyers[1] while they searched fjords from Trondheim to the northward during the 11th and 12th April. No enemy was encountered, but the *Isis* met the Norwegian gunboat *Nordkap* in Aluangen (66° 3′ N., 12° 55′ E.) who informed her that she had sunk a German tanker.[2]

At 1530, 12th, the destroyers rejoined the cruisers in approximately 66° 30′ N., 11° 30′ E., and the force then steered for the possible enemy rendezvous between 4° 30′ E., and 6° E. in 67° N. as given in A.T. 1607/11,[3] afterwards rejoining the Commander-in-Chief, Home Fleet, at 0930, 13th April off the Lofoten Islands. The destroyers were then sent to Skjel Fjord to fuel, and the cruisers remained with the flag till that afternoon, when they were again detached, this time to investigate conditions at Tromsö (Commander-in-Chief, H.F. 1717/13) being joined by the same four destroyers at 0700, 14th, in 69° 30′ N., 16° 05′ E.

Admiral Cunningham sent the *Berwick* with the *Inglefield* and *Imogen* to examine Ands Fjord, Vaags Fjord and various inlets in the neighbourhood of the proposed landing place of the Narvik expedition, while he himself in the *Devonshire* with the other two destroyers proceeded to Tromsö, where he arrived at 1500, 14th. There he made contact with the British Vice-Consul,[4] the Norwegian S.N.O., Captain Bredsdorff, and the G.O.C. of the district, General Fleischer. From them he learned that the situation there was quiet, and that the Norwegian authorities were confident of their ability to repel any German attempt to land from captured fishing boats or small craft ; also that considerable quantities of oil fuel were available in the port. After making various arrangements, such as the broadcasting of enemy reports, Admiral Cunningham sailed with the *Isis* and *Ilex*[5] that evening for Kirkenes, in compliance with orders from the Commander-in-Chief (C.-in-C. 1716/14), being joined early next morning (15th April) by the *Berwick* and *Inglefield* off North Cape. The

---

[1] *Inglefield, Imogen, Isis, Ilex.* See Sec. 15 *ante*.
[2] The *Kattegat*.
[3] See Sec. 15 *ante*.
[4] Lieut.-Commander Cumming, D.S.C., R.N. (ret.).
[5] The *Isis* and *Ilex* were detached at 0100, 15th, to rendezvous with the *Furious* which was on her way to Tromsö.

Force arrived at Kirkenes[1] at 1600 that afternoon, sailing for Tromsö the same evening as cover for a Norwegian troop convoy ; a second convoy was escorted by the *Imogen* a couple of days later.

Admiral Cunningham remained in these northern waters, based on Tromsö, cooperating with the Norwegian authorities, and working with the *Furious* in operations in connection with the arrival of the Narvik Expeditionary Force (Rupert), until the 19th April, when he sailed for Scapa (in response to an urgent signal from the Commander-in-Chief) with the *Berwick* and *Inglefield*.

20. Submarine activities,[2] 4th–14th April 1940 [PLANS 7, 8

While the focus of the Allied naval effort had thus been moving to the north, the southern area had not been entirely neglected. As already mentioned (*see* Sec. 12) the weight of the German air attacks on the Home Fleet in the afternoon of 9th April[3] had convinced the Commander-in-Chief of the impossibility of operating surface forces off the southern coasts of Norway without incurring very serious losses. It was therefore left to the Allied submarines to do what they could against the German sea communications with the southern ports. And fine work they did, though it was impossible for them unaided to cut the seaborne pipeline from Germany across the narrow waters of the Skaw and Skagerrak to Norway.

Special submarine dispositions had been ordered on 4th April, with the object of covering the ports involved in the operations under Plan R.4, should they be ordered, and on the night of 8th April they were disposed as follows :—

   3 in the Kattegat, *Sealion, Sunfish, Triton*.
   2 in the Skagerrak, *Trident*, O.R.P. *Orzel*.
   1 entering Skagerak, *Truant*.
   1 south-west of Skagerrak, 56° N., 6° E., *Seal*.
   3 off west coast of Denmark, *Spearfish, Snapper, Unity*.
   2 East of Dogger Bank, French *Amazone, Antiope*.
   6 on passage from the United Kingdom to the eastward, *Severn, Tarpon, Clyde, Thistle, Shark, Seawolf*.

As a result of the reports on 7th and 8th April of the German fleet being at sea the Admiralty in the afternoon of the 8th, after discussion with the Admiral, Submarines (Vice-Admiral Sir Max Horton) had ordered fresh dispositions designed to intercept the enemy heavy ships, with the result that by the morning of the 9th the submarines were moving to cover the approaches to the German ports in the Heligoland Bight, leaving the Norwegian ports somewhat neglected. Admiral Horton, however, had for some time been convinced that the invasion of Norway by the Germans was imminent—an opinion confirmed by the sinking of the *Rio de Janeiro* on the 8th[4], and in his original orders, timed 1931, 4th April, had laid down that if warships and transports were encountered the latter were to be taken as the primary objective. This instruction was allowed to stand ; and at 1324 the next day,

---

[1] The situation at Kirkenes was complicated by uncertainty as to the Russian intentions : this made the Norwegians reluctant to denude their north-eastern frontier of troops.

[2] These are fully dealt with in Naval Staff History, Submarines.

[3] It has been remarked that had the German aircraft which then attacked been armed with torpedoes and pressed home their attacks the fate of the *Prince of Wales* and *Repulse* might have been anticipated by some 18 months by the *Rodney* and *Valiant*.

[4] The report of this had been received before Admiral Horton's visit to the Admiralty that afternoon.

9th April, he signalled to the submarines that German merchant ships encountered in the Skagerrak east of 8° E. and in the area to the eastward of the German declared area should be treated as warships and sunk without warning.[1]

Actually, the submarines had already taken a hand in the game as evidenced by the sinking of the *Rio de Janeiro* by the *Orzel* on the 8th. This was followed up the same afternoon by the sinking of the tanker *Posidonia*[2] (on her maiden voyage) in the mouth of Oslo Fjord by the *Trident*. That night several submarines encountered enemy squadrons and convoys coming out of the Baltic, though no successes were scored ; but on 9th April the *Truant* sank the *Karlsruhe* off Kristiansand (*see* Sec. 12 *ante*) and on the night of the 10th/11th the *Spearfish* seriously damaged the *Lutzow*[3] with a snap shot on the surface off the Skaw. During the first week of the operations (8th–14th April), besides the ships mentioned above, seven other transports and merchant ships were sunk in the Skagerrak or Kattegat—four by the *Sunfish* and one each by the *Triad, Sealion* and *Snapper,* while the *Triton* made four hits on a convoy, though severe depth-charge attacks prevented her from observing the results.

These successes were not gained without loss. On 10th April the *Thistle,* which had unsuccessfully attacked a U-boat the day before, was off Stavanger and her Commanding Officer reported his intention of attempting to enter the harbour. Nothing further was heard of her ; it is now known that she was sunk by *U.4.* This loss was followed by the sinking by German A/S craft of the *Tarpon* off the west coast of Denmark[4] on the 14th.

The Germans, too, had made special submarine dispositions to cover their landing operations. Practically the whole of their available operational submarines were employed. Indeed, the almost total cessation of U-boat attacks on the Atlantic trade routes was one of the earliest indications that some large-scale operation was brewing elsewhere. They were disposed as follows :—

    (A) *Off Norwegian Ports*
        Narvik, 4 in Vest Fjord.
        Trondheim, 2 (inner approaches).
        Bergen, 4 (2 for each main entrance).
           1 to cover Haugesund.

    (B) *Attack Groups*
        N.E. of Shetlands, 6.
        East of Orkneys, 3 (small).
        East and west of Pentland Firth, 4 (small).
        West of the Naze, 3 (small).
        In eastern part of English Channel, 3.

---

[1] Hitherto submarines had been forbidden to sink merchant ships without ensuring the safety of their crews in accordance with international law. The decision to remove this ban in the area referred to was reached by the Cabinet on 9th April. The ' German declared area ' was bounded by lines passing through positions (*a*) 53° 36′ N. 4° 25′ E., (*b*) 53° 36′ N. 6° 2′ E., (*c*) 56° 30′ N. 6° 2′ E., (*d*) 56° 30′ N. 4° 25′ E. On 11th April the ban was further relaxed to include ' any ships, merchant or otherwise, under way within 10 miles of the Norwegian coast south of 61° N. and anywhere east of 6° E. as far south as 54° N. to be attacked on sight. Ships at anchor may be attacked if identified as enemy.' (V.A.S. 1956/11.)

[2] *Posidonia* (8100 gr. tons) was taken over by O.K.M. and renamed *Stedingen*. She was to have acted as a supply ship for Kristiansand (south) and for U-boats.

[3] The *Lutzow* was so seriously damaged by the torpedo, and later grounding in the Kattegat on her way home, that she was out of action for 12 months.

[4] 56° 45.5′ N. 8° 15′ E.

In contradistinction to the success of the British submarines, the German U-boats achieved practically nothing, only succeeding during the whole of April in sinking three British and two neutral merchant ships and one store transport (the *Cedar Bank*). When at an early stage in the operations (15th April) their disposition fell into the hands of the British,[1] the Commander-in-Chief, Home Fleet, expressed satisfaction that such an effort should have accomplished so little. It is now known that their torpedoes suffered from serious technical defects.[2] But for this fortunate circumstance, the story might have been different. Actually, many attacks were made by experienced submarine commanders—but without result. On this subject Admiral Doenitz, then Flag Officer, Submarines, waxed bitter. An entry in his War Diary (15th May 1940) reads :—

> 'I do not believe that ever in the history of war men have been sent against the enemy with such a useless weapon.'

21. General situation, 15th April 1940 [PLAN 6

Vice-Admiral Whitworth's attack at Narvik and the operations described in the foregoing sections marked the conclusion of the first phase of the campaign. Hitherto the chief naval interest had centred on attempts to bring to action the German naval forces and to blockade the detachments in Norwegian ports. From this time onwards it lay in convoying and maintaining the hastily improvised expeditions which the Allies were sending to the succour of the Norwegians, and in inshore operations in support of the troops when landed. Before following the fortunes of these expeditions the first of which were just arriving in Norwegian waters, however, it will be convenient to take stock of the general situation at the conclusion of the first phase as it existed in the evening of 15th April.

In the northern area Vice-Admiral Whitworth was cruising off the Lofoten Islands in the *Warspite*, standing by to support the operations against Narvik of the expedition which had arrived with the *Valiant* and escort at Vaags Fjord that day. The *Valiant* remained in Vaags Fjord on patrol till 1900, 15th, when she sailed for Scapa, screened by three destroyers.[3] On the same day Admiral of the Fleet Lord Cork, wearing his flag in the *Aurora*, met General Mackesy for the first time in Vaags Fjord, who had arrived there in the *Southampton* the previous day.

Vice-Admiral Cunningham, with the *Devonshire*, *Berwick* and *Furious* was operating in the Tromsö area.

The Commander-in-Chief, Home Fleet, having remained cruising off the Lofoten Islands during the 14th and met Vice-Admiral Whitworth off Skomvaer next day, shaped course to the southward in the evening of the 15th with the *Rodney* and *Renown*, arriving at Scapa on the 17th. Since the 14th, he had been exchanging signals with the Admiralty on the possibility of a frontal attack on Trondheim, to discuss which Rear-Admiral Holland, who had been studying the problem in London, was proceeding to Scapa to meet him. This proposal will be dealt with in the next chapter, but it was already giving the Commander-in-Chief much to consider.

---

[1] *See* Sec. 45 *postea*.

[2] The torpedoes suffered in two respects :—
   (a) The depth-keeping gear was defective and caused many misses.
   (b) The magnetic pistols were adversely affected by the proximity of the magnetic pole in the high latitudes and frequently failed to detonate.

[3] *Fearless, Griffin, Brazen.*

In the central area (Trondheim) Vice-Admiral Layton with the *Manchester, Birmingham, Cairo,* three destroyers and two transports was nearing Lillesjona, where he had been directed to transfer the troops to destroyers for passage to Namsos, temporarily occupied the day before by parties landed from the *Glasgow* and *Sheffield*, which remained cruising in the offing. Major-General Carton de Wiart, V.C., the military commander in this area, arrived in a flying boat at Namsos on the 15th, where Captain Nicholson in the *Somali* was awaiting him to discuss landing arrangements.

A landing party drawn from the *Hood, Nelson* and *Barham*, then in dockyard hands, had sailed from Rosyth in four sloops, the *Black Swan, Bittern, Flamingo* and *Auckland*, on the 14th and was storm-bound at Invergordon on its way to Aandalsnes (south of Trondheim). The *Suffolk*, on her way to join Admiral Cunningham in the Lofoten Islands, after landing the party in the Faeroes, had been recalled by the Admiralty to prepare for a bombarding operation in support of this landing, and arrived at Scapa in the evening of the 15th.

At Rosyth, Vice-Admiral Edward-Collins was embarking the second flight for Namsos—to be diverted next day to Aandalsnes—in the cruisers *Galatea* and *Arethusa* and the transport *Orion*.

Further afield, Vice-Admiral Wells (V.A.(A)) had been ordered to join the Home Fleet from the Mediterranean in the carrier *Glorious* and had left Gibraltar in the evening of the 14th; his usual flagship, the *Ark Royal* (soon to follow), was ordered to remain at Gibraltar for the time being.

Turning to the enemy, the situation was as follows. Their initial landings had gone almost exactly as planned. Their naval losses had been severe, but not higher than anticipated though the loss of Commodore Bonte's ten destroyers at Narvik had been a bitter blow[1]—and their surviving main units were by this time all back in German ports.

The initial supply arrangements for the assault forces at the two northern ports,[2] however, had virtually broken down; only one out of the six camouflaged steamers which were to meet the landing parties on arrival reaching her destination. The *Rauenfels* with ammunition for Narvik had been blown up on 10th April, the *Alster* with mechanical transport had been captured, and the *Barenfels*, after being diverted to Bergen, was sunk there while discharging her cargo for Narvik by air attack on the 14th. Of the Trondheim group, the *Sao Paulo* was sunk by mine off Bergen and the *Main* by a Norwegian destroyer; the third ship, the *Levante*, eventually reached Trondheim on the 12th, three days late. Yet another supply ship had been sunk at Stavanger by the Norwegian torpedo boat *Sleipner*[3] on the 9th.

The tankers, too, had been unfortunate, only the *Jan Wellem* from Murmansk reaching Narvik as planned, the other two, the *Kattegat* for Narvik and the *Skaggerak* for Trondheim, having both been scuttled by their crews to avoid capture.

'The expectation of the Army and the Air Force to be supplied in time with guns, ammunition, equipment and provisions for the troops that had been landed in the northern harbours was therefore frustrated.'[4]

---

[1] 'Ten of our modern destroyers, half of our destroyer fleet, are lying shot to bits, damaged or sunk in Ofot and Rombakenfjord.'—German Naval Staff War Diary.

[2] *See* Sec. 1 *ante*.

[3] *Sleipner*, 3—3·9-in.; 1–1·57 A/A guns; 2—21-in. torpedo tubes.

[4] B.R. 1840 (1) The German Campaign in Norway.

The German detachments in these two areas (Narvik and Trondheim) thus found themselves in a highly critical position until these deficiencies could be made good. The fate of their destroyers at Narvik, which had been unable to leave for want of fuel, left no doubt as to this. Intercepted Allied signals on 12th April had revealed the probability of an Allied landing at Namsos, and later messages indicated that another landing was impending at Vaags Fjord on the 15th. From the German point of view the fate of Narvik depended on holding the Trondheim area; ' the pivot of all operations was therefore Trondheim '[1] and the following directions were accordingly issued on the 14th.

(a) The Army (Group XXI) was to reinforce the garrison at Trondheim as soon as possible, taking possession of the railway Oslo–Dombaas and Aandalsnes.

(b) The Navy was to concentrate U-boats in the waters round Trondheim and Aalesund, and to arrange for the transport of the most important supplies by U-boats[2] to Trondheim.

(c) The Luftwaffe[3] to destroy enemy troops already landed; to prevent further landings in the Aandalsnes area; to occupy Dombaas with paratroops and to send airborne reinforcements to Trondheim.

Meanwhile, in the south, the follow-up troops and stores had arrived at their destinations between 9th and 12th April in the 1st Transport Division[4]—the ships sailing singly in disguise—more or less as planned. Losses[5] had occurred, from accident and enemy submarine attack, but not on a scale sufficient to cause serious interruption.

The 2nd Transport Division, sailing in convoy, lost two ships and a patrol vessel[6] to British submarines north of Gotenberg, but the remaining nine transports reached Oslo on the 12th; 900 troops, however, had been drowned and in future the passage of troops was restricted to fast warships and small craft using the shortest route between Jutland and the southern Norwegian ports. The 3rd Transport Division, 12 steamers carrying Army supplies, left home ports on the 13th and, sailing in five independent groups, arrived at Oslo 15th–16th April after losing two ships.[7] Thereafter the build-up proceeded steadily, the number of troops transported from Frederikshavn and Aalborg to Larvik and Oslo being about 3000 a day.[8]

On shore the German troops were advancing from Oslo up the railway lines leading to Trondheim through Lillehammer and Dombaas in the west and

---

[1] B.R. 1840 (1) The German Campaign in Norway.

[2] Several U-boats had been earmarked for this duty since the 10th. Within a week three sailed, each carrying 40 to 50 tons of small arms and A.A. ammunition.

[3] Luftflotte 5 for the conduct of all operations in Norway had been formed under the command of Colonel-General Milch on 12th April, and was operating from airfields near Trondheim, Stavanger and Kristiansand (south) in Norway, Aalborg in Denmark, Westerland in Sylt (Frisian Islands) and Lubeck and Luneberg in Northern Germany.

[4] *See* Sec. 1 *ante*.

[5] *Curityba* ran aground north of Helsingborg, 7th April; arrived Oslo, 10th. *Rio de Janeiro*, *Antares* and *Jonia* sunk by submarines.

[6] *Friedenau*, *Wigbert*, Patrol Vessel *1507*.

[7] *Florida* sunk by submarine in Kattegat; *Urundi* ran aground in Leads west of Faerdor.

[8] B.R. 1840(1) gives the following statistics of transportation (other than by warships) for the Norwegian campaign. 270 ships and 100 trawlers, totalling 1,192,000 g.r.t., carried up to 15th June :—

107,581 officers and men.
16,102 horses.
20,339 vehicles.
109,400 tons of supplies.

Of the above, 21 ships totalling 111,700 g.r.t. were lost, and of the 4344 officers and men in these ships, about 1000 were lost : a large part of their cargoes was salved.

through Kongsvinger, Elverum and Roros in the east. By 15th April the heads of their columns had reached Strandlökka near the southern end of Lake Mjösa and the western outskirts of Kongsvinger.

The Norwegian Army which numbered no more than six divisions, one of which was stationed in the extreme north, never had a chance to carry out an ordered mobilisation.[1] But by this time detachments were assembled at Storen and Steinkjaer in the Trondheim area. General Ruge had been appointed Commander-in-Chief on the 10th, but in the general confusion and with scanty communications had been unable to establish effective control.

The King of Norway, with the Crown Prince and the Government, closely pursued and ruthessly bombed whenever their whereabouts became known to the enemy, had retreated north through Hamar, Elverum and Lillehamar, and had found a temporary resting place at Otta (south-east of Dombaas).

Hunted and harried though they were, so long as they remained at liberty, the German invasion was doomed to failure politically, whatever might be effected militarily by brute force. Already Quisling's attempt to form a government had proved abortive; rejected by his fellow countrymen and discarded by the Germans, he had given way to an 'Administrative Council' set up[2] (with the approval of the King) under the Lord Chief Justice of Norway as the Civil Authority in the parts of the country in German occupation, and soon to be replaced in its turn by the Reich Commissioner Terboven on 24th April.

On 26th April the German wireless announced—somewhat belatedly—that a state of war existed between Germany and Norway.

---

[1] General Erichsen commanding the 1st Division succeeded in mobilising to the south-east of Oslo but he was isolated from Norwegian Headquarters and entirely without A.A. guns or aircraft. After a week of fighting he was faced with the alternative of surrender or internment in Sweden. He chose the latter.

[2] 16th April.

CHAPTER III

THE ALLIED COUNTER OFFENSIVE AND GENERAL EMPLOYMENT OF NAVAL FORCES

22. Plans and policy　　　　　　　　　　　　　　　　　　　　[PLAN 1

While all this had been going on in Norwegian waters, plans to counter the German invasion were being concerted as rapidly as possible by the Allied Governments. ' Completely outwitted '[1] and forestalled as they were, their plans were necessarily improvisations ; events proved that they were undertaken on a totally inadequate scale. The troops and ships earmarked for the discarded plan R.4 were at any rate available, but since the organisation and equipment of the troops had been designed for unopposed landings and the Germans were already in possession of the principal ports, new landing places had to be chosen ; as already mentioned, the first convoy sailed from the Clyde two days after the German landings, with the Narvik area as its destination.

The first hint of the new plans to reach the Commander-in-Chief, Home Fleet, was contained in A.T. 0820 of 9th April[2] already referred to, which told him to prepare attacks on the German ships of war in Bergen and Trondheim and said ' we shall probably want to land a force ' at Narvik. Some sixteen hours later, A.T. 0057/10 went a stage further :—

> 'The policy of the Allies is to give Norway as much assistance as possible. To do this it will be necessary to take Bergen and Trondheim. Narvik will also be taken. The order in which these operations will be undertaken has not been settled, but in the meantime it is important that no reinforcements of any kind should reach these three places.'

This signal crossed the signal 2231/9 which it will be remembered the Commander-in-Chief had sent giving his general ideas after the German air attack on his fleet that afternoon, in which he recommended attacking the enemy in the north with surface forces and military assistance, ' leaving the southern area mostly to submarines, due to German air superiority in the south '. With this view the Admiralty concurred in A.T. 1904/10 :—

> 'As enemy is now established at Narvik, recapture of that place takes priority over operations against Bergen and Trondheim. Expedition is being prepared as quickly as possible, and you will be further informed when plan and time-table are completed. In the meantime it is of primary importance to prevent Narvik's being reinforced by sea. Possibility of seizing and holding a temporary base near Narvik with small military force is under urgent examination : in the meantime you will presumably arrange for a temporary refuelling anchorage in the north . . . .
>
> Admiralty consider that interference with communications in southern areas must be left mainly to submarines, air and mining, aided by intermittent sweeps when forces allow.'

As things turned out, no operations (other than air attack) were attempted against Bergen ; and the Allied plan finally adopted was confined to landings in two areas—the Vest Fjord area in the north with Narvik as its objective and the Trondheim area some 300 miles further south. This necessarily entailed dispersion of force ; indeed at first there seems to have been considerable

---

[1] Churchill, THE SECOND WORLD WAR, Vol. I, p. 474.
[2] *See* Sec. 12 *ante*.

Sec. 22 THE ALLIED COUNTER OFFENSIVE AND GENERAL EMPLOYMENT OF NAVAL FORCES

indecision as to which area should constitute the main effort. The enemy, however, had no such doubts as to their main strategic object (*see* Sec. 21 *ante*) and concentrated all their efforts on securing Trondheim, with the result that the Allied forces landed in this area, which never attained a strength of above about 12,000 men, were forced speedily to withdraw.

The Narvik expedition eventually reached a strength of nearly 30,000, counting outlying detachments in the Bodo area—about 100 miles to the southward of Narvik—which, after the withdrawal from the Trondheim area, the Allies attempted to hold, in order to deny the Germans possible sites for airfields for operations against the Narvik expedition. This expedition was known as Rupert; its first units arrived at Harstad in the Lofoten Islands on 14th and 15th April, but it suffered various delays owing to weather and other causes and it was not until 28th May that the actual assault on Narvik took place. By that time Germany had overrun the Netherlands, which led to the decision to withdraw the British and French troops from Norway altogether.

In the central area landings were planned at Namsos, about 150 miles north of Trondheim by rail, and at Aandalsnes about the same distance to the south. It was hoped to initiate a pincer movement against Trondheim from these two areas, and by capturing the railway centre at Dombaas to seal off the town from the German forces advancing from the south. These expeditions were known respectively as Maurice (Namsos) and Sickle (Aandalsnes). Each was preceded by preliminary landings by naval parties in order to forestall the Germans and to ensure unopposed landings for the larger forces—Henry consisting of some 350 seamen and marines from ships then working in the neighbourhood at Namsos, and Primrose, about 700 men drawn from heavy ships in dockyard hands, with field howitzers, high angle pom-poms and two 4-in. guns of position, in the Aandalsnes area.[1]

It is to be noted that none of these expeditions was to land in the face of German opposition on shore. Rupert landed in Vaags Fjord, a long way from the enemy in Narvik. The orders for Henry said 'it is not intended that an opposed landing should be attempted' and the object of that landing was 'to ensure an unopposed landing for Maurice at Namsos'. Similarly, Primrose and Sickle both had orders not to land if the Germans should be already in Aandalsnes.

The plans for the landings in central Norway were only gradually evolved, the first naval orders—which dealt with Namsos—being contained in A.T. 0216/13. The same day the Government decided to land a small party at Aalesund (approaches to Aandalsnes) to 'create a diversion' and to hinder the passage of the enemy through the Inner Lead in those parts; but as stated above this grew into an advance against Trondheim similar to that from Namsos.

The general intention of these landings was finally conveyed to the Commander-in-Chief, Home Fleet, by the Admiralty in the following signal, timed 2340/13 :—

'(i) Government have now decided to land a force in the vicinity of Trondheim, so as to secure a footing from which that place can eventually be taken should it be decided to do so; and the following action is consequently being taken.
(ii) Operation Henry is being carried out.

---

[1] Each of these operations will be treated in detail in succeeding chapters.

PLANS AND POLICY   Sec. 22

(iii) A force of about 5000 men will arrive Namsos, probably a.m. 17th April, to hold place and try and advance to Stenkjaer. This will be known as Operation Maurice.

(iv) A force of marines and seamen from *Nelson, Barham* and *Hood*, about 600 strong, will land at Aalesund on about 17th April with object of neutralizing Inner Lead, south of Trondheim and create a diversion. This will be known as Operation Primrose.[1]

(v) Action is being taken to keep down scale of attack from Norwegian aerodromes, but attacks by flying boats and float planes must always remain possible.

(vi) In view of above coming to commitment, it is desirable to have more strength in south than at present.'

Three days later, these intentions were amplified by a message from the C.I.G.S. to General Carton de Wiart, who had been appointed Commander of Maurice (A.T. 0020/16) :—

'Capture of Trondheim considered essential. Plan proposed is as follows :—

Intend landing 600 marines at Aandalsnes (not Aalesund), 17th April, to be reinforced, if possible, at earliest opportunity. Propose you should exploit from Namsos, while force from Aandalsnes will also threaten Trondheim in conjunction with Norwegian forces. Meanwhile, combined operation for direct attack on Trondheim will be developed ? to take advantage of your pressure . . . only troops available for reinforcing Aandalsnes are Morgan's brigade.'

This leads up to some consideration of the vexed question whether a frontal attack should have been launched on Trondheim, and what were the chances of success, had such an attack been launched.

23. Question of direct attack on Trondheim   [PLAN 11

The project of a direct assault on Trondheim was much to the fore during these early days of the campaign. The following series of signals which passed between the Admiralty and the Commander-in-Chief, Home Fleet, gives an outline of what was intended and throws light on the reasons why the plan was given up.

So far as it concerned the Home Fleet, this proposal, named Operation Hammer, first appeared in A.T. 0142 of 14th April, sent a couple of hours after the message describing the expedition to Namsos :—

'Intention up to present has been to land at Namsos for the Trondheim area. For many reasons it would be advantageous to land the force inside Trondheim Fjord. Do you consider that the shore batteries could be either destroyed or dominated to such an extent as to permit transports to enter ? And, if so, how many ships and of what type would you propose to use ?

Request early reply, as any plan must depend on the above.'

On this, Sir Charles Forbes, who was then cruising off the Lofoten Islands, asked for details about the defences of Trondheim, both Norwegian batteries that might be in German hands and artillery that the invaders brought with them, and in his 1157/14 he gave his answers to the Admiralty questions :—

'Shore batteries could no doubt be either destroyed or dominated by battleship in daylight, swept and screened, if she had high explosive bombardment shells for main armament, but none of Home Fleet have.

This, however, is only the minor part of task.

The main difficulties are (1), surprise having been lost, to protect troopships from a heavy-scale air attack for over 30 miles in narrow waters, and (2) then to carry out an opposed landing, of which ample warning has been given, under continuous air attack. Nothing, to date, has led me to suppose the necessary

---

[1] A.T. 1347/14 explained : 'This operation is designed to synchronise with Operation Maurice.'

Sec. 23 THE ALLIED COUNTER OFFENSIVE AND GENERAL EMPLOYMENT OF NAVAL FORCES

freedom from air attack could be assured for length of time operation would take. In fact, reverse would be the case, as within three hours of being sighted Ju.88 bombers from Germany would be on spot; and if the information contained in your 0109/13 is correct, bombing would start almost immediately.

For foregoing reasons, I do not consider operation feasible, unless you are prepared to face very heavy losses in troops and transports.'[1]

The Admiralty answered him in A.T. 0121 of 15th April :—

'We still think that the operation described should be further studied.

It could not take place for seven days devoted to careful preparation. Danger from air would not be appreciably less wherever these large troopships are brought into the danger zone; in fact, it might be greater whilst the aerodrome at Trondheim is in action. Our idea would be that, in addition to R.A.F. bombing of Stavanger aerodrome, the *Suffolk* should bombard with high explosive at dawn, hoping thereby to put Stavanger aerodrome out of business. The aerodrome at Trondheim, which is close to the harbour, could be dealt with by F.A.A. bombers, and subsequently by bombardment.

(High explosive shell for 15-in. guns has been ordered to Rosyth. The *Furious* and 1st Cruiser Squadron would be required for this operation.)

Pray, therefore, consider this important project further.'

And instructions from the Chief of the Imperial General Staff to General Carton de Wiart at the same time, mainly about the landing of Maurice, contained this clause : ' Development of operations is dependent on capture of Trondheim ; combined plan being developed '.

Meanwhile, Sir Charles Forbes had received particulars of the Trondheim defences, estimates of the German and Norwegian strengths in troops in and about Trondheim, and news that the Germans had seized the coastwise batteries at the entrance of Trondheim Fjord—which is there only a mile and a half wide, leading out of Skjorn Fjorden, two and a half miles wide. He answered the Admiralty message in his 1733/15 :—

' (a) What is size of force to be landed ?

(b) What is precise position in which it is proposed to land them ?

(c) What is precise position of Trondheim aerodrome ? I have no shore map.

(d) What is role of 1st Cruiser Squadron ?—as they are at present doing very useful work at Kirkenes in accordance with A.T. 0054/14.

(e) If *Furious* is to be used, she will have to proceed to base to re-equip squadron, replenish stores, and embark fighter squadron ; and she cannot leave before refuelling at Tromsö on 17th April at earliest. This will also deprive Narvik of air co-operation, so suggest *Glorious*.

(f) I think you have misunderstood my 1157/14. I do not anticipate any great difficulty from naval side, except that I cannot provide air defence for transports whilst approaching and carrying out an opposed landing—the chief air menace being from Ju.88 machines from Germany. And I know, from personal experience, what an opposed landing is like, even without air opposition.

(g) Naval force required would be *Valiant* and *Renown* to give air defence to *Glorious* ; *Warspite* to carry out shore bombardments, as she is only 15-in. ship in fleet with 6-in. guns[2] ; at least four A.A. cruisers ; about 20 destroyers ; and numerous landing craft.

(h) I request, on my return to Scapa on morning of 18th April, D.C.N.S. or Admiral Holland may be there to discuss whole situation.'

---

[1] A.T. 0109/13 reported a dive-bomber group at Vaernes, 15 miles east of Trondheim, and possibly a group of Ju.88's at Narvik.

[2] *Warspite* had 8 15-in., 8 6-in., 8 4-in. H.A. *Valiant* had 8 15-in., 20 4·5-in. *Renown* had 6 15-in., 20 4·5-in. As it turned out, the *Valiant* actually prepared for bombarding, sailing from Scapa for Rosyth on the 19th to ship the special projectiles. The *Renown* sailed with her, but to dock and repair the damage received in the bad weather and her fight on the 9th. The *Resolution* (from the Halifax escort force) relieved the *Warspite* at Narvik, and the latter went to the Mediterranean.

QUESTION OF DIRECT ATTACK ON TRONDHEIM   Sec. 23

The answer to this came in A.T. 0250 of the 17th, of which this is a digest :—

(a) and (b) 'One brigade of regulars to take aerodrome by assault ; 1000 Canadian troops, part to capture forts, part to land near Hommelvik, and part to contact Norwegians near Levanger ; 200 Royal Marines to assist in capture of forts.'

(c) The true position of Vaernes aerodrome is 63° 27 N., 10° 56 E.

(d) 1st Cruiser Squadron : 'Not certain, but detailed plan may prove them necessary, and we must be prepared to put everything into this operation.'

(e) and (f) *Ark Royal* and *Glorious* to be used, with total of 45 fighter machines ; *Furious* not required.

(g) 'Do you propose to relieve *Warspite* by *Repulse*, or would you like *Resolution* to do so ?'

(h) Admiral Holland and the General commanding 'Hammer's' troops would come to Scapa on the 18th, 'provided agreement on general scope of operation is reached to-day,' otherwise on the 19th.

Rear-Admiral Holland arrived on board the Rodney at Scapa on 18th April, bringing with him the plan of the operation, but the General commanding the assault troops (Major-General Hotblack) had suddenly fallen ill in London, and Major-General Berney-Ficklin—hastily appointed to succeed him—was seriously injured together with two of his staff when his aircraft crashed on landing at Hatston airfield on the 19th. The plan as originally conceived had been altered to meet representations by Sir Charles Forbes so that all the assaulting forces would be carried in men of war instead of transports, and was summarised by him as follows[1] :—

(a) *Details of embarkation of assault force*

(i) Rosyth, 21st April : Divisional Headquarters in 'W' Cruiser, Brigade Headquarters and 'C' Battalion, 15th Brigade, in 'X' Cruiser and five destroyers, Canadian Battalion in two destroyers and five sloops.

Greenock, 20th April : 'A' Battalion, 15th Brigade, in 'Y' Cruiser and five destroyers. 'B' Battalion, 15th Brigade in 'Z' Cruiser and five destroyers.

(ii) All cruisers to carry approximately 300 men and 30 tons of stores each. Cruisers 'Y' and 'Z' also to carry two armoured landing craft and should therefore be *Southampton* class. Cruiser 'X' should be *Southampton* or *York* class.

(iii) In addition, a Royal Marine battery of 7 3·7-in. howitzers to be embarked. Three guns stores and crews and half Battery Headquarters in each 'Y' and 'Z' cruiser. One gun and crew in 'X' Cruiser.

(iv) Destroyers carrying Canadians to carry 100 men with blankets, tents and 7 days' rations. Remaining destroyers to carry 100 men, blankets and 48 hours' rations.

(v) Sloops to carry 150 men each, with blankets, tents and 7 days' rations.

(vi) Ships concerned to embark H.E. ammunition before sailing, as arranged by Commander-in-Chief, Rosyth, and Flag Officer-in-Charge, Greenock.

(vii) Time of arrival of Troops and gear to be signalled in due course.

(b) *Details of embarkation of reserve, 147th Brigade*

(viii) Naval base staff and stores embark on 19th April in *Sobieski* and *Duchess of Athol* at Clyde and in steamship *Orion* at Rosyth. These troops with blankets, tents and 7 days' rations to be transferred at Scapa on 21st April to cruiser detailed.

(ix) *Sobieski* to embark one new type motor landing craft and *Oronsay* one old armoured motor landing craft, both ex s.s. *Empire* after daylight.

---
[1] Home Fleet Narrative. These proposals were confirmed in A.T. 0117/19.

Sec. 23   THE ALLIED COUNTER OFFENSIVE AND GENERAL
                EMPLOYMENT OF NAVAL FORCES

The details of the naval side of this plan were worked out between 18th and 19th April, but late on the 19th the operation was cancelled.

Up to the 17th, the Chiefs of Staff had been in favour of the attempt; but 'during the 18th, a vehement and decisive change in the opinion of the Chiefs of Staff and of the Admiralty occurred. This change was brought about first by increasing realisation of the magnitude of the naval stake in hazarding so many of our finest capital ships, and also by War Office arguments that even if the fleet got in and got out again, the opposed landing of the troops in the face of the German Air Power would be perilous '.[1] On 20th April, A.T. 1140/20 to the Commander-in-Chief, Home Fleet, confirmed that ' Hammer is cancelled ' and some six hours later A.T. 1731/20[2] forecast the employment of the Hammer forces in the Aandalsnes area.

But before this Sir Charles Forbes, who from the first had regarded the project with misgivings, had evidently come to the conclusion that it was over-hazardous. A signal sent by him on the 18th, outlining his proposals for the future employment of naval forces, provided for supporting the army at Narvik, Namsos and Aandalsnes, but said of Trondheim only ' operate in inner routes against supplies for enemy military and air forces in Trondheim and Bergen area '.[3] As usual, there was difficulty in collecting enough destroyers to cope with the many calls upon them. His ' destroyers requirements ' were given in a signal sent at 0201, 19th (before A.T. 0117/19, summarised above, reached him), and amounted to 68, of which he earmarked 45 for Hammer; he then only had 63 at his command and a margin above the 68 to allow for loss or damage was essential. As regards the situation at Trondheim, reports made the German strength to be some 2000 men on the 16th or 17th, chiefly at Vaernes and in the forts that guard the entrance to the fjord, where there were said to be 6-in. and 8-in. guns. The troops were Austrian and Bavarian highlanders, young men, active and well-equipped. Whether they had mobile artillery was doubtful; but they were strong in the air—at Vaernes and on a frozen lake 5 miles south-east of Trondheim—and they were well off for anti-aircraft guns. Later reports said that more troops were arriving by air, land and sea.

The question whether this assault should have been attempted or not became the subject of considerable public controversy. For this reason, the Commander-in-Chief, Home Fleet, deemed it advisable to put on record his opinion

> . . . that it was a gamble that might have succeeded, but probably would not. It appeared to him that it was only in the fleet, which had had practical experience in the matter, that the scale of air attack that the enemy could develop on the Norwegian coast was properly appreciated. The experience of the attacks on the fleet on 9th and 11th April, and on the *Suffolk*[4] on 17th April, left no doubt in his mind that 45 F.A.A. fighters operating from carriers could not have afforded adequate protection in the circumstances of this assault, which, as he had pointed out, necessitated a long approach in narrow waters.

---

[1] Churchill, THE SECOND WORLD WAR, Vol. I, p. 494.

These reasons savour of the opinion expressed by the Commander-in-Chief, Home Fleet, in his signal 1157/14 (*see ante*). At the Admiralty, moreover, there was anxiety about the reserves of H/A ammunition, which were running low; and the experience of the *Suffolk*, which was seriously damaged by air attack on the 17th, may have influenced the decision. In any case, in view of the commitments at Narvik, Namsos and Aandalsnes, it is difficult to see how the cruisers, destroyers and sloops required for Hammer could have been provided.

[2] *See* Chapter V, Operation Sickle (*postea*).

[3] Commander-in-Chief, H.F., 1203/18 : *see* Sec. 24 *postea*.

[4] *See* Sec. 28 *postea*.

An opposed landing with very slightly superior forces had to be undertaken which, from previous experience and in view of what happened at Narvik, was bound to be a hazardous operation, and withal the combined operation had to be hastily planned and then performed without any practice at all, in fact *ad hoc*.[1]

With this view the German Naval Staff was in substantial agreement :—

' A direct assault on Trondheim would only have been possible in the first days of the German operations, while coastal batteries were still unprepared and before the German Air Force was able to operate effectively against the attacker. Even then the invader could only hope to consolidate his position if, by using extensive air transportation, he could establish air superiority in the Norwegian area and could land a powerfully equipped and modernly trained expeditionary force. In addition the British would have had to prevent any further reinforcements of German troops on the Skagerrak route to southern Norway. Thus it cannot be held against the British if, with their uncertainty as to the actual situation in southern Norway and with ignorance of the results of their submarine attacks in the Kattegat and Skagerrak, they did not decide on a direct attack against the harbours already in German occupation.'[2]

The French view, on the other hand, emerges from the following extracts from the minutes of conversations held in Paris on 22nd and 23rd April. At the first meeting the First Sea Lord (Admiral of the Fleet Sir Dudley Pound) and Vice-Admiral Sir Geoffrey Blake saw Admiral Darlan and Captain Auphan, when the French, runs the minute, ' were emphatic ' that the Norwegian theatre of operations ' is vital, and that nothing short of the actual outbreak of war in the Mediterranean should be allowed to deflect forces from the Allied effort there. They offered further naval help if required. . . .' ' They regarded the capture of Trondheim as vital.'

Next day, Sir Geoffrey Blake saw Admiral le Luc and Captain Auphan. ' The French did not disguise their profound regret that Hammer had been cancelled, and urged that, although the operation would now be a more difficult one, the question of undertaking it should be re-examined.'[3]

There was, too, a considerable body of opinion in the United Kingdom in favour of the attempt, typified by the debates which took place in Parliament.[4]

The question may well provide food for academic debate for many years to come ; but it may be noted that the view of the responsible Naval Commander on the spot, Admiral Sir Charles Forbes, and the considered opinion of the German Naval Staff, were in close agreement that at this stage of the operations —over a week after the original landings, by which time the German defence was a going concern—the attempt was unlikely to have succeeded ; and subsequent events of the Norwegian Campaign tend to confirm this opinion.

24. General employment of Home Fleet, April–June 1940 [PLAN 1

With the abandonment of operation Hammer the Home Fleet settled down to the business of convoying the various expeditions to and from Norway, and rendering such assistance as possible to the troops on shore. Cruisers, destroyers and sloops, as well as merchant ships, served as troopships ; and when troops sailed in unarmed ships one or two cruisers generally accompanied them, besides an anti-submarine screen of destroyers. Thus the convoys had no

---

[1] Home Fleet, Narrative, para. 230.

[2] B.R. 1840(1), page 60.

[3] It is probable that the French view was influenced by the desire to support any operations in distant Norway which might divert German forces from the attack on France in the near future, which was foreseen and which took place a month later.

[4] H. of C. Deb., Vol. 360, 1126.

Sec. 24 THE ALLIED COUNTER OFFENSIVE AND GENERAL EMPLOYMENT OF NAVAL FORCES

great strength (especially those for Aandalsnes), for every cruiser troopship carried several hundred men and sometimes a couple of hundred tons of stores, including guns and wagons. But seemingly the Germans did not intend to hazard their surface craft in attempts on the expeditions while on passage, though they sometimes brought off air attacks. A.T. 1701/19 informed the Commander-in-Chief, Home Fleet, that the Admiralty had ' no reliable reports of main German units later than the 12th, but that it was probable that all their large ships were in their home waters '.[1]

The Commander-in-Chief, Home Fleet, arrived back at Scapa from the Lofoten Islands on 17th April, and the next day he signalled to the Admiralty his ' outline proposals for the future employment ' of the fleet as follows :—

(a) Maintain close blockade of Narvik and support military forces there.

(b) Support military forces in Namsos and Aandalsnes area.

(c) Operate in inner routes against supplies for enemy military and air forces in Trondheim and Bergen area . . . .

(d) Submarines to operate in Skagerrak and off south-western coast of Norway against enemy lines of communication.

(e) Sweep by surface forces into Skagerrak to be undertaken to relieve pressure of enemy anti-submarine measures when weather conditions are suitable—*vide* my 2009/17th April. (Such a sweep ' not an operation of war except in fog, due to air attacks enemy can bring to bear '.)

(f) Kattegat to be intensively mined up to limit of Swedish territorial waters, both by magnetic and contact mines, starting from southward and working north.

(g) Continuous harassing of all enemy aerodromes in Norway, except in Narvik area, to be a special task of Royal Air Force.

In pursuance of this policy the *Warspite* flying Vice-Admiral Whitworth's flag remained in support of Lord Cork till 24th April, when she proceeded to Scapa and the Clyde *en route* for the Mediterranean, her place in the Narvik area being taken on 26th April by the *Resolution*, detached from the Halifax escort force. The *Repulse* sailed from Scapa on 17th April to protect the first French convoy to Namsos, but she was diverted to the assistance of the *Suffolk*, which had been disabled by air attack, and did not join the convoy till the last day of its passage (19th). She then took a single transport to Vaags Fjord afterwards returning to Scapa, where she stayed till June. As to the remainder of the capital ships of the Home Fleet, the *Rodney* remained at Scapa till the German raid on homecoming convoys from Narvik in June ; the *Renown* went to Rosyth for repairs, rejoining the fleet towards the end of May ; and the *Valiant* went out again at the end of April for service in the central Norwegian area.

The Home Fleet destroyers (apart from a dozen or so with Lord Cork in the Narvik Squadron) were required for convoy duty almost continuously throughout the campaign. Some had other service on the coast, and together with cruisers, A.A. cruisers, sloops and small craft did fine work in support of the military forces on shore, which will be described in succeeding chapters on the various landings.

Under clause (c) of the Commander-in-Chief's proposals four destroyers cruised in the Inner Lead about Trondheim in pairs between 21st and 28th April, with occasional breaks when ships had to go home for oil or were required for convoys. The *Ashanti* and *Mohawk*, *Somali* and *Tartar*, *Sikh* and

---
[1] Actually, apart from destroyers, submarines and small craft the *Köln* and *Emden* were the only undamaged ships at the disposal of the Germans at this date.

Nubian all took part in this patrol; they found no enemy at sea, but the *Nubian* and *Ashanti* suffered slightly from near misses in an air attack on the 28th. Vice-Admiral Layton supported the patrol during the nights of the 26th and 27th with the *Manchester* and *Birmingham* after landing troops at Molde and Aandalsnes; and two nights later (29th) mines were laid in Trondheim Lead by the *Ivanhoe*, *Icarus* and *Impulsive* (Operation Z.M.A.).

The month of May saw a considerable reduction in the Home Fleet effectives. The German threat to the Low Countries was becoming plainer every day and on 7th May Vice-Admiral Edward-Collins in the *Galatea*, with the *Arethusa*, was sent to Sheerness, and eight destroyers[1] to Harwich to work under the Commander-in-Chief, The Nore.

On the same day, the *Berwick* and *Glasgow* embarked the 2nd Battalion, R.M. Brigade, under Colonel R. G. Sturges, at Greenock, and sailed next morning for Iceland, escorted by the *Fearless* and *Fortune*. Reykjavik was occupied without incident on 10th May,[2] and the two cruisers then proceeded to Liverpool for long refits, the destroyers returning to Scapa.

On the 14th, increased tension with Italy caused the transfer of the eight destroyers detached to Harwich and in addition nine more,[3] with the A.A. cruiser *Carlisle* and three sloops, to the Mediterranean. Taking into account the numbers under repair from war damage, those working in the Narvik area under Lord Cork and those required for Narvik convoys, this latter detachment left the Commander-in-Chief, Home Fleet, with no destroyers for screening heavy ships for the rest of the month. Three more destroyers[4] were ordered to the Humber on 18th May, and on the 26th Vice-Admiral Layton, with the *Manchester*, *Birmingham* and *Sheffield* was also sent there and placed under the command of the Commander-in-Chief, The Nore.

25. Carrier and F.A.A. operations

The carriers and Fleet Air Arm played a conspicuous part throughout the campaign. The vital need was to neutralise the strong German Air Force, firstly by providing fighter cover over ports of disembarkation and ships engaged in it; secondly by giving air reconnaissance, air spotting and ground attack; and thirdly by air attack on enemy airfields, depots and transport, both ashore and afloat. For the first two requirements the home bases were too far distant for the employment of R.A.F. fighters; for the third, the limited numbers of R.A.F. bombers available and the distances to be flown rendered help by naval aircraft essential.

At the beginning of the campaign, the only carrier in home waters was the *Furious*. As already mentioned, she arrived in Norwegian waters on 11th April and when the Commander-in-Chief shaped course for Scapa on 15th April, she remained working under Lord Cork in the Narvik area until the 26th. She had no fighters embarked and by that time her two T.S.R. Squadrons had lost 50 per cent of their numbers;[5] she herself had sustained damage to her turbines by a near miss, and she then proceeded to Greenock for repairs.

---

[1] *Janus, Hyperion, Hereward, Havock, Kelly, Kimberley, Kandahar, Hostile.* The *Kelly* was damaged in an operation on 9th May (*see* Sec. 28 *postea*) and never got to Harwich.

[2] The Royal Marines arrived back in the Clyde on 24th May in the transports *Franconia* and *Lancastria*, which had brought an infantry brigade to relieve them on the 17th.

[3] *Hero, Hasty, Ilex, Imperial, Juno, Mohawk, Nubian, Khartoum, Kingston.*

[4] *Fury, Fortune, Foresight.*

[5] *See* App. F.

Sec. 25   THE ALLIED COUNTER OFFENSIVE AND GENERAL
          EMPLOYMENT OF NAVAL FORCES

The *Glorious* and the *Ark Royal* from the Mediterranean joined the Home Fleet at Scapa on 23rd April, and sailed for central Norway the same day under Vice-Admiral Wells, flying his flag in the *Ark Royal*, with the *Berwick*, *Curlew* and six destroyers[1] (Operation DX). Their object was to provide fighter protection for the southern expedition; to attack the enemy in Trondheim; and to land some Royal Air Force machines to work from the frozen Lake Lesjaskog (between Aandalsnes and Dombaas), known to the squadron as ' Gladiator Lake '.

The R.A.F. Squadron of Gladiators was flown off the *Glorious* between 1730 and 1800 on 24th April, and reached their landing ground without opposition, but the lake was shortly afterwards heavily bombed and all the R.A.F. aircraft were put out of action. All fighter support then devolved on the carriers' naval aircraft.

The carriers sent up fighters to patrol over Aandalsnes as soon as snow allowed in the evening of 24th April and each day afterwards up to the 28th a few aircraft patrolled over Aandalsnes or Namsos. In the course of these patrols, fighters engaged enemy aircraft attacking the railways, the airfield on ' Gladiator Lake ' and two convoys approaching Aandalsnes; they also helped to defend the *Flamingo* lying at that port. Apart from this work, the carriers kept anti-submarine and fighter patrols in the air ' whenever submarine or enemy aircraft attack was likely '.[2]

On 27th April the *Glorious* was detached to fuel, rejoining on 1st May; the *Sheffield* relieved the *Curlew* as radar guardship on the 28th, being relieved in her turn by the *Valiant* on the 30th, and oiling requirements occasioned changes in the destroyer screen; otherwise the squadron operated till the night of 1st May.

Admiral Wells worked from positions about 120 miles from the targets or patrol areas, going to seaward between operations—except the first day, when the aircraft had 400 miles to fly on passage alone, which the Admiral described as ' a very hazardous flight, most gallantly carried out '.[2] Bombing attacks on Trondheim were made by 34 aircraft on 25th April and by 18 (the *Glorious* having by then parted company) on the 28th. No German warships were seen there, but merchant shipping was attacked; and heavy damage was inflicted on the airfield and naval aircraft at Vaernes, especially by the raid on the 25th.

In the evening of the 28th the squadron drew off to seaward to rest the airmen ' who had been in action for five successive days ' and ' were showing definite signs of strain '.[2] The carriers, too, had not been without excitement; enemy aircraft attacked them on the 28th, when the *Ark Royal* shot down an enemy machine, and there were encounters with submarines on the 27th and 29th.

Admiral Wells moved in again on 30th April in order to provide cover for the troops retreating from Aandalsnes next day. The *Glorious* rejoined his flag on 1st May, bringing fresh aircraft to replace casualties and to cover the retreat from Namsos, scheduled for 2nd–3rd May, the Royal Air Force then taking over the protection of the Aandalsnes expedition. But throughout 1st May the squadron was subjected to air attacks, which occupied the attention of the fighters intended to augment the patrols over Namsos, and the German bombs

---

[1] *Hyperion, Hereward, Hasty, Fearless, Fury, Juno.*
[2] Report of V.A. (A). Operation DX.

fell sometimes ' unpleasantly close '. These attacks convinced the Vice-Admiral that he could no longer ' maintain a position from which aircraft could give support to our forces ' and, with the approval of the Commander-in-Chief, he accordingly withdrew that evening, and crossing the North Sea in 65° N., came west of the Shetlands to Scapa, arriving on 3rd May.

During these operations, the squadron estimated that they had destroyed 21 enemy aircraft (not counting the seaplanes in Trondheim Fjord), besides damaging a further 20 ; their own losses amounted to 13 aircraft destroyed and two rendered unserviceable.

With the failure of the campaign in central Norway the focus of naval interest once more shifted to Lord Cork's command. Vice-Admiral Wells only remained at Scapa long enough to make good aircraft losses, and sailed on 4th May in the *Ark Royal* for the Narvik area. There she remained till 24th May, providing fighters for the Narvik and Bodo areas, until R.A.F. landing grounds had been prepared, and launching almost daily attacks by Skuas and Swordfish on enemy railway lines, military stores, etc. During this period the *Furious* transported R.A.F. fighters and landed them at Bardufoss (21st May) and the *Glorious* six Walruses to Harstad (18th May), and Hurricanes to Bardufoss (26th May), as the newly prepared airfields became ready. After a brief interval between 25th and 30th May in Home Waters, the *Ark Royal* and *Glorious* once more proceeded to the Narvik area in connection with the final evacuation—a service from which the *Glorious* never returned.

The contribution of the Fleet Air Arm to the campaign was not limited to the work of the carrier-borne aircraft. Mention has already been made of the eminently successful attack by Skuas from Hatston on the *Königsberg* in Bergen (*see* Sec. 12 *ante*). A number of attacks were carried out from this base during April and May against enemy shipping, small war vessels and oil tanks. During three attacks in May the Squadron (806) was escorted by R.A.F. Blenheims. Surprise was attained on every occasion and British losses were small ; the success of the dive bombing method of attack seemed to be confirmed. Three attacks against oil tanks were particularly successful, resulting in the almost complete destruction of three separate oil depots.

Between 18th May and 6th June, a squadron of six Walruses was based on Harstad, whence they were employed on anti-submarine patrols, convoying, occasional ferrying and especially communication duties—a difficult problem in that mountainous country, broken by waterways and with few roads. Out of some 250 flights during the period, more than three-quarters were devoted to transporting British and French officers on such missions. The base was closed down on 6th June and the squadron re-embarked in the *Ark Royal* ; on the last day, however, the five remaining Walruses carried out a spirited bombing attack on German troops and installations at Solfolla.

In addition to these duties directly in connection with the Allied expeditions, minelaying operations were carried out by Swordfish (specially equipped with long distance tanks) from Hatston ; the first of these took place in the narrow Inner Lead channel south of Haugesund (between Bergen and Stavanger) on the night of 17th/18th May. And throughout the operations, land based F.A.A. fighters from Hatston and Wick maintained the air defence of Scapa, while Swordfish carried out anti-submarine operations as required. If any had previously doubted the necessity of a naval air arm or the scope of the operations it might legitimately be called upon to perform, surely the events in Norway from April to June 1940 gave the answer in no uncertain terms.

26. Employment of A.A. cruisers and sloops

The individual efforts of A.A. cruisers and sloops will appear in the succeeding chapters on the landing operations ; but some general indication of their services will not be out of place at this stage. In the words of the Commander-in-Chief, Home Fleet, ' the scale of air attack that would be developed against our military forces on shore and our naval forces off the Norwegian coast was greviously under-estimated when the operations were undertaken. In the result, when the situation on shore became desperate, we were committed and desperate measures had to be taken '.[1] In the absence of Allied fighters and adequate A.A. defences, any expedient which might mitigate the severity of the attacks on the Allied bases had to be resorted to. A.A. cruisers and sloops seemed the readiest means at hand, though they would be severely handicapped by operating in confined waters, surrounded by high cliffs.

Accordingly on 21st April the Commander-in-Chief, Home Fleet, received orders from the Admiralty that an A.A. ship or sloop was to be kept at Namsos and Aandalsnes, the *Black Swan, Auckland, Pelican* and *Fleetwood* being placed under his orders for this purpose (A.T. 1929/21). The next day further orders from the Admiralty (A.T. 1037/22) directed that two of these ships should be kept at both Namsos and Aandalsnes, and added the *Bittern* and *Flamingo* to the Force.

Meanwhile, H.M.S. *Carlisle*, flying the flag of Rear-Admiral Vivian, had arrived at Aandalsnes on 20th April, where she remained till the 22nd, later moving to Namsos ; there she stayed—except for a trip to Skjel Fjord for fuel —till the evacuation on the night of 2nd/3rd May. The *Calcutta* was at Namsos from 22nd to 27th, when she proceeded to Aandalsnes and was there during the final evacuation on the night of 1st/2nd May. The *Curacoa* arrived at Aandalsnes on the night of 21st/22nd April, but was seriously damaged by a bomb on the 24th and returned to the United Kingdom escorted by the *Flamingo*, which had arrived there that afternoon. The *Flamingo* returned to Aandalsnes early on the 26th, sailing the same night after expending all her ammunition.

The *Black Swan* and *Auckland* were already in Norwegian waters when the Admiralty orders reached the Commander-in-Chief. The *Black Swan* was hit at Aandalsnes on the 28th by a bomb which went right through the ship, doing surprisingly little damage, but enough to force her to return to the United Kingdom. The *Auckland* arrived at Namsos on 22nd April and sailed in the evening of the 24th, having fired practically all her ammunition. She returned to Aandalsnes on the 30th, and remained there till the final evacuation. The *Pelican* was hit by a bomb and had her stern blown off on 22nd April, while still some 50 miles from the shore on her way to Aandalsnes ; she eventually reached Lerwick on the 24th in tow of the *Fleetwood* which had just parted company from her for Namsos when she was hit. The *Fleetwood* was employed subsequently at Aandalsnes from the 29th to 30th ; then, having expended most of her ammunition, she returned to Scapa with some evacuated personnel. The *Bittern* was at Namsos from 24th to 30th April, when she was hit and set on fire by dive bombers ; after survivors had been taken off she was sunk by torpedo in 100 fathoms by order of Read-Admiral Vivian.

Commenting on this employment of these ships, the Commander-in-Chief, Home Fleet, remarked that it became evident at an early stage that the slight degree of protection that they could afford to the bases, being due mainly to the fact that they were primarily chosen as targets by the bombers, was out of all

---

[1] Home Fleet Narrative, para. 269.

proportion to their expenditure of ammunition and the damage they were sustaining. Although he realised that the moral effect of their presence was considerable he was of the opinion that the use of the ships for this purpose was wasteful and that considerable reinforcements would be required owing to the number of ships that had been damaged. This view he represented to the Admiralty on 26th April[1] and on the next day, owing to the heavy attacks on them, he ordered the A.A. guardships to withdraw during daylight hours.

27. A/S trawlers on the Norwegian coast

Some mention should be made here of the work of the A/S trawlers. On 13th April, the Admiralty ordered the 21st A/S Striking Force and the 23rd A/S Group to sail from Scotland for Namsos, and on the 17th the 12th and 22nd A/S Groups to sail for Aandalsnes. These were followed later by the 15th and 16th A/S Striking Forces, which went to Namsos.[2]

These trawlers were sent to Norway primarily to give A/S protection to H.M. ships and transports in the fjords, but no sooner had they arrived than they were subjected to frequent heavy air attacks, high level and dive bombing and machine gunning, which made it suicidal for them to carry out A/S patrols except during the few hours of darkness. They suffered severe casualties, eleven out of a total of 29 being sunk or driven ashore. During daylight hours, after the first day or two, they were forced to take shelter under high cliffs, partly to evade bombing and partly to rest their crews. While so placed, some of the crews endeavoured to camouflage their vessels with evergreen and small trees and themselves took refuge on shore, in some instances leaving their guns' crews on board to engage the enemy aircraft ; but even when on shore, the crews were machine-gunned on the hillside.

As most of the work of disembarking troops and stores and the evacuation were done at night, some of the trawlers did useful work ferrying between the transports and the shore, while others were employed on A/S patrols. ' Despite these arduous and hazardous conditions', wrote the Commander-in-Chief, Home Fleet, 'the morale and gallantry of officers and men remained magnificent'.[3]

As an example of what could be done by these little ships with scratch crews, if well led, the Commander-in-Chief went on to give some details from a report written by Lieutenant R. B. Stannard,[4] who was in command of the *Arab* :—

> ' In the early afternoon of 28th April, after a heavy bombing attack which had started fires among the stores and ammunition on the pier at Namsos, the *Arab* and *Angle* were ordered to tow off the transport *Saumur*, which was aground with a wire round her propeller. The *Angle* managed to get her off alone, so the *Arab* returned to the burning pier and her Commanding Officer, keeping her bows in by going slow ahead, ran two hoses over the forecastle and tried to put out the burning ammunition dump. While thus engaged, another air attack by sixteen planes developed, and as there was no hope of putting out the fire he left and went down the fjord.

---

[1] Commander-in-Chief 1030/26. In the same signal he recommended that immediate steps should be taken to establish A.A. ground defences and adequate R.A.F. fighter protection, both at Aandalsnes and Namsos ; and that endeavour should be made to ascertain whether any suitable localities for landing grounds existed north of Namsos, as he had by this time become convinced that the use of Mosjoen or Kongsmoen was essential as a landing place for army stores, if we were to maintain our forces in this area.

[2] *See* Appendix A(1) Composition of forces and brief statement of their movements.

[3] Home Fleet Narrative.

[4] H.M. The King approved the award of the Victoria Cross to Lieutenant Stannard for his gallantry during these operations.

Sec. 27   THE ALLIED COUNTER OFFENSIVE AND GENERAL
                 EMPLOYMENT OF NAVAL FORCES

On 30th April, after helping H.M.S. *Bittern* to drive off air attacks and helping other trawlers in various ways, he decided to put his crew ashore. He landed Lewis guns, food and blankets, and had them taken to a large cave, and then established a number of machine-gun posts at the top of the cliff. There the crew slept with look-outs on duty.

Next day, the *Aston Villa* made fast about 100 yards south of the *Arab*. There was continuous bombing and machine-gunning by high and dive bombers which came over in flights of six, nine and twelve planes. The positions ashore were also machine-gunned. The *Gaul* was hit and sank. The crews of the three trawlers then manned the positions ashore. The *Aston Villa* was set on fire by a direct hit from a dive bomber. Luckily only a few of her crew were still on board. The wounded were rescued and transferred in extemporised stretchers to the top of the cliff. As the *Aston Villa* was still on fire and in danger of blowing up, Lieutenant Stannard, with two others boarded the *Arab*, cut her lines and succeeded in moving her another 100 yards away before the explosion occurred.

Finally, when leaving the fjord in his damaged vessel to return to Scapa after five days at Namsos, he was attacked by a single German bomber which ordered him to steer east or be sunk. Instead, he continued his course, held his fire until the aircraft was about 800 yards away, and then opened fire with every gun on board and brought the aircraft down '.[1]

28. The Southern Area : Surface operations   [PLAN 1

Operations by surface craft off the southern coasts of Norway had been virtually ruled out—except on special occasions—by the Commander-in-Chief, Home Fleet, with the concurrence of the Admiralty, and this area was mainly left to submarines. Three operations by surface craft were, however, carried out ; the first—a bombardment of Stavanger airfield by the *Suffolk* on 17th April —certainly confirmed the Commander-in-Chief's appreciation of the power of the German Air Force. The bombardment (Operation Duck) was ordered by the Admiralty in support of the Naval landing at Aandalsnes (Operation Primrose) and its object was defined as ' to inflict the greatest possible damage to the aerodrome so as to restrict the operation of aircraft therefrom '.

The *Suffolk* (Captain J. W. Durnford) screened by the *Kipling, Juno, Janus* and *Hereward* towing T.S.D.S. sailed from Scapa in the afternoon of 16th April and crossed the North Sea at 26 knots ; at 0414, 17th April, the submarine *Seal* which had been ordered to mark position 'A' (58° 57′ N., 5° 10′ E.) was sighted and five minutes later a spotting Walrus was catapulted from the *Suffolk*. At 0432, the *Seal* was passed on a course of 110°, and at about this time rockets and A.A. gunfire were sighted, presumably coming from the defences of the airfield. This prevented the identification of a flare which a R.A.F. Hudson was to drop to indicate the position of the target. It was then getting fairly light ; the land could be seen, but with no detail ; the sea was calm, sky clear, with a light easterly wind. At 0445 speed was reduced to 15 knots and two minutes later the force turned to the bombarding course of 181°, a second Walrus being catapulted at about this time. Unfortunately wireless communication with the aircraft could not be established and in consequence the bombardment did not start till 0513, the range being about 20,000 yards. Three runs were carried out, in the course of which 202 rounds were fired. The failure of wireless communication with the aircraft was ' most disappointing and inevitably had an adverse effect on the bombardment '[2] ; nevertheless, casualties were caused to the German naval air contingent there, two petrol dumps were destroyed and other damage inflicted.

---

[1] Home Fleet Narrative.
[2] Commanding Officer, *Suffolk*, report.

After an hour in the air in the vicinity of the airfield, the two Walruses and the Hudson returned to Scotland, and at 0604 the force commenced its withdrawal at 30 knots, steering 270°. Orders had been received from the Admiralty the previous evening (A.T. 2300/16) for the force to sweep to the northward on completion of Operation Duck, in order to intercept enemy destroyers; Captain Durnford accordingly stood to the westward till 0704 and then altered course to the northward, reducing speed to 25 knots (to conserve fuel) and informing the Admiralty of his position, course and speed at 0720. Fighter escort had been arranged with Coastal Command, but this failed to make contact—it subsequently transpired, because the fighters had apparently expected the force to sweep north close inshore. Thus it came about that the squadron was entirely dependent on its own resources in event of air attack.

This was not long in coming. The first attack took place at 0825, when an emergency air attack report was made. From then on, the *Suffolk* was under continuous attack—both high level and dive bombing—for six hours and 47 minutes.[1] After about an hour and a quarter, Captain Durnford decided to withdraw to the westward, as offering the best chance of obtaining air support as early as possible. At 1037 the ship was hit by a heavy bomb, which caused very severe damage, put 'X' and 'Y' turrets out of action, reduced her speed to 18 knots and caused flooding to the extent of some 1,500 tons of water in 20 minutes. Repeated requests for fighter support, giving the position, failed to have any apparent effect.

Meanwhile, the attacks continued. By 1305 both steering motors were out of action but temporary repairs were effected 20 minutes later; near misses, which blew in lower deck scuttles and punctured the ship's side, caused further extensive flooding. Help was, however, on its way. At 1119, the Commander-in-Chief, Home Fleet, then nearing Scapa from the Lofoten Islands, ordered all Skuas at Hatston to be sent to the *Suffolk*'s assistance; he also sent the *Renown* and the *Repulse*, the latter of which was screening the first French convoy to the northward.[2] The Commander-in-Chief, Rosyth, informed the *Suffolk* at 1140 that three Blenheims and three Hudsons should reach her by 1230.

It was not, however, till 1415 that friendly aircraft were observed arriving; by 1430, nine were in company, but despite this there were four attacks between then and 1512—with the exception of the one which hit 'the most dangerous and accurate experienced.'[3] At 1620 the two battlecruisers were sighted ahead, and eventually the *Suffolk* managed to struggle into Scapa on 18th April with her quarterdeck awash.[4] She was beached at Longhope for temporary repairs and sailed for the Clyde on 5th May for permanent repairs.

Within a week of the *Suffolk*'s return to Scapa, a sweep into the Skagerrak by the French contre-torpilleurs *L'Indomptable*, *Le Malin* and *Le Triomphant* was arranged by the Admiralty. By this time the enemy anti-submarine

---

[1] Thirty-three attacks took place (21 high level, 12 dive bombing), in the course of which 88 splashes were observed. (*See* App. E.)

[2] 'The Commander-in-Chief, Home Fleet, was at sea when this operation was ordered and carried out. He took it for granted that a very strong air escort would be provided, since the *Suffolk* would be within range of enemy air bases, including those in Germany; and he also took it for granted, in view of the *Norfolk*'s experience at Scapa on 16th March, that the vulnerability of these ships to even a 250-kg. bomb was fully appreciated.' Home Fleet Narrative.

[3] Commanding officer, H.M.S. *Suffolk*, report. Captain Durnford remarked that the fighters in pursuit of the enemy appeared to have left the overhead area unguarded.

[4] For the last 164 miles she was steered by her screws, the steering gear having finally broken down at 1604, 17th.

Sec. 28 THE ALLIED COUNTER OFFENSIVE AND GENERAL
EMPLOYMENT OF NAVAL FORCES

measures were making themselves felt and the operation was aimed at the destruction of their patrols. The force left Rosyth in the afternoon of 23rd April, intending to cross the meridian of 6° 13′ E. at 2100 and that of Kristiansund south before 0500, 24th. The force entered the Skagerrak unobserved, and during the night sank two motor torpedo boats and a trawler and damaged a second trawler.[1] When retiring across the North Sea at high speed, the destroyers were heavily attacked by aircraft, despite a battle flight escort, but escaped without damage. Two aircraft of the escort, however, were shot down by enemy fighters.

On only one other occasion during the campaign did surface forces operate in the waters to the south-west of Norway. This was a sweep directed against enemy minelaying forces on 9th/10th May. By this time the withdrawal from central Norway had been completed and the centre of naval interest was shifting to the southward.

At 0900, 9th, the Commander-in-Chief, Home Fleet, received information from the Admiralty (A.T. 0827) of the probable positions of two enemy forces near the Little Fisher bank that evening. As it happened, the *Birmingham*, with the *Janus*, *Hyperion*, *Hereward* and *Havock* had left Rosyth bound to the southward at 0645, 9th. These ships were ordered by the Admiralty to steer 080°, 20 knots, after passing May Island ; and at the same time, Captain (D) 5 (Captain Lord Louis Mountbatten), in the *Kelly* with the *Kimberley* and the *Kandahar* with the *Hostile*, which were then just to the southward of St. Abbs Head, were ordered to turn to the northward and join the *Birmingham*. The Commander-in-Chief, Home Fleet, sailed a further unit of five destroyers, the *Fury*, *Foresight*, *Mohawk*, *Bulldog* and *Gallant* from Scapa at 1150.

Instructions to these forces were signalled by the Commander-in-Chief at 1024. The *Birmingham* and her destroyers were directed to pass through 56° 39′ N., 3° 37′ E. at 1930, 9th and then to steer 097° to meet an enemy force of three destroyers, one torpedo boat and four minelayers which were expected to approach that position from 56° 28′ N., 6° 10′ E. The *Fury* and her group were to be in 57° 21′ N., 2° 22′ E. at 1850, where six enemy motor torpedo boats were expected to be encountered. After sinking them, this group was to join the *Birmingham* at high speed. If nothing was sighted by 2230, all forces were to search back to the westward. Air escort by fighters was arranged for the *Birmingham*.

Lord Louis Mountbatten's destroyers joined the *Birmingham* in the afternoon, but the *Kimberley* soon afterwards had to return to Rosyth owing to shortage of fuel. The remainder of the forces continued to the eastward. The prospects seemed promising, but they were doomed to disappointment.

At 1940, an enemy report from a reconnaissance aircraft was received ; it placed the force expected—four minelayers, three destroyers and a transport barge [sic]—in 57° 12′ N., 5° 30′ E., steering 080°. Unfortunately, no amplifying report giving the speed was made. This position was about 70 miles east-north-east of the expected position (which the *Birmingham* had reached) and on the assumption that the enemy was retiring at speed, there was little chance of overtaking him before he reached the Skaw ; our forces therefore continued in accordance with their instructions. It was not till nearly seven hours later (0232, 10th May) that an amplifying report[2] giving the speed of the enemy as 6 knots was received, and it was then realised that contact would have been possible about 2300 the previous evening.

---

[1] This report seems to have been exaggerated. According to German information, only two A/S trawlers were engaged, of which one was damaged.
[2] Made at 2335/9 from Area Headquarters, Donibristle, after the sighting aircraft had landed.

Meanwhile the *Kelly* and *Kandahar*, which had been detached to hunt a submarine at 1935, had not received the original enemy report till 2018, when the *Birmingham* was nearly out of sight ahead. Both destroyers immediately proceeded at high speed to join her, but visibility was falling and they did not in fact do so during the operation. They were, however, joined at 2050 by the *Bulldog*, which had become detached from the *Fury*'s force at 1730 when sinking a floating mine and had afterwards (at 1958) ineffectively engaged what appeared to be a motor yacht, which escaped to the eastward at high speed making smoke. Unfortunately, the *Bulldog* made no enemy report.

At 2235 the *Kelly* and *Kandahar*, being then in 56° 48′ N., 5° 9′ E. sighted enemy motor torpedo boats. One,[1] which was lying almost stopped in the track of our destroyers, fired torpedoes at the visibility distance of about four cables and hit the *Kelly* under the bridge. During the next hour and a half there were several contacts with motor torpedo boats; the *Kandahar* reported two at 2240, the *Birmingham* one at 2256 and the *Hostile* one at 2353. Attempts to sink these were unsuccessful, and they retired under their own smoke.

Meanwhile the *Kelly* had been badly damaged—a fact which was not known till 0013, 10th May, when a signal timed 2300, 9th, from the *Bulldog* was received. The *Bulldog* took the *Kelly* in tow, and subsequently reported that no other ships were in company and she was steering 262° at 7 knots. Visibility was very bad, and at 0010, 10th, an enemy motor torpedo boat rammed both destroyers, further damaging the *Kelly*. The *Bulldog* sustained minor damage only, and the motor torpedo boat was thought to have sunk.

As a result of these reports, the *Birmingham* and all destroyers taking part in the operation were ordered to cover the withdrawal of the *Kelly*, and Vice-Admiral Layton in the *Manchester*, with the *Sheffield*, was sailed from Scapa to assist. Air protection for the whole force was arranged. But that night big events were taking place to the south; Holland and Belgium were invaded, and at 0616, 10th, the *Birmingham* and all the destroyers except two as escort for the *Kelly* in tow were ordered to proceed towards Terschelling at maximum speed.

Admiral Layton made contact with the tow at 1507, 10th, and covered the withdrawal till the next afternoon, when he was ordered to Rosyth by the Commander-in-Chief, owing to the suspected presence of U-boats. The whole force was bombed by enemy aircraft off and on the whole time. Tugs reached the *Kelly* and had her in tow by 0430, 12th May, and she eventually reached the Tyne at 1600, 13th, 'very largely due' in the words of the Commander-in-Chief, Home Fleet, 'to the fine determined spirit shown by Captain the Lord Louis Mountbatten, G.C.V.O.'[2]

29. The Southern Area : Submarine activities 15th April–May

For the first three weeks of the campaign, Allied submarines continued to harass the German supply lines in the Skagerrak and Kattegat. As time went on, however, two factors were increasingly against them, viz. shorter hours of darkness and increased German anti-submarine measures, and added to these was the need to conserve and re-dispose them for the impending invasion of the Low Countries. For these reasons, the patrols in the Skagerrak and Kattegat with the exception of the minelayers *Narwhal* and *Seal* were mainly withdrawn

---

[1] It was thought this M.T.B. might have been co-operating with a Dornier aircraft which had been engaged by the *Kelly* at 2052.

[2] Home Fleet Narrative.

on 28th April,[1] many of the smaller submarines being employed in the southern part of the North Sea during the invasion of the Low Countries and subsequent events, while the larger submarines continued the attack on enemy communications further north along the Norwegian coast.

But before they were withdrawn from the Eastern Skagerrak and Kattegat attacks on the German convoys were of almost daily occurrence and many successes were scored. Thus on 15th April the *Sterlet* sank the *Brummer* which was escorting a convoy, and the *Snapper* two A/S trawlers ; on the 18th, the *Seawolf* seriously damaged two ships in convoy, setting one on fire and sinking her ; the *Triad* attacked a convoy on the 20th, and the *Tetrarch* a large transport on the 24th—both, however, without success. On 1st May the *Narwhal*, while on a minelaying operation, sank the s.s. *Buenos Aires* and damaged the *Bahia Castillo*. All these attacks took place within 30 miles of the Skaw or to the northward. Further west, the French *Orphée* attacked two U-boats about 90 miles south-west of the Naze and claimed one sunk on 21st April.[2]

Three British submarines came to grief in the latter part of April, however— the *Sterlet*, sunk by enemy A/S craft in the East Skagerrak[3] on the 18th ; the *Truant*, damaged by an explosion, possibly a magnetic torpedo, on the 25th, while on passage[3] to Sogne Fjord with Liaison Officers and S.A. ammunition ; and the *Unity*, which accidentally met an Allied convoy in a fog and was rammed and sunk by the Norwegian s.s. *Atlejarl*, in 55° 13′ N., 1° 20′ E.

Off the west coast of Norway, the *Trident* drove aground and badly damaged a 4000-ton merchant vessel[4] on 2nd May in Kors Fjord (Bergen area) after a 10-mile chase in broad daylight, and two days later the *Severn* chased and sank a German prize, the Swedish s.s. *Monark*, on passage from Stavanger to Germany.

A sad incident occured on 5th May, when the *Seal*, which had been laying mines in the Kattegat, was seriously damaged by a mine or depth charge. Attempts to reach Swedish territorial waters off Goteborg failed, and she was captured and towed ignominiously into a German port.

Next day (6th) the *Sealion* attacked two large transports to the southward of Oslo Fjord, and on the 8th the *Taku*, two 3000-ton merchant vessels escorted by torpedo boats west of the Skagerrak ; she was severely hunted, but survived undamaged. Neither of these attacks achieved success, but on 20th May the *Spearfish*, after capturing their crews, sank two Danish fishing vessels to the east of the Dogger Bank, and on the 23rd the *Tetrarch* sank one Danish fishing vessel some 70 miles south of the Naze, and sent another in prize to Leith—a distance of 340 miles.

Minefields were laid by the French *Rubis* on the 10th and 25th May ; by the *Narwhal* on the 1st and 11th, and by the *Porpoise* on 15th May.

30. The Conjunct Expeditions [PLAN 1

The foregoing sections give a brief summary of the principal naval activities during the period of the Allied operations in Norway. It is now proposed to turn to the amphibious expeditions which they were designed to support.

---

[1] This decision was taken on 23rd April.

[2] *U.22* was lost in the North Sea in April 1940, due to a cause unknown.

[3] 58° 03′ N., 11° 19′ E.

[4] She was, however, subsequently salved.

From a naval point of view, four main localities were involved in these operations, viz. :—

CENTRAL NORWAY: *OBJECTIVE TRONDHEIM*[1]

Namsos (Operations Henry and Maurice). First landing 14th April : evacuation 2nd May.

Aandalsnes (Operations Primrose and Sickle). First landing 17th April : evacuation 1st May.

NORTHERN NORWAY: *OBJECTIVE NARVIK*[2]

Harstad (Operation Rupert). First landing 14th April : evacuation 8th June.

Bodo area (between the Central and Northern areas). First landing 29th April in an attempt to check German interference at Narvik after the evacuation of the Trondheim area. Evacuated 29th May.

The ensuing chapters follow the fortunes of each of these expeditions in some detail. Both the central and northern campaigns opened with the landings of parties on Norwegian soil on the same day—14th April ; but whereas the former venture was over in under three weeks, the latter dragged on until the capture of Narvik on 28th May and the final evacuation some ten days later. For this reason the campaign in Central Norway will be dealt with first ; but it must be remembered that operations in the Narvik area were being conducted concurrently.

---

[1] The military forces in the Namsos area were under the command of Maj.-Gen. Carton de Wiart, V.C. ; those in the Aandalsnes area under Maj.-Gen. Paget. Lt.-Gen. Massy was appointed Commander-in-Chief, Forces operating in Central Norway, on 19th April, but he exercised his command from the United Kingdom, as the course of events did not permit of opening a H.Q. in Norway.

[2] The military forces in Northern Norway were commanded by Maj.-Gen. Mackesy till 13th May, when he was superseded by Lt.-Gen. Auchinleck. On 20th April Admiral of the Fleet Lord Cork was appointed in supreme command of all expeditionary forces in this area.

CHAPTER IV

THE LANDINGS AT NAMSOS

31. Operation Henry   [PLAN 11

It will be remembered that none of the projected Allied landings was to take place if the Germans were in a position to oppose it (otherwise than from the air) and consequently it was of the utmost importance to forestall the arrival of enemy troops at the chosen places by whatever means were available. This was the reason for Operation Henry—a purely temporary measure designed to ensure that on the arrival of the first flight of troops at Namsos, they would not find it already occupied by Germans.

Vice-Admiral Cunningham had reported Namsos and the adjacent fjords clear of the enemy on 12th April, then proceeding north to rejoin the Commander-in-Chief off the Lofoten Islands, but the troops destined for Namsos could not arrive for some days. Further south, Captain Pegram with the *Glasgow*, *Sheffield* and six destroyers[1] was operating in the Aalesund area; early on 13th April[2] he was searching for a pocket battleship, a cruiser and many large merchant ships reported by aircraft the previous day, when he intercepted A.T. 0216/13 addressed to the Commander-in-Chief:—

> 'In order to forestall the Germans at Namsos and to ensure an unopposed landing for a larger force, which will arrive at Namsos [about the 16th] propose, if you see no objection, that *Sheffield* and *Glasgow* should each prepare a landing party of about 150 men. A decision as to whether these parties will be required to land should be received by *Glasgow* and *Sheffield* about 1500 today (Saturday). Party should have provisions for seven days. Time of landing will be at the discretion of the Commanding Officer, H.M.S. *Glasgow*. Operation will be called "Henry"'.

The Commander-in-Chief had ' no objection, as a very temporary measure; but, as both ships' main armaments will be practically out of action for this period, consider it essential R.A.F. bombers should clear up pocket-battleships, cruisers, destroyers, and 15,000-ton storeship in Molde area'. The Admiralty therefore told Captain Pegram to carry on, and A.T. 1627/13 gave him particular instructions (extract):—

> 'Your object is to secure Namsen Fjord, so that a force of two battalions can be landed, a.m., 17th April. Landing parties should secure quays at Namsos and Bangsund and bridge across River Namsen; road south from Bangsund to be secured, if possible. Norwegians should be given every encouragement and assistance with rifles and ammunition.
>
> About 4000 German troops in Trondheim area; outposts reported at Stenkjaer. Norwegian units reported at Snass (64° 25′ N., 12° 18′ E.) and Verdalsoren area (63° 47′ N., 11° 30′ E.).
>
> Cruisers are to withdraw to the westward when fjord has been secured. Daily contact is to be made with landing party by destroyer'.

Captain Pegram prepared to land his party at dawn on the 14th, shifting the men into two destroyers off Kroken, on the east shore in the widest part of Namsen Fjord, a dozen miles short of Namsos, where the cruisers would wait. Captain Nicholson with the 6th Flotilla would then conduct the landing at Namsos, while the three ships of the 4th Flotilla covered the mouth of the

---

[1] *Somali, Mashona, Matabele* (of 6th Flotilla), *Afridi, Sikh, Mohawk* (of 4th Flotilla).
[2] *See* Sec. 19 *ante*.

fjord. But Captain Pegram had sent all six destroyers to Aalesund ' to mop up the many large merchant vessels ' (which turned out to be Norwegian) ; once there they stayed all the 13th, the Senior Officer, Captain Nicholson, being impressed with the importance of that neighbourhood, on which the local authorities insisted, and expecting that the landing might be diverted there from Namsos. 'Admiral Tank-Nielson', he reported ' considers Romsdals Fjord the most strategic point on the west coast ; main importance lies in position of railway and road and the existence of ammunition stocks at Molde '. Captain Pegram therefore decided to land in the evening, despite the greater risk from the air ; but for a time this danger made him hesitate, presumably on hearing of the destroyers' experiences on the 13th, when a score of German aircraft bombed them during their visit to Aalesund and Molde. Although the destroyers drove off the enemy with the loss of three machines, and without injury to themselves, the strength of the attack showed that ships would run considerable danger in the fjords.

The party landed from the destroyers ' without difficulty ' at dusk on the 14th, ' although,' said Captain Pegram, ' I am certain our presence was known to the enemy ' through reconnaissance aircraft. About 350 seamen and marines landed under Captain Edds, R.M., of the *Sheffield*. They took with them demolition gear to destroy the wharves and bridges in case of need, and extra rifles and cartridges to supply the wants of their Norwegian allies. A staff officer of the main expedition had arrived in the afternoon, flying to Norway ahead of his general ; and, in consultation with him, it was decided to send the *Glasgow*'s party to Bangsund, and to take post south of it, while the *Sheffield*'s landed at Namsos and took post to the eastward. The British staff officer and the Norwegian officers saw no difficulty in ' Henry's ' holding its own for a time, but they did not feel sanguine about future movements : snow covered the district ; Namsos and Bangsund were small, they gave little concealment, and they were short of fresh water ; ' the southward move of any force much larger than one battalion must be both slow and conspicuous from the air '.

After landing ' Henry ', Captain Nicholson stayed at Namsos in the *Somali* to arrange for the landing of ' Maurice ' and to meet its commander, General Carton de Wiart, who arrived in a flying boat on the 15th. The other two ships of the 6th Flotilla went out to meet and assist the troopship convoy on its arrival. Captain Pegram, with the *Glasgow*, *Sheffield* and the three destroyers of the 4th Flotilla (two of which had oiled from the cruisers under way in Namsen Fjord) went out also to cruise in the offing near Kya Light, and afterwards to join Admiral Layton, who was bringing over the British troops of ' Maurice ' and expected to reach Namsen Fjord by dusk on the 15th. The discouraging report from the army officers, quoted above, decided the Government to hold up the landing, however, and the first troops did not land until the following night. ' Henry's ' task then ending, the *Sikh* and *Matabele*, after landing some troops of ' Maurice ', brought off the naval parties from Namsos and Bangsund, and carried them to their proper ships early on the 17th.

32. Operation Maurice : First landings, 16th–17th April [PLAN 11

Under the original plan, as mentioned previously,[1] Vice-Admiral Edward-Collins was to have conducted the naval side of this expedition, the first flight of which then consisted of two battalions under Brigadier Morgan, embarked in the cruisers *Galatea* and *Arethusa* and the transport *Orion*. These were to have arrived at Namsos on 17th April, followed a few days later by a full

---
[1] *See* Sec. 19 *ante*.

brigade, with wagons, stores, ammunition and petrol embarked in transports. Admiral Whitworth's victory at Narvik on the 13th, however, produced a wave of optimism as to the task of the northern expedition and in the evening of the 14th the Government diverted to Namsos one of the two brigades then on passage to Narvik under Admiral Layton ' because expected opposition at the latter place had been considerably reduced by naval action '.

That evening Admiral Layton's convoy divided, he himself in the *Manchester*, with the *Birmingham*, *Cairo* and three destroyers, and two transports, the *Empress of Australia* and *Chrobry*, carrying the 146th Brigade (battalions of the Lincolnshire, the King's Own Yorkshire Light Infantry and the York and Lancaster regiments) steering for Namsos, while the remainder of the convoy escorted by the *Valiant* and nine destroyers continued for Narvik.[1] This detachment then became the first flight for Central Norway.

On the 15th, however, the account of conditions in and about Namsos led the Government to put off the landing and to order the convoy to go to Lillesjona, more than 100 miles farther north. They gave the last order probably on receiving a signal from Captain Nicholson, who reported ' facilities for landing and accommodation of large numbers of troops at Namsos very inadequate . . . impossible to deal with more than one transport at anchor at a time . . . very grave risk to town and transports unless command of air is certain '. On the other hand, he said, ' If transports could be sent elsewhere, destroyers could embark troops and land them at Namsos and Bangsund. . . . This would enable troops to be dispersed by rail from Namsos and by road from Bangsund. All disembarkation of troops should take place at dusk, and might be continued well into the night, provided weather is clear '. The following signal gave the new arrangements—A.T. 1722/15, addressed to Admiral Layton :—

> ' General Carton de Wiart will probably join you Lillesjona. Subject to what Carton de Wiart may report after visiting Namsos, it is probable that a decision will be given that troops should be transferred to destroyers at Lillesjona and proceed in destroyers to Namsos, taking as much stores with them as possible. It is hoped that, after discussion with General, you will be able to land first flight at Namsos tomorrow, Tuesday, at dusk. Early arrival is of first importance from political point of view '.

Admiral Layton welcomed the change of plan. To begin with, the size of the transports caused embarrassment, especially the *Empress of Australia*, which had in-turning screws ; he had already arranged to send the troops on board destroyers in Namsen Fjord, but Lillesjona was clearly to be preferred. Then the *Cairo* and the old destroyers with him were running short of oil, which the Admiralty provided for by diverting to Lillesjona the oiler *War Pindari*, on her way to Tromsö. Lastly, like everybody else, Admiral Layton felt anxious about the danger from the air. Under the original plan for the landing, there had been two anti-aircraft ships told off to protect the troopships. Now there was only the *Cairo* ; the Admiralty had ordered the *Curlew* to join the convoy, but bad weather delayed her, which was unlucky, said Admiral Layton, ' as it appeared that every possible anti-aircraft protection would be needed '. The convoy kept out at sea until dark on the 15th to avoid being shadowed from the air, and anchored in Lillesjona early on the 16th. Four of Captain Pegram's destroyers joined on the way to the anchorage. The *War Pindari* arrived in the forenoon and oiled the destroyers before they took the troops from the transports. Later still, General Carton de Wiart arrived in the *Somali* from Namsos, which place he had reached by air the day before. In the evening the *Curlew* arrived ; and the *War Pindari* sailed for Tromsö, having finished

---

[1] *See* Secs. 19 and 21 *ante*.

her task for Admiral Layton, but left behind one of her escorting destroyers, the *Nubian*, that the *Somali* might go home for ammunition, which she had run out of the day before in encounters with German aircraft.[1]

The influence of the air appears also in messages the General sent the War Office during the night (15th–16th). In the first, after giving his first thoughts about landing the troops, he emphasized ' the difficulties presented by enemy air activity, whereas we have no planes at all '. In the second, 0126/16, he says :—

> ' Concealment of troops by day is very difficult. There is little cover and still a great deal of snow. However, if it is essential to advance, the sooner it is done the better.
>
> I cannot at present judge situation at Trondheim ; but it will be essential that strong action should be taken as regards enemy air activity when I attack. If there is to be naval attack at Trondheim, and it is successful, General Audet should attack as soon as possible after it. If you could inform me of date of this attack, it would help decide definite date of my attack. My orders to General Audet would be to attack if naval operations succeeded. If you could ensure his having close liaison with Navy, this would be possible '.[2]

He had already sent the commander of the 146th Brigade his first thoughts about a landing. While held up by weather on his way across the North Sea, thinking the troops would land at Namsos on the 15th, he said they should take their stand covering Henry, the naval party, and make ready to advance at short notice towards Trondheim. While going from Namsos to join the brigade, he said he proposed landing two battalions from destroyers during the night 16th–17th : two companies to land at Bangsund, the rest at Namsos, and the destroyers should be ready to leave Lillesjona at noon. This plan was carried out, though a couple of hours late, during an attack from the air. The *Afridi*, *Nubian*, *Sikh*, *Matabele* and *Mashona* went alongside the transports as they finished oiling and took on board the two battalions, while the Germans dropped bombs in the anchorage, narrowly missing the two transports and the *War Pindari*, each of which had destroyers alongside during the attack. They sailed in the afternoon, the Lincolnshire and half the York and Lancaster going to Namsos, the other two companies of the York and Lancaster to Bangsund. The General went in with his men, making his headquarters on board the *Afridi*, and from her he reported thus to the War Office a little before midnight :

> ' Have brought 1000 men to Namsos today, and hope to bring remainder of Phillips's brigade tomorrow . . . Am occupying Grong, Bangsund and probably positions astride Beitstad Fjord, 25 miles south of Namsos. No fresh information of the enemy. Enemy aircraft still bombing at leisure'.

The King's Own Yorkshire Light Infantry should have landed from destroyers next day, the transport *Chrobry* going in at the same time with all the stores of the brigade. But, said Admiral Layton,

> ' when it became clear the air attacks were persisting, I had to review the plans made with the General. It was true that air attacks were not so far on a very large scale, though practically continuous ; but I could see no reason why they should not increase, and continue at short intervals ; and it was impossible to ignore the risk of a disastrous hit on a liner full of troops. I was confirmed in my opinion by a visit I paid to the troopships in the course of the afternoon, when it became clear to me that the morale of the young and untried soldiers was likely to suffer if they were subjected to prolonged attacks of this kind while still embarked.

---

[1] The *Somali* was attacked three times at Namsos on 15th April and had 60 bombs aimed at her without effect, but she spent all her ammunition and at the end fired practice ammunition ' for moral effect'.

[2] The first troops of General Audet's command reached Namsos in the night, 19th–20th.

> I therefore decided that it would be necessary to leave the anchorage before daylight the next morning. This made it impossible to use the destroyers as arranged. Accordingly, I decided to move the third battalion from the *Empress of Australia* to the *Chrobry*, and send the latter in alone to Namsos'.

The soldiers and all but 170 tons of the stores having been shifted into the *Chrobry*, the convoy sailed about 0330 on the 17th, and stood out to sea for the day. The *Highlander* had run on shore in the night, while patrolling outside Lillesjona, and she had to go home, leaving only the *Vanoc* and *Whirlwind* for a screen, but before she actually parted company she forced a German submarine to dive, some distance ahead, and thus enabled the convoy to avoid attack. About 1000 the screen gained strength by the return of the ships that had landed the first battalions, General Carton de Wiart returning with them in the *Afridi*. Later still in the forenoon, with the General agreeing, Admiral Layton sent home the *Empress of Australia*, escorted by the *Birmingham* and two old destroyers. 'There seemed no alternative', says the Admiral, 'to letting the 170 tons of stores still in her go back to the United Kingdom and be shipped back in a smaller vessel, and the sooner this was done the better'. The rest of the convoy turned back in time to reach Namsen Fjord at sunset, about 1945. There the *Chrobry* parted company for Namsos, with the *Curlew* and the five 'Tribals' for escort, while the Admiral, in the *Manchester*, went out to sea again for the night, and the *Cairo* went north to Skjel Fjord for oil. The soldiers landed during the night without interruption from the enemy; but at 0200, the 18th, 'the military working parties were withdrawn, presumably in order to take cover before daylight: this cessation left 130 tons of stores still on board the *Chrobry*, and the G.O.C. agreed to these remaining'. All the ships returned to the Admiral in 65° N., 7° 50′ E., at noon.

33. Naval movements and landing of French, 17th-20th April [PLAN 11

Ever since landing their parties for 'Henry', the *Glasgow* and *Sheffield* had been cruising off the coast. Captain Pegram had sent his destroyers to join Admiral Layton at Lillesjona, when the signals showed him that they would be needed to land 'Maurice', but he kept his cruisers away from the land, lest their presence near Namsos should arouse suspicion in the enemy. He went back to Namsen Fjord early on the 17th to take on board his landing parties; and, having no further orders, he then stretched away to the southward to help the *York*, which, with the *Effingham*, *Calcutta* and *Ashanti*, was searching for five German destroyers, reported by aircraft off Stavanger the evening before and perhaps trying to land a force at Aandalsnes. The *York* and her consorts finding nothing, Captain Pegram turned north again in the afternoon, and later received a signal from the Admiralty telling him to go to Namsen Fjord to give anti-aircraft protection for the *Chrobry*'s landing, and to oil the *Mashona* and *Nubian*, after which the *Glasgow* and *Sheffield* were to go to Scapa. The two cruisers gave some 200 tons of oil each to the *Mashona* and *Nubian* in Namsen Fjord during the night, joined the Admiral outside next day, and then went to Scapa to get oil themselves, arriving there on the 19th.

Admiral Layton's service on that part of the coast was ending, too. The next troops for 'Maurice' were French. General Audet was bringing the first three battalions of his chasseurs-alpins in four troopships, escorted by the French Admiral with the *Emile Bertin* and some French destroyers. They should have arrived on the 18th, but were a day late, so Admiral Layton took the opportunity to send in the *Chrobry* again to land the last of her stores in the evening of the 18th, and she went home next day with a cargo of timber from

Namsos. Meanwhile, Sir Charles Forbes ordered home nearly all the British ships to prepare for the intended landing at Trondheim (Operation Hammer). Accordingly Admiral Layton steered towards Rosyth on the 19th, and made ready the *Manchester* for taking troops and stores on board. The *Matabele* had gone home for oil on the 18th, the *Sikh* and *Mashona* took the *Chrobry* home, the *Afridi* and *Nubian* started for home after landing General Carton de Wiart and some Norwegian pilots they had collected to meet the French. This left the *Cairo* only, for the *Curlew* had to go home, too, for oil ; and Admiral Layton ' viewed this position with some anxiety, especially as the next convoy was to be the first French one and in view of the growing probability of submarines operating off the entrance to Namsen Fjord '. Evidently Sir Charles Forbes saw things in the same light, for he ordered the *Manchester* to go back, but she had run 400 miles to the southward on her way home and could not get back in time ' for the first and critical French landing ', so Admiral Layton ' adjusted course and speed with a view to meeting the convoy on its return journey '.

Fortunately the *Cairo* was still on the spot and she led the French convoy in to Namsos. German aircraft attacked it during its passage through the fjords in the evening of 19th April, as they had attacked the British part of ' Maurice ' at Lillesjona. They hit the *Emile Bertin*, flagship of Admiral Derrien, early in the attack, about 1800, and she went home.[1] The *Cairo* and the French destroyers took the troopships to Namsos : *El d'Jezair* (Admiral Cadart), *El Mansour*, *El Kantara*, each of 5,000–6,000 tons, and the *Ville d'Oran*, above 10,000 tons. They had no further casualty, though the last-named transport was slightly damaged. The troops landed in the night with all but a few tons of ammunition and stores, and the convoy went home, escorted by the *Cairo*, being joined by the *Manchester* in the evening of the 20th, which remained in company till off the Shetlands next day and then proceeded to Scapa.

34. German air attacks on Namsos

A few hours after the ships had gone on the 20th, German aircraft attacked Namsos itself, there being no defence. The *Nubian* came back that night, and Commander Ravenhill says : ' The whole place was a mass of flames from end to end, and the glare on the snows of the surrounding mountains produced an unforgettable spectacle '. General Carton de Wiart came on board to say that ' the storehouses on the jetties had been destroyed and that, owing to the evacuation of the Norwegians, all his transport had disappeared ; in consequence, any stores landed would be exposed to almost certain destruction before there was any hope of removing them, even troops might not be got to safety in time . . . unless the Germans could be drastically restricted in their air activities within a very short time, the expedition was doomed '. And early on the 21st the General thus reported the state of affairs to the War Office :—

' Enemy aircraft have almost completely destroyed Namsos, beginning on railhead target, diving indiscriminately. At present impossible to land more men or material. If I am to continue operations, it seems that I must largely depend on road-borne supplies, either through Mosjoen (150 miles away by road) or from Sweden . . . . Acute shortage of cars and petrol here. I see little chance of carrying out decisive or, indeed, any operations, unless enemy air activity is considerably restricted. Audet wishes Gamelin informed of situation. Phillips's brigade at present Verdal, Stenkjaer, Foldafoss. French take over around Namsos.'

---

[1] The *Montcalm* took the place of the *Emile Bertin* in the Home Fleet.

There were more attacks from the air on the 21st, though less harmful than the day before. The *Auckland* sloop, coming in the afternoon to relieve the *Nubian*, was attacked with bombs and machine-gun fire throughout her passage up Namsen Fjord. The following remarks in Commander Ravenhill's letter of proceedings, written as the *Nubian* went back to Scapa, describe an experience common to all small ships employed at the expeditionary bases :—

> 'Just before my departure (on the 22nd), a French naval officer came on board and expressed the gratification of the French General at the effect the presence of the ships had had in curtailing enemy air activity. He asked me to press very strongly for the continued presence of the ships. Personally, I doubt whether the presence of so small a force of ships does stop the enemy making raids: the gunfire certainly makes the bombing wilder, and has the effect of easing pressure tremendously on the land forces, as the enemy appear to go exclusively for the ships when there are any present. I was not surprised when I heard a severe raid had taken place in the evening after my departure, and I don't suppose my presence would have averted it.
>
> A very great strain is imposed on the personnel of these A.A. ships when employed on this type of duty. Owing to the high mountains, no warning can be obtained of the approach of hostile aircraft; and in ships whose entire armament is manned for A.A. fire it is essential to be in at least the second degree of readiness during daylight hours from about 0300 to 2100. Reversion to third degree of readiness during the six hours of darkness does not provide much relaxation. The ships are continually underway, day and night, and when the attacks come there is little room to manoeuvre. There is continued tension, and the knowledge that before the day is over there is almost certain to be at least one severe attack and that nothing can come to your assistance is trying to the nerves.
>
> I am not trying to pretend that *Nubian* has performed any arduous duty, as we had a very short period under these conditions, but enough to realise what it might be like for any length of time.
>
> If ships have to be used for A.A. defence of a port which lies so close to an enemy air base as does Namsos, I submit that at least three ships are necessary to be effective, and they will have to be carefully disposed, so as to obtain freedom of manoeuvre in the restricted waters without getting in each other's way.'

35. Final Reinforcements, Namsos [PLAN 11

In the meantime, the next body of French troops had sailed from Scapa in the 10,000-ton transport *Ville d'Alger*, escorted by the *Calcutta* and a couple of French destroyers, to which Admiral Layton added the *Birmingham* for the latter part of the passage across the North Sea. They were to arrive on the 21st, but as things stood the General would not let them land, so the transport, arriving before they could stop her, was ordered to sea again. The *Calcutta* brought her in next day, 22nd, and a storeship came the same evening. The storeship went alongside to unload; but the big Frenchman could not manage it, so she had to anchor, the troops going on shore in the *Auckland* and a destroyer, and she sailed again without landing her heavy stores, among them some anti-tank guns and an anti-aircraft battery.

No more infantry landed at Namsos. General Carton de Wiart had mentioned the possibility of having to withdraw as early as the 21st, as follows (*Nubian's* 2335/21) :—

> 'Phillips's brigade attacked by enemy landed from cruiser and torpedo boat early this morning, 21st April: our troops being pressed, but situation not yet clear. Am endeavouring to push up French troops; but lorries promised by Norway staff have not yet materialized. Enemy aircraft again very active and dominating situation.

Fear our position becomes untenable, for although jetties not destroyed, approaches very difficult, owing to debris and craters. Only three small storehouses standing, so no room to hide stores. Railhead damaged. No labour available. All civilians left Namsos. No cars left.

Should you decide on evacuating, send ships not larger than 5,000 tons maximum and fear it requires two nights to embark '.[1]

The German troops mentioned had artillery, and landed at Stenkjaer, which ships could reach through narrow fjords from Trondheim. Next day a German destroyer shelled the troops at Verdalsoren, some 15 miles farther south. And on the 23rd the General signalled again that he feared ' there is no alternative to evacuation ' unless he could have superiority in the air. In these circumstances, the next convoy of chasseurs-alpins joined the Narvik expedition instead. On the other hand, guns and stores were landed at Namsos on 27th and 28th April, including those the *Ville d'Alger* had carried home again and another battery of anti-aircraft guns and a battery of howitzers manned by the Royal Marines.

---

[1] It is interesting to notice that the Germans, who were not fully aware of the effect of their air attacks or of the weakness in numbers and equipment of the Allied troops in Central Norway, regarded the situation in the Trondheim area as much more serious from their point of view than it actually was. Thus it came about that on 21st April, just when General Carton de Wiart was describing his position as ' untenable,' Hitler was informing the Naval Staff that he had decided to use fast liners, including the *Bremen* and *Europa*, to carry reinforcements to Trondheim. This plan was dropped, as the result of representations by the Naval Staff that it could not guarantee safe passage ; but that it should have been put forward is a measure of the anxiety the Germans were feeling at the time.

CHAPTER V

THE LANDINGS AT AANDALSNES, AALESUND AND MOLDE

36. Operation Primrose [PLANS 1, 11

While the expedition to Namsos was fizzling out to its inevitable conclusion the Aandalsnes venture was having little better fortune.

The original intention was to occupy Aalesund, half-way between Bud and the peninsula of Stadtlandet, ' with the object of neutralizing ' the Indreled on that part of the coast and to ' create a diversion ' south of Trondheim, while troops were landing at Namsos, north of that place. This operation received the code name of ' Primrose ', and was to be carried out by marines and seamen drawn from certain ships of the Home Fleet then in dockyard hands. Meanwhile, however, the Norwegians made known their anxiety for Romsdals Fjord, where they feared a German attack, and which Admiral Tank-Neilsen called ' the most strategic point on the west coast '. This fjord is some 40 miles north and east of Aalesund and farther inland. Near its mouth, actually outside the fjord proper, lies Molde, which has a little harbour like Aalesund; at the inland end of the fjord is Aandalsnes, from which the railway runs south through Dombaas, 60 miles away, and through Lillehammer to Oslo, a branch line from Dombaas running back northward to Trondheim, distant about 100 miles from Dombaas. The Norwegian Army had its general headquarters at Lillehammer, while a column of troops some 2000 strong lay between Aandalsnes and Dombaas, and there were stocks of munitions at Molde. For these reasons, presumably, and to make ready for the enveloping attack on Trondheim from north and south, the British Government changed the destination of ' Primrose ' to Aandalsnes.

The parties had begun to make ready two days before the expedition was decided on, in compliance with A.T. 1209 of the 11th, addressed to the *Hood, Nelson* and *Barham*, which ran as follows : ' Marine detachments of 100 men from each ship and seamen field gun's crews may be required for a special operation to occupy small islands for limited period shortly ; parties would be required to be self-supporting for one month, and to land and mount 12-pdr. gun or 3·7-in. howitzer ; necessary preliminary preparations to be made '. Orders next day increased each party by 70 men ; and on the 13th came orders for the 21st Light Anti-aircraft Battery, Royal Marines, and two detachments of the 11th Searchlight Regiment, Royal Marines, to join the expedition. On the same day Lieutenant-Colonel Simpson, R.M., was appointed in command of the force, which was to be transported to Norway in the sloops *Black Swan, Flamingo, Auckland* and *Bittern*. Some 45 officers and 680 men actually sailed, with three 3·7-in. howitzers and eight anti-aircraft pom-poms for the field force, and two 4-in. guns for Aalesund ; but the searchlights stayed behind.

Colonel Simpson came to Rosyth in the morning of the 14th, and the rest of the expedition arrived during the day. The *Barham*'s party arrived first from Liverpool, then the *Hood*'s from Plymouth, the anti-aircraft battery from Tynemouth, the *Nelson*'s from Portsmouth, and last, a little before midnight, the searchlight detachments from Yeovil. Men and gear went on board the sloops as they arrived, for the expedition had orders to sail the same day, so had not time for 'any pre-arranged and useful order' of stowage. For instance, the seamen and marines from the *Nelson* sailed in different ships, to make room for the anti-aircraft guns to sail in two ships also and avoid the risk of having all in one basket, but the *Nelson*'s had not expected nor prepared for this when loading their train. Although Captain Poland of the *Black Swan* spared the greater part of one month's supply of victuals for the expedition from the three months' outfit in his flotilla, that the force might use the space thus saved for essential equipment instead of the victuals they had brought with them, they had still to go without some of their stores; among other things there was no room for the searchlights. As it was, the ships drew a foot more water than their normal draught, and had to stow much heavy gear on their upper decks, besides carrying an extra number of men equal to their own crews, 'most unfavourable' weather forecasts notwithstanding. 'It is for consideration', wrote Colonel Simpson afterwards, 'whether, in similar circumstances, a delay of some hours in sailing is not justifiable in order to allow a reasonable loading plan'.

The *Auckland* did sail that evening, with the *Barham*'s party and one of the 4-in. guns, that she might gain a footing at Aalesund betimes and keep pace with the Namsos expedition, whose first troops were also embarking at Rosyth that day. Owing to the late arrival of the rest of the force, the other three ships could not sail until 0330 on the 15th. But they soon overtook the *Auckland*. She had met with a gale of wind in the night, and finding he could not keep the speed required to arrive by dawn on the 16th, Commander Hewitt decided to wait for his consorts. They joined him off Buchan Ness, and steered away for Invergordon soon afterwards to shelter. The sea was rising, the ships could barely steam 10 knots, their crowded passengers were sea-sick. 'It would not have been possible to arrive at our destination at or near dawn on the desired day', said Captain Poland in his subsequent report, 'and 'Primrose' would also have been a very wilted flower by the time it arrived'. At Invergordon they received A.T. 1926/15, which changed their destination to Aandalsnes :—

> 'Inform Lieut.-Colonel Simpson that . . . force is now to proceed to Aandalsnes, which is understood to be in Norwegian hands. If Germans are in Aandalsnes, no landing is to be made, and situation reported. It is possible that other military forces will be landed later at Aandalsnes . . . .'

The gale which forced them in to Invergordon gave Colonel Simpson time and opportunity at last to meet his officers and to explain his plans for the landing and for future service, though there was not much he could do before the expedition arrived, as he lacked maps and knew little of the country he was bound for, the NORWAY PILOT being his only source of knowledge.

The wind and sea abating, the expedition set out again on the 16th. During the passage, two further signals affecting the operation were sent. A.T. 1633 of the 16th ordered 1000 soldiers, under Brigadier Morgan, to follow as soon as possible; and A.T. 1507/17 told Colonel Simpson to mount his 4-in. guns at Aalesund and to land men to hold that place as well as Aandalsnes.

The force arrived at Aandalsnes at 2200 on the 17th; and the *Black Swan* went alongside the quay to unload, with the *Bittern* outside her, while the other two ships patrolled in the fjord. When the *Black Swan* finished the *Bittern* took her place, the *Flamingo* going alongside her in turn, and so they proceeded. All had finished by 0700 on the 18th, much helped by the use of a 5-ton travelling crane on the quay—an unexpected resource—and unmolested by the enemy, though they had sighted and fired on a German aircraft a few hours before they arrived. Then the *Auckland* and *Bittern* put to sea again to take the *Barham*'s party and the 4-in. guns to Aalesund, and another party went to Molde, to form a base there, with Captain Denny as Naval Officer-in-Charge. Thus the expedition had an easy passage, apart from the weather, and it landed without hindrance. Yet there had been reason for anxiety in reports on the 16th that Germans from seaplanes might forestall ' Primrose ' and that German destroyers had been seen off Stavanger. On receiving the first report, Captain Poland made up his mind to disregard his routeing orders and to go direct from Fair Island to his destination, chancing discovery from the air as he steered along the Norwegian coast, instead of standing farther north before crossing the North Sea.

German aircraft bombed Aandalsnes nearly every day from the 20th onwards. The attacks grew worse, so all the work of the base was done at night, the men taking shelter in the woods and on the hillsides during the raids. In the end the Germans destroyed the town, most of which was built of wood, but the marines' anti-aircraft gunners claim to have protected the railway and the quay successfully. The *Hood*'s field howitzer went into action against some German parachute troops between Dombaas and Dovre the day after landing, and helped the Norwegians in rounding them up. Otherwise, ' Primrose ' encountered enemy land forces only on the last day of the expedition, when a few marines at an outpost beyond Verma covered the retreat from that place. For the rest, ' Primrose ' became part of ' Sickle ' when the latter expedition arrived. Brigadier Morgan sent his first battalions forward to Dombaas and beyond, as soon as he could learn the state of affairs, leaving only light anti-aircraft guns at Aandalsnes. ' He relied upon me ', said Colonel Simpson, ' to hold the Aandalsnes area with its vital railhead and landing place ', and this remained the principal object of the naval party. Colonel Simpson had made his own arrangements with this in view at his landing. The marines established ' six platoon posts, with one in reserve, covering important tactical positions such as road bridges, the electrical power station at Verma, about 28 miles inland, and possible lines of enemy approach, as well as the aerodrome at Lesjaswick (Lake Lesjaskog—' Gladiator Lake '), about 40 miles inland. Some positions were changed as the situation altered, but the functions of the detachments remained the same '. The anti-aircraft pom-poms were posted at various points about the town. The seamen served mainly as a working party at the base. Captain Denny wrote from Molde ; ' It is fortunate that the first party to be landed was a seaman and Royal Marines' force and that this party largely remained in the vicinity of Aandalsnes ; the unavoidable absence of any proper base personnel and equipment in the earlier stages of the expedition produced a local situation which, in my opinion, was only mastered through the adaptability to be expected of naval units '.[1]

As for Aalesund, its party arrived there in the afternoon of 18th April. The Norwegians received the party with enthusiasm, all but its 4-in. guns, which they held would invite attack from the air, and against that they had no defence. The local Norwegian commander thought the guns unnecessary for controlling the Indreled, since dangerous areas had been declared off Bud and Stadtlandet on the 8th, nor did he expect attack by sea now that Aandalsnes was occupied. On his behalf Commander Hewitt of the *Auckland* asked for two 3-in. high-angle guns, and ' strongly recommended ' taking away the coast defence weapons, unless some sort of anti-aircraft guns could be provided

---

[1] Captain Denny added : ' This force, it must be remembered, was ashore throughout the period of the operation, and consequently were exposed for the longest period to the effects of air bombardment ; in general, they behaved like seasoned veterans.'

for the port. In the meantime, Major Lumley, of the *Hood*, whom Colonel Simpson had placed in command at Aalesund, set about digging the gun-pits, though he had leave to put off mounting the guns, which in fact were never mounted. Apart from the objection to having the guns at all, Major Lumley found they lacked several essential articles of equipment. It was the same with the 3-in. high-angle guns, when they came on the 23rd; 'many essential items had been omitted'. One or two transports coaled at Aalesund before going home after landing men or gear at Aandalsnes, but little else happened there during the stay of the British party except the almost daily attacks from the air.

37. Operation Sickle [PLAN 11

Meanwhile, before the 'Primrose' force had even reached Aandalsnes, the decision had been taken to increase the scale of operations in this area, and preliminary orders issued for Operation Sickle. The first hint of this operation came on 16th April and was contained in a message from the C.I.G.S. to General Carton de Wiart (A.T. 0020/16)[1] which stated that the naval party would be reinforced, if possible, but that the only troops immediately available were those under Brigadier Morgan's command. These consisted of two weak territorial battalions, the 5th Leicestershire and the 8th Sherwood Foresters, with four Bofors anti-aircraft guns, hitherto destined for Namsos.

Later that day orders were sent to Vice-Admiral Edward-Collins, who conducted the first flight of the expedition, and to Brigadier Morgan. Those to the Admiral (A.T. 1633/16) ran as follows :—

> 'It has been decided to land a military force at Aandalsnes as soon as possible, in addition to 'Primrose' force. *Galatea, Arethusa, Carlisle, Curacoa* and two destroyers are placed under your command, and a total of approximately 1000 troops under Brigadier Morgan are to be embarked in these ships. Forces to sail as soon as ready. Cruisers can go alongside at Molde, and it is recommended that troops from cruisers should be disembarked at that place, being subsequently ferried to Aandalsnes . . . It is of great importance to get troops out of ships as soon as possible on account of air attack . . . Your action on arrival must depend on situation; unless immediate action is essential, a landing at dusk is considered advisable on account of air attack.'

Brigadier Morgan's instructions followed in A.T. 2014/16 :—

> 'Your role to land Aandalsnes area, secure Dombaas, then operate northwards and take offensive action against Germans in Trondheim area. Not intended that you should land in face of opposition. Second echelon your force will follow you two days later. As you are without transport, you should rely on Norwegian rolling stock and locally impressed transport. You will be kept informed of progress and timings of other British forces operating Trondheim area.
>
> Your force independent command under War Office until receipt further orders. Intention later place you under commander general operations Trondheim area.
>
> During the voyage and during landing operations, senior naval officer will be in command. He will decide, in co-operation with you, where and when to land.'

And in A.T. 2217 of the 17th :—

> 'Denial to Germans of use of railway through Dombaas northward becomes vital. Indications point to improbability of your encountering serious German opposition between Aandalsnes and Dombaas, if you move quickly. Consider full possibility of pushing even small detachments on to Dombaas really rapidly, and act as you judge best. When you have secured Dombaas, you are to prevent Germans using railway to reinforce Trondheim. Am sending small demolition party . . . You should make touch with Norwegian G.H.Q., believed to be in area Lillehammer, and avoid isolating Norwegian forces operating towards Oslo.'

---

[1] *See* Sec. 22 *ante*.

Most of the troops and stores had to shift from the transport *Orion*, on board of which they had been under the earlier arrangements for Namsos ; and the work, says Admiral Edward-Collins, was ' much hampered by the impossibility of berthing a cruiser directly under the derricks of the *Orion* and the fact that the stores had been loaded as received, and those required were generally at the bottom of the holds '. However, the expedition sailed from Rosyth early on 17th April in the cruisers and anti-aircraft ships named in the orders and in the *Arrow* and *Acheron*. In the evening of the 18th they found the *York* outside Buddybet, the northern approach to Molde and Aandalsnes, where she was cruising to protect the expeditions' arrival ; the Admiral released her from her watch, likewise the *Effingham*, which was covering the southern approach. Inside the fjords were the *Black Swan*, *Flamingo* and *Bittern* sloops : German aircraft had attacked these ships in the afternoon, but ' Sickle ' arrived and landed without interference. The Admiral had learnt from the *Black Swan* that cruisers could go alongside at Aandalsnes, so he left the *Curacoa* and *Arethusa* to land at Molde, and took the rest of the expedition to Aandalsnes, arriving between 2000 and 2100, the 18th. The *Galatea* went alongside at once, the two destroyers taking turns to go alongside her to land their troops and to receive fuel from her ; then the *Carlisle* took the *Galatea's* place, and at 0300 on the 19th the ships sailed. At Molde, of course, the work was finished earlier ; local craft collected by Captain Denny (Naval Officer-in-Charge) ferried the troops and stores thence to Aandalsnes, some arriving before the Admiral left. The *Galatea* and *Arethusa* arrived back at Rosyth without incident on 20th April.

The landing at Aandalsnes, said the Admiral ' was completed more rapidly than I had expected . . . a 5-ton travelling crane on the quay was of great assistance in expediting the unloading of stores '. He went on :—

> ' It is my belief that operation ' Sickle ' was carried out without the knowledge of the enemy, and that this was probably due to the absence of any troop transport with the force, from which aircraft could deduce its object.[1]
>
> In spite of sea-sickness and the general discomfort of the voyage, all the troops landed in good order ; and by 0100 an advance party had entrained and left for Dombaas Junction, which there appeared to be every prospect they would reach without opposition. I consider this a very creditable performance on the part of the ships and troops concerned. I consider the facilities at Aandalsnes excellent for the landing of a small force ; but it is most desirable that adequate shore air defence be provided at the earliest possible moment to prevent damage to the quay and railway station, which are the great assets of the place. The quay, though good, is very short, and there is only one crane ; one large well-aimed bomb would wreck both.'

In the evening of the 19th, the *Carlisle* (Flag, Rear-Admiral Vivian) turned back on her way home, and relieved the *Black Swan* as Senior Naval Officer at Aandalsnes, taking the place of the ' Primrose ' sloops as anti-aircraft guardship. Admiral Vivian's experience and that of his successor, Captain Aylmer in the *Curacoa*, proved the wisdom of landing the troops at night. German aircraft that appeared on the 19th after the troopships had sailed did not drop bombs, perhaps owing to the good shooting of the *Black Swan ;* but bombing attacks greeted the *Carlisle* within three hours of her coming on the 20th, and continued all day. The *Curacoa* arrived on the 22nd to find full employment up to the evening of the 24th, when she was hit and had to go home. Here is Captain Aylmer's account of affairs in a signal made a few hours before his ship was disabled :—

> ' Aandalsnes and *Curacoa* have been repeatedly bombed each day : high, low, and dive bombing attacks, and machine-gunned in the fjord. During daylight

---

[1] This has been confirmed from German sources.

hours hostile aircraft are never absent from the sky. Attacks usually well pressed home. Some damage to town; many near misses on *Curacoa*. In dive bombing, bombs appear set delay approximately 12 seconds and burst deep; this undoubtedly saved *Curacoa's* stern from serious damage. Hits on ship must be expected while doing anti-aircraft guardship. Personnel continuously closed up at action stations and getting no rest. Services of friendly aircraft in this area urgently required and will be most welcome. Reliable sources give seven hostile aircraft brought down by anti-aircraft fire and others damaged. *Curacoa* running short 4-in. ammunition: am drawing from small stock ashore, when fuzed.'

Enemy aircraft constantly attacked Aalesund, too, particularly when ships lay there, but Molde came off lightly until the last few days of the expedition. The letters of proceedings discuss various methods of coping with the attacks. All commanding officers agreed that ships must keep underway during daylight, with good speed at command. The high ground bordering the narrow fjords made gunfire difficult—generally a case of 'snap shoots' as Captain Poland of the *Black Swan* had it—and radio direction finding was no help in these conditions. All paid tribute to the steadiness and spirit of the men in long periods of constant duty. One officer mentioned the 'tremendously heartening effect' of having another anti-aircraft ship in company. Sir Charles Forbes, however, had come to the conclusion that the employment of ships for this purpose was wasteful.[1] On 26th April he 'recommended Admiralty to send A.A. batteries and Royal Air Force fighters to counter enemy air action at bases on Norwegian coast in preference to using ships' and next day he said he should not 'keep a sloop or A.A. cruiser at Aandalsnes during daylight hours. Does not effectively protect base and they shoot away all their ammunition in one day'.[2]

38. Sickle Reinforcements [PLANS 1, 11

Unlike the principal flights, the first reinforcement for 'Sickle' came in transports: 600 men in the little *St. Magnus* and *St. Sunniva*, escorted by the destroyers *Jackal* and *Javelin*. The storeship *Cedarbank* in the same convoy was torpedoed and sunk on passage by a U-boat—a serious loss, since she carried A.A. guns and equipment, and transport—but the remainder arrived in daylight[3] on 21st April, a day of snowstorms and low clouds, however, which screened the port from enemy aircraft—one of the few days at Aandalsnes free from attack. Such immunity was exceptional, and the next day (22nd) aircraft disabled the *Pelican* sloop some 50 miles from the coast on her way there to

---

[1] *See* Sec. 26 *ante*.

[2] An ominous note had been struck by A.T. 0003/20 from the First Sea Lord to the Commander-in-Chief, which ran :—

'Recent expenditure of destroyer long range anti-aircraft ammunition has been heavy if the total size of the reserve held is appreciated. This is now reduced to 13,000 rounds of which 6,000 are abroad. Deliveries in the next three weeks should reach 6,000 rounds after which further supplies are not immediately in sight. Although I am unwilling to suggest restriction in the use of any anti-aircraft gun, it is obvious that expenditure of this nature at the recent high rates must be curtailed. Action has been taken to accelerate supply to the maximum and you will be informed when the margin is ample.'

Clearly it was of great importance to keep this information from the fleet, but the Commander-in-Chief had to bear it constantly in mind.

[3] The other reinforcements arrived after dark except a convoy which arrived the afternoon of the 27th; indeed, they had specific orders to arrive at dusk and 'to sail at daylight even if disembarkation is incomplete'.

Sec. 38   THE LANDINGS AT AANDALSNES, AALESUND AND MOLDE

give anti-aircraft protection. That evening the *Arethusa*[1] arrived, laden chiefly with stores. She brought among other things some much-wanted 4-in. ammunition for the sloops, machine-guns for the Norwegians, a battery of Oerlikon anti-aircraft guns and the advance party and some stores for the Royal Air Force station on Lesjaskog Lake. She landed everything in a little over four hours that night, which was thought a good evolution; but her captain remarked that 'a great saving of labour for the ship's company and a reduction of the chaos which occurs when embarking stores for these expeditions could be made if there was a sea transport officer at the place of embarkation who knew what had to be embarked and who could inform the ship's officers what they had to take and whom it was for'. Admiral Edward-Collins, in forwarding the report, concurred: 'I fully agree . . . the recent operations have been in the nature of rush evolutions; but the old proverb of more haste, less speed, has been very much in evidence.'[2]

As soon as Hammer (the direct attack on Trondheim) was given up, further reinforcements for Sickle were decided on. Major-General Paget went out to take command, two brigades of regular infantry were earmarked, and possibly some field artillery might have followed. As it turned out, only one brigade reached Aandalsnes before the Government decided to withdraw. The following signal shows, however, a distinct advance in the importance of the expedition (A.T. 1731/20th April):—

> 'It is intended to land a considerable force in the Aandalsnes area with the ultimate object of capturing Trondheim in conjunction with General de Wiart's force at Namsos. Two brigades originally allocated to 'Hammer' will be landed in Aandalsnes area, so as to gain control of the Dombaas area and isolate Trondheim from the south. Further troops will follow.
>
> (2) This operation will still be referred to as 'Sickle.'
>
> (3) 'Maurice' is being reinforced by French troops.
>
> (4) The first of the brigades referred to in paragraph 1 will probably land p.m. 23rd and p.m. 25th April.
>
> (5) Immediate steps are being taken to obtain small transports suitable for entering the fjords; in the meantime it will be necessary for H.M. ships to be used for transporting troops.'

The 15th Brigade actually went, three battalions of Yorkshire regiments, about 2700 all told, with nine anti-tank guns and a battery of Bofors anti-aircraft guns. They sailed in two parties: Admiral Edward-Collins taking the 1st York and Lancaster Regiment and the 1st King's Own Yorkshire Light Infantry, the anti-tank guns and half the Bofors guns; and Admiral Layton taking a battalion of the Green Howards, the rest of the Bofors guns and their crews, General Paget and his staff, and the headquarters troops. There seem to have been ideas of withdrawing already, owing to the threatened destruction of the base by air attack, for the Admiralty made this signal to Captain Denny at Molde (A.T. 2013/21):—

> 'It must be accepted that piers at Aandalsnes may be destroyed by aircraft at any time: termination of operation on this account cannot be accepted, and you should accordingly be prepared to unload ships into small craft and land stores anywhere you can. Report what could be done about motor transport and guns in these circumstances.'

This one brigade landed successfully at Molde and Aandalsnes.

---

[1] The *Arethusa* left Rosyth alone on 22nd April, the day after her return from landing troops of the first flight. (*See* Sec. 37 *ante*.)

[2] Much confusion and delay occurred in landing stores, ammunition, etc., because no working parties were organised by the Army to clear them from the jetties, as they were put ashore.

Admiral Edward-Collins left Rosyth on the 22nd with the *Galatea*, *Sheffield*, *Glasgow*, and the *Vansittart* and *Campbell*, *Ivanhoe* and *Icarus*, *Impulsive* and *Witch*. The flagship carried about 400 men, the two larger ships 700 each, the destroyers 60 each. Besides the land forces they took one of the belated searchlights with its crew and two 3-in. high-angle guns for the naval party at Aalesund, officers and men for the naval base, and a quantity of stores. They arrived in the evening of the 23rd without incident, the *Sheffield* and two destroyers going to Molde, while the rest went on to Aandalsnes. The *Sheffield* went alongside to unload, as did the *Galatea* at Aandalsnes, but the *Glasgow* anchored and sent men and gear on shore in destroyers and local small craft. Having finished their task the cruisers sailed separately for home, each with a couple of destroyers in company, but the *Glasgow* rejoined the flag in the evening, 24th, a few miles north and east of the Shetlands. Soon afterwards, a couple of aircraft attacked them without result. Apart from that, as Admiral Edward-Collins pointed out : ' It is remarkable that my ships have now carried out this operation three times without molestation.'[1]

Admiral Layton left Rosyth on the 24th. He had the *Manchester* and *Birmingham* just home from serving with ' Maurice ' at Namsos, the *York* and the destroyers *Arrow*, *Acheron* and *Griffin*, each ship taking her quota of troops and stores, a little under 1600 men and some 300 tons of stores altogether. The *Manchester* went alongside at Molde in the evening of the 25th, and her ' unloading . . . was carried out with unexpected rapidity '. The *Birmingham* and *York* anchored at Aandalsnes, the destroyers and local craft ferrying troops and stores to the quay. Early in the morning (26th) the *York* and the destroyers sailed for the United Kingdom, but the *Manchester* and *Birmingham* stayed on the coast to support the destroyers cruising in the Trondheim approaches.

On the way north towards Trondheim, before the *York* and destroyers were out of sight, Admiral Layton's ships fell in with German armed trawlers disguised as Dutchmen.

The *Birmingham* sank one, a minelayer, which on falling in with the destroyers had hoisted German colours and managed to ram the *Arrow*, necessitating her return home escorted by the *Acheron*. A little later the *Griffin* captured another trawler fitted for supplying submarines and armed with torpedoes.

These encounters led the Commander-in-Chief to suspect the presence of enemy transports astern of the trawlers, and he accordingly ordered Admiral Layton to sweep to the southward, who altered course accordingly at 1045. Shortly afterwards six destroyers hove in sight, steering to the south-westward. These proved to be the aircraft carriers' relieved screen proceeding to Sullom Voe for fuel. Admiral Layton thereupon ordered them to spread on a line of bearing on their way south and to keep a lookout for enemy supply ships, while he himself with the *Birmingham* covered the area to the eastward of them till 1600, 26th, when he turned to the northward to take up a covering position for the night off the entrance to Trondheim Fjord.

The *Manchester* and *Birmingham* remained in this vicinity till the forenoon of the 28th and then they returned to Scapa, for by this time the retreat from Aandalsnes had been decided on and it was necessary for them to fill up with oil before playing their part in the withdrawal.

During this service they had not been free from air attack. German aircraft had dropped a few bombs, some of which nearly hit the *Birmingham*, in the

---

[1] The *Arethusa* belonged to Admiral Edward-Collins's squadron.

afternoon of the 25th, three hours before the convoy entered Buddybet; another machine attacked the *Manchester* early on the 26th, after she had cleared the fjords again. Yet another attacked the *Manchester* and *Birmingham* in the evening of the 27th, a hundred miles or so from the coast, as they were going in for the night patrol. But the main weight of the air attacks was falling on the inshore operations. That afternoon (27th), a supply convoy had been seriously harassed—four ships escorted by the *Afridi*, *Witherington* and *Amazon*. So fierce was the attack that only two ships unloaded, one at Molde, the other at Aandalsnes, and the latter did not land all her cargo. The convoy sailed again at 0200 next morning, the escort strengthened by the *Sikh* and *Mohawk*, withdrawn from their patrol in Trondheim Leden; aircraft attacked the convoy again from 1000 to 1400 on the 28th. This convoy should have arrived in the evening of the 26th, but was late; and a warning had been sent from Aandalsnes in the morning of the 27th saying, ' Ships must not berth alongside until 2100, and leave by 0200, proceeding to sea for day with escort, otherwise ships will be lost by air attack '; but this warning may not have reached the *Afridi*.

39. The situation on shore, 27th-28th April [PLANS 1, 11

To return to Aandalsnes. General Paget arrived on 25th April to hear from Captain Denny that his base and line of communication must soon fail unless protected from the enemy in the air. Forty-eight hours later came a definite proposal to give up the expedition. On the 27th, the General having gone to the front, the commander of the army base staff told the War Office he was ' planning to evacuate Aandalsnes between 1st and 10th May '. The work of the base was restricted to the dark hours, between 2000 and 0600, both afloat and on shore; the wooden piers were all burnt, and only the concrete quay remained; the roads were pitted with craters and badly scarred by heavy traffic in melting snow. They were also losing small craft: by the end of the month, for instance, they had lost by air attack seven anti-submarine trawlers out of 12— the first to go being the four cricketers, *Larwood* and *Jardine*, *Bradman* and *Hammond*. Patrols of fighter aircraft from Admiral Wells's carriers did something to protect the base and the troops, yet the General felt bound to put these words in a memorandum he sent home on the 27th: ' Our own air: conspicuous by its absence '. The squadron of Gladiators, flown from the Glorious to Lesjaskog Lake on the 24th, had been virtually destroyed next day, and the ice melting, the lake could no longer serve as a landing ground.

As for the troops at the front, Brigadier Morgan's two battalions had ' had a dusting ', and were now to come out of the fighting zone. The first two battalions of the 15th Brigade took post at Otta, 30 miles beyond Dombaas on the way to Lillehamrner, while its last battalion lay farther back near Dombaas itself. The Norwegians had ' probably about the remains of two brigades ' in the district; they had worked on skis on the flanks of Morgan's men, but were ' liable to disappear without warning '. The enemy ' may have up to two or three divisions ', with probably Bavarians and Austrians accustomed to skis, and served by 6-in. howitzers working very effectively with aircraft, whereas the British had neither guns nor planes. General Paget asked for help in the air, for field artillery (25-pounders), for anti-aircraft guns both long- and short-range, for more infantry. ' Unless immediate help is forthcoming on above lines at once ', said the memorandum of 27th April, ' the whole force may be jeopardized within a period of from four to five days '.

This was no exaggeration. Three days later, on 30th April, the advance troops of the German Army Group XXI made contact with elements of the Trondheim occupation force at Storen (the railway junction some 30 miles to the southward of Trondheim) and in the words of the German Naval Staff appreciation, 'the situation of the Allied troops south of Trondheim can be regarded as desperate'.

But the position had already been recognised by the Allied High Command as hopeless and that night the re-embarkation from the Molde and Aandalsnes area began.

CHAPTER VI

THE WITHDRAWAL FROM CENTRAL NORWAY

40. The Decision to withdraw, 28th April

As previously mentioned, General Carton de Wiart had begun to consider withdrawing from Namsos as early as 21st April, within five days of his arrival there. General Paget, when he reached Aandalsnes on the 25th—a bare week after the first British troops had moved out to meet the enemy—likewise saw that he might soon find that area untenable; and this opinion he had reiterated in his memorandum of the 27th.

Early next day (28th) came the order for a general withdrawal from Central Norway (A.T. 0339) :—' It has been decided to re-embark the force landed at Namsos and Aandalsnes areas as soon as possible. . . .'. The principal cause of the giving up of these southern expeditions was the German strength in the air. This allowed them to send an army to Norway by sea, unhindered except within the limited capacity of submarines and mining. Once established in Norway, their working with an adequate air force gave German soldiers further advantages. Aircraft transported small parties of troops and quantities of supplies, they directed the fire of artillery, and especially they destroyed the Allies' bases almost at leisure, interrupted only by a few machines working from carriers or flying occasionally the long distance from the British Isles, and by a few short-range guns on shore backed by the long-range fire of one or two sloops, destroyers, or anti-aircraft ships. The immediate occasion of the retreat seems to have been this gradual destruction of the bases, on which the troops depended for almost every need, whether of victuals, fuel or ammunition; but so long as the Germans retained command of the sea in the Skagerrak and were thus able to reinforce their troops in Southern Norway at will, the final decision in Central Norway could scarcely be in doubt. ' It is impossible ', said the First Lord of the Admiralty, when explaining to Sir Charles Forbes the decision to withdraw from Aandalsnes, ' for 3000 or 4000 men without artillery or air superiority to withstand advance of 70,000 or 80,000 thoroughly equipped Germans '. At the same time he said, ' Feel sure you must be very proud of the way your A.A. craft and, above all, the Fleet Air Arm are comporting themselves '.[1]

41. Plan of the evacuation [PLAN 11

The first plan was to bring off the troops of both expeditions at the same time. Each would need two nights, 1st–2nd and 2nd–3rd May; but most of ' Primrose ' and ' Sickle ' would come from Molde, using Aandalsnes on one night only, and that might have to be a day sooner than the others. The Admiralty put several transports at Sir Charles Forbes's disposal, some of them large ships. The War Office directed that the men should be withdrawn ' regardless of loss of equipment '; they calculated there were 6200 men to come from Namsos and 5500 from the Aandalsnes district. Aircraft from Admiral Wells's carriers

---

[1] A.T.1939/29 April. A.T.1904 of the 10th had given the Admiralty ruling that ' interference with communications in southern areas must be left mainly to submarines, air and mining, aided by intermittent sweeps when forces allow '.

were to cover the retreat, protecting landing places and troopships and attacking the enemy's troops. There was also a plan to attack the forts near Trondheim in order to divert attention : ' It has been agreed a bombardment of the forts, at Trondheim, should be undertaken by battleships or 8-in. cruisers, when desired by G.O.C., during periods of evacuation '. Ships of war ' escorting one or two liners ', said a later signal, should arrive off the approaches at dusk on the first night of embarking, and ' after dark, liners and escorts turn and steer westwards, remainder of force carrying out bombardment of fort at entrance '. Sir Charles Forbes replied to this that the *Valiant* might leave Admiral Wells, with whose carriers she was cruising, in time to attack the forts at dawn on 2nd May, but he had no liners nor destroyers for screening them, ' every destroyer fit to fight and available is being used '.

For the evacuations, he ordered Vice-Admiral Edward-Collins to take charge of the Aandalsnes operations on the first night, and Vice-Admiral Layton to take charge on the second night, while Vice-Admiral Cunningham was to be in command at Namsos on both nights. In order to provide the necessary cruisers and destroyers, he requested that the *Southampton* and *Aurora* should be released from Narvik, and that the *Sheffield*, then giving cover to the *Ark Royal* should be detached to rendezvous with Admiral Edward-Collins. He also asked for the loan of three French contre-torpilleurs.[1]

The actual arrangements differed from the original plan, which could be a point of departure to work from only. ' Primrose ' and ' Sickle ' embarked in two nights, 30th April–1st May and 1st–2nd May, but nearly all came from Aandalsnes, not counting the party from Aalesund. Only some 50 people embarked at Molde ; no troops could go there, owing to the damage to the roads about the town and to the lack of small craft for ferries. ' Maurice ' embarked in one night at Namsos, 2nd–3rd May. Furthermore, air attacks on the carriers on 1st May hampered their work and caused Admiral Wells to give it up that evening ; nor did the bombardment of the Trondheim forts take place.

No German surface ships interfered with the withdrawal. There were one or two asdic contacts with submarines, but the enemy attacked the convoys from the air only, and chiefly the ships from Namsos. Yet between the 1st and 4th May there were always convoys of troops at sea, with generally the cruisers and sometimes the destroyers full of passengers. As a rule each convoy came home divided into small groups of ships, which crossed the North Sea between roughly 63° and 66° N., until they reached the longitude of the Shetlands, when they turned to pass west of those islands and the Orkneys. Admiral Wells, who reached Scapa with the carriers on 3rd May, had the *Valiant* in his squadron from 30th April onwards. Besides her, there were three capital ships in the Home Fleet : the *Resolution*, working under Lord Cork in the Narvik–Tromsö area far to the northward ; the *Rodney* and *Repulse* at Scapa with Admiral Forbes, the last-named ship ready ' to meet possibility of attack on ships engaging in evacuation ', and her screen of destroyers earmarked.

Before the evacuation of troops took place, the *Glasgow* was sent to Molde to take away the King of Norway. She arrived there with two destroyers, the *Jackal* and *Javelin*, late on 29th April and sailed again the same night, attacked from the air as she cast off from the burning quay—she had come alongside, says Captain Denny, ' with fire hoses playing, the whole scene being brilliantly lit by the flames of the burning town '. She took on board the King, the Crown Prince, members of the Government and of the Allies' legations, and

---

[1] These could not be spared, as they were required for service in the Mediterranean. It was later decided, too, that the *Aurora* should not take part in the operation.

part of the base staff and so on, anticipating the general withdrawal—about 280 people all told, besides a quantity of gold bullion. They went to Malangen Fjord, near Tromsö, where the Norwegian passengers shifted into a Norwegian man-of-war to go to Tromsö, and the British ships went home.

42. The Retreat from Aandalsnes, Molde and Aalesund [PLAN 11

Captain Pegram of the *Glasgow* found at Molde that Captain Denny had not received the signals about withdrawing. Captain Denny and Brigadier Hogg, commander of the army base staff, expected ships on the 29th, the day before that actually arranged;[1] they had planned to send away 1000 men from Aandalsnes that night and supposed the *Glasgow* had come for that purpose. The growing scale of attack from the air added to the difficulties. The *Black Swan* had been hit on the 28th, after a couple of strenuous days in which she had fired 2000 rounds of 4-in. and 4000 of pom-pom ammunition; and she had sailed for Scapa next day, making 12 knots in a heavy sea despite a three-foot hole in her bottom.[2] On 29th–30th April, for the first time, the enemy attacked throughout the night. The *Fleetwood*, which had relieved the *Black Swan*, speedily expended her ammunition, and went home early on the 30th, taking 340 troops—part of those collected against the arrival of ships from home on the 29th—a prodigious number of passengers for a vessel of her size. 'A.A. fire from ships subject to continuous attacks themselves all day', said Captain Poland, 'will never meet situation; strong A.A. backed up by full aircraft support essential'. Still the departure of the sloops meant taking away the only long-range weapons there were, apart from those in the ships that came to carry troops away on the 30th, until the arrival on 1st May of the *Auckland* and *Calcutta*, sent in haste by Sir Charles Forbes from Scapa.

Owing to the air attacks, nobody could tell whether ships would still be able to go alongside, when the time came, or whether men and gear must come off in boats. Apart from that, General Paget could give little notice of the moment for withdrawing from the battle. Moreover, communication was precarious between the base and the fighting zone and between the two ports themselves, and after the *Fleetwood* sailed the expedition had no communication with the ships coming to its relief. In these circumstances there was little scope for preparing beforehand. 'The comparative success achieved', remarked Captain Denny, 'was due more to good fortune than to thorough organisation such as displayed at Gallipoli'. And the good fortune, he added, lay in the absence of attack from the air each night the expedition embarked. Admiral Layton considered, from the way the Germans bombed possible troop-billets right up to the end, that they did not expect an immediate retreat.[3]

Admiral Edward-Collins arrived for the first night's work at Aandalsnes at 2230 on the 30th with the *Galatea* and *Arethusa*, the *Sheffield*, wearing the flag

---

[1] A.T.2127/29, announcing the decision to commence the evacuation on the night of 30th April/1st May, was made in Flag Officer's cypher and as it did not include instructions to pass the message to the military authorities, the Commander-in-Chief, H.F., presumed that the War Office would inform the G.O.C., Aandalsnes.

[2] The Commander-in-Chief, concurring with R.A., Destroyers, considered the *Black Swan*'s conduct on the occasion 'outstanding and in accordance with the very highest traditions'.

[3] The German Naval Appreciation, from air reports, was that the enemy intended 'to re-embark troops landed at Aandalsnes as quickly as possible during the night, and to use them at another place, that is at Namsos'.

THE RETREAT FROM AANDALSNES, MOLDE AND AALESUND Sec. 42

of Rear-Admiral Clarke,[1] and *Southampton*, six destroyers[2] and the small transport *Ulster Monarch*, having sent the *Tartar* and the *Ulster Prince* to Molde the same night. All had come from Scapa except the *Sheffield* and *Southampton*, which joined at sea, the former from cruising with Admiral Wells and the latter from the Narvik squadron. There had been neither time nor information enough to give written orders, and the Admiral made his final arrangements during the passage. Brigadier Hogg signalled during the afternoon, as the ships approached the coast : ' Probably unsafe to berth transports, but worth while trying with destroyers ; if this fails, propose using destroyers' boats along south shore eastwards of Aandalsnes '. But the Admiral determined to go alongside if he could, ' as most fortunately proved to be the case. We should never have embarked the numbers concerned in the time available in ships' boats from the beach in the dark '. Accordingly, he went in the *Galatea* straight alongside the concrete quay, the one proper landing place that survived. The *Walker*, outside the flagship, carried troops to the *Sheffield*, which had anchored off the town. The *Arethusa* went alongside after the *Galatea* had finished, and took on board the last party that night from Aandalsnes itself. Some 1800 men embarked in the three cruisers. ' Although dead beat and ravenously hungry ' they went on board ' in a well-disciplined and orderly manner ' but many ' were without arms or equipment '.

There were two outlying parties near Aandalsnes to gather in, besides Captain Denny's people at Molde : about 300 men had been sent to Alfarnes, 6 miles north of Aandalsnes at the mouth of another fjord, and about 100 marines were at Veblungsnes, a mile or so from Aandalsnes on the west point of the river's mouth. Admiral Edward-Collins had sent the *Wanderer* and *Sikh* to Alfarnes as the squadron came in, and the *Southampton* when he found he did not need her for the main body. The *Wanderer* took the ground with 150 troops on board, and the *Sikh* had to tow her off ; eventually the *Sikh* and *Southampton* brought the whole party away. The *Westcott* and *Walker* brought off the marines in their boats ; Colonel Simpson, who was wounded, and two or three people with him at Veblungsnes had gone on board the *Mashona* already. Meanwhile, the *Tartar* and *Ulster Prince* had embarked Captain Denny and the remainder of his staff, Admiral Diesen and other Norwegian officers, and a few soldiers and others—all there were to come from Molde, in fact, but General Ruge and his staff, the General refusing to leave unless he could be sure of going direct to another port in Norway. Thus each ship had her work to do, except the transport *Ulster Monarch*, which went away empty. The Admiral had told off destroyers to support the main embarkation with their guns and others to carry out an anti-submarine patrol in the fjord, but the business of embarking troops left little opportunity for other services ; it was as well there was no enemy about. The only opposition came from the air later, as the ships were leaving the outer fjords between 0300 and 0400 on 1st May, when German aircraft dropped a few bombs near some ships without effect. ' Once again ', says Admiral Edward-Collins, ' and contrary to all expectations, Romsdals Fjord was entered, the operation completed, and forces withdrawn without loss or damage through enemy action '.

The ships had sailed as they finished their tasks, and they crossed the North Sea again in ones and twos. They had on board some 2200 men, but no guns. The number still to come was unknown. In a signal to Admiral Layton, then on his way to Aandalsnes with two cruisers and three destroyers for the second

---
[1] Rear-Admiral M. L. Clarke, D.S.C., had hoisted his flag as R.A. 2nd in command 18th C.S. on 21st April.
[2] *Somali, Mashona, Sikh, Wanderer, Walker, Westcott.*

night's work, Admiral Edward-Collins put the number of British troops at 1500 with possibly Norwegian troops and refugees as well, but he warned his successor that ' as a result of continual bombing night and day, all . . . at Aandalsnes are shaken, and it appeared no one there really knew the position at the front '. The *Ulster Monarch* joined Admiral Layton ' in view of the indefinite numbers ' ; unluckily she had to turn back with a cracked piston, but the *Somali* and *Mashona* did a second night's service. Later in the day, Sir Charles Forbes ordered the *Southampton* and some more destroyers to go once again to Aandalsnes in case a third night should prove necessary, the War Office having worked out that there might be 2900 British troops still to come away, some of whom might not be able to reach Aandalsnes from the fighting zone in time to embark in Admiral Layton's ships. However, two nights sufficed.

Aandalsnes suffered the usual attacks from the air on 1st May. A Royal Air Force patrol flew above the town for its protection in the morning, and first the *Auckland* and then the *Calcutta* arrived from home, the *Auckland* having seen the attack on Admiral Edward-Collins as she came through another fjord south of him. The Germans dropped bombs occasionally throughout the day, but made a determined attack on the two ships late in the afternoon for above an hour and a half. During this attack there came peremptory orders from Sir Charles Forbes to withdraw : he had already told the two ships to go out, ' if bombing is severe ', until required for the night's work. They went out accordingly, Commander Hewitt of the *Auckland* remarking : ' It was most heartening to observe that *Calcutta* adjusted her speed so as to remain in company—this in spite of the fact that she was the more heavily attacked ' ; and the two ships cheered one another when the attack was over. They reached open water outside Buddybet in time to meet and to turn back with Admiral Layton. Aircraft had made several attacks on Admiral Layton's ships during the afternoon. No sooner did he enter Buddybet in the evening than more appeared, perhaps the same machines that had lately harassed the *Calcutta* and *Auckland*, and the squadron was attacked intermittently for an hour or so as it steamed through the fjords. The fire of the two large cruisers and the *Calcutta* and *Auckland* brought down one machine, but bombs from another very nearly hit the flagship.

Admiral Layton now had the *Manchester* and *Birmingham* and five destroyers[1] besides the two A.A. ships. Sir Charles Forbes had offered him two small transports as well, but their speed was only 16 knots and ' a quick get away would be essential ' so he refused them, though he accepted the *Ulster Monarch* from Admiral Edward-Collins on learning how uncertain was the number of troops he had to deal with. Like his predecessor, he had given no written orders, ' the situation being so doubtful ', but contented himself with giving general instructions by word of mouth before leaving Scapa. As the squadron approached the coast of Norway, he had sent the *Somali* to Aalesund to collect the Primrose detachment there. Off Molde, which was covered with a pall of smoke, the *Diana* parted company to carry General Ruge and his staff from Molde to Tromsö. The other ships came to Aandalsnes a little before 2300 on the 1st. The cruisers anchored, being too long to go alongside, while two of the three destroyers went to the quay, which was still undamaged, and in an hour or so nearly 1300 men were ferried to the two cruisers. General Paget then said there remained but a rearguard of some 200 men. The Admiral wanted to sail betimes, that the ships might reach open water before dawn, when he expected fog ; he did not want to be held up in the fjords with the ships

---

[1] *Inglefield, Delight, Diana, Somali, Mashona.*

full of troops. The *Birmingham* therefore sailed as soon as she had her quota, and the *Manchester* followed shortly afterwards with the destroyers. This left the *Calcutta* and *Auckland* for the rearguard. The *Calcutta* found some 700 men, whom she got on board in 15 minutes, and the *Auckland* took the true rearguard, about 240 men, who ' embarked with such commendable promptitude that the ship was alongside for only 7 minutes '. They all reached home with no more than patches of fog to contend with in the fjords, the ships carrying much the same numbers from Aandalsnes as the night before, about 2200, to which the 250 from Aalesund in the *Somali* must be added. The five remaining anti-submarine trawlers attached to the expedition went home also.

43. The Retreat from Namsos [PLAN 11

When the order came on 28th April to withdraw, there were at Namsos the *Carlisle*, anti-aircraft ship, flying Rear-Admiral Vivian's flag, the *Bittern* sloop, and some trawlers. There were also two French storeships with their escort of two destroyers, whose presence enabled General Carton de Wiart to take the first step towards withdrawing by sending back a French battalion of 850 men then in Namsos itself; they sailed for Scapa on the 29th. A small party (about 100 chasseurs–alpins and a section of British light A.A. guns) left in the *Janus* next day for Mosjoen—the first of a series of landings in this area designed to impede the advance of the enemy on Narvik after the withdrawal from Central Norway.[1]

The *Carlisle* which had gone north to Skjel Fjord to oil on the 29th returning on the 30th found the *Bittern* disabled by a bomb, and Admiral Vivian had to order her to be sunk. Attacks from the air had also disabled three trawlers, which had to be sunk, too, leaving five fit for service. Having consulted with the General, who said ' the presence of a cruiser was of great moral value, but of little value for direct defence ', Admiral Vivian then proposed to the Commander-in-Chief that the *Carlisle* and three trawlers should go to sea during daylight hours to preserve them for their coming duties; for the *Carlisle* would be wanted to protect the troopships from air attack, while the trawlers were to serve as ferries. This signal crossing one from Sir Charles that gave orders in the same sense, the *Carlisle* sailed at daylight. Fog prevented her return at night, and early on 2nd May, when about 130 miles from the coast, she joined Vice-Admiral Cunningham, who was coming to fetch away the expedition.

Admiral Cunningham had the *Devonshire* and *York*, the *Montcalm* (Admiral Derrien), five destroyers[2] and the transports *El d'Jezair* (Admiral Cadart), *El Kantara* and *El Mansour*, while four destroyers[3] had gone ahead in circumstances to be described later. He had sailed from Scapa on 29th April meaning to bring off half the expedition in the transports in the night of 1st–2nd May and the other half in the cruisers the night following; and Sir Charles Forbes warning him that the work might have to be done all in one night, he had an alternative plan for that contingency. ' I was fortunate ', he writes, ' in that time admitted of my interviewing Admirals Derrien and Cadart, and of my being able to explain my intentions in detail to the majority of the commanding officers of cruisers and destroyers in my force, to issue certain written instructions, and to acquaint French warships and transports of what cruising dispositions I proposed to use '.

---

[1] *See* Chapter VIII *postea*.
[2] *Afridi, Nubian, Hasty, Imperial*; French *Bison*.
[3] *Kelly, Grenade, Griffen, Maori*.

In outline the first plan was as follows. The three transports and six destroyers would leave the flag at 2000 on 1st May off Kya Light, some 20 miles south-west of the mouth of Namsen Fjord and 40 short of Namsos. They were to fetch the first half of the troops, about 3000 men; and as soon as each transport had her load she would sail independently with one destroyer. The Admiral would cruise off Kya Light during the night, with the cruisers and three destroyers, ready to meet the loaded transports in the morning and to escort them to the westward until the time came for the cruisers to go in with six destroyers for the rest of the troops. He would make Kya Light again at 2000 on 2nd May on his way in. On arrival off Namsos, the cruisers were to keep underway, while destroyers and trawlers brought off the troops as before, and this time the destroyers, too, were to carry troops, as were the *Carlisle* and *Bittern*.

Admiral Cunningham gave out his alternative plan by signal on 30th April, by which time he knew that one battalion had left Namsos already, so that the number still to come was but 5400 men. He proposed to reach the mouth of Namsen Fjord at 2100 on the appointed day, when the three transports were to go in with four destroyers, followed in half an hour by the *York* and a destroyer, while the *Devonshire*, *Montcalm* and the other destroyers stayed outside. Each transport was to embark 1700 men at the stone pier and sail again with one destroyer when ready; the *York* and her destroyer were to stop a couple of miles short of Namsos to receive troops from trawlers, and would sail with the *Carlisle* after the last transport; the fifth destroyer would stay for stragglers. The convoy would go home in two, perhaps three, groups of ships. In the main, this second plan was actually followed.

In the evening of the 30th, when the signal describing the above arrangements had been made, Admiral Cunningham passed the carrier squadron then on the way to cover the retreat from Aandalsnes with its fighter aircraft, and Admiral Wells signalled that he should send up fighters over Namsos on 2nd May; but this unhappily fell through, owing to the German air attack on the 1st. German aircraft molested Admiral Cunningham also on 1st May, and two machines, attacking in the afternoon, nearly hit the *Devonshire* and a transport with their bombs. Then the squadron ran into thick and widespread fog in the evening, some 40 miles short of Kya Light, which forced the Admiral to turn out to sea and prevented him from sending the transports to Namsos that night. The *Maori* went on, however, having missed the signal to turn to seaward, and reported herself near Kya Light about 2200 with a visibility of 2 cables. On this, Captain Lord Louis Mountbatten suggested his joining the *Maori* with his own three ships, *Kelly, Grenade, Griffin*, ' with a view to the four of us taking off most of the troops due to be evacuated from Namsos on this, the first night '. Admiral Cunningham approved, so the little flotilla groped its way in by sounding and asdic, the fog growing thicker than ever, only to find it quite clear in Namsen Fjord at 0500 on the 2nd. Namsos thus exposed ' once more to bombing attacks ', Lord Louis decided to go out again and hide in fog banks until he might join the squadron on its way to Namsos in the evening. He met the Admiral again about 2000 with the *Maori* slightly damaged by a near miss (she had 23 casualties), a German aircraft having sighted the destroyers on the edge of a fog bank too low to cover their masts.

The delay caused by the fog made Admiral Cunningham specially anxious to do his business in one night. He had signalled the gist of his plan for this to Namsos, suggesting 1st–2nd May as the date. General Carton de Wiart had received the signal through Admiral Vivian, but had to answer that it would not do; he could not disengage all his troops in time for that night; moreover he must have two nights for the whole task. When the squadron turned back out of the fog in the evening of 1st May, Admiral Cunningham had once more proposed to Admiral Vivian that they should embark the whole expedition the following night; again Admiral Vivian, who was then at sea in the *Carlisle*, answered that two nights were needed, which agrees with a signal the General made to the War Office, that it was 'not a question of shipping, but of hours of dark'. But next morning, the 2nd, Admiral Cunningham decided to send ships enough to Namsos to bring off all the troops that night, if the weather allowed, and made known his intention to the Admiralty by signal. His reasoning appears in his report as follows :—

> '840 of the 6200 troops which I had originally been informed would be evacuated from Namsos had already been removed . . . on the night of 28th/29th April, leaving about 5400 to be embarked. I had sufficient transport for this number, but, as far as time required to embark was concerned, I appeared to be limited by (*a*) the number of large ships that could be safely operated at Namsos at one time ; (*b*) the facilities, piers, ferrying craft, etc., available, which were reported as sadly lacking ; (*c*) the reiterated statements of C.S.20, and military authorities through him, that evacuation could not be carried out on one night only, because of the above.[1]
>
> I was uncertain of the state of affairs ashore and how long evacuation could be delayed with safety from the military point of view ; and I could not lose sight of the fact that should the fog persist or recur after to-night I might be faced with the necessity of attempting to carry out the remainder of the evacuation in daylight, a project which all the evidence tended to show would be extremely hazardous, if not impossible . . . I was convinced that to attempt to spread evacuation over two nights would be courting disaster. I therefore decided in any case to throw enough shipping into Namsos on first night to permit of complete evacuation and, if the General was unable to disengage his troops in time to take advantage of the opportunity thus afforded, to endeavour to evacuate the remnant in the remaining cruisers and destroyers the following night.
>
> In coming to this decision, I was much influenced, firstly by the gallant bearing of Admiral Cadart and by his confidence in his ability to place two of his transports simultaneously, and subsequently the third, alongside the stone pier ; and secondly by my own conviction, formed from discussions on 29th April with Captain Lees of H.M.S. *Calcutta* and Commander Ravenhill of H.M.S. *Nubian*, both lately returned from Namsos, that the present reports upon the damage to the wooden pier were somewhat overdrawn.'

Admiral Vivian had joined Admiral Cunningham in the morning of 2nd May, fog preventing the *Carlisle*'s return to Namsos the night before. Early in the afternoon came a signal from the Admiralty to say the General reported things 'getting serious' and he wished to see a naval officer who knew the plan for withdrawing the expedition. Admiral Cunningham then gave Admiral Vivian the detailed plan of the 30th for embarking all in one night, and sent him ahead to Namsos. As soon as he arrived, about 2000 that evening, Admiral Vivian consulted with Generals Carton de Wiart and Audet. He told them it was essential that the last troopship should be loaded by 0200 next morning, the 3rd, so that all might be clear of the fjord by 0330, and that guns and stores should be embarked only if it could be done at the same time as the men. The Generals agreed.

In the meantime Admiral Cunningham had approached the coast, seeking shelter in banks of fog from shadowing aircraft. The French transports had fuel enough for one night more only, so the Admiral prepared to do the work with the ships of war alone, should the fog persist. However, Admiral Vivian reported clear weather inshore, and soon after 1830 the squadron ran out of the

---

[1] C.S.20 was Admiral Vivian. Presumably the General's signal, that it was not a question of shipping, had not yet reached Admiral Cunningham.

fog some 40 miles from the mouth of Namsen Fjord. Then the transports and their escorts parted company, while the Admiral cruised off Kya Light with the *Devonshire, Montcalm* and four destroyers.

Captain Vian in the *Afridi* led the transports in, followed by the *York* and *Nubian*, and joined in the fjord by the *Kelly, Grenade* and *Griffin*. Admiral Cadart went straight alongside the stone pier in the *El d'Jezair* about 2230, and the *El Kantara* secured outside him. The *El Mansour*, underway off the town, and the *York*, further out, as had been arranged, both got their loads from trawlers and destroyers, which fetched the troops from the wooden pier. The transports sailed as soon as they had their loads, followed by the *York* and *Carlisle*, all accompanied by destroyers. The *El Mansour* cleared the fjord at 0230, about the time the last transport was leaving the pier that morning of 3rd May. Admiral Cunningham joined a second destroyer to her escort and sent the *York* and *Nubian* to overtake her. So, too, the *Montcalm* and *Bison* joined the *El Kantara* and her destroyer, while the *Devonshire, Carlisle* and four destroyers joined the *El d'Jezair*.

The first group of ships crossed the North Sea independently, and reached Scapa without adventure. But German aircraft harassed the rest of the squadron that day for nearly seven hours. Admiral Cunningham had hoped to find shelter in fog until well away from the coast, but the fog cleared as the sun rose, so they had ' perfect bombing weather '. The enemy attacked five times between 0845 and 1530, at distances of from 140 to 220 miles from their airfield at Vaernes near Trondheim ; they succeeded in destroying two ships, the *Bison* and *Afridi*, at a cost of two or three machines shot down out of some 50 that attacked.[1] For the first three attacks—0845–1030—the aircraft came in waves of a dozen, and singled out the *Devonshire* and *Montcalm*, dropping bombs very near those ships, and disabling the *Bison* in the last attack of the three. Her survivors were rescued by the *Grenade, Afridi* and *Imperial* ; ' Commander R. C. Boyle, R.N., of the *Grenade* very gallantly secured the stern of his ship to the sinking *Bison*, despite burning oil and exploding ammunition and was responsible for saving the lives of many of the *Bison*'s ship's company by this act '.[2] At 1400, whilst rejoining the squadron after sinking the wreck of the *Bison*, the *Afridi* was hit by two bombs, and she eventually capsized, losing about 100 killed, including some of the *Bison*'s people and some men of the York and Lancaster regiment—the only army casualties incurred in the evacuation—that she had on board. In the last attack, at 1530, the enemy bombed the *Griffin* and *Imperial*, but without effect, as these ships were rejoining the flag with survivors from the *Afridi*.

After the attacks in the forenoon, Admiral Cunningham concentrated his ships and Admiral Derrien's, forming cruisers and transports in single line ahead ' for mutual support ' with the *Carlisle* astern. They arrived at Scapa on the 5th, a day later than the *York*'s group. The Admiral writes of this passage from Norway :—

> ' The manner in which the transports *El d'Jezair* and *El Kantara*, under the command of Contre-amiral Cadart, were manœuvred at high speed to conform to the movements of the escorting vessels during the air attacks is worthy of the

---

[1] Admiral Cunningham says the *Carlisle* gave ample warning of every attack, and her ' assistance in this respect and by reason of the accuracy of her anti-aircraft fire proved invaluable ' ; but she had only an hour and a half's allowance of ammunition left after the third attack.

[2] Commander-in-Chief, Home Fleet (H.F. Narrative, par. 254.)

highest praise; they also hotly engaged all aircraft sighted, and thereby contributed their quota to the general defence of the convoy. The loyal and understanding co-operation afforded to me by Contre-amiral Derrien and his squadron greatly lightened my task and contributed materially to the success of the operation . . . and the bearing of officers and men in all ships of my force, under extremely trying conditions, was fully in accordance with the highest tradition.'

The arrival at Scapa of Vice-Admiral Cunningham's force from Namsos brought to a close the sorry story of the campaign in Central Norway. Though it was impossible not to regret the turn events had taken, declared the Commander-in-Chief, Home Fleet, he could not but admire the way in which all units under his command had done their duty and overcome every difficulty with which they had been confronted; and he accordingly sent the following message to all concerned :—

'To Home Fleet, British, Polish, French and Norwegian Warships and merchant vessels attached to the Home Fleet :—

During the last three weeks you have been engaged upon two of the most difficult operations of war that naval forces are required to undertake. You may be proud that you have carried out these operations with the loss at sea of only about twelve officers and men of the Army in the face of heavy air attacks. I am proud to command a fleet that has shown itself capable of meeting the heavy demands made upon it with such determination and success.'

CHAPTER VII

THE EXPEDITION TO NARVIK: PHASE I
(14TH APRIL–7TH MAY)

44. Inception of Operation Rupert

In the meantime, while the brief campaign in Central Norway was reaching its inevitable conclusion, the expedition to Narvik, though not as yet seriously threatened by the enemy, had also received a check. The rosy hopes of a speedy recapture of the port, before the enemy recovered from the effects of Admiral Whitworth's blow on 13th April, speedily vanished, for reasons which will be apparent later. Once missed, the opportunity did not recur. Moreover, an unusually protracted spell of bad weather and deep snow compelled the postponement of a serious attempt till the latter part of May.

To recapitulate, the Government decided on 10th April to send this expedition, which was, in fact, the child of 'Avonmouth' in Plan 'R.4'; its first troops left British waters on the 12th; but half these troops went to Namsos instead, the Government then expecting 'reduced opposition' at Narvik, and desiring to recover Trondheim as soon as possible. So early as the 11th, at a meeting of the naval staff that night, Admiral Phillips (Deputy Chief of the Staff) had questioned the wisdom of sending 'all our readily available' troops to Narvik. He argued that it had been decided at a time when Norway seemed at the point of coming to terms with Germany, when ' it would be essential to secure our important interests in the Narvik area'; now he 'considered that the taking of Narvik would not help the Norwegians directly, nor would it improve our position in the eyes of the world to any great extent' whereas 'Namsos was the key to retaking Trondheim, and . . . a footing in that area was important from a military point of view'. However, the Admiralty and the War Office decided to go on with 'Rupert' as arranged, and to give 'further consideration' to a landing at Namsos. The change of plan on the 14th and the diversion to Namsos of other troops later meant that 'Rupert' had but one brigade of infantry until 27th April, when three battalions of Chasseurs-Alpins joined. Yet this does not seem to have affected the fortunes of the expedition greatly; for, apart from other things, without troops trained and equipped to fight in deep snow, very little could be done before the 'long awaited' thaw, which came only at the end of the month.

45. Opening moves: Conflicting instructions [PLAN 14

The *Southampton*, screened by the *Escapade* and *Electra*, arrived in Vaags Fjord early on the 14th, having on board General Mackesy, commanding the land forces; Captain Maund, the naval chief of staff; and two companies of the 1st Scots Guards. In the first place they went to Harstad on the west shore of the fjord, where the army base was to be. The General having consulted with the authorities at the place, and learning that the 6th Norwegian Division under General Fleischer lay in the Bardu district north-east of Narvik, they crossed then to the mainland, and the Scots Guards landed near Salangen in Sag Fjord to work with the Norwegian troops.

Lord Cork had sailed in the *Aurora* from Rosyth to take command of the expedition by sea at the same time as General Mackesy left Scapa. He, too, meant to go first to Harstad to join the General; for he had not met him before. On the 14th, however, as the *Aurora* approached the coast, a signal from Admiral Whitworth, then in Vest Fjord with the *Warspite* and some destroyers, put the German strength in Narvik at some 2000 men, probably with little artillery, and emphasized his 'impressions' of the night before, that the Germans were 'thoroughly frightened' by saying :—

> 'I am convinced that Narvik can be taken by direct assault without fear of meeting serious opposition on landing. I consider that the main landing force need only be small, but it must have the support of (his squadron) or one of similar composition.'[1]

Thereupon Lord Cork, whose 'impression on leaving London was quite clear that it was desired by H.M. Government to turn the enemy out of Narvik at the earliest possible moment, and that I was to act with all promptitude in order to attain this result', ordered the *Southampton* to meet him that night in Skjel Fjord. He thought of attempting Narvik next morning with the 350 Scots Guards from the *Southampton* and a party of seamen and marines from all the larger ships and from the *Penelope* and destroyers repairing at Skjel Fjord. He made this signal to the General :—

> 'In view of successful naval action at Narvik yesterday, 13th April, and as enemy appear thoroughly frightened, suggest we take every advantage of this before enemy has recovered. If you concur and subject to information we shall receive tonight 14th April, from *Warspite*, I should be most willing to land military force now in *Southampton* at Narvik at daylight tomorrow, Monday, from *Aurora* and destroyers. Supporting fire could be provided by cruisers and destroyers, and I could assist with a naval and marine landing party of 200 if you wish.'

But nothing came of this plan. Owing to the peculiar wireless-telegraphy conditions in Norway, the *Southampton* did not receive Lord Cork's first signal until the afternoon, by which time her troops had landed in Sag Fjord to join the Norwegians—'one of the first objects laid down for the army by the War Office'. And, says Lord Cork, 'any idea of making an attempt with naval forces would have, in any case, been rendered difficult by receipt of A.T. 2347/14, in which appears : "We think it imperative that you and General should be together and act together and that no attack should be made except in concert." During the night, therefore, the *Aurora* went round towards Vaags Fjord.

The main body of the troops arrived next day, 15th, meeting the *Aurora* outside by the mouth of And Fjord in the morning. They were the 24th Brigade : the 1st Irish Guards, 2nd South Wales Borderers, and the rest of the 1st Scots Guards. They came in three large transports, with the *Protector* netlayer and *Vindictive* repair ship, convoyed by the *Valiant* and nine destroyers. The little harbour of Harstad having but a narrow entrance, the transports were to anchor in Bygden, a channel between two islands 10 miles across the fjord, whence destroyers and local shipping would ferry soldiers and stores to the base. But as they were steaming through And Fjord, a 'military outpost' reported a submarine in Vaags Fjord. The *Fearless* and *Brazen*, screening ahead, proceeded through Topsundet and carried out an attack with five depth charges, 'which literally blew the U-boat to the surface in the middle of the pattern. The crew abandoned their vessel, *U.49*, and started screaming in the most

---

[1] See Sec. 18 *ante*.

dreadful fashion '[1]; nearly all were saved, and while engaged on this rescue work, the *Brazen* picked up papers which gave the whole of the U-boat disposition for the invasion of Norway.[2]

The convoy arrived at Vaags Fjord in due course, landing troops and stores that afternoon and the day following. German aircraft harassed them at the anchorage and during the passage to Harstad, as they did the troops for Namsos at Lillesjona. They did no material damage; but the General remarks that his force had no defence against these attacks, which 'complicated the operation' of landing.

While this was going on, Captain de Salis was reconnoitring Narvik harbour and Rombaks Fjord with the *Faulknor* and *Zulu*, two of the destroyers Admiral Whitworth had working in Vest Fjord; and that night Captain de Salis signalled his opinion that a landing on Rombaks Fjord, to advance on Narvik from the north-east, would not be opposed by fixed defences, and might be covered by destroyers' guns. Lord Cork had intended to assault the place on the 16th, when disappointed of his plan for the day before. The chances of success would depend largely on how much Admiral Whitworth's action had affected the spirit of the enemy and how far ships' guns could support the infantry; for the Germans had probably as many men as the British, and they seem to have had a few Norwegian guns as well, whereas the British had no artillery.

But at this stage an unexpected difficulty confronted him; for at his first meeting with General Mackesy on the 15th he 'was astonished to hear' that the General's orders, given him just prior to sailing, 'ruled out any idea of attempting an opposed landing. Thus the General and myself left the United Kingdom with diametrically opposite views as to what was required'.

General Mackesy gives his views in his final report:—

> 'During 14th April and the following days, all available information pointed to Narvik itself being strongly held, and to the fact that the naval action of 13th April had by no means demoralized the garrison as a whole. The probability was that the garrison had, in fact, been increased by nearly 1000 good fighting men from the sunken German ships; this was fully confirmed by subsequent intelligence reports. My troops had been embarked for a peaceful landing at a friendly and organised port and could not be ready for active operations for some days . . .
>
> The country was covered by snow up to four feet and more in depth; even at sea level there were several feet of snow. Blizzards, heavy snowstorms, bitter winds, and very low night temperature were normal. Indeed, until the middle of May, even those magnificent mountain soldiers the French Chasseurs-Alpins suffered severely from frostbite and snow blindness. Troops who were not equipped with and skilled in the use of skis or snow-shoes were absolutely incapable of operating tactically at all. I had no such troops at my disposal when I first landed. Shelter from the weather was of vital importance.
>
> It soon became certain that the enemy held Narvik in considerable strength. All the existing defences had been handed over intact by the Norwegian garrison. A personal reconnaissance convinced me that topography favoured the defence, and that an opposed landing was quite out of the question so long as the deep snow and existing weather conditions persisted, and so long as my force lacked landing craft, tanks, adequate artillery support, adequate anti-aircraft defence and

---

[1] Home Fleet Narrative, para. 219.

[2] See Sec. 20 *ante*.

The Admiralty promulgated these dispositions on 16th and 17th April, and at 0210, 17th, directed Rear-Admiral (D) to arrange for an anti-submarine striking force of nine destroyers to operate against the U-boats in the Orkney and Shetland areas; but it was found impossible, owing to other commitments, to provide this number.

air co-operation. The problem was, of course, not merely one of landing, but one of carrying out a subsequent advance of several miles; yet, owing to the configuration of the ground, not even during the first mile could support be given by ships' guns.

I decided, therefore, that my first objective must be to secure the Oijord and Ankenes peninsulas, north and south of Narvik, from which in due course observed fire could be brought to bear on the enemy defences. Both these peninsulas were held by the enemy.'

Lord Cork gave up his thoughts of immediate attack, and he reported so on the 16th. On this the Admiralty urged the importance of an ' early capture ', warning him at the same time that certain battalions of chasseurs-alpins would not be coming, though apparently earmarked for Narvik hitherto, that the *Warspite* and some of his destroyers would be soon wanted elsewhere, that the Germans would reinforce and supply their garrison by air. But Lord Cork himself, now that ' the chance of a coup de main had passed ' had to own defeat by the snow. ' I personally tested this ', he says, ' and also landed a section of marines to do the same, and found it easy to sink to one's waist, and to make any progress was exhausting '. Instead of a direct assault, he proposed to bombard Narvik from the sea, ' in the hope that the result might cause the enemy to evacuate or surrender the town '. If that failed—as it did—they must wait upon the weather; and as a step towards the General's plan of securing a foothold either side of the port, the Irish Guards landed on the 19th in Bogen Inlet, on the north shore of Ofot Fjord, and the South Wales Borderers went to Ballangen, on the south shore, a week later. As for the chasseurs, General Mackesy protested that without them he was ' definitely inferior ' to the enemy, so he asked for other troops in their room, but the War Office said they had none to send.[1]

On the 20th the Government appointed Lord Cork supreme commander of the expedition.

46. Operations in Ofot Fjord, 16th-26th April [PLAN 14

Throughout the operation of ' Rupert ' force a detached squadron in Ofot Fjord harassed the enemy continuously in a smaller way. The service seems to have started from a request of General Mackesy's on the 16th to destroy shipping in Rombaks and Herjangs Fjords, through which the Germans supplied their outlying posts, especially about Gratangen, 15 miles north of Narvik. This request Lord Cork had passed on to Admiral Whitworth, who suggested cruisers and destroyers should be used to attack shipping, piers, and bridges in and near the fjords, including the merchantmen in Narvik, which ' were left afloat on 13th April because it was believed that Narvik harbour could be occupied almost immediately '. Captain de Salis commanded at first with a couple of destroyers. Then Captain Hamilton came in the *Aurora* with more destroyers—it was in the *Aurora* on the 20th that General Mackesy made the reconnaissance he mentions in his report quoted above. The *Enterprise*, which had arrived from home on the 17th, joined Captain Hamilton after that reconnaissance; they destroyed a railway bridge on the 21st and fired on Narvik next day ' to harass the enemy ' on the promontory. Captain Hamilton reports that, out of two cruisers and five destroyers at his command, ' one cruiser and at least two destroyers were continuously on patrol night and day, and on frequent occasions all ships available were employed simultaneously '.

---

[1] General Mackesy's protest is in his signal, 2105/17, to the War Office. Presumably the French troops that did not then join ' Rupert ' were those General Audet took to Namsos.

On 24th April, the bombardment took place.[1] Lord Cork, wearing his flag in the *Effingham*, which had arrived from Southern Norway on the 20th, personally directed the operation ; with him were General Mackesy and Brigadier Fraser, Commander of the 24th Brigade. The other ships to attack were the *Warspite, Aurora, Enterprise* and *Zulu*, while the *Vindictive*[2] embarked the Irish Guards from Bogen ready to land them should the cannonading give an opportunity.

The thick weather, with heavy snowstorms, forbade support by aircraft from the *Furious* ; nor could German machines interrupt the attack. The *Aurora* and *Zulu* first attacked from Rombaks Fjord for some 40 minutes, going thence to engage enemy positions in Herjangs Fjord. Then, about 0700, the other three ships attacked 'the fixed defence areas' about Narvik, as Admiral Whitworth describes it. The main bombardment lasted about three hours, but Lord Cork's hopes were disappointed. 'The climatic conditions were . . . entirely against' a landing ; 'the low visibility entirely prevented any estimate of the effect achieved by the bombardment' ; and it appeared later that 'nothing indicated any intention to surrender', though the attack 'had considerable effect'.

The next day there was a further heavy fall of snow, and as weather conditions compelled postponement of any direct attack on Narvik, attention was given to movements of troops designed to bring pressure on the enemy to the north and south of the Narvik peninsula on the 26th. Ballangen (as already mentioned) was occupied by the South Wales Borderers, and further dispositions were made as the arrival of reinforcements permitted (*see* Sec. 47).

47. Changes in Squadron : Army reinforcements [PLAN 14

Directly after this affair, Vice-Admiral Whitworth sailed for the United Kingdom in the *Warspite*, her place being taken by the *Resolution*,[3] which arrived next day. As already mentioned, the *Furious*, after suffering damage from an air attack near Tromsö and with only eight aircraft remaining serviceable, and the *Southampton*, required for duty at the withdrawal from Aandalsnes, also left Lord Cork's command ; Vice-Admiral Cunningham, with the *Devonshire* and *Berwick*, had already left the Tromsö area on 19th April. The Narvik destroyers varied continually, reliefs being supplied by exchanging with convoy escorts. By arrangement with the Commander-in-Chief, Home Fleet, there was to be a standing flotilla of ten destroyers, half for Vest Fjord and half for Vaags Fjord, besides a screen for the capital ship ; but in actual practice, no standing flotilla ever materialised. However, there were generally some fifteen all told until the Germans invaded the Low Countries, when the Admiralty recalled destroyers from Norway for employment in the southern part of the North Sea, and the total then came down to eight. The destroyers led a busy life. For instance, the *Electra* records on 8th May that for the first time since 3rd April she lay with steam at longer notice than half an hour, while the *Fame*'s report says she had steam on her main engines continuously from 10th May to 8th June.

---

[1] General Mackesy was opposed to this bombardment on humanitarian grounds, out of consideration for the Norwegian inhabitants of Narvik ; but his views were not supported by the Defence Committee, which considered the protest he made to Lord Cork.

[2] The *Hostile, Havock, Hero* and *Foxhound* screened the *Warspite* on the occasion. The *Electra* attended the *Vindictive*.

[3] The *Resolution* remained with Lord Cork until 18th May, when he sent her home 'to avoid exposing her to constant bombing' (by which she had already been slightly damaged) with the request, however, that she should be earmarked for his service for ten days longer.

Against this reduction in the ships of war, there was an increase in the strength of the land forces. Three battalions of chasseurs-alpins arrived on 27th April: two battalions went to Gratangen to work with the Norwegians north of Narvik, the third went to the Ankenes peninsula, joining the South Wales Borderers, who came there from Ballangen. A week later two battalions of the Foreign Legion and four of Poles arrived: the Foreign Legion went to the Ballangen neighbourhood, while the Polish battalions took up stations in reserve. Besides infantry, the French brought twelve field guns and ten small tanks. Moreover, a few 'much needed' motor landing craft arrived at the end of April, and with them came a battery of 25-pounders, the only British field artillery other than naval guns to land in Norway. The army received a few light anti-aircraft guns in April, too, both British and French; but no heavy pieces came until 6th May, just three weeks after the arrival of the first infantry.

With the coming of fresh troops—and of the thaw—Lord Cork turned again to plans for attacking Narvik. The stout-hearted General Bethouart had arrived from Namsos on 28th April to command the French contingent, and the Admiral took him to spy out the land in the *Codrington* the same day. ' I imagine ', remarks Captain Creasy of the *Codrington*, ' the only occasion on which a destroyer with the Union flag . . . has ever engaged an enemy ', for she fired on German gun positions and the railway near Narvik during the reconnaissance. On 1st May, Lord Cork went once more into Ofot Fjord ' to keep in touch with events '; this time his flagship, the *Effingham*, with the *Resolution* and *Aurora*, bombarded German positions in Beisfjord and about Ankenes to help the Borderers in their attempts to make headway on the peninsula.[1] The fruits of these two days, apparently, was an order to prepare for a direct assault on Narvik by British troops on the 8th. This plan fell through, but it was followed by a plan to land the Foreign Legion in Herjangs Fjord to seize Bjerkvik and clear the Germans out of all that country, while chasseurs and Norwegians from Gratangen way attacked southward from Elvenes and through the valley Graesdalen, further eastward, and then to march on Oydejord.

Meanwhile, since the retreat from Central Norway, the British Government had been sending small parties of troops to Bodo, Mo and Mosjoen, south of Narvik, to hinder the enemy's advance northward. A company of Scots Guards had already been sent from the Narvik force to Bodo before the end of April; and from then onwards this imposed an increasing strain on the 'Rupert' forces, both naval and military. On 7th May this area was added to Lord Cork's command.

It will be convenient, therefore, at this stage to follow the fortunes of these operations before dealing with the final events of the campaign against Narvik.

---

[1] Further successful bombardment of this area was carried out by the *Resolution* and *Aurora* on the 3rd; in the course of these operations the Polish destroyers *Grom* and *Blyskawica* suffered damage from gunfire.

CHAPTER VIII

OPERATIONS AT BODO, MO AND MOSJOEN

48. Object of Operations [PLAN 12

The object of the supplementary landings which took place in the Bodo–Mosjoen area on the collapse of the campaign in Central Norway was to delay the German advance northward towards Narvik, and especially the increasing reach of their air power.

The Government had considered sending small bodies of troops to intermediate positions between the main areas of hostilities while the British and French troops were still fighting in Central Norway. Thus as early as 21st April a trawler was sent to report on the facilities of Mosjoen, at the head of Vefsen Fjord, some 90 miles north eastward from Namsos; and on the 25th there came a suggestion from Sir Charles Forbes to use Mosjoen or Kongsmoen ' if suitable landing ground could be found in their vicinity ', apparently to relieve Namsos, where they were feeling the strain of continual attacks from the air on an overcrowded base. Two days later he again ' urged on the Admiralty . . . necessity of landing in Mosjoen or Mo area, properly organised ', the *Penelope* having reported several spots suitable for landing grounds on the island of Heroy in that neighbourhood.[1] In view of the decision that day to withdraw from Central Norway, the Commander-in-Chief added : ' Landing will now only be with object of denying area to enemy air force to start with. If he establishes air force in Mosjoen or Bodo area, same state of affairs will shortly take place at Narvik as at Aandalsnes and Molde '.

49. The First Landings [PLAN 12

Positive orders came on 29th April, when Lord Cork was told he must occupy the head of Salt Fjord, near the mouth of which lies Bodo, to prevent the enemy from arriving by parachute. Accordingly, he sent first a destroyer, which reported there were no Germans nor shipping of any sort in the neighbourhood, and then a company of the Scots Guards, which landed at Bodo and worked eastward. General Carton de Wiart had orders the same day to send a party from Namsos to Mosjoen, so the *Janus* (Commander Tothill) sailed the following night with 100 chasseurs–alpins and a section of British light anti-aircraft guns; she landed her party late on 2nd May unopposed and unobserved. Commander Tothill remarked on this point :—

> ' The success of the operation depended entirely on not being observed by reconnaissance planes. Mosjoen is within range of enemy dive bombing planes; the fiords are in places narrow, with no room to manœuvre and, owing to the shortness of darkness, the fiords have to be navigated during daylight hours. Now that the enemy air force are no longer occupied with forces operating further to the southward, sea communication with Mosjoen is not considered to fall within the limits of a justifiable risk.'

---

[1] Kongsmoen is the same as Kongsmo in 64° 55′ N., 12° 35′ E., at the head of Indre Folden Fjord and half-way between Namsos and Mosjoen.

Captain Yates of the *Penelope* received and passed on much general intelligence during his ship's stay at Skjel Fjord, repairing to go home after her grounding near Bodo.

By this, presumably, he meant that troops must rely on the country to replenish supplies.

On 1st May, the Admiralty ordered Lord Cork to send a destroyer to Mo to prevent an enemy landing, and made the 'excellent proposal'[1] to the Commander-in-Chief, Home Fleet, that a Destroyer Division should be established to patrol the coast from Namsos to the northward, to prevent the movement of enemy troopships by sea. Unfortunately, owing to shortage of destroyers, this suggestion could not be carried out. Two flying boats were sent from the United Kingdom to reconnoitre airfields in the Bodo area, but they were caught in the water and put out of action by enemy aircraft on 4th May.

The next military landing took place at Mo, situated at the head of North Ranen Fjord, some 45 miles to the northward of Mosjoen. The troops consisted of the 1st Independent Company—300 men or double the strength of an ordinary battalion company—which arrived from the United Kingdom in the transport *Royal Ulsterman*, escorted by the *Mohawk*, on 4th May and accomplished their landing 'apparently unobserved'.

Three more independent companies went out a few days after the party for Mo, two companies to Mosjoen, in the *Ulster Prince* with Colonel Gubbins, the Senior Officer of all these out-lying forces, and one to Bodo, in the *Royal Scotsman*. They sailed from home together, escorted by four destroyers, parting company off the coast of Norway to go to their respective destinations; both landed on the 9th, and the *Ulster Prince* brought away the chasseurs-alpins from Mosjoen. Altogether, five independent companies went to Norway, the last arriving at Bodo on 13th or 14th May in the *Royal Ulsterman*, escorted by the *Matabele*.

50. Area placed under Narvik command

Before this, however, various changes had taken place in Norway. On the 4th, Lord Cork had asked the Admiralty to explain 'the general policy regarding Bodo, Mo and Mosjoen', saying also: 'It seems most important to hold in force the Mo road leading north', but 'it appears the forces being sent are hardly adequate for this purpose, and with such weak detachments in the air another naval commitment comes into being'. The Admiralty answered on the 5th, as Lord Cork records, 'that it was not possible to maintain large forces in face of enemy air superiority well in advance of established fighter aerodrome, that Bodo was the only place south of Narvik where such could be established, that small parties only would be maintained at Mo and Mosjoen with the object of obstructing enemy advance and to prevent landings by sea and air'; and on the 7th the Government put the independent companies directly under the Narvik command. The Germans were then pressing northward, the Norwegians in those parts were tiring, and as soon as he arrived at Mosjoen, on the 9th, Colonel Gubbins seems to have decided he must begin to withdraw, agreeably to his instructions to harass and delay the enemy, but to go back gradually to Mo and Bodo. Thereupon, Lord Cork arranged to send reinforcements, apparently anticipating a signal from home (A.T. 0053/10), which ran thus: 'Essential Bodo should be held pending full examination of problem involved, which is now in progress; if necessary, garrison must be reinforced from resources at your disposal'.

---

[1] Lord Cork's despatch.

Sec. 51   OPERATIONS AT BODO, MO AND MOSJOEN

51. German landing at Hemnes   [PLAN 12

But the Germans moved first. In the evening of 10th May they landed some 300 troops at Hemnes, in Ranen Fjord, 15 miles west of Mo, part from aircraft and part from a captured coasting steamer, while another captured steamer probably landed troops at or near Mosjoen the same evening. Lord Cork had news of their coming up the coast, the first message reaching him at 1100 and reporting two steamers in the Inner Lead a little north of Namsos; and he ordered the *Calcutta* and *Zulu* to intercept them.[1] The steamer for Hemnes arrived there about 1900, and her troops landed after the town had been bombed and set on fire, other troops coming by air at the same time. The British ships arrived two hours afterwards, too late to stop the landing of troops, but in time to sink the transport with nearly all the stores still on board. They went on to Mo, which they found unmolested, and the *Zulu* picked up some soldiers who had escaped from Hemnes, where part of the independent company at Mo had been stationed; then they went to join the *Penelope*, which was to sail in tow from Skjel Fjord that night to go home under their escort.

Colonel Gubbins heard of the German movement by sea at some time in the afternoon or early evening of the 10th, and he believed they would land at Elsfjorden, south of the Hemnes peninsula. Had he doubts before about withdrawing, the enemy's landing behind him must have made plain the need to do so. He left Mosjoen that night, and retired by land and by water up Vefsen Fjord, and went to Sandnesjoen on the western shore of Alsten Island in the Inner Lead, some 20 miles from Mosjoen and 45 miles from Mo. The Germans occupied Mosjoen soon after he had gone. The army headquarters passed on this news to Lord Cork and suggested that a 'little warship should try to keep in touch with Gubbins'. As we have seen, Lord Cork had now but few ships at his command. The *Calcutta* and *Zulu* had sailed already for Hemnes, and must return to escort the *Penelope* as soon as they had finished their work there; other ships were about to sail for Mo with the Scots Guards; the French attack on Bjerkvik was making ready; and, apart from these things, the usual services in Vaags Fjord and Ofot Fjord had to go on. However, in the afternoon of the next day, the 11th, he recalled the *Jackal* and *Javelin*, which had arrived that morning with a convoy from home, and sailed again when they had oiled, having Admiralty orders to go home immediately. He told them to go on to Mo and 'report fully on situation ... from naval point of view'; to gain touch with Colonel Gubbins, who was last reported at Sandnesjoen, and help him to 'establish himself'.

Commander Napier, of the *Jackal*, knew no more than this signal told him, but he met the *Penelope*'s convoy and gained 'a little information' from the *Calcutta*. He went on at 25 knots to Mo, where he landed an officer, who learned, among other things, that Colonel Gubbins was still at Sandnesjoen, and wished Commander Napier to go to him, but first to bombard Sund near the town of Hemnes. This he did, each ship firing 30 rounds with no opposition, and he remarked in a signal to Lord Cork that 'this position is particularly open to naval attack'. On the way back down Ranen Fjord he met the *Enterprise*, with other ships, bringing the Scots Guards to Mo, so he went on board her to give what news he had. He arrived at Sandnesjoen at 0300, the

---

[1] The *Calcutta* had proceeded to sea the day before to reinforce the *Jackal* and *Javelin* which were escorting an east-bound convoy, and was some 50 miles W.N.W. of Skomvaer, when Lord Cork's signal (timed 1150/10) reached her at 1301. The *Zulu* was at Skjel Fjord. They effected a rendezvous off Myken Light about 1700 (the earliest the *Zulu* could get there), and shaped course for Mo, which had been indicated in a further signal from Lord Cork as the possible destination of the enemy.

12th, to find Colonel Gubbins with 450 men ready and waiting to go to Bodo. ' I was deeply impressed with the personality and leadership of the commanding officer ', he writes, ' and the quality of his officers and men. They had lost all their gear, were short of food and sleep, and had been hard at it fighting a delaying action against superior forces, unsupported, in a strange country, and subjected to the complete German air superiority. They were of a very fine type, and their cheerfulness and enthusiasm beyond praise '. The *Jackal* took the Colonel and 100 men accordingly ; the rest were already on board a local steamer which the *Javelin* escorted by another route ; both parties reached Bodo by midday. The *Jackal*, arriving first, spared the little column several thousands of small-arms cartridges and two months' allowance of provisions, and went out to meet the *Javelin ;* together they distracted the attention of some German aircraft, while the transport went safely in. Then they set course for Scapa, still dodging bombs for another hour or so. ' It appeared to me ', remarks Commander Napier, ' that an air position is rapidly developing in Northern Norway similar to that complete ascendancy established with such unfortunate results in Aandalsnes and Namsos areas '.[1]

52. Mo and Bodo reinforced [PLAN 12

In the meantime, three companies of the Scots Guards with four field and four light anti-aircraft guns had sailed on 11th May for Mo, if it should prove to be still in friendly hands, or for Bodo otherwise. The *Enterprise*, *Hesperus* and *Fleetwood* carried the troops between them, the stores going in the transport *Margot ;* and the *Cairo* was joined to the convoy at the request of Captain Annesley of the *Enterprise*, who asked also for protection by fighters from the *Ark Royal*. The ships reached Mo in the morning of the 12th, having fired on the wharf at Hemnes on their way. The troops were all on shore before 0800, but the Germans attacked from the air and hindered the unloading of the *Margot*, which took nine hours even with the help of a working party from the *Hesperus*. Two or three fighters patrolled overhead for some hours, as they had for a time during the convoy's passage the day before, but no more aircraft could be spared, for the *Ark Royal* had to provide patrols over the *Penelope* at the same time. The *Cairo* and *Fleetwood*, said Captain Annesley, were of the greatest value on the occasion, armed as they were entirely with high-angle guns, though the *Fleetwood* spent all her ammunition. Apparently the *Enterprise* sailed alone for Bodo in the afternoon, firing on Hemnes again as she went out, and ' was bombed continuously from Hemnes to open sea '. The *Cairo* brought away the rest of the convoy later ; they escaped further attention from the German bombers, being ' favoured by bad visibility and low clouds '.

Both the *Enterprise* and *Cairo* signalled to Lord Cork afterwards suggesting the use of small craft for supplying the troops in future, the *Cairo* adding : ' Passage through Ranen Fjord could not be made in clear weather by slow convoy without extreme probability of loss and damage due to large scale of attacks by dive and level bombers '. And Captain Annesley remarked on these points again after consulting with Colonel Gubbins and a Norwegian naval captain at Bodo : ' All emphatic that no large ships, with possible exception A.A. cruisers, should enter Ranen Fjord. . . . Supplies should be conveyed in puffers or small coasters, and troops in destroyers '. They also suggested destroyer patrols in the approaches to Ranen and Vefsen Fjords and motor boats for service inshore. The army asked that the *Cairo* should stay at Mo

---

[1] A signal from the army headquarters to the War Office says 500 to 1000 Germans with four guns and several tanks were reported advancing north of Mosjoen on the 13th.

until they could mount heavy anti-aircraft guns there, as ships had been stationed off Namsos and Aandalsnes in April, and that other ships should cruise near Hemnes to hamper the German advance and stop reinforcements from coming down Els Fjorden. Unluckily there were not ships for every service required or desirable.

On 13th May came the Foreign Legion's landing at Bjerkvik. Directly afterwards General Auchinleck took over from General Mackesy, and deciding to use all the British troops in the force to the southward, he put Brigadier Fraser in command of the whole, with orders ' to hold Bodo permanently and Mo for as long as he could '. The Norwegian Generals Ruge and Fleischer also stressed the importance of these places; indeed, they longed ' to pass from the defensive to the offensive and recapture Mosjoen '. Brigadier Fraser embarked in the *Somali* in the evening of the 13th, when she had finished her part in the Bjerkvik landing, and she sailed from Tjeldsundet with the French destroyer *Foudroyant* next morning. They were to visit Mo, that the Brigadier might see how the land lay before he set up his headquarters at Bodo; and whilst he was on shore at Mo, the ships were to harass the German communications on the Hemnes peninsula and in Els Fjorden. This they did in the evening of the 14th, the *Foudroyant* shelling Hemnes and sinking boats and seaplanes in the fjord, while the *Somali* fired on a party of the enemy near Finneid, where there was a British outpost. Early next morning, the 15th, on the way back to Bodo with the Brigadier, news came that the Polish transport, *Chrobry*, which was taking the Irish Guards and other troops to Bodo, had been bombed in Vest Fjord some 30 miles short of her destination. The *Somali* and *Foudroyant* steered towards her, but aircraft attacked them in their turn as they steamed through Traen Fjorden, south of Bodo, and a near miss damaged the *Somali* so much that Captain Nicholson decided to go straight home, escorted by the *Foudroyant*. As Brigadier Fraser had thus to go home, too, he signalled his impressions to General Auchinleck; he thought that ' to continue holding Mo is militarily unsound so long as German air superiority continues '.[1] On the other hand, Lord Cork told the Admiralty the same day, ' I feel we must hold on and fight at Mo; if that goes the whole Narvik situation becomes precarious '.

53. Loss of the *Chrobry* and *Effingham* [PLAN 12

The *Chrobry* had sailed from Tjeldsundet in the evening of 14th May, escorted by the *Wolverine* and *Stork*. She had on board her the 24th Brigade Headquarters, the Irish Guards, some anti-aircraft guns, and a troop of the 3rd Hussars, besides some sappers and a field ambulance. German aircraft attacked the ships before they left the anchorage without effect, but they saw no more of the enemy till a little before midnight, when dive bombers attacked the *Chrobry* three times in five minutes in the middle of Vest Fjord, setting her on fire, exploding ammunition, and killing several army officers and men. The *Wolverine* went alongside the blazing troopship and took on board nearly 700 men, while the *Stork* lay off to guard against further attack. Then the *Wolverine* made the best of her way to Harstad. Meanwhile, the *Stork* had driven off three more aircraft that threatened attack, and when her consort left her she turned to rescuing the rest of the troopship's passengers and crew, going afterwards to Harstad also; she did not wait to sink the troopship, for

---

[1] Brigadier Fraser later succeeded in transferring to the *Curlew* and returned to Harstad; but he was suffering from a wound previously received at Ankenes, and was invalided home by a Medical Board.

she had 300 passengers to think of, and aircraft were still about. In the end, aircraft from the *Ark Royal* sank the *Chrobry* on the 16th, the guns, the tanks, and the rest of the equipment going to the bottom in her.[1]

Early on the 17th the South Wales Borderers sailed for Bodo, a battalion of Poles having relieved them on the Ankenes peninsula. They sailed in the *Effingham* from Harstad, escorted by the *Coventry* (flag, Rear-Admiral Vivian), *Cairo* and two destroyers.[2] Instead of taking the short way through Tjeldsundet, they went outside the islands to lessen the risk of attack from the air. When approaching Bodo in the evening, however, they tried a short cut, this time to lessen the danger from submarines, and the *Effingham* and the *Matabele* ran on shore between Briksvaer and the Terra Islands. The destroyer escaped with slight damage, but the *Effingham* was lost. The other ships and some local vessels sent for from Bodo took off the troops and ship's company and part of the large consignment of stores the cruiser was carrying, including some of the machine-gun carriers; attempts to tow off the ship into deep water failed, so she was torpedoed where she lay.

In the end the Borderers and the Irish Guards went to Bodo by detachments in destroyers and local small craft ('puffers'), landing between 20th and 25th May. On the 21st Colonel Gubbins had been made a brigadier and appointed to command all the outlying troops—some 4000 men with four field pieces. He had small chance indeed against the growing strength of the German advance from the south. By the 23rd they, too, were believed to have 4000 men, but with ample artillery and tanks, in the Mo-Mosjoen area and, according to General Auchinleck, 'the operations . . . were marked throughout by an unrelenting pressure on the enemy's part, both on the ground and in the air, and by a steady resistance by our troops, handicapped as they were by an almost complete absence of any support in the air or any means of hitting back at their enemy'.

The whole business, whether of maintaining the force in action or of bringing it away, naturally depended very largely on the shipping available. Lord Cork's destroyers now numbered eight, besides which he had two sloops and some 30 trawlers. Most of the latter were anti-submarine craft or minesweepers; but a small trawler force under Acting-Commander W. R. Fell arrived from England at Skjel Fjord on 18th May for work in the Bodo area. These vessels proved quite unsuitable but Commander Fell organised a force of 10 puffers and took them south a few days later, where they became known as the Gubbins Flotilla. 'They performed remarkable work and were almost continuously in action for seven days'.[3]

By then the efforts in the Bodo area were nearing their conclusion, for on the 25th the Government decided to order the complete withdrawal of all forces from Norway. The evacuation of Bodo force will be dealt with in Chapter X.

---

[1] The signal 'Rupert' force to War Office, 1915/14th May, details the troops that were to have sailed in the *Chrobry*, but the field guns referred to in this signal were countermanded.

[2] *Matabele, Echo.*

[3] Lord Cork's despatch.

CHAPTER IX

THE EXPEDITION TO NARVIK: PHASE II
(7TH–28TH MAY)

54. Development of Base: Harstad Area [PLAN 14

While the operations described in the previous chapter were in progress to the southward and preparations were maturing for the direct assault on the port of Narvik, much attention was being paid to the development and defence of the base in the Harstad area.

The facilities at Harstad left much to be desired, and the unloading of transports was a continual difficulty. There were only two wharves and the average rate of discharge was two ships in five days. Disembarkation of personnel was usually done while the ships were in Bygden anchorage; destroyers and H.M.S. *Protector* did good service in connection with this work. Large numbers of local craft were hired for the various water transport services; but they were not very reliable, being prone to disappear into neighbouring fjords at the sound of an air raid warning and to remain there for a considerable time afterwards.[1] As there were over 140 raids on Harstad during the eight weeks of the operations, a good deal of time was lost by this practice.

The use of Harstad—itself on an island—as Military Headquarters and main point of disembarkation meant that the Navy had a very large area to protect against submarines and aircraft; at the same time offensive patrols to harass the enemy in the Narvik region had to be maintained. In addition Skjelfjord (some 90 miles distant) required protection so long as the *Penelope* and other damaged ships were there (till 10th May).

A preliminary request for guns for fixed defences and for harbour defence Asdics was sent on 22nd April and on the 28th the Admiralty informed Lord Cork that the M.N.B.D.O. would be sent to mount the guns and asked for site prospecting to be carried out. The next day Read-Admiral Lyster was appointed to command the defences and their development; he arrived by air on 5th May, and assumed the responsibility.

Meanwhile, the following proposals had been signalled to the Admiralty on the 1st:—

The main Naval Base to be in Tjeldsundet with a large ship anchorage to the west of Holsflva, other ships in Lavangsfjord and west of Skaanland: advanced anchorages at Bogen and Ballangen. A minefield extending $1\frac{1}{2}$ miles 310° from Baroen on Baroy Island. 6-in. battery south of Lodingen Church, 4·7-in. battery north of Kvitnes. 12-pdr. battery on west side of Tjelsundet 1 mile south of Staksvollholm. Further batteries considered desirable for south and north ends of Tjelsundet. Minefields N.E. and south of Steinvaer. Harbour defence Asdics off S.W. corner of Baroy Island and Botvaer Island, with control station off Lodingen. Port war signal station on Rotvaer Island. B.1 indicator net and gate west of Staksvollholm. Indicator net or mines at northern entrance to Tjelsundet from Taakeboen beacon to Hella.[2]

---
[1] Discontinuance of the warning system led to a strike among the Norwegian labourers and small craft crews.

[2] The finalised details of these proposals are given in Lord Cork's despatch.

These proposals never actually came to fruition. The *Mashobra* arrived with the Royal Marine Fortress unit under Lieutenant-Colonel H. R. Lambert, on 10th May; their work, both in mounting A.A. guns and preparing the surface defences, 'merited the highest praise'.[1] But by the time the evacuation was ordered, none of the coast defence guns had been mounted, though the sites had been prepared; mining had not got beyond the planning stage; and though progress had been made in laying the nets and booms they had not been completed.[2] The defence of the bases throughout the operations, therefore, really depended on surface patrols, which were established early and worked regularly, supplemented by A/S air patrols when the necessary Walrus aircraft were available.

Actually, after the sinking of *U.49* on 15th April, no contacts with enemy submarines occurred, though there were many reports of their being sighted. An Irish Guardsman fishing at Bogen landed a used escape apparatus belonging to *U.64*.

The possibility of enemy minelaying by aircraft always had to be envisaged, but this most awkward form of attack does not seem to have been resorted to until 29th May, when five enemy aircraft were seen laying mines in Tjeldsundet South Channel; subsequent sweeping operations exploded four mines, two by non-magnetic sweep and two by magnetic.

But defence against enemy bomber attack was the prime necessity. This started on the day the first convoy arrived and continued throughout the campaign, greatly increasing in frequency and intensity after the Allied withdrawal from the Trondheim area.

'Fighter aircraft of the Fleet Air Arm[3] and Royal Air Force, in those periods when they were available, wrought great havoc among the enemy and afforded a very welcome relief'[1]; but from the earliest days the establishment of airfields was a major preoccupation. The problem presented unusual difficulties, the land being covered by snow, three or more feet deep, but the work of clearing the Norwegian airfield at Bardufoss was put in hand, and a suitable ground was found at Skaanland in Lavangs Fjord, between Harstad and Tjelsundet. It was hoped to have these landing grounds in operation by 15th May, but the lateness of the thaw caused a 'depressing delay'[1] and it was not till 21st May that the first Gladiator Squadron landed at Bardufoss.

So for the greater part of the campaign, reliance had to be placed on A.A. artillery and H.M. ships with good A.A. armament. This need was emphasised in a telegram to the Admiralty on 25th April; the reply came on the 30th, that 48 3·7-in. H.A. guns and 48 Bofors (in addition to 12 already in the area) would be sent; two A.A. cruisers were to join Lord Cork's forces on completion of certain other operations. 'The next day, as if to emphasise the matter, the enemy obtained a direct hit on the building used for Naval accommodation in Harstad, fortunately killing only two ratings. At the same time they bombed the Hospital Ship *Atlantis*, anchored wide away from all other ships, and a Norwegian Hospital ship, causing many casualties in the latter'.[1]

The first 3·7-in. A.A. guns arrived on 6th May, and four of them were in action at Harstad on the 9th, four more being on their way to Bardufoss, which had already received Bofors guns on the 7th. 'Men bombed on shore could now begin to feel that they had some chance of hitting back; a psychological factor of considerable importance'.[1]

---

[1] Lord Cork's despatch.

[2] At the evacuation, all nets were sunk and all traces were removed.

[3] *See* Sec. 25 *ante*.

Sec. 54   THE EXPEDITION TO NARVIK: PHASE II (7TH–28TH MAY)

The allotment of the limited guns available was made on the principle that it was only possible to give a minimum degree of protection to really vital areas and that smaller and less important areas must go without.[1]

The final distribution of anti-aircraft artillery at the end of May was:—

Situation	Heavy Guns	Light Guns
Bardufoss	12	12
Sorreisa	—	2
Elvenes	—	4
Tromsö	4	4
Harstad	12	5
Skaanland	15	10
Ballangen	—	4
Ankenes	—	4
Bjerkvik	—	4
Bodo	—	2
Loaded for Bodo	4	4
In a 'Q' ship	—	1

55. The Landing at Bjerkvik 12/13th May   [PLAN 14

To return to the operations against Narvik itself, which had made little direct progress since the bombardment on 24th April.

The detached squadron, strengthened for a few days early in May by the *Resolution*, continued its activities in Ofot Fjord. It stopped traffic by water; it worked with the South Wales Borderers along the shore near Ankenes; it fired on parties of German troops and on piers and bridges, ammunition stores and gun positions; it tried, but unsuccessfully, to stop the enemy from moving men and stores by air; and in the intervals the destroyers searched outlying fjords for submarines and carried out regular anti-submarine patrols. The Germans retaliated chiefly from the air. They failed in an attempt upon the *Aurora* with the General on board her; but later on, when attacking 'on an average once daily', they sank the *Grom* (4th May), disabled a turret in the *Aurora* (7th), and damaged one or two other ships.[2] Later on, in the middle of May, Rear-Admiral Vivian relieved Captain Hamilton with the *Coventry*, and for a while the *Cairo*, but having other duties as well these ships spent less time in the fjord than had Captain Hamilton's cruisers.

The plan finally adopted for the assault on Narvik was to be carried out in two stages, firstly a landing at Bjerkvik at the head of Herjangs Fjord, with the object of securing Oydejord and obtaining control of Rombaks Fjord; and secondly, after these positions had been consolidated, a direct attack on Narvik from Oydejord across Rombaks Fjord.

The landing in Herjangs Fjord was planned to take place in the early hours of 13th May, served by the following ships: *Effingham*, *Resolution* and *Aurora*; *Somali*, *Havelock*, *Fame*, *Wren* and *Basilisk*; *Vindictive* and *Protector*—with

---

[1] On 20th May it was decided that the best disposition would be as follows, but for various reasons, this could not be adhered to:—

Situation	Heavy Guns	Light Guns
Bardufoss	8 (16)	12 (24)
Harstad and Skaanland	24 (48)	18 (36)
Bodo	8 (16)	12 (12)
Tromsö	8 (24)	16 (24)

The figures in brackets show the number of guns considered necessary to give really adequate protection in each area. (General Auchinleck's despatch.)

[2] *See* App. H.

two trawlers, four assault landing craft, and three motor landing craft. They were to assemble near Ballangen the day before to embark the Legion, and sail about 2100 to reach their destination 20 miles away by midnight. An advance guard of 120 men of the first battalion were to make the whole passage in the four assault landing craft under their own power; the rest of the 1500 infantry in the *Vindictive* and *Protector* and the two cruisers, from which they were to land in ships' boats and assault landing craft in turns; there were also five tanks, which took passage in the *Resolution*, and were to land in the motor landing craft.[1] The trawlers' task was to tow the motor landing craft to the fjord, and then to patrol against submarines outside. This left the destroyers, unhampered by other duties, to support the soldiers with their fire from positions within a few cables' lengths of the shore, while the big ships lay further out. Lastly, fighter protection for ships and troops, reconnaissance of the enemy's positions, and bombing attacks were to be supplied by aircraft from the *Ark Royal* which had been working off the coast since the 6th.

Three tanks were to land first, followed by the advance guard already in its landing craft, then the rest of the first battalion—' when ordered by the flagship '—in flights of 350 in men-of-war's boats or 120 in the assault landing craft; all to land on the beach, near Bjerkvik, at the top of the fjord. The second battalion was to go on shore in the same way later, headed by the other two tanks, but landing at Meby about a mile to the right of the first battalion. Lord Cork's original orders laid down that there should be no ' preliminary bombardment unless the enemy open fire on the force during the approach or is sighted by ships or aircraft '. For this, the *Resolution*, the cruisers, and all five destroyers had target areas allotted to them along the foreshore, the targets being chiefly machine-gun posts in houses, along the beach, and on the wooded hillsides beyond the villages; and the orders ran: ' Every effort should be made to locate targets in these areas, but fire is not to be withheld because targets have not been located, as the object is to produce the maximum volume of fire on possible enemy positions '. Lord Cork revised this plan later by ordering the leading destroyers, as soon as they should reach their stations off the pier, ' to open fire without further orders and destroy all houses in Bjerkvik, particularly those near the landing beach; if troops are seen leaving houses they are to be engaged in preference to the houses '. A naval officer was to go on shore with the second flight of infantry to control the fire of the ships in support of the troops as they moved inland.

The ships arrived punctually in their stations at midnight the 12th/13th. General Bethouart was in the *Effingham* with the Admiral, as was General Auchinleck, who had arrived from the United Kingdom the day before to succeed General Mackesy. The *Somali*, *Havelock* and *Fame* immediately opened fire on the village of Bjerkvik, while the *Resolution* hoisted out the tanks, and the *Effingham* and *Aurora* hauled up the boats they had already in tow. This preliminary bombardment lasted a quarter of an hour, setting houses ablaze and exploding stores of ammunition, but the Germans continued to reply with machine-guns, so the Admiral ordered a general bombardment that went on till 0100, the 13th. Then, in the growing light, the tanks went on shore, and the advance guard, and the second flight in its open boats, followed by the rest of the first battalion in due course. Most of the battalion had to edge away to the left and land near Haugen, a mile or so west of Bjerkvik; helped by the tanks, however, the legionaries soon fought their way back to the village and began their northward advance up the Elvenes road to join hands with the chasseurs.

---

[1] This was the first occasion on which tanks were landed in a combined operation.

The ships had shifted their fire inland, ' a creeping barrage ', the *Wren* called it, but at 0200 they left off, their work over until the time came to prepare the way for the second battalion. The enemy's fire obliged these latter troops, too, to seek a better landing place. With the ships firing overhead, they began to land about 0300, rather south of Meby ; they worked north-eastward to seize Elvegaarden, at the foot of the mountain Mebyfjieldet, and secured the coastwise road to Oydejord—their two tanks, says an officer of the Legion, ' frisking about like young puppies, firing all the time, in the midst of fields which were here free from snow '.

About 0600 General Bethouart reported to Lord Cork that he no longer required the support of H.M. Ships, beyond those normally on patrol in that area, and went on shore. Soon afterwards Lord Cork and General Auchinleck returned to Harstad in the *Effingham*, the other big ships departing as the last troops left them, while some of the destroyers stayed to support the attack. Later in the day the Polish battalion from Bogen arrived by land to join the Legion.

That afternoon (13th May), on arrival at Harstad, General Auckinleck assumed command of the military and air forces in accordance with his instructions from the War Office.[1]

Thus the attack succeeded, and with very little loss to the legionaries. It is hard to judge from the scanty reports how much the ships' guns contributed to this result. Captain Stevens of the *Havelock* remarked that ' enemy machine-gun posts were immediately, but only temporarily, silenced by a few rounds of 4·7-in. shell. These posts were well concealed and probably equipped with light automatic guns, which could be lowered and raised as easily as a rifle '. General Auchinleck called the bombardment heavy and the landing completely successful in spite of ' appreciable opposition ' from the German machine-guns. ' Although I was present in the capacity of a spectator only ,' he went on, ' I am constrained to express my admiration for the way in which the whole operation was conceived and effected by all concerned. I was particularly struck by the businesslike efficiency of the French Foreign Legion. . . . That the landing was not interfered with by enemy aircraft was almost certainly due to the fortunate weather conditions prevailing at the time. At this period there were no land-based aircraft available in Norway with which to counter enemy air attacks, and a bombing raid might well have turned the operation from a success into a failure '.

The weather also affected the *Ark Royal*'s aircraft. Patrols of three fighters at a time flew above the embarking troops near Ballangen in the evening of the 12th, but by 2200 the clouds were as low as 500 ft., so they had to give up. Nor could flying start again before 0200 on the 13th, which meant that the first fighter patrol for the landing arrived only when the second battalion was going on shore, and the bombers had not time to reach the positions near Lake Hartvig, 3 miles east of Bjerkvik, that Lord Cork wished them to attack during the landing—instead, rather later in the morning, they attacked the railway near Sildvik and Hunddalen, about 9 and 12 miles beyond Narvik respectively. Low clouds and fog made effective reconnaissance impossible. Several aircraft had to land in Vaags Fjord, prevented by thick fog from returning to their

---

[1] General Auchinleck was appointed G.O.C.-in-C. designate of the Anglo-French land forces and of the British Air Component in the theatre of operations. It was the intention of the C.I.G.S. that he should take over when the Government decided to end the system of unified command under Lord Cork, but that if, on arrival, local conditions appeared to necessitate the step, he was to assume the command, placing himself under Lord Cork.

ship, after carrying out their various tasks. On the other hand, no German aircraft appeared at all on either day; and after the landing Lord Cork made the following signal to Admiral Wells in the *Ark Royal*: ' Many thanks for your close support this morning. It was most comforting to see them '.[1]

The French soon occupied Oydejord, and went on to master the north shore of Rombaks Fjord, General Dietl withdrawing his troops to the mountains to the north and east. General Auchinleck points out that possession of this shore would give a larger choice of landing places, avoiding ' difficult beaches which were believed to be strongly defended by machine-guns '. It would allow of using the French field guns to support the landing, and it would make possible some degree of surprise, for the landing craft could assemble secretly under a mile from their destination instead of being ' marshalled in Ofot Fjord in daylight in full view of the enemy '. The ships stationed in Vest Fjord worked with the French troops to gain possession; and Commander Walter of the *Fame* took 150 chasseurs–alpins to Lilleberg, half-way to the narrows, and landed them in ' puffers ' in the little harbour on the 21st, the *Cairo* and the big French destroyer *Milan* coming inside the fjord in support; there the chasseurs joined forces with other French soldiers and pushed further eastward. On the other side of Narvik a Polish battalion relieved the South Wales Borderers on the Ankenes peninsula, that the Borderers might reinforce Bodo, while the Poles made ready to attack towards the head of Beisfjord.

56. Preparations for assault on Narvik

So far as the army was concerned, the assault on Narvik might have taken place a day or two after the little expedition to Lilleberg. But the danger from the air seemed to grow worse. In contrast with the lucky day of the landing at Bjerkvik, despite the gallant efforts of the *Ark Royal*'s few machines up to her leaving for home on 21st May, in the fortnight after Bjerkvik, the German aircraft destroyed or damaged above a dozen ships of war, transports and storeships, beginning with the troopship *Chrobry*, on the 14th, and ending with the *Curlew*, which they sank in Tjeldsundet on the 26th. Lord Cork and the generals therefore resolved they must have adequate protection for the assault: in the Admiral's words, ' either such weather conditions as were likely to largely reduce or abolish any danger of air attack or the ability to provide efficient fighter protection overhead '. The need of shore-based aircraft to counter enemy attacks appeared more urgent with each German raid, but the airfields at Bardufoss, and at Skaanland, for the Royal Air Force fighters that the *Glorious* and *Furious* were to bring from home, were not yet ready. The squadron from the latter ship landed at Bardufoss on the 21st, but Skaanland could not receive aircraft until the 26th. This determined the date of the assault; for besides the wish to have as many aircraft as possible for that occasion, the two remaining motor landing craft were busy up to the last moment transporting guns and stores of all kinds for the airfields.[2] The view

---

[1] The *Ark Royal* could not spare fighters before the evening of the 12th, though Lord Cork asked to have them in the forenoon, because they had been protecting the *Penelope*, which was going home in tow after her temporary repair in Skjel Fjord, and the *Enterprise* and her convoy of troops, who landed that day at Mo.

[2] The delay at Skaanland meant that the *Glorious* had to go home again to oil before landing her squadron of aircraft; and in the end Skaanland would not do, so all the machines worked from Bardufoss.

The *Cairo* records that she engaged enemy aircraft every day but two between 11th and 27th May, and in that period she expended 5,700 rounds of 4-in.

Sec. 56   THE EXPEDITION TO NARVIK: PHASE II (7TH–28TH MAY)

of the commanders appears in the following signal, which Lord Cork made on 20th May in answer to messages from home that 'expressed . . . increased disappointment at stagnation round Narvik and at delay in occupying town' and urged its immediate capture :—

> 'I fully understand that the occupation of the town of Narvik is desired, and am anxious to report its capture. The most important work at the moment, however, is the completion and protection of the aerodromes, and for these all motor landing craft are required. If we are to maintain our position here, it is of paramount importance that we can operate aircraft as quickly as possible and be able to counter German bombers; indeed, it might be described as a necessary preliminary to a combined operation on whatever scale . . .
>
> It would be folly under existing conditions, to switch off from the essential preparation of aerodromes to that of attacking Narvik, a place which does not affect the main issue and can be got on with at the end of this week. A delay there does not matter. A delay with aerodromes has become dangerous.'

Only a few days after this—the 24th—the Government decided to retreat from Norway altogether. They wished, however, to have the port of Narvik and the railway destroyed, and they thought the defeat of the German troops in the district would make easier the task of withdrawing. The commanders agreed, General Auchinleck remarking that, 'apart from the desirability of making sure whether the facilities for shipping ore from Narvik had, in fact, been destroyed as thoroughly as had been reported, the chances that a successful attack would do much to conceal our intention to evacuate . . . would outweigh the possible disadvantages involved in extending our commitments by establishing troops in close contact with the enemy on the Narvik peninsula, where his main force was thought to be located'.

Accordingly, they resolved to attack in the night of 27th–28th May, by which time the second squadron of fighters should be ready for service.

57. Plan of Operations [PLAN 14

'The plan is open to criticism in details—its great merit, however, was in that it was the plan of those who had to carry it out. The weak point in the plan was that owing to the paucity of transport available—a less bold man than General Bethouart might well have made this an excuse for inaction—it was necessary to leave the First Flight . . . unsupported for an unduly long time . . .'[1]

The two battalions of the Foreign Legion, the Narvik battalion of the Norwegian Army, and four tanks were to attack across Rombaks Fjord. They would land on the beach east of Orneset, at the mouth of the fjord, supported by the fire of the ships and of two batteries of French field pieces and one of Norwegian mountain guns posted on Hill 145 about a thousand yards inland from Oydejord. The first flight would come round from Lindstrand or Saegnes in Herjangs Fjord, in the three assault and two motor landing craft (the only vessels of these types remaining) and keep the shore close on board as long as possible to hide themselves, whereas later flights were to embark at Oydejord and thence cross direct. The first flight would thus number 290 men, which the generals thought dangerously weak, especially as these troops must fight alone for three-quarters of an hour before the next flight could join them; moreover, as the motor landing craft would then be wanted for the tanks, the next few flights of infantry would muster only 90, with perhaps a few more

---

[1] Lord Cork's despatch.

in fishing smacks. As it happened, all went well in that respect, but General Auchinleck wrote of 'the barest margin of safety' and commented on the landing as follows :—

> 'Had the enemy been able to launch an immediate counter-attack the result might have been disastrous. It must always, in my opinion, be unwise to embark on operations of this character unless landing craft are available to land a first flight of adequate strength and, in addition, provide an adequate floating reserve to meet unforeseen contingencies. Moreover, the absence of bomber aircraft deprived the attack of one of the most effective means of repulsing an enemy counter-attack . . . The broken and intricate nature of the ground prevented accurate observation by the supporting ships and artillery. The risk, however, was in my opinion worth taking, and as things turned out it was justified.'

Besides this main attack, the chasseurs from Lilleberg and farther east were to feint towards the head of Rombaken, the inner part of Rombaks Fjord; and the Poles, with two field guns and two tanks, were to attack Ankenes and march towards the head of Beisfjord to threaten the German line of retreat south-east of Narvik.

The soldiers had much less support from the sea than they might have had in April or for the attack projected early in May. Lord Cork had now no capital ship; and he had only one ship with 6-in. guns, the *Southampton* (Flag, Rear-Admiral Clarke), the *Enterprise* and *Aurora* having gone home. The table below gives the arrangements for the preliminary bombardment: each ship lay about 1000 yards off shore with a firing range of roughly 2000 yards, except that the *Southampton* was over 4000 yards from Fagernes.

Ship	Target
In Rombaks Fjord:	
Beagle	Stromnes railway station.
Fame	The mouths of two railway tunnels behind Forsneset.
Havelock	The mouth of a tunnel behind Djupviken.
Walker	The mouth of a tunnel behind the landing beach near Orneset.
In Ofot Fjord:	
Cairo (Flag)	The hill east of Vaasvik 'to destroy enemy positions there'.
Firedrake	Ditto. The hill east of Lillevik.
Coventry	The ridge north of Framnesodden.
Southampton	(1) Fagernes promontory 'to destroy enemy positions there and to prevent reinforcements proceeding from there to the Ankenes Peninsula'.
	(2) The village of Ankenes, east of the church—actually, she fired on the second target first.

The orders said 'there has been considerable enemy activity in the railway tunnels east of Narvik, but with what object is not known'; apparently the Germans were believed to use the tunnels as shelters for troops and guns. The bombardment was to start twenty minutes before the first flight of legionaries reached the shore. The ships inside Rombaks Fjord were to leave off as the first landing craft passed them. Signals from the flagship would govern the firing of the ships outside. After the landing, naval officers attached to the troops would signal the targets to be attacked by reference to a gridded map. Besides the eight bombarding ships, there was the *Stork* sloop to protect the landing craft from air attack.

58. The capture of Narvik, 28th May 1940 [PLAN 14

The ships arrived in their stations independently just after 2330, the 27th, with Generals Auchinleck and Bethouart on board the *Cairo* in which Lord Cork was wearing his flag. They immediately began engaging, as did the field guns above Oydejord. The bombardment, said General Auchinleck, ' was heavy and accurate, but close support of the attacking troops was hampered throughout by the broken nature of the terrain and the difficulty of accurate observation in the birch scrub which covered the lower slopes of the hills ' ; and Captain Stevens of the *Havelock* remarked—as he did after Bjerkvik— that ' while 4.7-in. fire immediately silenced enemy machine-guns, it did not apparently succeed in destroying them, ' though he quickly destroyed a German machine-gun and its crew with his own half-inch machine-gun at 1800 yards range. The first flight of legionaries landed punctually at midnight without loss, the opposition ' weaker than expected ' according to Lieutenant Francklin, who commanded the landing flotilla. The next party, however, was not ready at Oydejord when the landing craft came there ; German field guns and mortars opened a galling fire on the pier, while the party was embarking ; and the French sent round their later flights to embark at Saegnes in Herjangs Fjord, which ' slowed up the operation very considerably' and prevented the use of fishing smacks to supplement the landing craft, owing to the shallow water. None the less, the first battalion of the Legion and the Narvik battalion were both on shore by 0400, the 28th, or sooner, which was well within the time table. On the other hand, the first couple of tanks— apparently the only tanks put on shore that side—stuck in the soft mud and sand of their landing beach at Taraldsvik, and did no service.

It was as well that the landing so far had gone punctually, for German bombers appeared about 0500, apparently 30 or more, with the air to themselves. The Royal Air Force fighter patrols which had been arranged to protect the ships and troops became fog-bound at Bardufoss some twenty minutes before the Germans appeared over Narvik. For two hours the German aircraft attacked. They seem to have helped their comrades on the ground in a counterstroke that gave the Allies a hard fight to hold what they had won, and to have hindered the landing of the second battalion of legionaries. Although the aircraft actually hit the *Cairo* only[1] each ship had to manoeuvre to avoid bombs in a way that made it impossible to support the troops with gunfire. Luckily the ships had virtually finished their task, and General Bethouart wanted now but two destroyers, and was ready to go on shore himself. Lord Cork withdrew accordingly about 0630, leaving Admiral Vivian to attend on the soldiers with the *Coventry*, *Firedrake* and *Beagle*, to which were added the *Delight* and *Echo* in the afternoon.

According to one report the German counter-stroke came when they saw the ships retire. The Allies were then attacking Hill 457, a plateau south-east of the landing beach, and the Germans drove them back across the railway and up the hill by Orneset. They also brought machine-guns to bear on the beach, where part of the second battalion of the Legion was still coming on shore, so another landing place was found further to the westward. The first battalion renewed its attack, with the *Beagle* and the field guns at Oydejord supporting, and before long the legionaries and the Norwegians gained the plateau. Later on the second battalion seized the high ground north and west of Narvik.

---

[1] The *Cairo* was hit by two small bombs and lost 30 men, killed and wounded. The casualties to the landing forces from the bombing amounted to only one small landing craft loaded with ammunition.

German aircraft attacked the troops again in the evening, and nearly hit the *Coventry*; this time some British fighters came to the rescue, though with what effect the reports do not say.

By 2200 that night, the whole of Narvik peninsula west of a line from Fagernes to Forsneset had fallen to the Allies. To the south, the Poles had stiff fighting round Ankenes. They eventually established themselves on the side of a hill above that village, overlooking Narvik harbour. The *Southampton* had supported them in the morning, firing on Ankenes and Nyborg and across the harbour on Fagernes; for a time, too, the *Firedrake* engaged German machine-guns near the Ore Quay. Admiral Clarke remarked that ' in general, the shore signal station was not helpful in communicating clearly what was wanted, in fact, it did not appear always to know', and that none of the *Southampton*'s targets ' was really identified, although the result of the bombardment appeared to be what was wanted '—certainly the Poles seem to have been entirely satisfied.

In the two days following the capture of Narvik, the French continued their advance along both sides of Rombaks Fjord as far as the narrows by Stromsnes (where the *Eskimo* had been torpedoed on 13th April). General Fleischer's division lay north and east of the fjord in touch with the Chasseurs-Alpins, except that his Narvik battalion lay as garrison in its name town. The Poles reached the head of Beisfjord, and had three battalions in the district between Ankenes and the head of the fjord by the end of the month. All these troops were in touch with the enemy.

The German General Dietl was in fact in a critical situation, and had it been possible for the Allies to carry the operations to their logical conclusion, must soon have been faced with the alternatives of surrender or withdrawal across the Swedish frontier. Actually, provisional arrangements were made for the latter.

' Thus ended an operation ', wrote General Auchinleck, ' which, in my opinion reflects great credit on the judgment and pertinacity of General Bethouart and on the fighting qualities of his troops. Reconnaissance after the capture of the town revealed the full difficulties of landing on the beaches close to the town and the wisdom of the plan finally adopted. Though he knew of the decision to evacuate Norway before the operation started, General Bethouart persevered with his plan; and the vigour with which the advance eastwards was pressed after the capture of the town drove the enemy back on to his main position covering Sildvik and Hunddalen, thus making it difficult for him to attempt a counter-attack against Narvik at short notice; this enabled the subsequent evacuation to be carried out under more favourable conditions than at one time seemed likely '. But he said too :—

> 'The plans for the landing on the peninsula north of Narvik had continually to be changed and postponed, owing to the lack of proper landing craft, particularly of motor landing craft, which were required to land tanks. These motor landing craft were also in constant demand for the vital task of landing heavy anti-aircraft guns for the protection of the base area. The landing at Narvik was also successful thanks to the most effective co-operation of the Royal Navy, the excellent support given by the guns of H.M. ships, and the skill and determination of General Bethouart's troops; but with the facilities available the transfer of three battalions across a narrow fjord some 1500 yards wide took over seven hours, and the strength of the first flight had to be limited to 300 men. The landing of such a small advanced party on a hostile shore entailed considerable risk; and in view of the likelihood of such operations having to be repeated in other theatres of war, it is urgently necessary that an ample supply of modern landing craft should be provided without further delay. It is unfair to expect any troops to undertake such hazardous operations with such inadequate means.'

CHAPTER X

THE RETREAT FROM NORTHERN NORWAY

59. The Decision to Withdraw

The British and French Governments' decision to leave Norway altogether reached Lord Cork during the night of 24th/25th May in the following signal from the Chiefs of Staff (A.T. 2004/24) :—

> 'His Majesty's Government has decided your forces are to evacuate Northern Norway at earliest moment.
>
> Reason for this is that the troops, ships, guns and certain equipment are urgently required for defence of United Kingdom.
>
> We understand, from military point of view, operations evacuations will be facilitated if enemy forces are largely destroyed or captured. Moreover, destruction of railways and Narvik port facilities make its capture highly desirable. Nevertheless, speed of evacuation, once begun, should be of primary consideration in order to limit duration maximum naval efforts. Two officers will be sent at once from United Kingdom to concert evacuation plans with you and General Auchinleck. Evacuation of all equipment, vehicles and stores will clearly take too long: following are required to be evacuated in order of importance from point of view of defence of United Kingdom, (a) personnel, (b) light anti-aircraft guns and ammunition, (c) 25-pounders, (d) heavy anti-aircraft guns and ammunition. Tactical conditions must rule ; but, so far as they permit, plan should be framed accordingly.
>
> Norwegian Government have not yet been informed and greatest secrecy should be observed.'

The following morning Lord Cork discussed the matter with General Auchinleck ; both were agreed that the safety of the force made secrecy vital and that the information should only be imparted to those Senior Officers it was imperative should know it. Next day (26th) General Bethouart was informed. He received the news with ' characteristic calm, though one point upon which he was insistent was that for reasons of national honour he could not abandon the Norwegian Army he had been working with, in the lurch on the field of battle. The whole question was discussed and it was agreed that pressure on the enemy must be kept up until the last, that the attack on Narvik . . . must go on, and that this operation would of itself be the best possible way of concealing our intentions from the enemy '.[1]

There remained the difficult question of breaking the news to the Norwegians. Clearly, it was only fair that this should be done as soon as possible. After communication with the Foreign Office, the decision was taken on 1st June that Sir Cecil Dormer (H.B.M. Minister to Norway) should inform the King of Norway in the morning of 2nd June and that the Norwegian Cabinet and the Commander-in-Chief, General Ruge, should be informed later that day. Vice-Admiral Cunningham, who had been operating in the Tromsö area since 10th May, was also told and directed to arrange for the passage of the King and Government.

' Naturally, at first, there was a feeling of soreness and disillusionment among the Norwegians on learning of the evacuation, but on the whole the decision was received as being inevitable under the circumstances and every help was

---
[1] Lord Cork's despatch.

given to facilitate the withdrawal'. Cordial letters were exchanged between Lord Cork and the Norwegian Admiral Diesen, who undertook to send all effective Norwegian ships, including submarines, to the Shetlands and to destroy the rest.

As a first step, it was decided to evacuate the troops from the Bodo area. Brigadier Gubbins had already reported that he must retire not later than 1st June unless reinforcements could be sent to him and this was under consideration, but the idea was necessarily abandoned in view of the new policy, and orders for withdrawal were accordingly issued.

60. Withdrawal from Mo and Bodo [PLAN 12

The situation in the Bodo area when the decision was taken to withdraw was as follows.

The Scots Guards had been falling back from Mo since 18th May; a week later they reached Rognan, at the head of Saltdals Fjord, some 40 miles by water to the eastward of Bodo and 12 miles south of the main position near Fauske, where the Irish Guards and the five independent companies lay. The Brigadier's plan was to bring back the Scots Guards from Rognan to Hopen, about 10 miles east of Bodo, when the troops near Fauske were to retreat through them and embark; the Scots Guards were to retreat in turn through the South Wales Borderers, posted nearer in, and the whole force was to leave Bodo in destroyers in three flights between 29th May and 1st June.

Commander Fell's flotilla of puffers had reached the area on 24th May, and it was on these craft that the programme principally fell in the first place. His first task was to ferry troops to Bodo on the 25th. Thenceforward the flotilla worked unceasingly in the service of the troops between Rognan and Bodo until the last straggler had embarked on 1st June. The ships and their native crews might change—they were not fighting units and 'most of the Norwegian crews took flight or sabotaged their engines, if left for a moment unguarded' under fire—but the work went on with new puffers and new crews.

On 29th May, the day the retreat from Bodo began, the Admiralty had signalled to Lord Cork that 'aircraft carriers and four fast liners will arrive Bodo area on 2nd June for evacuation of garrison' and 'it appears undesirable to attempt embarking Bodo garrison without fighter protection from carriers'. It was, however, decided not to wait and to carry on with the evacuation by destroyers as planned, though less than half a dozen aircraft could be spared from the two British squadrons at Bardufoss and the airfield at Bodo only became operational on 26th May. Nor were there any anti-aircraft guns worth mentioning.

During the last few days before the embarkation German bombers raided Bodo and attacked the troops several times, but the enemy's main concern was with attacks on the base at Harstad and the shipping in the fjords to the northward. On 26th and 27th May the few Royal Air Force fighters shot down three or four Germans, a number almost equal to their own strength. On the 28th the enemy arrived in force and destroyed the town and damaged the airfield. Fortunately they missed the quay from which the embarkation was to take place and they did not appear while the troops were actually going on board; the evacuation was successfully completed on 29th, 30th and 31st May, 1000 men being taken direct to the United Kingdom in the *Vindictive* and the remainder to Harstad in destroyers[1] and small craft. A considerable amount of equipment was brought away, but four 25-pdr. guns, four Bofors, and three Bren carriers which had been salved from the *Effingham*, together with such material as could not be moved by the men had to be abandoned.

Mention should be made of the useful work of s.s. *Ranen*, a small Norwegian passenger steamer which had been taken up and armed with one Bofors, one Oerlikon and numerous machine guns as a decoy ship. Commanded by Commander Sir Geoffrey Congreve and manned by a mixed party of naval ratings, Irish Guardsmen and Borderers, she harried the enemy in their advance up the coast from Bodo. She also added to General Dietl's perplexities by cutting the telephone cables by which the Germans communicated their progress northwards.

61. Plan of general withdrawal

Meanwhile, plans had been got out for the general withdrawal.

By this time Germany had all Holland and nearly all Belgium in her power; her advancing armies, well inside France, seriously threatened the Channel ports. The evacuation of the British Army from Dunkirk was in full swing[2] and the Admiralty had warned Sir Charles Forbes that the risk of invasion by airborne and seaborne troops, perhaps assisted by 'the Fifth Column', was thought to be 'very real'. In these circumstances, plans for retreat—which followed hard upon the heels of the final plans for taking Narvik—must rely as little as possible on outside help, whether for ferrying the troops and stores to the transports or for protection during the passage home. As Admiral Forbes put it : 'The naval effort during evacuation will of necessity be large and prolonged, unless a disaster is courted, and will take place at a time when our naval effort might well be required in the North Sea, 1000 miles away'.

Lord Cork's plan had three phases. Under the first he sent home certain stores, including some French tanks and guns, before the end of May in ships he had already in Norway, escorted by some of his own trawlers. For the main embarkation, to be carried out in the two later phases, he needed ships to take the rest of the stores and some 24,500 troops—all the expeditionary force except the 1000 men that went direct from Bodo. These transports were to arrive in two groups during the first week in June.

As for ships of war, the Admiral expected to have one large cruiser, three anti-aircraft cruisers and about 10 destroyers of his own ; he asked for five more destroyers to maintain his patrols, whilst the bulk of the flotilla ferried troops to the transports at rendezvous in the outer fjords or at sea, but the Admiralty could spare him only three. As things turned out, the *Curlew* was sunk before the end of May, and the *Cairo* and a destroyer had to go home disabled, all the result of attacks from the air ; thus the actual strength was considerably less than Lord Cork had counted on.[3]

---

[1] *Firedrake, Vanoc, Arrow, Havelock, Echo.*
General Auchinleck in his despatch remarked :—
    'The swiftness and efficiency with which the evacuation was carried out reflects great credit on Brigadier Gubbins and his staff. The destroyers of the Royal Navy were very well handled and carried out the programme laid down to the minute.'

[2] The evacuation from Dunkirk started on the 26th May and ended on the 4th June.

[3] *See* Appendix C (3).

On the other hand, the expedition was to have invaluable protection in the air up to the last moment of embarking, and indeed during the passage home, for Vice-Admiral Wells arrived off the coast with the *Ark Royal* and *Glorious* in the evening of 2nd June. The *Ark Royal* had fighters to patrol above the embarking troops and bombers to attack the German troops and communications —for instance, the airfield at Bodo and troops at Fauske, both places so lately in British hands, besides their old targets of a few weeks before, the railway at Hunddalen and Sildvik. When the last troops sailed she went most of the way home with them, and her aircraft patrolled round the convoy. The *Glorious* had come to carry home the Royal Air Force fighters from Bardufoss. That the cloudy weather of their last few days in Norway favoured the departing troops does not lessen the credit due to the Royal Air Force, who in General Auchinleck's words had inspired their opponents with a 'genuine fear' of their prowess, and who shared in the work of protecting the troops until a few hours before the rearguard left the shore.

The following arrangements were made to protect the expedition during its passage home. All the ships of the Narvik squadron were needed for embarking troops or giving local protection to the end, so Lord Cork originally intended to keep the first group at one of his distant rendezvous until the last soldiers had embarked, when four destroyers would go ahead to join it, while the rest of the squadron escorted the other troopships and the main storeship convoy. But the Commander-in-Chief, Home Fleet, asked the Admiralty on 30th May to keep him posted with the situation, 'particularly as regards' the sailing of the two groups of troopships, 'and also whether battlecruiser may be required to provide cover'. Although Lord Cork does not seem to have intercepted this signal, he answered it in effect next day, when he told Admiral Forbes his arrangements, and said 'much appreciate if some covering protection could be given'. Then, the Admiralty having desired that the troops should return as soon as possible to fit in with other movements they had to provide for, Lord Cork further informed him that the first group would leave the rendezvous on the 7th in charge of the *Vindictive*, but without other escort; and he asked, 'Could covering force be provided, and convoy met, where you consider necessary—all destroyers in area required for rapid embarkation last flight'. Sir Charles replied that 'cover and anti-submarine escort will be sent to meet Group One', adding later that the *Valiant* (Captain Rawlings) would sail from Scapa on the 6th to accompany this first group as far south as 61° N., and then go north again to meet the second group in its turn, also that destroyers would join the first group and stay with it to the Clyde.

Admiral Forbes had meant originally to send the *Renown* and *Repulse*, but on the 5th 'two unknown vessels', possibly raiders, were sighted about 200 miles north-east of the Faeroes steering towards the Iceland–Faeroes passage, and Vice-Admiral Whitworth with the two battlecruisers, the *Newcastle*, *Sussex* and five destroyers[1] was sent to intercept them. Two days later, Admiral Whitworth's force proceeded to the coast of Iceland, on a report of an enemy landing there; but on the 8th the Admiralty ordered the *Renown* and two destroyers back to Scapa, as it was considered 'there should not be less than two capital ships available to proceed south in case of invasion'.

Thus it came about in the event that during the evacuation the Home Fleet heavy forces were considerably dispersed.

---

[1] *Zulu, Kelvin, Maori, Forester, Foxhound.*

62. The withdrawal [PLAN 15

The transports for the two later phases of the withdrawal went out singly or in small groups, some with escorts for the whole or part of the way, some with none. Most of the storeships went to Harstad to load, and sailed again in the evening of 7th June as an independent group—the slow convoy—with an escort of its own that joined it next day when the last troops had sailed ; but a few storeships loaded at Tromsö, whence they sailed also on 7th June, meeting an escort of trawlers later. The fifteen troopships, two of which were not used, went first to one or other of two distant rendezvous appointed by Lord Cork about 180 miles from the coast,[1] where the two main groups were to assemble before closing the coast to receive troops, and where individual ships were to wait after loading or between partial loadings until their group was ready to go home. Rear-Admiral Vivian in the *Coventry*, in general charge of the embarking, met the main groups at sea as they approached the coast to give them their instructions and to protect them from air attack while near the shore, and three or four of the hard-worked destroyers gave them anti-submarine protection in the intervals between turns of ferrying. Three of the troopships were small cross-channel steamers, two of which shipped men and stores at Harstad ; the others got their passengers from destroyers in outlying fjords or at rendezvous some 40 miles out at sea. The soldiers left the shore at night, when experience taught that German aircraft gave least trouble, though it was daylight all round the clock. They embarked from places in Ofot Fjord and Tjeldsundet, from Harstad and the little fjords or sounds north of it, sometimes from puffers into destroyers, sometimes direct into destroyers, which carried them to the troopships, and all the time the airmen of both Services watched over them, and destroyers and the *Stork* and trawlers patrolled against possible submarines. The first main group of troopships, six large merchantmen and the *Vindictive*, took nearly 15,000 men in three early morning loadings between 4th and 6th June. The second group, four large and three small merchantmen, took a little under 10,000 men on 7th and 8th June.

Moreover, 'a great deal more stores and equipment was loaded' than the General had hoped, though most of the anti-aircraft guns and many wagons were abandoned.

All the troops had left the shore by the early morning of the 8th without hindrance from the enemy. General Auchinleck had been anxious lest German troops advancing from the Bodo district should embarrass the departure of the troops round Narvik, who were in touch with the enemy to the last. But General Bethouart skilfully withdrew his rearguard, a battalion each of Poles and the Foreign Legion ; and the nearest the Germans got to interfering was the landing of a few men by parachute near Ballangen in the afternoon of the 7th, as reported by the *Stork*. When in due course they re-occupied Narvik, they found it in a sorry state. Ore quays and electric power had been totally destroyed and the railway line for 2 miles east of Narvik partially destroyed. It was estimated that the ore quays and electrical supply would take nine months to repair ; and this, combined with clearing the harbour, in which some 20 ships had been sunk, would preclude the export of ore in appreciable quantities for about a year.[2]

During the last few days before the retirement, steps were taken to deny to the enemy anything of value that could not be taken away in the area held

---

[1] Rendezvous A. Lat. 70° 30′ N., Long. 7° 20′ E.
    Rendezvous B. Lat. 69° 30′ N., Long. 6° 40′ E.

[2] Actually the first iron ore steamer sailed from Narvik on the 8th January, 1941.

by the Allies. The M.N.B. ship *Mashobra* which had been bombed on the 25th May and beached was blown up; the 7,000-ton oiler, *Oleander*, severely damaged by a near miss on the 26th, was sunk; disabled trawlers were destroyed; harbour defence booms and nets were sunk and all traces removed. An attempt was made to tow away the A.L.C.s, but finally they and the M.L.C.s were scuttled.

Nor was the destruction confined to what the Allies had brought with them. For example, Sir Geoffrey Congreve in the *Ranen*, with the trawler *Northern Gem*, destroyed the oil tanks at Solfolla '[1] (on the north shore of Vest Fjord) in the night of the 7th June. ' This successful exploit ended with a most spirited engagement, on his part, with the enemy '.[2] The bombing attack by the Walrus aircraft on the installations at Solfolla has already been mentioned (*see* Sec. 25 *ante*).

The last men to be embarked in the transports were the ground staff of Bardufoss airfield. The Gladiators had been flown on board the *Glorious*, but it was feared that the eight Hurricanes that remained efficient would have to be abandoned. The Royal Air Force had orders to keep in action to the last, and then destroy their aircraft, should the enemy air activity necessitate it; but the cloudy weather and their own quality enabled them to take their aircraft away in the *Glorious*. ' The courageous action of the pilots in volunteering to fly their machines on to the flying deck of *Glorious* and of Group Captain Moore in allowing it to be done resulted in all eight being got safely away—an achievement which deserved a better fate than that which befell the gallant men who had carried it out successfully.'[3]

The organisation of the convoys carrying the expedition to the United Kingdom was as follows :—

GROUP I
escorted by the *Vindictive*

Monarch of Bermuda	*Franconia*
Batory	*Lancastria*
Sobieski	*Georgic*

GROUP 2
escorted by *Coventry, Southampton, Havelock, Fame, Firedrake, Beagle, Delight*

Oronsay	*Ulster Prince*
Ormonde	*Ulster Monarch*
Arandora Star	*Duchess of York*
Royal Ulsterman	*Vandyck*[4]

SLOW CONVOY
STORESHIPS FROM HARSTAD
escorted by *Stork, Arrow,* 10 trawlers

Blackheath	*Theseus*
Oligarch	*Acrity*
Harmattan	*Coxwold*
Cromarty Firth	*Couch*

---

[1] Lat. 68° 40' N., Long. 14° 34' E.
[2] Lord Cork's despatch.
[3] Lord Cork's despatch.
All these pilots were lost in the *Glorious* on the way home.
[4] The *Vandyck* failed to make the rendezvous and was subsequently sunk off Andsnes by German aircraft.

Sec. 62   THE RETREAT FROM NORTHERN NORWAY

STORESHIPS FROM TROMSÖ

escorted by 4 trawlers

Oil Pioneer	*Arbroath* (A.S.I.S.)
Yermont	*Nyakoa* (A.S.I.S.)

some Norwegian vessels.

Under the arrangements come to with the Commander-in-Chief, Home Fleet (*see* Sec. 61), the first group set out from the distant rendezvous early on 7th June and duly met the *Valiant* and her screen of four destroyers[1] about 0100, 8th, in 65° 30′ N., 1° 50′ W., roughly half-way between the rendezvous and 61° N., where the *Valiant* was to part company. The five destroyers[2] for the troopships were late, but in spite of thick fog off the Faeroes they joined the convoy at about 2300 that night in roughly 61° N., 6° W.; then the *Valiant* and her screen turned north again, while the convoy stood on for the Clyde. The troopships' passage was uneventful except for an attack on the 8th by a single aircraft, which the *Vindictive* drove away by her fire.

The store convoys sailed from Harstad and Tromsö on the 7th, and that evening Vice-Admiral Cunningham embarked H.M. the King of Norway, the Crown Prince and various notables[3] in the *Devonshire* at Tromsö, sailing at 2030 independently for the Clyde.

The last group of transports had cleared And Fjord by 2300, 8th June, and left its distant rendezvous in the morning of the 9th, escorted by the *Southampton*, *Coventry* and five destroyers. Rear-Admiral Vivian was placed in charge of the convoy and Lord Cork, who was accompanied by Generals Auchinleck and Bethouart, wore his flag in the *Southampton*. The *Glorious* had been detached at 0300, 8th, owing to shortage of fuel, and ordered to proceed home independently with the *Acasta* and *Ardent* as screen; but the *Ark Royal*, with her screen of three destroyers,[4] accompanied the convoy, some of her aircraft searching for enemy surface craft in the most probable direction of their approach and others providing overhead cover against air attack.

At midnight, 9th/10th June, being clear of Norwegian waters, the operations came under the command of the Commander-in-Chief, Home Fleet, and Lord Cork accordingly hauled down his flag, having directed that the *Southampton* was to remain with the convoy for the passage.

But before this, misfortune had overtaken the expedition. Since the middle of April, both men-of-war and transports had crossed and re-crossed the North Sea, in ones or twos or in weakly protected convoys, with never a sign that German surface craft might interrupt their passage. On 8th June, however, they suddenly appeared in force off Northern Norway, where they caught and sank six ships going home independently of the convoys.

---

[1] *Tartar, Mashona, Bedouin, Ashanti.*

[2] *Atherstone, Wolverine, Witherington, Antelope, Viscount.*

[3] The party included H.M. the King of Norway, the Crown Prince and their attendants; H.B.M. Minister, the French and Polish Ministers, and members of the *Corps diplomatique*; the Norwegian Prime Minister, 10 ministers, staffs and families; certain members of the Norwegian Air Force; political refugees; 33 British officers and 306 other ranks—a total of 435 men and 26 women.

[4] *Diana, Acheron, Highlander.*

63. The German Naval Sortie (Operation Juno) [PLAN 15

The presence of the German ships off Northern Norway was entirely fortuitous so far as the British evacuation was concerned. Of this, the secret had been well kept; the Allied Commanders had disguised the movements of troops and shipping with 'conflicting rumours and bogus instructions' and the Germans were quite unaware of what was in hand.

The object of their operation, known as Operation Juno, was to relieve the German land forces in Narvik by attacking enemy transports and warships in the Narvik–Harstad area, and for this purpose a force consisting of the *Scharnhorst* and *Gneisenau*, the *Hipper* and four destroyers, the *Galster, Lody, Steinbrink* and *Schoemann* under Admiral Marschall, had left Kiel at 0700, 4th June, with orders to carry out a surprise attack on And and Vaags Fjords, the destruction of enemy warships, transports and installations found there being the object: if, however, later reports showed that an attack on Ofot Fjord and Narvik itself would be profitable, this would then become the principal task.

At 2000, 6th June, the force was in 68° N., 2° 30′ W., and during the night the *Hipper* and destroyers completed with oil from the store ship *Dittmarschen*, which had previously been ordered to a waiting position in this neighbourhood.

It was not until the 7th June that the first report of an Allied convoy being at sea off the coast of Norway reached the German ships. This placed four large and three small ships in 67° 57′ N., 3° 50′ E., steering southerly at 0700, 7th, that is some 150 miles south east of the Germans.

Admiral Marschall took no notice of this report, as he supposed them to be empty transports returning to the United Kingdom; but later that day, at 1955, came a report of an Allied convoy on a westerly course just off the entrance to And Fjord at 1325 and two aircraft carriers about 45 miles north of Andenes at 1400; and then, suspecting that a general withdrawal from Norway was in progress,[1] he decided to postpone the attack on Harstad, which he had planned for the night of the 8th/9th,[2] and steered to intercept these ships instead, informing the Admiral, Group West, at 0300, 8th June, of his intention. This change of plan was not approved by Group Command, West, and a signal in reply was sent at 0430 pointing out that the main objective remained the 'destruction of enemy naval forces in the area Harstad–Narvik'.

An hour later Admiral Marschall fell in with his first victims. These were the 5000-ton tanker *Oil Pioneer* from Tromsö, with her escorting trawler, the *Juniper*, which the German ships sighted at 0531/8th, and sank an hour and a half later in 67° 26·5′ N., 4° 23′ E., picking up 25 survivors from the tanker, and four from her escort.

The *Scharnhorst* and *Hipper* then each flew off an aircraft to search for further prey. These soon reported a 12,000-ton merchant ship and a hospital ship to the north, and a cruiser and a merchant ship to the south. The *Hipper* was ordered to deal with the former, which proved to be the 20,000-ton troopship *Orama* and the hospital ship *Atlantis*, which had left the Norwegian coast the day before, the troopship being sent home alone and empty[3] because she had arrived without sufficient oil or water to wait for the rest of her group. The *Hipper* sank the *Orama* at 1106 in 68° 2′ N., 3° 36′ E., picking up a total

---

[1] Admiral Marschall's War Diary.
[2] Log of *Scharnhorst*, 6th June, 1940.
[3] About 100 German prisoners were embarked in her.

of 275 survivors. The Germans were successful in jamming the S.O.S. signals of all these three ships; as the *Atlantis* observed strictly the provisions of the Geneva Convention and did not use her wireless, they respected her privilege of immunity from attack and let her go unmolested.

The *Scharnhorst* and *Gneisenau* meanwhile, after vainly searching for the ships reported to the south, had turned to a northerly course and the whole force proceeded in company till 1400, when the *Hipper* with the destroyers was detached and ordered to Trondheim[1] while Admiral Marschall, who still had no reconnaissance reports of Harstad and was convinced that Vaags Fjord no longer offered a worth while objective, continued to the north with the battlecruisers, in the somewhat vague hope of falling in with the aircraft carriers which had been located in the Andenes area several times during the last few days. His luck was in and he had not long to wait. At 1545 a masthead was sighted to the eastward; course was altered to close and in a few minutes it was identified as a large aircraft carrier, with destroyer escort.

64. The sinking of the *Glorious*, *Ardent* and *Acasta* [PLAN 15

This proved to be the *Glorious*, which, after being detached at 0300 that morning, had proceeded on a course 250° at 17 knots. The wind was N.W., 2–3, and a north westerly swell was running; visibility was extreme. No reconnaissance aircraft were up, and none had been since parting from the *Ark Royal*, for the whole previous day and night had been spent piloting the R.A.F. Hurricanes on board.[2] It was shortly after 1600 that the Germans were sighted to the northwestward; the *Ardent* was ordered to investigate, while the *Glorious* turned to the southward, bringing the enemy on to her starboard quarter steering south-east, and orders were given to range the Swordfish; but it was too late, and none of them got away.

At 1631 the *Scharnhorst* opened fire at a range of 27,800 yards, soon followed by the *Gneisenau*; the *Ardent* made for the enemy at high speed, and both destroyers started laying a smoke screen, which was very effective and caused the guns of both battlecruisers to cease fire for some time. Shortly after the action commenced, however, the *Glorious* had received a hit in the forward upper hangar which started a fire; this was got under control, but it destroyed the Hurricanes, and prevented any torpedoes being got out. The fire curtains had to be lowered. A salvo hit the bridge about 1700, and a heavy shell struck her aft about 1715. The Commander was then apparently in charge of the ship. The *Glorious* was of course completely outranged and her 4·7-in. guns could do little against the enemy. One main wireless aerial was shot away at an early stage of the action.

The order to abandon ship was given about 1720, and some 20 minutes later, listing heavily to starboard, she sank. The *Ardent* after firing two four-tube salvoes at the enemy, had been sunk about 1728, leaving the *Acasta*, faced by overwhelming odds, to fight gallantly to the last. With her guns still firing she steered to the south-east, temporarily concealed by smoke. There seemed a chance of escape, but this was not Commander Glasfurd's idea. He passed a message to all positions ' you may think we are running away from the enemy; we are not, our chummy ship (*Ardent*) has sunk, the *Glorious*

---

[1] Admiral Marschall considered that these ships would have no further opportunity of oiling at sea, once the British heard of the sinkings. They were therefore to complete with fuel at Trondheim and then give protection to the German convoys between there and Bodo.

[2] One T.S.R. aircraft and one section of Gladiators were being kept at 10 minutes' notice.

is sinking, the least we can do is to make a show '—and altering course through the smoke screen towards the enemy, he fired a four-tube salvo, of which one torpedo hit the *Scharnhorst* abreast the after 11-in. turret. A final salvo hit the *Acasta* at 1808, and the order was given to abandon ship; her heroic Commander was last seen taking a cigarette from his case and lighting it, as he lent over the bridge waving encouragement to his men.[1] Then she sank. But her single torpedo had a big result; the *Scharnhorst* was severely damaged and her speed reduced; Admiral Marschall abandoned his cruise and with both battlecruisers steered for Trondheim, where they arrived at 1430, 9th June. To this alone the Earl of Cork's troop convoy to the northward owed its safety.

The sinking of the *Glorious* and the two destroyers was attended by heavy loss of life, the naval losses amounting to 1474,[2] and the R.A.F. to 41—a total of 1515. A large number of men got on to Carley floats, but it had not been possible to provide provisions and water in all of them, owing to fire damage. It was very cold (temperature 46°); there was a sea running, which capsized the *Acasta*'s boats, and within a few hours men were collapsing from exhaustion. On one float, which started with 22 officers and men, the number was reduced to four by next morning. Poignancy is added to the story by the fact that survivors sighted a British cruiser some 5 miles to the north-west on the 9th and later in the day two aircraft from the *Ark Royal*, in the course of a search for the enemy, passed close over the rafts but did not see them; had they done so, many might even then have been saved.

It was not until 0030, 11th June—some 54 hours after the ships sank, that 38 (three officers, 35 ratings) from the *Glorious*, and one rating from the *Acasta* were picked up by the small Norwegian vessel *Borgund* and landed in the Faeroes. Another Norwegian fishing vessel, the *Svalbard II*, rescued five men from the *Glorious*, who, with two survivors from the *Ardent*, picked up by a German seaplane, were made prisoners-of-war. Among the hundreds lost were nearly all those airmen who had performed the supremely difficult task of flying their land machines on board the *Glorious*. And in addition was the loss of one of our few aircraft carriers, whose services in this Norwegian campaign had enhanced their value—a most serious blow.

65. British reactions, 9th June 1940 [PLANS 15, 16]

The first news to reach the British that German ships were at sea came from the *Atlantis*, which met the *Valiant* about 0900, the 9th, just 24 hours after the *Orama* was sunk. Once again[3] the German battlecruisers had traversed the North Sea undetected by British air reconnaissance.[4]

---

[1] The details of the *Acasta*'s fight are taken from an account written by her sole survivor, Able Seaman C. Carter.

[2]

	Officers	Ratings	Total
Glorious ..	76	1086	1162
Acasta ..	8	152	160
Ardent ..	10	142	152
	94	1380	1474

[3] *See* Sec. 15 (*ante*).

[4] The inadequacy of British air reconnaissance caused grave concern to the Commander-in-Chief, Home Fleet, who on 15th June called the attention of the Admiralty to it, and made various suggestions for its improvement. (Commander-in-Chief, Home Fleet, 1541/15 June.) He also pressed for the reintroduction of a daily intelligence signal, giving disposition of enemy main units, which since 21st May 1940 had been discontinued.

The *Valiant* was on her way back to join Admiral Vivian's convoy. She broadcast the hospital ship's account of a battleship and two destroyers attacking a two-funnelled transport (the *Orama*), and increased speed towards the troopships, then some 400 miles to the northward, and about 100 miles from where the *Atlantis* had seen the enemy. The *Valiant*'s signal brought one from Admiral Cunningham, in the *Devonshire* with the King of Norway on board. The *Devonshire* must have been 100 miles or so westward of the *Glorious*, when that ship sighted the enemy and turned away to the south-eastward. She, and she only, had received an enemy report the *Glorious* made to Admiral Wells. It was 'a barely readable signal'; for technical reasons it was 'probably corrupt and referred to some other matter'; and Admiral Cunningham decided not to break wireless silence, for 'to do so would have involved serious risk of revealing *Devonshire*'s position at a time when air attack was likely, which in the circumstances was in the highest degree undesirable'. Next day, however, when German shadowing aircraft had sighted the *Devonshire*, and the *Valiant*'s signal ' indicated the possible vital importance of this message', the Admiral made his 1031/9, which ran: '*Valiant*'s 0901/9, following was read, reception very doubtful on 3700 kc/s, at 1720/8. Begins—Vice-Admiral (A) from *Glorious* : my 1615, two P.B. Time of origin, 1640—ends. *Glorious*'s 1615 not received'. Not until the afternoon of the 9th when the Germans claimed in a wireless news bulletin to have had two squadrons of ships at sea, including the *Scharnhorst* and *Gneisenau*, and to have sunk the *Glorious* and a destroyer, the *Orama*, the *Oil Pioneer*, and a ' U-boat chaser ' (*Juniper*), was there serious anxiety about the carrier.

The Commander-in-Chief, Home Fleet, however, had taken steps to support the returning expedition as soon as the *Valiant*'s signal reached him on the 9th. He ordered that ship to make the best of her way to Admiral Vivian's convoy, which in fact she was doing already, having begun to work up to full speed on hearing of the enemy from the *Atlantis* ; and he made a signal to the *Glorious* to join the *Valiant*, if she had oil enough. The *Repulse, Newcastle, Sussex* and three destroyers, then at sea between Iceland and the Faeroes he ordered also to join Admiral Vivian. He raised steam in the *Rodney* and *Renown* at Scapa, and sailed with them and six destroyers in the afternoon to protect the convoys.

These ships—four capital ships, two cruisers and 13 destroyers, counting the *Valiant* and her screen—were all Sir Charles Forbes had now under his command (except for one or two more destroyers oiling or cleaning boilers) after the detachment of Home Fleet cruisers and destroyers to the Humber, Sheerness and Mediterranean (*see* Sec. 24). As always, there was an overall shortage of destroyers, and at this time many had been engaged in bringing away the Army from France, with heavy damage and loss ; indeed, the want of destroyers had led Sir Charles to tell the Admiralty on the 3rd that ' in event of heavy ships being required to proceed to sea, battlecruisers only will be sailed unless occasion is vital '.

To go back to the convoys. Admiral Vivian also received the signals from the *Valiant* and *Devonshire*, and the Admiralty's reproduction of the German broadcast on 9th June. These signals explained wreckage reported by the *Ark Royal*'s patrolling aircraft and bodies seen by the *Southampton* that day, for the route the troopships followed lay not far from the Germans' track of the day before ; indeed, survivors of the *Glorious* said they saw the convoy and friendly aircraft pass them by. In the afternoon, German aircraft shadowed and attacked the *Valiant* on her way to join the troopships. ' I reported the attack ', said Captain Rawlings, ' as I was leading aircraft straight to the convoy and considered they would probably steer further to the westward'. When this report came, Admiral Wells recommended that the convoy should keep further westward, away from the enemy's air station at Trondheim, and that his aircraft should inform the *Valiant* of the new course and deal with the convoy shadower. Lord Cork agreed, so the convoy turned in the evening, anticipating an Admiralty order to do so. The aircraft duly informed the *Valiant* and drove off the shadowing enemy, and she and her destroyers joined about 2200 near 67° 30' N., 1° W. The same night, however, several aircraft tried to attack the *Ark Royal*; her fire and the *Valiant*'s kept them at arm's length, whilst her fighters shot down one and damaged others. Next morning, the 10th, the *Newcastle*, *Sussex* and *Repulse* arrived, the first two departing to join the Harstad store convoy on the battlecruiser's approach, and at midday the *Ark Royal* left to join Sir Charles Forbes, then some 70 miles off to the eastward. The *Repulse* and *Valiant* parted company from the convoy on the 11th, and went to Scapa. On the 12th, the convoy came safe to the Clyde. The storeships also arrived safely. The *Newcastle* and *Sussex* took the Harstad convoy to Scapa, and the Tromsö ships came home later, escorted by a couple of trawlers.

Apart from the ships sunk by Admiral Marschall's squadron, only one other ship came to grief—the *Vandyck*, armed boarding vessel. She was a spare troopship in the second group, but instead of going back alone, like the *Orama*, she had orders to cruise on a station 130 miles to seaward, while the other ships loaded, and to join them at the distant rendezvous in time to go home on the 9th. By some mistake she seems to have gone to one of the inner rendezvous, from which she reported herself by signal some hours after the convoy had proceeded, though she was afterwards reported as having spoken a trawler more than 100 miles away within two hours of making her original signal. Aircraft and a destroyer sent to find her failed to do so, and the Naval Attaché at Stockholm informed the Admiralty on the 11th that she had been sunk off Andenes the day before by German aircraft.

66. Movements of the Commander-in-Chief, Home Fleet [PLANS 15, 16

The Commander-in-Chief, having left Scapa at 1250, 9th June, in the *Rodney*, wearing the Union at the main for the first time at sea,[1] with the *Renown* and destroyer screen, steered to the northward at best possible speed until the evening of the 10th to cover the returning troop convoy.

At 1625 on the 9th he received a message from the Admiralty (A.T. 1330/9) informing him that he was in command of all forces in the northern area of the North Sea, *i.e.* including those hitherto commanded by Lord Cork, who hauled down his flag that night. Aircraft of Coastal Command, reconnoitring Trondheim at 0846, reported four enemy cruisers there, subsequently modified to a battlecruiser, two cruisers and about seven destroyers; this was in fact Admiral Marschall's force. The *Hipper* and the four destroyers had reached Trondheim on the morning of the 9th, and the *Gneisenau* and damaged

---

[1] Sir Charles Forbes had been promoted to Admiral of the Fleet on 8th May, 1940. This was the first occasion in history—as was pointed out to Sir Charles Forbes by H.M. The King—that an Admiral of the Fleet had flown the Union at the main as Commander-in-Chief of a fleet in time of war. (Lord St. Vincent, on taking command of the Channel Fleet in 1806, was authorised to wear the Union at the main as a special mark of distinction, because he had formerly been First Lord of the Admiralty; but he was not promoted to Admiral of the Fleet till 15 years later.)

Scharnhorst a few hours later in the afternoon. Despite Admiral Marschall's important success in sinking the *Glorious*, the German Naval Staff was not pleased with his action in withdrawing his force to Trondheim, and ordered him to resume operations forthwith against the British convoys, about which numerous reports were coming in. Accordingly, he sent the *Gneisenau* and *Hipper* to sea on 10th June; they were reported—as 'a *Scheer* and a *Hipper*'—in 64° 35′ N., 9° 45′ E., steering 300°, at 1400 that day by the submarine *Clyde*. But it was clear to Admiral Marschall that by this time the convoys were beyond their reach, and they were recalled to Trondheim that night.[1]

After receiving the aircraft report of the force in Trondheim, Admiral Forbes at 1000, 10th, ordered the *Ark Royal* to leave the troopships and join him, the Admiralty having asked him to arrange a torpedo attack by aircraft, should the Royal Air Force find the enemy in port; but on receipt of the *Clyde*'s report, the Admiralty cancelled the operation against Trondheim and ordered the Commander-in-Chief to concentrate on the ships reported. Sir Charles Forbes accordingly at 1600 stood to the eastward and south-eastward towards them, with aircraft scouting ahead; at the same time he asked Vice-Admiral Wells if he could send an air striking force as the 'only hope of getting the ships'. An extensive reconnaissance failed to find the enemy and at midnight, having no further report of them, he turned back to 320°, to provide cover for the slow convoy and storeships from Narvik, which were still at sea. By the morning of the 11th the last convoy was well to the westward, though the fleet kept meeting trawlers and merchantmen, chiefly Norwegian, 'all over the ocean'.

The same afternoon, the 11th June, the Royal Air Force machines attacked the ships at Trondheim, reporting there a capital ship and two cruisers, and claiming a hit with a 250 lb. bomb on each cruiser. The *Gneisenau* and *Hipper* had returned by that time from their short sortie, having realised that the convoys were beyond their reach, and there were consequently in Trondheim, when the aircraft attacked, two capital ships (*Scharnhorst*, *Gneisenau*), one cruiser (*Hipper*), and four destroyers. None of the ships was hit or damaged in the attack.

The Commander-in-Chief with the fleet was then somewhere beyond 67° N., and the Admiralty suggested that naval aircraft should attack; the fleet accordingly moved south that evening, in thick weather. Passing the last Tromsö store convoy next morning, the 12th, the Admiral turned eastward, having decided to attack with 15 Skuas, from 65° N., 4° 40′ E., early next morning, provided he could reach the flying-off position undiscovered. German aircraft shadowed the fleet in the afternoon. 'It does not look hopeful for tomorrow, his reconnaissance is too efficient', signalled the Commander-in-Chief to Admiral Wells. However, 15 Skuas left the carrier in the appointed position

---

[1] The German Naval War Staff was dissatisfied with Admiral Marschall's whole conduct of the operation. In its view, his decision to attack the convoys was "operationally false"; it involved a risk of revealing the position of the battlecruisers before their main task of attacking Harstad had been carried out, and it could produce no relieving effect on the land situation at Narvik. The Naval Staff also considered that the torpedo hit on the *Scharnhorst* might have been avoided by better tactical conduct of the action, and that the ships should not have withdrawn to Trondheim immediately afterwards. That he did eventually intercept and sink the *Glorious*, the Staff ascribed to "an extraordinary stroke of luck".

This seems less than just to Admiral Marschall, as had he persisted in going to Harstad on the night of the 8th/9th, he would have found nothing there to attack: and whether by luck or skill, he did score an important success in sinking the *Glorious*. The net result so far as he was concerned was that he was relieved of his command as Commander-in-Chief, Afloat, and replaced by Vice-Admiral Lütjens, who perished a year later in the *Bismarck*.

MOVEMENTS OF THE COMMANDER-IN-CHIEF, HOME FLEET   Sec. 66

in time to attack at 0200, the 13th. They believed that they hit the *Scharnhorst* with at least one bomb; this was true, but the bomb failed to explode, a tragic turn of fate as eight of the aircraft were lost in the attack. Some Royal Air Force machines bombed the neighbouring airfield of Vaernes at the same time to distract attention from the Skuas, while others gave the naval machines fighter protection. The fleet returned to Scapa as soon as the surviving Skuas returned, the *Ark Royal* and her screen entering harbour on the 14th, the two capital ships (*Rodney* and *Renown*) with their screen on the 15th at 1700.

The campaign for Norway was at an end.

CHAPTER XI

COMMENT AND REFLECTIONS

67. The Commander-in-Chief, Home Fleet's remarks

The various reports on the campaign in Norway naturally teem with lessons, suggestions and recommendations.

Most of these are of a topical or technical nature, and have been either confirmed or rendered obsolete by the experiences of the later years of the war—for example, suggestions as to the best ways of dealing with air attack on surface craft, and remarks on the value and limitations of the handful of A.L.C.s and M.L.C.s in the Narvik operations, the forerunners of the vast fleets of landing craft which reached their climax on the Normandy beaches in 1944. Such lessons, though possibly of archæological interest, would serve no useful purpose now, and therefore no attempt is made to enumerate them.

Nevertheless, much of permanent value may be culled from this campaign. As already pointed out, it was the first large-scale operation in history involving the employment of all three arms—sea, air and land. The Commander-in-Chief, Home Fleet, in his general remarks on the operations, stressed the necessity of correctly balancing these components in any operation of war.

' There was little doubt in his mind that the general basis of the (German) plan was the conviction that our sea power in the north could be broken by means of air power and submarines. . . .

It had, the Commander-in-Chief considered, been proved again, *but was apt to be forgotten*,[1] that a preponderance in power of each form of fighting force was required, each in its own element, to control that element. For instance, naval forces were required to control sea communications ; air forces or military forces could not do so, but could help the naval force, each in its own element. Air forces were required to control the air ; naval and military forces could not do so, but could help. Military forces were required to control the land ; the two other forces by themselves could not do so, but could help. . . .[2]

On our part, the scale of air attack that would be developed against our military forces on shore and our naval forces off the Norwegian coast was grievously under-estimated when the operations were undertaken. . . .'[3]

It was this latter factor—the scale of air attack—that went a long way to ensuring the German success in Norway. After the air attack on the Home Fleet in the first afternoon of the campaign, it was speedily recognised—at least in the Fleet—that ships could not operate with a reasonable chance of success in proximity to shore bases operating air forces virtually unopposed in the air. On the other hand, as the campaign progressed, the counter to this new menace, which when properly developed would largely neutralize it, became apparent, viz., the presence of friendly fighters.

---

[1] Author's italics.

[2] In special circumstances there are, of course, exceptions to this rule, *e.g.* a powerful fort can control the sea within range of its guns, or a really strong air force can control the sea or land within a reasonable distance of its airfields, if—as happened in Norway— the other side has virtually no air force present.

[3] Home Fleet Narrative, para. 269 (extract).

68. System of Command

From the British naval point of view, perhaps the most important aspect of the campaign was the system of high command, especially as regards the relations between the Admiralty and the Commander-in-Chief, Home Fleet.

The right and duty of the Admiralty to exercise general control of all naval forces has always been recognised; but just how detailed this control should be, in order to produce the best results, is a difficult and delicate problem. The Admiralty keeps the Commanders-in-Chief informed of the general policy and strategy (including, naturally, enemy intelligence), and allocates the forces deemed necessary to implement them. In the 18th century an attempt was made to pass on the experience of the Senior Officers at the Admiralty by means of the 'Fighting Instructions'. More than that, in those days of slow and uncertain communications, could not be done.

A great change was brought about at the beginning of the 20th century by the invention of Wireless Telegraphy. This enables the Admiralty to exercise constant direct control over the doings of the Commanders-in-Chief afloat, and, if so desired, to communicate direct with subordinate Commanders. It is now recognised that the 18th century fighting instructions, though admirable in their inception, succeeded in paralysing the initiative of the Commanders afloat for nearly a century; and there seems a possibility that too rigid distant control by wireless might well produce similar results. At some stage the Commander afloat must assume unfettered control; the difficulty is to determine precisely when.

The importance of having a clearly defined working arrangement had been recognised both ashore and afloat before the war, and correspondence on the subject had taken place between the First Sea Lord and the Commander-in-Chief, Home Fleet; but the question had not been definitely settled and there was some doubt as to precisely how things would work out in practice. The Norwegian campaign presented the first full scale opportunity for testing the arrangements.

In the event the Admiralty controlled the operations in considerable detail. It would almost appear that this on occasions introduced an element of uncertainty into the situation.[1]

The importance of the Commander-in-Chief afloat not revealing his position by the use of wireless enters the problem nowadays and may be advanced as an argument in favour of the Admiralty making operational signals direct to various units of the fleet. But there are other methods of communication, for example, the despatch of the *Codrington* by Admiral Forbes on 10th April to a rendezvous with directions to the cruisers, or the aircraft sent by the German Admiral Lütjens to Trondheim, with orders to make an important signal three hours after leaving him.[2]

The whole matter of course bristles with difficulties, but it is of such importance as to merit the most serious consideration and discussion in time of peace, if it is to work smoothly in the early days of any war. The difficulties

---

[1] *See* Secs. 8, 11, 12, 14, 28.

[2] The Commander-in-Chief will almost always be in a position to *request* Admiralty to issue instructions to his forces, if from difficulty in communications or other causes, he is unable to control them himself. This was done by Admiral Sir John Tovey a couple of years later in the course of operations against the *Tirpitz* in support of a convoy to North Russia.

are not lessened by the fact that personalities are bound to enter into it. An understanding which might work well between one Admiralty Administration or C.N.S. and one Commander-in-Chief, might produce confusion or friction between others.

On the whole, the events of the Norwegian Campaign seem to indicate that as a general rule, subject to the ultimate responsibility and consequent duty of the Admiralty to take what measures they think fit in an emergency (as, for example, the sudden arrival of unexpected enemy intelligence) the aim should be for them normally to limit themselves (a) to giving the Commander-in-Chief directions as to broad policy and strategy on a high level, including early warning of projected operations; and (b) to keeping him well posted in intelligence, both enemy (especially, of course, new operational intelligence) and information of other friendly forces, etc., which may be operating within the area of his command.

It is interesting to note that the Germans also found difficulties in adjusting the relationship between the Naval High Command ashore, and the Commander-in-Chief afloat, as a result of which Admiral Marschall after his not unsuccessful handling of Operation Juno was relieved of his command because he exercised his judgment to modify the plan to meet a new situation that had arisen since he put to sea, and which could not have been known to the Naval Staff when the operation was planned. Apart from the fact now known, that on 8th June the attack on Harstad would have been too late and that Admiral Marschall's initiative led to the destruction of the *Glorious*, surely the exercise of his discretion under such circumstances should have been well within the competence of the Commander-in-Chief afloat.

The appointment of Lord Cork—an Admiral of the Fleet, senior to the Commander-in-Chief, Home Fleet—to a command within the operational area of the latter was an unusual feature in the Command set up of the Norwegian campaign, which, despite the careful definition of the geographical limits of Lord Cork's command, might well have introduced complications. Lord Cork had been in close contact with the First Lord of the Admiralty for several months, examining the question of Baltic strategy, and the latter and the First Sea Lord ' were both agreed . . . that Lord Cork should command the Naval forces in this amphibious adventure in the north '.[1] There were no doubt strong reasons for the appointment in this particular case, though Lord Cork's seniority was likely to produce a delicate situation alike in his relations with the Commander-in-Chief, Home Fleet, and even more so with the Military Commander of the Narvik expedition, Major-General Mackesy.

The divergence between the instructions given to Lord Cork and those given to General Mackesy requires no comment; but the episode well illustrates the difficulty of gearing the normal administrative machinery to the necessities of war, after a comparatively long period of peace.

69. The importance of wireless silence

The importance of ships so far as possible keeping wireless silence in order to avoid giving away their positions has already been touched on in connection with the exercise of command afloat. But there is another and even more

---
[1] Churchill, THE SECOND WORLD WAR, Vol. I, p. 483.

important reason, applying equally to shore stations as well as ships, for limiting the use of wireless : the danger that the enemy may have succeeded in breaking the codes and cyphers in use.[1] This happened in the Norwegian campaign. As early as 12th April the Germans intercepted and decyphered a signal from Vice-Admiral Cunningham indicating Namsos and Mosjoen as suitable for landing (*see* Sec. 21 *ante*), and three days later they similarly learned that the *Chrobry* and *Batory* were earmarked for landings at Namsos and that General Carton de Wiart was the Commander in this area.

The problem of whether and when to break wireless silence must usually be a difficult one, and the decision must be made by the officer concerned after a most careful appreciation of the situation as known to him at the time.

Vice-Admiral Cunningham's decisions on 8th and 9th of June are of interest in this respect. At 1740, 8th June, the *Devonshire* intercepted a ' barely readable ' signal (timed 1640) from the *Glorious* to the Vice-Admiral, Aircraft Carriers, which subsequent events proved probably an amplifying report identifying two pocket battleships. The *Devonshire* at the time was proceeding alone to the United Kingdom ; she had on board the King of Norway and most of the Norwegian Cabinet, and was then some 300 miles to the westward of Harstad. Clearly it was no time to draw attention to herself and the Vice-Admiral decided to maintain wireless silence. Next forenoon, at 0938, the *Devonshire* intercepted the *Valiant*'s report from the *Atlantis* of the attack on the *Orama*. The *Devonshire* was then to the eastward of the Faroes ; wireless silence had already been broken to request air and destroyer escort, and the *Valiant*'s signal gave an ominous significance to the *Glorious*'s message intercepted the day before ; Admiral Cunningham immediately passed it to the Commander-in-Chief, to whom it brought the first hint that there might be cause for anxiety about the carrier.

No hard and fast rule can be laid down, except that wireless should be used as sparingly as possible, having due regard for the efficient performance of the operations in hand.[2] A common doctrine, thoroughly permeating the fleet, will tend to reduce the necessity for many of such signals. A good example of this occurred a year after the Norwegian campaign during the chase of the *Bismarck*. Captain Vian, with a division of destroyers, was steering to the east-north-east under orders to join the Commander-in-Chief, when he intercepted a signal placing the *Bismarck* some 75 miles to the southward of him. He immediately altered course without orders to the south-east to intercept ; making contact most opportunely just as the sun set, he then shadowed and harassed her throughout the night. ' *I knew*[3] you would wish me to steer to intercept the enemy . . .', he subsequently wrote to the Commander-in-Chief.[4]

---

[1] These, of course, were lessons of the War of 1914–18. Since then the advance of science, enabling more accurate bearings to be taken, and new technique have enhanced their importance, and will no doubt continue to do so.

[2] Several instances occurred during the war where security in this respect was overdone *e.g.* a decision in the *Cumberland* in October 1939 to maintain wireless silence, which resulted in information not reaching the Commander-in-Chief, South Atlantic, that in his opinion might have led to the early destruction of the *Graf Spee* ; and in connection with the *Cornwall*'s encounter with Raider No. 33 (which she sank) in May 1941, the Admiralty remarked ' . . . rigid adherence to wireless silence resulted in essential reports not being made . . .'

[3] Author's italics.

[4] Incidentally, it is pertinent to remark that had the *Bismarck* kept wireless silence, she might well have escaped.

70. Tactical Loading of Expeditionary Forces

A lesson of importance which emerges from the campaign is the necessity for loading an expeditionary force tactically, even though it may not be anticipated that its landing will be opposed. Plan R.4 was abandoned by orders from the Admiralty at the very outset; but had the troops been kept embarked and had they been tactically stowed, it is easy to see in retrospect what a very important role they might have played. For example, the cruisers at Rosyth could have reached Stavanger before the Germans[1]; or, alternatively, had they been sent to the north, and been able to land their troops immediately after Admiral Whitworth's action on 13th April, there seems little doubt that Narvik could have been occupied at once.

But it is doubtful whether the loading arrangements were sufficiently flexible for the troops to have landed for active operations, even if they had been kept embarked. The fact that on the splitting of convoy N.P.1, when the 146th Brigade was diverted to Namsos, its Brigadier was on board one of the ships which continued to Harstad, is an indication of the sort of contretemps which might have been experienced.

71. Risks and chances

The campaign well illustrates what might be termed the 'lost principle of war', viz., that nothing decisive can be achieved without taking risks.[2] This does not mean, of course, that risks should be blindly courted; but it does mean that having been recognised and carefully assessed, and every possible provision made to minimise them, they must be accepted for an adequate object.

Thus the very audacity of the German plan for the original landings—a great risk, recognised and accepted by Admiral Raeder—largely contributed to its triumphant conclusion; and in a lesser degree, the decision of the Admiralty to accept the risk to the *Warspite* in penetrating Ofot Fjord at the second Battle of Narvik produced the one resounding Allied success in the whole campaign.

The campaign is also interesting as emphasising the narrow chances[3] on which important events so often turn. On the whole, the chances favoured the Germans; perhaps they deserved it. The sighting of the *Hipper* at the moment she chanced to be on a westerly course for no reason except to fill in time had the effect of causing the Commander-in-Chief, Home Fleet, to steer away from the Norwegian coast in the afternoon before the invasion; similarly, the U-boat report of Captain Warburton-Lee's destroyers steering *away* from Narvik (also filling in time) must have misled Commodore Bonte. Had the U-boat sighted and reported them steering towards Narvik before they turned south-westerly, there can be little doubt the German destroyers would have been more on the alert and the result of the ensuing action would have been very different.

---

[1] *See* Sec. 8 *ante*.

[2] 'The boldest methods are the safest; nothing great can be achieved without risk.'—Nelson.

'It seems to be a law inflexible and inexorable that he who will not risk cannot win.'—John Paul Jones.

'All naval expeditions . . . have always failed, because the Admirals . . . have learned—where I do not know—that war can be made without running risks.'—Napoleon.

[3] 'Something must be left to chance: nothing is sure in a sea fight beyond all others.'—Nelson.

'There is no human affair which stands so constantly and so generally in close connection with chance, as war.'—Clausewitz.

Other examples which will occur to the reader are the escape of the *Hipper* from Trondheim on 10th April, when a fortuitous delay in sailing saved her from her diversionary course taking her straight into Sir Charles Forbes' battle fleet ; the sinking of the *Rio de Janeiro*, which might have compromised the whole German plan of invasion, had the correct inference been drawn and acted upon ; and the colour given to Admiral Raeder's planned diversion in the north by the chance encounter with the *Glowworm*, while she was seeking Admiral Whitworth's force the day before the invasion.

72. The Principles of War as applied in the Campaign

That the occupation of Norway was a great military success for Germany cannot be denied. But it must never be forgotten that it was a treacherous and unprovoked attack—ruthlessly carried out—on a small friendly nation against whom she had no shadow of complaint. There had been no diplomatic hint,[1] let alone *pour-parlers*, ultimatum, or declaration of war when the blow fell ; and it was on this refusal to be bound by the hitherto accepted usage of civilised nations, or any moral principles whatever,[2] that their whole plan of invasion hinged. In the year 1940 the implications of ' total war ' were not generally understood outside Germany ; despite what had happened to Belgium in 1914, and quite recently to Austria, Czechoslovakia and Poland, civilized nations did not expect even Germany suddenly to fall upon a neighbour for no better reason than that it suited her.

It is important to realise the immense initial advantage conferred on the Germans by this attitude when considering other factors that contributed to their success.

From the naval point of view, they accurately appreciated the risks from the first ; serious losses were anticipated, and in fact occurred, but no capital ship was lost. There was, however, one very serious weakness in their plan, which directly led to the loss of Commodore Bonte's ten destroyers at Narvik. If the destroyers could not make the passage to Narvik and back at the required speed without re-fuelling, they should have used cruisers for this purpose and the destroyers to convey the troops to Bergen and Trondheim,[3] rather than trust to the arrival of independently routed, unescorted oilers to get them home.

Turning to the Allied effort, the Higher Command had not the same freedom of action as the enemy, whose gangster methods, already referred to, had secured

---

[1] Unless the exhibition by the German Minister in Oslo—at a party to which Members of the Norwegian Government were invited shortly before the invasion started—of a film depicting the ' terror ' bombing of Warsaw can be considered as such.

[2] Some German apologists are already (1950) attempting to depict the invasion as a ' race for Norway ' between the Allies and themselves (which they won), with the implication that there was not much to choose between the two. This, of course, is a travesty of the facts. While the Allies were formally approaching the Norwegians by recognised diplomatic channels and genuinely seeking some solution of their legitimate grievance over the unhampered iron ore traffic, the Germans were conspiring with such traitors as Quisling to seize the whole country. The Allied precautionary measure, Plan R.4, was only to be put into execution after Germany had invaded Norway, or when there was clear evidence she was about to do so ; and then it was to be carried out with every consideration for Norwegian susceptibilities. The German plan, on the other hand, relied on treachery and terror bombing from the outset for its fulfilment. Contrast this with the Admiralty instructions with regard to laying the minefields (admittedly a technical breach of neutrality) in which the sentence occurs ' . . . should force have to be used we must refrain from replying to Norwegian fire until the situation becomes intolerable.' (A.T.1925/5.)

[3] The Germans were aware that they would not meet a British submarine north of Trondheim, so the destroyers were not needed to screen the battlecruisers.

Sec. 72   COMMENT AND REFLECTIONS

them the initiative, and the scope of whose operations came as an unpleasant surprise;[1] pre-war policy, moreover, had tended to retard rearmament, and there was a serious shortage both of materiel and trained personnel. Nevertheless, it is questionable whether the best use was made of such resources as did exist.[2]

In this connection, it is worth while to consider briefly the Principles of War (agreed between the three fighting Services)[3] as applied to the operations in Norway, both as a test of their validity, and as possibly providing an explanation of some of the events that occurred.

In the early days the Allied *aim*[4] did not seem to have been clearly thought out, much less maintained. The abandonment of Plan R.4 will occur to the reader ; and later, was the main effort to be at Trondheim, or elsewhere in Central Norway ? Or in the north at Narvik ? This appearance of vacillation at the very top,[5] percolating through, was likely to affect *morale* adversely sooner or later ; the fact that the morale of all forces so finely stood the strain can be accounted for partly by the British character and partly because the final withdrawals were not delayed too long. The Germans, on the other hand, carefully defined and adhered to their aim. For the first phase, it was to capture the capital and to secure a foothold in the principal ports ; as soon as this was accomplished, their next aim was to consolidate the position at Trondheim, and to this end all their efforts were directed, until the collapse of the Allied campaign in that region. Their morale, already high, was naturally enhanced by their steady advance. *Offensive action* was the keynote of their whole campaign. The Allies, too, took offensive action locally, and were eventually successful at Narvik ; but the advisability of offensive action under such handicaps as obtained in Central Norway,—almost complete lack of air power and, in addition, feeble anti-aircraft protection against a powerful air force well within range—may be open to doubt.

The fourth principle, *security*, with its somewhat pointed reference to the ' adequate defence of vulnerable bases '[6] could not be attained so long as the enemy held unfettered control of the air. Other instances where neglect of this principle brought its consequences will occur to the reader—notably the omission in the German plan to ensure oil for the Narvik destroyers and Commodore Bonte's inadequate arrangements, which cost him his life and enabled Captain Warburton-Lee, with a force only half his own, to inflict a signal defeat on him. This action, of course, also illustrated the value of *surprise*, as did Admiral Whitworth's (to a lesser degree) three days later ;

---

[1] A report of the German landing at Narvik was at first not credited, and the Prime Minister (the Rt. Hon. Neville Chamberlain) expressed the opinion that this actually referred to *Larvik* (at the entrance to Oslo Fjord).

[2] Mr. Winston Churchill has made it plain that the *system* of higher direction in force at this time suffered from inherent weaknesses, which rendered the efficient conduct of the war impossible. (THE SECOND WORLD WAR, Vol. I, pp. 528–530, English Edn.) This subject is outside the scope of a Naval Staff History, but if the narrative of the campaign indicates that the principles of war, on which much thought had been expended by the Service Staffs in the inter-war years, were discarded at the first serious clash of arms, and that unfortunate results ensued, surely all other lessons pale into insignificance.

It is from this angle that the following points are raised, and in no spirit of criticism of Service Ministries or Staffs—still less individuals, all of whom were doing their best under circumstances of extraordinary stress and complexity.

[3] Naval War Manual, 1947, pp. 6–8.

[4] Apart from the overall aim of keeping the Norwegians in the fight and beating the Germans *somehow*, sometime.

[5] This was of course known to only a few very Senior Officers, but its effects (constant changes of orders, etc.) would be bound to be noticed generally before long.

[6] Naval War Manual, 1947, p. 7.

unfortunately there were no balanced forces readily available to exploit the advantage. But the outstanding example of surprise was the whole German campaign.

As to *concentration of force* the modest forces available at first to the Allies were immediately dispersed between Narvik and Central Norway ; while the eventual employment of some 35,000 troops and considerable naval forces—with inadequate air support—to evict some 3000 Germans from Narvik may be held to have infringed the principle of *economy of effort*. *Per contra*, the successful initial German occupation of five of the principal Norwegian ports by no more than 8700 troops (suitably supported by sea and air) could scarcely have been effected more economically.

Lack of *flexibility* in the Allied arrangements was instanced by the difficulty of switching troops, already nearing Vest Fjord, from Harstad to Narvik, when Admiral Whitworth's victory on 13th April offered a fleeting chance of immediate success.

Regarding *cooperation*, there was ample good will ; but the diverse instructions given to Lord Cork and General Mackesy show what a long path had to be travelled before the true cooperation reached in the latter stages of the war was achieved. As was only to be expected at this early period of the war, various weaknesses in the administrative arrangements revealed themselves as the campaign progressed.

73. Conclusion

Though it must be admitted that the Allied ' ramshackle campaign ' in Norway was a failure from the military point of view, it provided sufficient breathing space for the Norwegians to steady themselves after the first shock, and enabled the King and Government, by transferring their activities to the United Kingdom and remaining ' in being ', to defeat the German political aim.

The bright spot in an otherwise dismal story is the fine style in which the Allied morale, of all services and all nations—despite conflicting orders, lack of equipment, prolonged and almost unopposed air attack and constant reverses—stood the strain. The Royal Navy in particular can be proud of its share in the venture, and apart from its assistance in air defence and other activities inshore in support of the landings, the fact that it succeeded in transporting, maintaining and finally evacuating the other Services with a loss of only 13 troops killed and nine wounded[1] and 41 airmen[2] while afloat under its care, may justly be regarded as a source of pride and satisfaction.

---

[1] Embarked in the *Afridi* when bombed 3rd May 1940.
This does not include casualties in the *Chrobry*, which was in the nature of an inshore operation : 6 officers were killed on this occasion, but nearly all the troops were saved.

[2] Embarked in the *Glorious*, 8th June 1940.

APPENDIX A

ALLIED WARSHIPS EMPLOYED IN CONNECTION WITH OPERATIONS IN NORWAY, APRIL–JUNE 1940, WITH MAIN ARMAMENT AND COMMANDING OFFICERS

  I. HOME FLEET.
 II. MINELAYERS.
III. H.M. SHIPS OTHER THAN HOME FLEET.
 IV. FRENCH SHIPS.

APPENDIX A

ALLIED WARSHIPS EMPLOYED IN CONNECTION WITH OPERATIONS IN NORWAY, APRIL–JUNE 1940

I. HOME FLEET
(From " Pink " List, 9th April 1940)

SECOND BATTLE SQUADRON

Rodney (9 16-in., 12 6-in., 6 4.7-in. H.A.) .. Flag, Admiral Sir Charles Forbes, G.C.B., D.S.O., Commander-in-Chief, Home Fleet.
Captain F. H. G. Dalrymple-Hamilton.
Warspite (8 15-in., 8 6-in., 8 4-in. H.A.) .. Captain V. A. C. Crutchley, V.C., D.S.C.
Valiant (8 15-in., 20 4.5-in.) .. .. Captain H. B. Rawlings, O.B.E.
Nelson[1] (9 16-in., 12 6-in., 6 4.7-in. H.A.) Captain G. J. A. Miles.
Barham[2] (8 15-in., 12 6-in., 8 4-in. H.A.) .. Captain C. G. Cooke.

BATTLECRUISER SQUADRON

Renown (6 15-in., 20 4.5-in. H.A.) .. Flag, Vice-Admiral W. J. Whitworth (V.A.C.B.C.S.).
Captain C. E. B. Simeon.
Repulse (6 15-in., 12 4-in., 8 4-in. H.A.) .. Captain E. J. Spooner, D.S.O.
Hood[3] (8 15-in., 12 5.5-in., 8 4-in. H.A.) .. Captain I. G. Glennie.

AIRCRAFT CARRIER

Furious (12 4-in. H.A./L.A.) .. .. Captain T. H. Troubridge.

A.A. CRUISERS

Cairo[4] (8 4-in. H.A./L.A.) .. .. .. Captain P. V. McLaughlin.
Calcutta[4] (8 4-in. H.A./L.A.) .. .. Captain D. M. Lees.

FIRST CRUISER SQUADRON

Devonshire (8 8-in., 8 4-in. H.A.) .. .. Flag, Vice-Admiral J. H. D. Cunningham, C.B., M.V.O.
Captain J. M. Mansfield, D.S.C.
Berwick (8 8-in., 8 4-in. H.A.) .. .. Captain I. M. Palmer, D.S.C.
York (6 8-in., 4 4-in. H.A.) .. .. Captain R. H. Portal, D.S.C.
Sussex[5] (8 8-in., 8 4-in. H.A.) .. .. Captain A. R. Hammick.
Norfolk[6] (8 8-in., 8 4-in. H.A.) .. .. Captain A. J. L. Phillips.
Suffolk[7] (8 8-in., 8 4-in. H.A.) .. .. Captain J. W. Durnford.

SECOND CRUISER SQUADRON

Galatea (6 6-in., 4 4-in. H.A.) .. .. Flag, Vice-Admiral Sir G. F. Edward-Collins, K.C.V.O., C.B.
Captain B. B. Schofield.
Arethusa (6 6-in., 4 4-in. H.A.) .. .. Captain G. D. Graham.
Penelope (6 6-in., 8 4-in. H.A.) .. .. Captain G. D. Yates.
Aurora (6 6-in., 8 4-in. H.A.) .. .. Captain L. H. K. Hamilton, D.S.O.

---

[1] Refit Portsmouth till mid-June.
[2] Refit Liverpool till early July.
[3] Refit Plymouth.
[4] Detached from 20th C.S.
[5] On passage from East Indies : then refit till 25th May.
[6] Repairs Clyde till 6th July.
[7] Refit and repairs, Govan, till 10th April.

APPENDIX A—*continued*

Eighteenth Cruiser Squadron

Manchester (12 6-in., 8 4-in. H.A.)	Flag, Vice-Admiral G. Layton, C.B., D.S.O., Commanding 18th C.S. Captain H. A. Packer.
Sheffield (12 6-in., 8 4-in. H.A.)	Flag, Rear-Admiral M. L. Clarke, D.S.C., 2nd in Command, 18th C.S. (21/4–6/5). Captain C. A. A. Larcom.
Southampton (12 6-in., 8 4-in. H.A.)	Flag, Rear-Admiral M. L. Clarke, D.S.C. (6/5). Captain F. W. H. Jeans, C.V.O.
Glasgow (12 6-in., 8 4-in. H.A.)	Captain F. H. Pegram.
Birmingham (12 6-in., 8 4-in. H.A.)	Captain A. C. G. Madden.
Edinburgh[1] (12 6-in., 12 4-in. H.A.)	Captain C. M. Blackman, D.S.O.
Newcastle[2] (12 6-in., 8 4-in. H.A.)	Captain J. Figgins.

Destroyer Flotillas

Woolwich (Depot Ship)	Flag, Rear-Admiral R. H. C. Hallifax (R.A. (D)).

Second Destroyer Flotilla

Hardy (5 4.7-in., 8 21-in. tubes)	Captain (D)2 B. A. W. Warburton-Lee.
Hotspur (4 4.7-in., 8 21-in. tubes)	Com. H. F. H. Layman.
Havock (4 4.7-in., 8 21-in. tubes)	Lt.-Com. R. E. Courage.
Hero (4 4.7-in., 8 21-in. tubes)	Com. H. W. Biggs.
Hereward[3] (4 4.7-in., 8 21-in. tubes)	Lt.-Com. C. W. Greening.
Hyperion (4 4.7-in., 8 21-in. tubes)	Com. H. St. L. Nicholson.
Hunter (4 4.7-in., 8 21-in. tubes)	Lt.-Com. L. de Villiers.
Hostile (4 4.7-in., 8 21-in. tubes)	Com. J. P. Wright.
Hasty[4] (4 4.7-in., 8 21-in. tubes)	Lt.-Com. L. R. K. Tyrwhitt.

Third Destroyer Flotilla

Inglefield (5 4.7-in., 10 21-in. tubes)	Captain (D)3 P. Todd.
Isis (4 4.7-in., 10 21-in. tubes)	Com. J. C. Clouston.
Ilex (4 4.7-in., 10 21-in. tubes)	Lt.-Com. P. L. Saumarez, D.S.C.
Imperial[5] (4 4.7-in., 10 21-in. tubes)	Lt.-Com. C. A. de W. Kitcat.
Delight (4 4.7-in., 10 21-in. tubes)	Com. M. Fogg-Elliott.
Imogen (4 4.7-in., 10 21-in. tubes)	Com. C. L. Firth, M.V.O.
Diana[6] (4 4.7-in., 10 21-in. tubes)	Lt.-Com. E. G. Le Geyt.

Fourth Destroyer Flotilla

Afridi (8 4.7-in., 4 21-in. tubes)	Captain (D)4 P. L. Vian, D.S.O.
Gurkha (8 4.7-in., 4 21-in. tubes)	Com. A. W. Buzzard.
Sikh (8 4.7-in., 4 21-in. tubes)	Com. J. A. Gifford.
Mohawk (8 4.7-in., 4 21-in. tubes)	Com. J. W. M. Eaton.
Zulu (8 4.7-in., 4 21-in. tubes)	Com. J. S. Crawford.
Cossack (8 4.7-in., 4 21-in. tubes)	Com. R. St. V. Sherbrooke.
Maori (8 4.7-in., 4 21-in. tubes)	Com. G. N. Brewer.
Nubian[7] (8 4.7-in., 4 21-in. tubes)	Com. R. W. Ravenhill.

---

[1] Refit, Tyne, till end of June.
[2] Defects, Tyne.
[3] Repairs, Portsmouth, till 17th April.
[4] Repairs, Dundee.
[5] Repairs, Tyne, till 13th April.
[6] Docked, Hull.
[7] Repairs, Tyne, till 12th April.

APPENDIX A—*continued*

Fifth Destroyer Flotilla

Kelly[1] (6 4.7-in., 10 21-in. tubes)	Captain (D)5 Lord Louis Mountbatten, G.C.V.O.
Kashmir (6 4.7-in., 10 21-in. tubes)	Com. H. A. King.
Kelvin (6 4.7-in., 10 21-in. tubes)	Lt.-Com. J. L. Machin.
Kipling[2] (6 4.7-in., 10 21-in. tubes)	Com. A. St. Clair Ford.
Kimberley (6 4.7-in., 10 21-in. tubes)	Lt.-Com. R. G. K. Knowling.
Kandahar[3] (6 4.7-in., 10 21-in. tubes)	Com. W. G. A. Robson.
Khartoum[4] (6 4.7-in., 10 21-in. tubes)	Com. D. T. Dowler.
Kingston[4] (6 4.7-in., 10 21-in. tubes)	Lt.-Com. P. Somerville, D.S.O.

Sixth Destroyer Flotilla

Somali (8 4.7-in., 4 21-in. tubes)	Captain (D)6 R. S. G. Nicholson, D.S.O., D.S.C.
Ashanti (8 4.7-in., 4 21-in. tubes)	Com. W. G. Davis.
Matabele (8 4.7-in., 4 21-in. tubes)	Com. G. K. Whiting-Smith.
Mashona (8 4.7-in., 4 21-in. tubes)	Com. W. H. Selby.
Bedouin (8 4.7-in., 4 21-in. tubes)	Com. J. A. McCoy.
Punjabi (8 4.7-in., 4 21-in. tubes)	Com. J. T. Lean.
Eskimo (8 4.7-in., 4 21-in. tubes)	Com. St. J. A. Micklethwaite, D.S.O.
Tartar (8 4.7-in., 4 21-in. tubes)	Com. L. P. Skipwith.

Seventh Destroyer Flotilla

Jervis[5] (6 4.7-in., 10 21-in. tubes)	Captain (D)7 P. J. Mack.
Janus (6 4.7-in., 10 21-in. tubes)	Com. J. A. W. Tothill.
Javelin (6 4.7-in., 10 21-in. tubes)	Com. A. F. Pugsley.
Jersey[6] (6 4.7-in., 10 21-in. tubes)	Lt. W. R. Patterson, O.B.E.
Juno (6 4.7-in., 10 21-in. tubes)	Lt.-Com. A. M. McKillop.
Jupiter (6 4.7-in., 10 21-in. tubes)	Com. D. B. Wyburd.
Jackal[7] (6 4.7-in., 10 21-in. tubes)	Com. T. M. Napier.
Jaguar[8] (6 4.7-in., 10 21-in. tubes)	Lt.-Com. J. F. W. Hine.

Eighth Destroyer Flotilla

Faulknor (5 4.7-in., 8 21-in. tubes)	Captain (D)8 A. F. de Salis.
Fearless (4 4.7-in., 8 21-in. tubes)	Com. K. L. Harkness.
Foxhound (4 4.7-in., 8 21-in. tubes)	Lt.-Com. G. H. Peters.
Fury (4 4.7-in., 8 21-in. tubes)	Com. G. F. Burghard.
Forester (4 4.7-in., 8 21-in. tubes)	Lt.-Com. E. B. Tancock, D.S.C.
Fortune (4 4.7-in., 8 21-in. tubes)	Com. E. A. Gibbs, D.S.O.
Fame[9] (4 4.7-in., 8 21-in. tubes)	Lt.-Com. W. S. Clouston.
Foresight[10] (4 4.7-in., 8 21-in. tubes)	Lt.-Com. G. T. Lambert.
Firedrake[11] (4 4.7-in., 8 21-in. tubes)	Lt.-Com. S. H. Norris, D.S.C.

[1] Repairs, Blackwall, till 27th April.
[2] Repairs, Tyne, till 16th April.
[3] Refit and repairs, Hull, till 11th May.
[4] Repairs, Falmouth, till 15th May.
[5] Repairs, Tyne, till 3rd July.
[6] Repairs, Hull, till July.
[7] Repairs, Blyth.
[8] Repairs, Dundee.
[9] Repairs, Grimsby, till 10th April.
[10] Repairs, Grimsby, till 1st May.
[11] Defects, Cardiff, till 1st May (?).

APPENDIX A—*continued*

First Destroyer Flotilla[1]

Codrington (5 4.7-in., 8 21-in. tubes)	Captain (D)1 G. E. Creasy, M.V.O.
Grenade (4 4.7-in., 8 21-in. tubes)	Com. R. C. Boyle.
O.R.P. *Blyscawica* (7 4.7-in., 6 21-in. tubes)	Com. Stanislaus Nahorski.
O.R.P. *Grom* (7 4.7-in., 6 21-in. tubes)	Com. Alexander Hulewicz.
O.R.P. *Burza* (4 5.1-in., 6 21.7-in. tubes)	
Greyhound (4 4.7-in., 8 21-in. tubes)	Com. W. R. Marshall-A'Deane.
Glowworm (4 4.7-in., 8 21-in. tubes)	Lt.-Com. G. B. Roope.
Griffin (4 4.7-in., 8 21-in. tubes)	Lt.-Com. J. Lee-Barber.
Gallant[2] (4 4.7-in., 8 21-in. tubes)	Lt.-Com. C. P. F. Brown.
Grafton[3] (4 4.7-in., 8 21-in. tubes)	Com. C. E. C. Robinson.

Twelfth Destroyer Flotilla[4]

Electra (4 4.7-in., 8 21-in. tubes)	Lt.-Com. S. A. Buss.
Echo[5] (4 4.7-in., 8 21-in. tubes)	Com. S. H. K. Spurgeon, D.S.O., R.A.N.
Escort[6] (4 4.7-in., 8 21-in. tubes))	Lt.-Com. J. Bostock.
Escapade (4 4.7-in., 8 21-in. tubes)	Com. H. R. Graham.
Encounter (4 4.7-in., 8 21-in. tubes)	Lt.-Com. E. V. St. J. Morgan.
Eclipse (4 4.7-in., 8 21-in. tubes)	Lt.-Com. I. T. Clark.

Miscellaneous

Protector (Netlayer)	Captain W. Y. La R. Beverley.
Vindictive (Repair Ship)	Captain A. R. Halfhide, C.B.E.

Submarine Command

Vice-Admiral Sir Max K. Horton, K.C.B., D.S.O. (V.A. S/M), H.Q., London.

Second Submarine Flotilla

Depot Ship, *Forth* (Rosyth)	Captain G. C. P. Menzies, Capt. (S)2.
Thistle (6 21-in. tubes, bow, 4 external)	Com. W. F. Haselfoot.
Triad (6 21-in. tubes, bow, 4 external)	Lt.-Com. E. R. J. Oddie.
Trident (6 21-in. tubes, bow, 4 external)	Com. A. J. L. Seale.
Triton (6 21-in. tubes, bow, 4 external)	Lt.-Com. E. F. Pizey.
Truant (6 21-in. tubes, bow, 4 external)	Lt.-Com. C. H. Hutchinson.
Seal[7] (6 21-in. tubes, bow, minelayer)	Lt.-Com. R. P. Lonsdale.
Porpoise[7] (6 21-in. tubes, bow, minelayer)	Com. P. Q. Roberts.
O.R.P. *Orzel* (12 21.7-in. tubes)	Lt.-Com. J. Grudzinski.
Tribune[8] (6 21-in. tubes, bow, 4 external)	Lt.-Com. H. J. Caldwell.
Triumph[9] (6 21-in. tubes, bow, 2 external)	Lt.-Com. J. S. Stevens.
O.R.P. *Wilk*[10] (6 21.7-in. tubes)	Lt.-Com. B. Krawezyk.

---

[1] Nore Command (Harwich) temporarily attached to Home Fleet.
[2] Refit, Southampton.
[3] Refit, Hull, till 15th April.
[4] Rosyth Command, temporarily attached to Home Fleet.
[5] Refit, Leith.
[6] Repairs, Rosyth.
[7] Temporarily attached.
[8] Repairs, Greenock.
[9] Repairs, Chatham, till end September.
[10] Refit, Dundee, till 5th May.

APPENDIX A—*continued*

THIRD SUBMARINE FLOTILLA

Depot Ship, *Cyclops* (Harwich)	Captain P. Ruck-Keene, Capt. (S)3.
Sealion (6 21-in. tubes, bow)	Lt.-Com. B. Bryant.
Seawolf (6 21-in. tubes, bow)	Lt.-Com. J. W. Studholme.
Shark (6 21-in. tubes, bow)	Lieut. P. M. Buckley.
Snapper (6 21-in. tubes, bow)	Lieut. W. D. A. King.
Sterlet (6 21-in. tubes, bow)	Lieut. G. H. S. Haward.
Sunfish (6 21-in. tubes, bow)	Lt.-Com. J. E. Slaughter.
Salmon[1] (6 21-in. tubes, bow)	Com. E. O. B. Bickford, D.S.O.

SIXTH SUBMARINE FLOTILLA

Depot Ship, *Titania*[2]	Captain J. S. Bethell, Capt. (S)6.
Unity (4 21-in. tubes, bow, 2 external) ..	Lieut. J. F. B. Brown.
Spearfish (6 21-in. tubes, bow)	Lt.-Com. J. H. Forbes.
Swordfish (6 21-in. tubes, bow)	Lieut. P. J. Cowell.
Clyde[3] (6 21-in. tubes, bow)	Lt.-Com. R. L. S. Gaisford.
Severn[3] (6 21-in. tubes, bow)	Lt.-Com. B. W. Taylor.
Sturgeon[4] (6 21-in. tubes, bow)	Lieut. G. D. A. Gregory, D.S.O.
Narwhal (6 21-in. tubes, bow, minelayer)	Lieut. C. S. Green.
Ursula[5] (6 21-in. tubes, bow, 2 external) ..	Com. G. C. Phillips, D.S.O.

TENTH SUBMARINE FLOTILLA
16th French Submarine Division

Depot Ship *Jules Verne* (Harwich) ..
Amazone (6 21.7-in., 2 15.7-in. tubes) ..
Antiope (6 21.7-in., 2 15.7-in. tubes) ..
La Sibylle (6 21.7-in., 2 15.7-in. tubes) ..

II. MINELAYERS

Teviot Bank	Com. R. D. King-Harman (ret.).

TWENTIETH DESTROYER FLOTILLA

Esk (2 4.7-in. guns, 60 mines)	Captain (D)20 J. G. Bickford, D.S.C. Lt.-Com. R. J. H. Couch.
Impulsive (2 4.7-in. guns, 60 mines) ..	Lt.-Com. W. S. Thomas.
Ivanhoe (2 4.7-in. guns, 60 mines) ..	Com. P. H. Hadow.
Icarus (2 4.7-in. guns, 60 mines)	Lt.-Com. C. D. Maud.
Intrepid[6] (2 4.7-in. guns, 60 mines) ..	Com. R. C. Gordon.
Express[7] (2 4.7-in. guns, 60 mines) ..	

III. H.M. SHIPS OTHER THAN HOME FLEET
BATTLESHIP

Resolution (8 15-in., 12 6-in., 8 4-in. H.A.).	Captain O. Bevir.	3rd B.S. (America and W.I.).

---

[1] Refit, Chatham, till 10th May.
[2] Tyne, refit till early June. Com. (S) ashore at Blyth.
[3] Temporarily attached.
[4] Refit, Tyne, till 20th April.
[5] Docked, Blyth.
[6] Repairs, Middlesbrough.
[7] Repairs, Hartlepool.

APPENDIX A—*continued*

AIRCRAFT CARRIERS

Ark Royal (16 4.5-in.)	Flag, Vice-Admiral L. V. Wells, C.B., D.S.O. Captain C. S. Holland.	⎫ Mediterranean.
Glorious (16 4.7-in. H.A./L.A.) ..	Captain G. D'Oyly Hughes, D.S.O., D.S.C.	⎭

CRUISERS

Enterprise (7 6-in., 3 4-in. H.A.) ..	Captain J. C. Annesley, D.S.O.	⎫ America and
Effingham (9 6-in., 8 4-in. H.A.) ..	Captain J. M. Howson.	⎭ W.I. Command.

A.A. CRUISERS

Coventry (8 4-in. H.A./L.A.)	Flag, Rear-Admiral J. G. P. Vivian. Captain D. Gilmour.	⎫
Curlew (8 4-in. H.A./L.A.)	Captain B. C. B. Brooke.	⎬ 20th C.S.
Curacoa (8 4-in. H.A./L.A.)	Captain E. A. Aylmer, D.S.C.	
Carlisle (8 4-in. H.A./L.A.)	Captain G. M. B. Langley, O.B.E.	⎭

DESTROYERS

Acasta (4 4.7-in., 8 21-in. tubes) ..	Com. C. E. Glasfurd.	⎫ 18 D.F. Western
Ardent (4 4.7-in., 8 21-in. tubes) ..	Lt.-Com. J. F. Barker.	⎭ Approaches.
Arrow (4 4.7-in., 8 21-in. tubes) ..	Com. H. W. Williams.	16th D.F., Portsmouth.
Basilisk (4 4.7-in., 8 21-in. tubes) ..	Com. M. Richmond, O.B.E.	⎫ 19th D.F.,
Brazen (4 4.7-in., 8 21-in. tubes) ..	Lt.-Com. Sir Michael Culme-Seymour, Bt.	⎭ Dover.
Havelock (3 4.7-in., 8 21-in. tubes) ..	Captain (D.9) E. B. K. Stevens, D.S.C.	⎫ 9th D.F., Western
Hesperus (3 4.7-in., 8 21-in. tubes) ..	Lt.-Com. D. G. F. W. MacIntyre.	⎬ Approaches.
Highlander (3 4.7-in., 8 21-in. tubes) ..	Com. W. A. Dallmeyer.	⎭
Vanoc (4 4-in., 6 21-in. tubes) ..	Lt.-Com. J. G. W. Deneys.	⎫ 11th D.F.,
Veteran (4 4-in., 6 21-in. tubes) ..	Com. J. E. Broome.	⎬ Western
Walker (4 4-in., 6 21-in. tubes) ..	Lt.-Com. A. A. Tait.	Approaches.
Whirlwind (4 4-in., 6 21-in. tubes) ..	Lt.-Com. J. M. Rogers.	⎭
Wolverine (4 4-in., 6 21-in. tubes) ..	Com. R. H. Craske.	15th D.F., Western Apps.
Wren (4 4.7-in., 6 21-in. tubes) ..	Com. H. T. Armstrong.	18th D.F., Western Apps.

SLOOPS

Auckland (8 4-in. H.A.)	Com. J. G. Hewitt.	⎫
Bittern (6 4-in. H.A./L.A.)	Lieut. T. Johnston.	
Black Swan (6 4-in. H.A.)	Captain A. L. Poland, D.S.C.	
Flamingo (6 4-in. H.A.)	Com. J. H. Huntley.	⎬ Rosyth.
Fleetwood (4 4-in. H.A./L.A.)	Com. A.N. Grey.	
Pelican (8 4-in. H.A.)	Com. L. A. K. Boswell, D.S.O.	
Stork (6 4-in. H.A./L.A.)	Com. A. C. Behague.	⎭

IV. FRENCH WARSHIPS

CRUISERS

Emile Bertin (9 6-in., 4 3.5-in. H.A./L.A.)	Flag, Rear-Admiral Derrien.
Montcalm (9 6-in., 8 3.5-in. H.A./L.A.)	

DESTROYERS

Bison (5 5.4-in., 6 21.7-in. tubes) ..
Milan (5 5.4-in., 7 21.7-in. tubes) ..
Maillé Brézé (5 5.4-in., 7 21.7-in. tubes) ..
Foudroyant (4 5.1-in., 6 21.7-in. tubes) ..
L'Indomptable (5 5.4-in., 9 21.7-in. tubes)
Le Malin (5 5.4-in., 9 21.7-in. tubes) ..
Le Triomphant (5 5.4-in., 9 21.7-in. best) ..

149

APPENDIX A (1)

A/S TRAWLERS EMPLOYED ON NORWEGIAN COAST

Name	Remarks
21st Striking Force *Danemon* *Lady Elsa* *Man of War* *Wellard* **23rd A/S Group** *Indian Star* *Melbourne* *Berkshire* *Rutlandshire*[1]	Arrived Namsos area 16th April. Ordered by C.-in-C., H.F., to proceed to Skjel Fjord on 20th April after a heavy air attack in which the *Rutlandshire* was sunk. The surviving trawlers remained in the Narvik area.
22nd A/S Group *Warwickshire*[1] *Hammond*[1] *Larwood*[1] *Bradman*[1] *Jardine*[1]	Arrived Aandalsnes area 21st April.
12th A/S Group *Stella Capella* *Cape Argona* *Cape Cheluyskin*[1] *Blackfly*[2]	Escorted petrol carrier to Namsos, arriving 23rd April. Then to Skjel Fjord and to Molde, 27th April. Remained in Molde area till evacuation 30th April/1st May.
11th A/S Striking Force *Cape Siretoko*[1] *Argyleshire* *Northern Pride*[3] *Wisteria*[4]	Arrived Molde–Aandalsnes area 27th April and left after final evacuation 30th April/1 May.
15th A/S Striking Force *Cape Pessaro*[1] *St. Goran*[1] *St. Kenan* *St. Lomas* **16th A/S Striking Force** *Aston Villa*[1] *Gaul*[1] *Angle* *Arab*	Arrived Namsos area 27th April. Left Namsos after final evacuation of 2nd/3rd May for Narvik area.

APPENDIX A (2)

NAVAL COMMANDS IN NORWAY

I. Narvik Area

Flag Officer, Narvik, and C.-in-C., Northern Expeditionary Force.	Admiral of the Fleet, the Earl of Cork and Orrery, G.C.B., G.C.V.O.
Chief of Staff	Captain L. E. H. Maund, R.N.
Flag Officer, Harstad	Rear-Admiral A. L. St. G. Lyster, C.V.O., D.S.O.
O.I.C., M.N.B.D.O., Harstad	Lt.-Colonel H. R. Lambert, D.S.C., R.M.
C.O., F.A.A., Narvik Area	Captain R. S. Armour, R.N.

II. Central Area

N.O.I.C., Molde (Aandalsnes area)	Captain M. M. Denny, R.N.
S.O.R.M., Aandalsnes	Lt.-Colonel H. W. Simpson, R.M.
S.O.R.M., Aalesund	Major H. Lumley, R.M.

---

[1] Sunk or driven ashore.
[2] Damaged in collision; remained Skjel Fjord.
[3] Attached from 12th A/S Striking Force.
[4] Attached from 19th A/S Striking Force.

APPENDIX B

GERMAN WARSHIPS MENTIONED IN NARRATIVE, WITH MAIN ARMAMENT, ETC.

APPENDIX B

GERMAN WARSHIPS MENTIONED IN NARRATIVE: NORWAY, APRIL–JUNE 1940

Name and Main Armament	Remarks

BATTLECRUISERS

Gneisenau (9 11-in., 12 5.9-in. H.A./L.A., 14 4.1-in. H.A.). — Flag, Admiral Lütjens (C.-in.-C). Damaged by *Renown*, 9th April.

Scharnhorst (9 11-in., 12 5.9-in. H.A./L.A., 14 4.1-in. H.A.). — Captain Hoffman. Damaged by *Acasta* (torpedo), 8th June.

ARMOURED SHIPS[1]

Lützow (6 11-in., 8 5.9-in., 6 4.1-in. H.A.) — Captain Thiele. Damaged Oslo coastal batteries, 9th April; and by *Spearfish* (torpedo), 11th April.

Admiral Sheer (6 11-in., 8 5.9-in., 6 4.1-in. H.A.). — Refitting during Norwegian operations.

CRUISERS

Blücher (8 8-in., 12 4.1-in. H.A.) .. — Flag, Rear-Admiral Kummetz. Sunk, Oslo coast defences, 9th April.

Admiral Hipper (8 8-in., 12 4.1-in. H.A.) — Captain Heye. Rammed and damaged by *Glowworm*, 8th April.

Leipzig (9 5.9-in., 6 3.5-in. H.A.) .. — Under repair (Kiel) during Norwegian operations.

Koln (9 5.9-in., 6 3.5-in. H.A.) .. ..

Königsberg (9 5.9-in., 6 3.5-in. H.A.) .. — Captain Ruhfus. Sunk. Bombed by F.A.A., Bergen, 10th April.

Karlsruhe (9 5.9-in., 6 3.5-in. H.A.) .. — Captain Rieve. Sunk. Torpedoed by *Truant*, 9th April.

Emden (8 5.9-in., 3 3.5-in. H.A.) .. ..

Nürnberg (9 5.9-in., 8 3.5-in. H.A.) — Under repair (Kiel) till 10th May 1940.

OLD BATTLESHIP (1905)

Schleswig Holstein (4 11-in., 10 5.9-in.) ..

GUNNERY TRAINING SHIPS

Bremse .. .. — Damaged, Bergen coastal batteries, 9th Apil.

Brummer .. .. — Sunk. Torpedoed by submarine, 15th April.

DESTROYERS

Wilhelm Heidkamp (5 5-in. H.A./L.A., 8 21-in. tubes). — Broad pendant, Commodore Bonte, S.O., Narvik. Torpedoed and sunk, 10th April.

Georg Thiele (5 5-in. H.A./L.A., 8 21-in. tubes). — Damaged, 10th April; destroyed 13th April, Narvik.

Hans Ludemann (5 5-in. H.A./L.A., 8 21-in. tubes). — Damaged, 10th April; destroyed 13th April, Narvik.

Anton Schmidt (5 5-in. H.A./L.A., 8 21-in. tubes). — Torpedoed and sunk, 10th April, Narvik.

Hermann Künne (5 5-in. H.A./L.A., 8 21-in. tubes). — Damaged, 10th April; destroyed 13th April, Narvik.

Dieher von Roeder (5 5-in. H.A./L.A., 8 21-in. tubes). — Damaged, 10th April; destroyed 13th April, Narvik.

---

[1] 'Pocket battleships'.

APPENDIX B—*continued*

NAME AND MAIN ARMAMENT — REMARKS

DESTROYERS—*contd.*

Wolfgang Zenker (5 5-in. H.A./L.A., 8 21-in. tubes). — Destroyed, Narvik, 13th April.
Erich Giese (5 5-in. H.A./L.A., 8 21-in. tubes) — Destroyed, Narvik, 13th April.
Erich Koellner (5 5-in. H.A./L.A., 8 21-in. tubes.) — Destroyed, Narvik, 13th April.
Bernd von Arnim (5 5-in. H.A./L.A., 8 21-in. tubes). — Damaged, 10th April; destroyed, 13th April, Narvik.
Friedrich Eckholdt (5 5-in. H.A./L.A., 8 21-in. tubes).
Theodor Riedel (5 5-in. H.A./L.A., 8 21-in. tubes).
Bruno Heinemann (5 5-in. H.A./L.A., 8 21-in. tubes).
Paul Jacobi (5 5-in. H.A./L.A., 8 21-in. tubes).

TORPEDO BOATS

Kondor (3 4.1-in. H.A./L.A., 6 21-in. tubes)
Möwe (3 4.1-in. H.A./L.A., 6 21-in. tubes)
Falke (3 4.1-in. H.A./L.A., 6 21-in. tubes)
Wolf (3 4.1-in. H.A./L.A., 6 21-in. tubes)
Seeadler (3 4.1-in. H.A./L.A., 6 21-in. tubes)
Greif (3 4.1-in. H.A./L.A., 6 21-in. tubes)
Albatros (3 4.1-in. H.A./L.A., 6 21-in. tubes) — Wrecked, Oslo, 9th April.
Luchs (3 5-in., 6 21-in. tubes) .. ..
Leopard (3 5-in., 6 21-in. tubes) .. ..

APPENDIX C (1)

DISPOSITION OF THE HOME FLEET, NOON, 9TH APRIL

I. OFF THE COAST OF NORWAY

(a) Detached under Vice-Admiral Whitworth : *Renown*—near 67° N., 10° E.

Repulse, Penelope, Bedouin, Punjabi, Eskimo, Kimberley—about to join the flag in 67° N., 10° E.

Esk, Icarus, Ivanhoe, Greyhound—patrolling the Vest Fjord minefield.

Hardy, Havock, Hotspur, Hunter, Hostile (joined p.m.)—going up Vest Fjord to Narvik.

(b) With C.-in-C., Home Fleet—near 60° N., 3° E. : *Rodney, Valiant, Galatea, Arethusa, Devonshire, Berwick, York, Emile Bertin, Codrington, Griffin, Jupiter, Electra, Escapade, Brazen, Tartu, Maille Breze.*

(c) Detached under Vice-Admiral Layton—making towards Bergen : *Manchester, Southampton, Glasgow, Sheffield, Afridi, Gurkha, Sikh, Mohawk, Somali, Matabele, Mashona.*

(d) On passage to join Vice-Admiral Layton from United Kingdom : *Aurora.*

(e) Going to fetch Convoy H.N.25 from Bergen rendezvous : *Tartar, Blyskawica, Grom, Burza.*

II. OTHER SHIPS AT SEA

(a) On passage to join Admiral Forbes : *Warspite, Furious, Ashanti, Maori, Fortune.*

(b) On passage to base short of fuel, disabled, etc. : *Birmingham, Fearless, Hyperion, Hero, Zulu, Cossack, Kashmir, Kelvin, Impulsive, Delight.*

(*Note.*—The *Delight* had been screening the *Furious* from the Clyde ; the others were in the North Sea.)

(c) Escorting Convoy O.N.25 : *Javelin, Janus, Juno, Eclipse, Grenade.*

III. IN HARBOUR—SULLUM VOE OR SCAPA

Cairo, Calcutta, Inglefield, Isis, Ilex, Imogen, Escort, Encounter, Faulknor, Foxhound, Forester, Brestois, Boulonnais, Foudroyant, Le Chevalier Paul.

Total ..
- 5 capital ships.
- 13 cruisers.
- 1 aircraft carrier.
- 2 anti-aircraft ships.
- 62 destroyers.

APPENDIX C (2)

DISPOSITIONS DURING THE RETREAT FROM CENTRAL NORWAY
30TH APRIL–3RD MAY

I. THE CONVOYS

(*Note.*—The figures against a ship's name show the approximate number of passengers she brought away; numbers under 20 not shown.)

(*a*) From Aandalsnes, etc., 30th April–1st May—Vice-Admiral Edward-Collins: *Galatea* (660), *Arethusa* (520), *Sheffield* (590), *Southampton* (200), *Wanderer*, *Walker* (70), *Westcott* (50), *Sikh* (120), *Tartar*, *Somali*, *Mashona*, *Ulster Prince* (50), *Ulster Monarch*.

(*b*) From Aandalsnes, etc., 1st–2nd May—Vice-Admiral Layton: *Manchester* (860), *Birmingham* (390), *Calcutta* (720), *Inglefield*, *Delight*, *Mashona*, *Somali* (250), *Auckland* (240).

The *Diana* took General Ruge and 30 Norwegian staff officers from Molde to Tromsö.

(*c*) From Namsos, 2nd–3rd May—Vice-Admiral Cunningham: *Devonshire*, *York* (1170), *Montcalm*, *Carlisle*, *Afridi* (40), *Nubian*, *Maori*, *Kelly*, *Hasty*, *Imperial*, *Grenade*, *Griffin*, *Bison*, *El d'Jezair* (1300), *El Kantara* (1100), *El Mansour* (1750).

II. OTHER SHIPS OFF THE COAST OF NORWAY

(*a*) With Lord Cork about Narvik: *Resolution*, *Effingham* (flag), *Aurora*, *Enterprise*, and about a dozen destroyers.

(*b*) Taking the King of Norway, etc., from Molde to Tromsö: *Glasgow*, *Jackal*, *Javelin*.

(*c*) The Carrier Squadron—Vice-Admiral Wells: *Valiant*, *Berwick*, *Ark Royal* (flag), *Glorious*, and a destroyer screen (varied between three and ten).

III. AT SCAPA WITH C.-IN-C., HOME FLEET

Rodney (flag), *Repulse*, *Curlew*, and half a dozen destroyers.

Note.—There were some 30 destroyers besides those mentioned above. A few had special duties (*e.g.*, three were screening the *Warspite* on her way to the Mediterranean), the rest were engaged with convoys, chiefly between the Narvik command and British ports.

APPENDIX C (3)

DISPOSITIONS, 8TH JUNE

I. ON PASSAGE FROM NORTHERN NORWAY

(*a*) With first group of troopships near Faeroe Islands : *Valiant, Tartar, Mashona, Bedouin, Ashanti.*

(*b*) Proceeding independently:—
   (i) *Devonshire* (Flag, Vice-Admiral Cunningham).
   (ii) *Glorious, Ardent, Acasta.*

(*c*) On passage to assembly rendezvous for second group of troopships :—
   (i) *Southampton* (Flag, Admiral of the Fleet Lord Cork), *Coventry* (Flag, Rear-Admiral Vivian), *Havelock, Fame, Firedrake, Beagle, Echo, Delight.*
   (ii) *Ark Royal* (Flag, Vice-Admiral Wells), *Diana, Acheron, Highlander.*

(*d*) Others:—
   (i) *Arrow, Walker* and *Stork*—with Harstad store convoy.
   (ii) *Campbell*—to join Tromsö store convoy.
   (iii) *Veteran, Vanoc*—to join Vice-Admiral Cunningham after ferry duties. Actually, owing to shortage of fuel, these destroyers did not join him.

II. OTHER SHIPS AT SEA

(*a*) On passage from Scapa to meet first group of troopships : *Atherstone, Wolverine, Witherington, Antelope, Viscount.*

(*b*) Returning to Scapa from coast of Iceland : *Renown* (Flag, Vice-Admiral Whitworth), *Zulu, Kelvin.*

(*c*) Off the coast of Iceland : *Repulse, Newcastle, Sussex, Maori, Forester, Foxhound.*

III. AT SCAPA

Rodney (Flag, Admiral of the Fleet Sir Charles Forbes, C.-in-C., Home Fleet), *Inglefield, Amazon, Electra, Escort, Escapade, Fearless, Whirlwind.*

Note.—Some of these destroyers may have been at sea or at Sullom Voe.

APPENDIX C (4)

DISPOSITIONS OF ALLIED SUBMARINES DURING BRITISH MINELAYING AND GERMAN INVASION OF NORWAY, 8TH–9TH APRIL

I. 8TH APRIL

Kattegat :
Sealion
Sunfish
Triton

Skagerrak :—
Trident
Orzel (Polish).

Entering Skagerrak :—
Truant

Outside Skagerrak :—
Seal .. .. 57° N., 6° E.

West Coast, Denmark :—
Spearfish
Snapper
Unity

East of Dogger Bank :—
Amazone (French)
Antiope (French)

On passage out :—
Severn
Tarpon
Clyde
Thistle
Shark
Seawolf

On passage home :—
Swordfish

Under sailing orders :—
Ursula
Triad

II. 9TH APRIL

Kattegat :—
Sealion
Sunfish
Triton

Skagerrak :—
Trident
Orzel
Truant
Spearfish

South-west Coast, Norway :—
Seal
Clyde
Thistle

Outside Skagerrak :—
Severn .. 57° N., 7° E.
Tarpon .. 57° N., 5° E.
Ursula .. 57° N., 4° E.

West Coast, Denmark :—
Snapper
Unity

East of Dogger Bank :—
Amazone .. 55° N., 4° E. ⎫ Both
Antiope .. 53° N., 3° E. ⎭ days

Heligoland Bight :—
Shark
Seawolf

On passage out :—
Triad
Sterlet

Under sailing orders :—
La Sybille (French)

Notes.—(1) These dispositions are for 0600 each day, according to the daily position signal made by Vice-Admiral, Submarines. The number of submarines in the Kattegat, Skagerrak or off the Norwegian coast rose from 10 on 9th April to 14 on the 12th. The strength decreased from the 14th, however, and by the 18th there was only half that number in those waters.

(2) The object of the patrol is stated in a signal made by Vice-Admiral, Submarines, dated 1931/4 April : 'To attack and then report enemy transports and warships ; when transports escorted by warships are encountered it is more important to attack the transports.'

(3) The first result of these measures was the sinking of a German troopship near Kristiansand by the *Orzel* at midday, 8th April, and of a laden tanker in the mouth of Oslo Fjord by the *Trident* early that afternoon. On the 9th the *Truant* sank the cruiser *Karlsruhe* off Kristiansand, and in the night, 10th/11th, the *Spearfish* damaged the *Lutzow* near the Skaw.

(4) Four submarines were lost during the Norwegian operations : the *Thistle*, *Tarpon* and *Sterlet* in April, and the *Seal* early in May.

APPENDIX D

SIMILARITY OF GERMAN SILHOUETTES

The similarity of the silhouettes of the German ships of various classes frequently caused confusion and uncertainty to their opponents. The reports of submarines and aircraft on 8th April (*see* B.S., Sec. 8 *ante*), and Admiral Whitworth's engagement on 9th April (*see* B.S., Sec. 10 *ante*) are examples of this; and it is almost certain that on 24th May 1941 the *Hood* at first mistook the *Prinz Eugen* for the *Bismarck*.

Vice-Admiral Whitworth in his report of the action of 9th April 1940 against the *Gneisenau* and *Scharnhorst* remarked : ' Both were known to be either of the *Scharnhorst* or *Hipper* class, but throughout the action observation of the details of the enemy was so difficult that even direct comparison with the silhouette cards failed to establish the identity.'

Evidence from control personnel after the action and fragments of an 11-in. shell found on board the *Renown* seemed to confirm that the leading ship was a battle cruiser and the second ship a cruiser of the *Hipper* class, and they were so referred to throughout in the original reports. Could it have been established that *both* German battle cruisers were in the Lofoten Islands area at this stage of the operations, it would have been of great value to the Commander-in-Chief, Home Fleet, and the Admiralty.

The Commander-in-Chief subsequently remarked that this difficulty in identification must always be borne in mind when enemy reports were received.

The similarity of the German silhouettes was not a deliberate policy adopted for purposes of deception, but arose from the fact that all their later ships were designed under the same Chief Constructor, who applied so far as possible the same arrangement and features to all classes, which resulted in their remarkably similar appearance.

It is worth noting that if—all other things being equal—such similarity in appearance can be produced, it is almost certain to cause confusion and might well entail serious consequences for the enemy, while it is difficult to see that it could have any disadvantage for friends.

APPENDIX E
SUMMARY OF AIR ATTACKS ON H.M.S. *SUFFOLK*—17TH APRIL 1940

Attack	Time	Distance of nearest splash (*in yards*)	Type of attack
1	0825	1000	H.L.B.
2	0831	70	H.L.B.
3	0842	100	H.L.B.
4	0901	40	H.L.B.
5	0903	25	H.L.B.
6	0914	80	H.L.B.
7	0919	40	H.L.B.
8	0922	75	H.L.B.
9	1030	20	D.B.
10	1037	HIT	D.B.
11	1046	150	D.B.
12	1048	120	D.B.[1]
13	1100	70	D.B.
14	1120	120	H.L.B.
15	1134	120	H.L.B.[2]
16	1141	100	D.B.
17	1149	150	H.L.B.
18	1207	120	H.L.B.
19	1208	20	H.L.B.
20	1226	130	H.L.B.

[1] This attack was reported as being an aerial torpedo, but no track was seen coming towards the ship. The aircraft came very low—to about 150 feet.

[2] This was definitely an incendiary bomb, being silver in colour and entering the water with a 'sizzle.'

APPENDIX E—*continued*

Attack	Time	Distance of nearest splash (in yards)	Type of attack
21	1231	160	H.L.B.
22	1236	80	D.B.

At 1305—Steering motor out of action

23	1315	20	H.L.B.
24	1323	40	D.B.
25	1325	5	D.B.[1]

At 1328—Steering motor in action again

26	1332	60	D.B.
27	1333	140	H.L.B.
28	1345	75	H.L.B.
29	1347	30	D.B.[2]
30	1430	5	H.L.B.
31	1445	10	H.L.B.
32	1503	20	D.B.
33	1512	10	H.L.B.

Total number of bomb splashes seen   88
Total number of attacks   33
High level bombing attacks   21
Dive bombing attacks   12

---

[1] The machine dived at a 70° angle of sight and sprayed the hangar with machine gun fire. It flew astern of the ship from starboard to port after dropping the bomb and turned E.S.E. emitting smoke and losing height. The machine was not seen to come down.

[2] After this dive bombing attack, the machine appeared to be on fire, lost height, dropped her load of bombs, and later came down in the sea about four miles away on the starboard quarter.

APPENDIX F

H.M.S. *FURIOUS*

STATISTICS OF OPERATIONS IN NORWAY DURING THE PERIOD 11TH APRIL 1940 TO THE 24TH APRIL 1940

1. Distance flown by aircraft .. .. 23,870 miles.
2. Bombs dropped—250 lb. S.A.P. .. .. 116 in number.
                20 lb. H.E. .. .. 293 in number.
                Total weight .. .. $15\frac{1}{4}$ tons.
3. Torpedoes dropped 18
4. Aircraft totally lost 9
5. Aircraft hit by enemy 17
6. Aircraft damaged beyond facilities for repair on board .. Nil
7. Photographs taken 295
8. Casualties—

	Killed.	Wounded.	Missing.	Injured.
Officers	2	3	1	1
Air Gunners ..	1	2	1	1

APPENDIX G

SOME EXTRACTS OF GENERAL AUCHINLECK'S DISPATCH, DATED 19TH JUNE 1940

(M.017624/40)

In the Narvik as in the other expeditions to Norway, the German mastery in the air gained the day for them, the taking of the port after a six weeks' campaign notwithstanding. Indeed, the delay before the attack was largely the effect of the German strength in the air. The following extracts of General Auchinleck's dispatch deal with this subject:—

Paragraph 38.—' On 13th May the Germans had a powerful air force in southern Norway and several excellent air bases from which to operate it. We, on the other hand, had not a single aerodrome or landing ground fit for use. The enemy thus had complete mastery in the air, except on the somewhat rare occasions when the Fleet Air Arm were able to intervene with carrier-borne aircraft. The vigour and daring of the pilots of the Fleet Air Arm, when they were able to engage the enemy, earned the admiration of the whole force; but even their strenuous efforts could not compensate for the absence of land-based aircraft . . . .'

Paragraph 40, when it was decided to send Royal Air Force machines to work from Bardufoss.—' The need for some support in the air for both the sea and land forces was urgent, particularly for H.M. ships, which were suffering heavily from the daily and almost continuous attacks made on them in the narrow waters round Narvik by the thoroughly efficient enemy bomber aircraft. Nevertheless, Group-Captain Moore, rightly, in my opinion, resisted all pressure to induce him to call for the aircraft to be sent before he was quite satisfied that the landing grounds could be said to be reasonably ready to receive them.'

Paragraphs 114–116.—' Surprise landings from aircraft had far-reaching effects, owing to the ability they conferred on the enemy to outflank positions or take them in the rear. The action on the Hemnes Peninsula, south of Mo, provides an outstanding example of these tactics. The sequence of this action was, first, bombing and low-flying attacks on our troops holding the position. These attacks were followed almost immediately by landings from seaplanes in two places on each flank of the peninsula. Once these landings had been secured, they were promptly reinforced by small coastal steamers; and further reinforcements were brought up to the outflanking detachments by seaplanes on succeeding days . . . .

The outstanding example of the supply by air is the maintenance of the German detachments in the Narvik area . . . . His troops, to the number of 3000 or 4000, have been successfully supplied by air for many weeks . . . .

As regards the control of sea communications, the enemy's supremacy in the air made the use inshore of naval vessels of the type co-operating with this force highly dangerous and uneconomical. Though it might have been possible to use high-speed coastal motor-boats, armed with small guns, to prevent movement of enemy craft in these waters, the use of trawlers, owing to their extreme vulnerability to air attack, was not considered practicable. On the other hand, the inshore waterways were used at will by the Germans, who constantly employed local boats and steamers to ferry their troops about, thus entailing more dispersion of the defending forces on land. In an attempt to send considerable reinforcements and wheeled vehicles to Bodo, the Polish steamer *Chrobry* was sunk before she reached port. The unloading of large supply ships, which, owing to the limited facilities available, would have taken many hours, had to be ruled out as impracticable; and reinforcements to Bodo could therefore be sent only by destroyer or by small local craft. Thus, the provision of adequate reinforcements in guns and vehicles was made extremely difficult.'

As for anti-aircraft artillery, General Auchinleck states that he had only half the strength he asked for; yet he only asked for two-thirds of the War Office calculation of what would be required (Appendix E to the dispatch).

The General has also remarks about water transport.

Paragraph 17.—' The force was maintained through the base area which had been established from the outset at Harstad, the forward delivery to units and formations in contact being made by locally procured water transport to Fjord Head, where approximately 10 days' reserve supplies, etc., were held. Inland water transport was thus the main agency for forward maintenance. Yet, although a study of the map would have shown that this was so, no provision had been made to send with the force at the outset the necessary personnel to organise and operate inland water transport in the way that railway units are sent to operate railways in the theatre where the railway is the main transport agency.'

APPENDIX G—*continued*

Paragraph 48.—'. . . the weak link in the administrative system was the locally procured inland water transport which the navy had endeavoured to organise. It was weak because the craft were owner-driven diesel-engined fishing craft of 10 to 50 tons, and also because of the lack of adequate control or organisation. In consequence, though willing workers, the personnel could not be relied upon, whilst the distances to be covered were great. All immediately procurable craft ("puffers") and seven small coastal steamers, two of which were used as hospital carriers, were located at Harstad and in the vicinity of the forward field supply depots.'

Paragraph 50.—' Great difficulties were experienced in the handling of heavy equipment and stores at places other than Harstad, as there was no means of putting them ashore except by motor landing craft. These were few in number, and were also required for tactical operations. In consequence, the establishment of anti-aircraft guns in position and the creation and stocking of aerodromes at Bardufoss and Skaanland were seriously delayed . . . .'

APPENDIX H

NAVAL LOSSES AND DAMAGE (ALLIED AND GERMAN)

Note.—Total losses are shown in *ITALIC CAPITALS*. For damage to A/S Trawlers, *see* App. A (1)

ALLIED

SHIP	REMARKS
CAPITAL SHIPS	2 DAMAGED
H.M.S. Renown	Slight damage, gunfire, German battle cruisers, 9th April.
H.M.S. Rodney	Slight damage, bomb, 9th April.
AIRCRAFT CARRIERS	1 SUNK, 1 DAMAGED
H.M.S. Furious	Damage to turbines, near miss, bombs, 18th April.
H.M.S. *GLORIOUS*	Sunk, gunfire, German battle cruisers, 8th June.
CRUISERS	2 SUNK, 8 DAMAGED
H.M.S. Aurora (6-in.)	Damaged, bomb, Ofot Fjord, 7th May.
H.M.S. Cairo (A.A.)	Damage, bombs, Narvik, 28th May.
H.M.S. Curacoa (A.A.)	Severe damage, bomb, 24th April.
H.M.S. *CURLEW* (A.A.)	Sunk, bombs, Skjel Fjord, 26th May.
H.M.S. *EFFINGHAM* (6-in.)	Grounded, total loss, 17th May.
French *Emile Bertin*	Damage, bombs off Namsos, 19th April.

GERMAN

SHIP	REMARKS
	3 DAMAGED
Gneisenau	Damage, gunfire, *Renown*, 9th April.
Lützow	Severe damage, torpedo, *Spearfish*, 11th April.
Scharnhorst	Severe damage, torpedo, *Acasta*, 8th June.
	4 SUNK, 2 DAMAGED
BLÜCHER (8-in.)	Sunk, coast defences, Oslo Fjord, 9th April.
Bremse (Training)	Damage, coast defences, Bergen, 9th April.
BRUMMER (Training)	Sunk, torpedo, *Sterlet*, 15th April.
Hipper (8-in.)	Rammed by *Glowworm*, 8th April.
KARLSRUHE (6-in.)	Sunk, torpedo, *Truant*, 9th April.

APPENDIX H—continued

H.M.S. *Enterprise* (6-in.)	Damage, near misses, bombs, Narvik area.	
H.M.S. *Glasgow* (6-in.)	Slight damage, near miss, bombs, 9th April.	
H.M.S. *Penelope* (6-in.)	Damaged, grounding, 11th April.	
H.M.S. *Southampton* (6-in.)	Slight damage, near miss, bombs, 9th April; ditto, 26th May, Narvik area.	
H.M.S. *Suffolk* (8-in.)	Severe damage, bombs, 17th April.	*KÖNIGSBERG* (6-in.) — Damage, coast defences, Bergen, 9th April. Sunk F.A.A. dive bombing, 10th April.
COAST DEFENCE VESSELS		
H. Nor. M.S. *EIDSVOLD*	} Sunk, gunfire and torpedoes, Narvik, 9th April.	
H. Nor. M.S. *NORGE*		
DESTROYERS	9 SUNK, 12 DAMAGED	10 SUNK
H.M.S. *ACASTA*	} Sunk, gunfire, German battle cruisers, 8th June.	*ANTON SCHMITT*
H.M.S. *ARDENT*		*BERND VON ARNIM*
H.M.S. *AFRIDI*	Sunk, bombs, evacuation from 3rd May.	*DIETHER VON ROEDER*
H.M.S. *Arrow*	Damaged, rammed, German trawler, 26th April.	*ERICH GIESE* *ERICH KOELLNER* } Destroyed, 1st and 2nd Battles of Narvik.
French *BISON*	Sunk, bombs, evacuation from Namsos, 3rd May.	*GEORG THIELE* *HANS LUDEMANN*
O.R.P. *Blyskawica*	Damaged, gunfire, Narvik area, 2nd May.	*HERMANN KUNNE*
H.M.S. *Cossack*	Damaged, gunfire, 2nd Battle of Narvik.	*WILHELM HEIDKAMP*
H.M.S. *Eclipse*	Damaged, bombs, 11th April.	*WOLFGANG ZENKER*
H.M.S. *Eskimo*	Damaged, torpedo, 2nd Battle of Narvik.	

165

APPENDIX H—*continued*

	ALLIED		GERMAN	
SHIP	REMARKS		SHIP	REMARKS

DESTROYERS—*continued*

SHIP	REMARKS
H.M.S. *Fame*	Damaged, gunfire, Narvik area, 23rd May.
H.M.S. *Firedrake*	Damaged, gunfire, Narvik area, 23rd May.
H.M.S. *GLOWWORM*	Sunk, gunfire and ramming *Hipper*, 8th April.
O.R.P. *GROM*	Sunk, bombs, Ofot Fjord, 4th May.
H.M.S. *GURKHA*	Sunk, bombs, off Bergen, 9th April.
H.M.S. *HARDY*	Damaged, gunfire, and beached; total loss: 1st Battle of Narvik.
H.M.S. *Hesperus*	Slight damage, near misses, Narvik area.
H.M.S. *Hotspur*	Damaged, gunfire, 1st Battle of Narvik.
H.M.S. *HUNTER*	Sunk, gunfire, 1st Battle of Narvik, 10th April.
H.M.S. *Kashmir*	Severe damage, collision, 9th April.
H.M.S. *Kelly*	Severe damage, torpedo, M.T.B., 9th May.
H.M.S. *Kelvin*	Severe damage, collision, 9th April.
H.M.S. *Matabele*	Slight damage, grounding, 17th May.
French *Milan*	Damaged, bomb, 23rd May, Narvik area.
H.M.S. *Punjabi*	Damaged, gunfire, 2nd Battle of Narvik.

APPENDIX H—continued

H.M.S. Somali	..		Damaged, near miss, bomb, off Bodo, 15th May.
H.M.S. Vansittart	..		Damaged, bomb, off Narvik, 10th May.
H.M.S. Wanderer	..		Damage, grounded, Alfarnes, 30th April.
H.M.S. Walker	..		Damaged, near miss, bomb, 27th May, Narvik area.
SUBMARINES			4 SUNK, 2 DAMAGED
H.M.S. Seal	..		Damaged, mine or depth charge, Kattegat; captured by Germans, 5th May.
H.M.S. STERLET	..	U.22	Sunk by A/S Craft, Skagerrak, 18th April.
H.M.S. TARPON	..	U.49	Sunk by A/S Craft off Denmark, 14th April.
H.M.S. THISTLE	..	U.46	Sunk by U.4 off Stavanger, 10th April.
H.M.S. Truant	..		Damaged, explosion, possibly magnetic torpedo, 25th April.
H.M.S. UNITY	..		Sunk, rammed by s.s. Atlejarl.
			SUNK.
			Lost in North Sea, possibly by French Orphée, 21st April.
			Sunk by Brazen and Fearless. Vaags Fjord.
			Sunk, Warspite's aircraft, Herjangs Fjord.
SLOOPS			
H.M.S. Black Swan	..		Damaged, bomb, 28th April.
H.M.S. BITTERN	..		Severe damage, bomb; sunk, 30th April.
H.M.S. Pelican	..		Severe damage, bomb, 22nd April.

Index

The numerical references refer to SECTIONS, not pages.

Only those names of individuals and ships that are specifically mentioned in the text of the narrative are included in the index: for other names the appropriate Appendix must be consulted, viz. :—

Appendix A — Allied war ships with main armament and Flag and Commanding Officers.
Appendix A (1) — A/S Trawlers.
Appendix A (2) — Naval Commands ashore in Norway.

A

Aachen, S.S., sunk, Narvik, 10 April, 13 (note).

Aalesund, 19; landing at, 36; 38.

Aandalsnes, Introduction, 19, 21; Allied landings planned, 22; 24, 25, 26; preliminary landing (Primrose) and enemy bombing, 36; Sickle landing, enemy bombing, 37, 38; decision to evacuate, 39, 40; plan of withdrawal, 41; evacuation, 42, 48, 51, 52.

Acasta, H.M.S., Destroyer, 19 (note), 62; torpedoes *Scharnhorst* and herself sunk, 63 (and note).

Acheron, H.M.S., Destroyer, at Operation Sickle, 37; reinforcements to Aandalsnes, escorts damaged *Arrow*, 38; 62 (note).

Acrity, S.S., 62.

Actions (Surface Craft), *Glowworm* against *Hipper*, 5; *Renown* against battlecruisers, 10; 1st battle of Narvik, 13; 2nd battle of Narvik, 18; destroyers and E-boats, 10 May, 28; sinking of *Glorious, Ardent* and *Acasta*, 61.

Admiralty, Inform C.-in-C., H.F., of German movements, cancel *Teviot Bank's* minelaying, 4; direct destroyers in Vest Fjord to join Admiral Whitworth, 7, 8; instructions to Admiral Whitworth, 7; inform C.-in-C., H.F., Plan R4 abandoned, 8 (and note); information and instructions to C.-in-C. and annul C.-in-C's. dispositions, 8/9 April, 8, 68, 71; directions, 9 April, to Admiral Whitworth, Captain Warburton-Lee, and C.-in-C., 11, 12; annul attack on Bergen, 12 (and note); messages to Captain Warburton-Lee, 13; to Admiral Whitworth and *Penelope*, 14; information to C.-in-C., 15; order battleship attack at Narvik, and urge occupation, 18; re-dispose Submarines, 8 April, 20; question of attack on Trondheim (Operation Hammer), 21, 22, 23; 26; 28; instructions to Captain Pegram (Operation Henry), 31; and to Admiral Layton (Operation Maurice), 32; 36; instructions to Admiral Edward-Collins (Operation Sickle), 37; 38; 40 (note), 41; 42 (note); 43; 44; urge early occupation Narvik, 45; 48; 49; on Bodo area, 50; 51; 61; place all forces in Northern area under C.-in-C., H.F., 66; control of forces afloat, 68.

Air Attacks, *British*, on German battlecruisers, 7 April, 4 (and note); on ships in Bergen, 12; on Trondheim, 15, 25, 66; Narvik, 17, 18; shipping, 25; battlecruisers, 66.

German, on Oslo area, 9; Home Fleet, 12, 15; Scapa Flow and 2nd C.S., 12, 18 (note); on R.A.F. Gladiators on Lake Lesjaskog, 25, 26; 27; on *Suffolk*, 28 (and note), App. E; on French destroyers, 28; at Namsos, 32, 33, 34; sink *Bison* and *Afridi*, 43; on Aandalsnes area 31, 36, 37, 38, 39, 40, 41, 42; on *Enterprise*, Bodo area, 52, 60; sink *Chrobry*, 52, 53; on Harstad area, 54, 56 (and note), and ships in Ofot Fjord, 58; at capture of Narvik, 58; on Bodo, 60; 62; on *Valiant*, 65; influence on campaign, 67.

Aircraft Carriers, 2; *Furious* joins C.-in-C., H.F., 8 (and note), 12; 15; 17; 18; 19; 21; *Glorious* and *Ark Royal* join H.F., 21, 25; general employment, 25; 41; 55; 62; 63.

Airfields, importance of Stavanger, 8; Germans capture Norwegian, 9; Luftwaffe operational, 21 (and note); Vaernes damaged by air raids, 25; Stavanger bombarded by *Suffolk*, 28; repairs and construction, Bardufoss and Skaanland, 54; and importance, 56; at Bodo, 60.

Air reconnaissance locates German heavy ships, 7 April, 4 (and note), *Hipper*, 8 April, 8 (and note); *Köln* at Bergen, 9 April, 12; failure to locate German battlecruisers, 9–12 April, 15, and 4–9 June, 65 (and note); 18; 49; 62; 64; reports forces in Trondheim, 66.

Afridi, H.M.S., Destroyer, 4 (note) 19 ; 31 (note); lands troops Namsos, 32; 33; 38; at evacuation of Namsos, bombed and sunk, 43 (and note), 73 (note).

Albatros, German torpedo boat, 1 ; engaged by *Olav Tryggvason*, 9.

Alster, S.S., German storeship, 1 (note) ; captured by *Icarus*, 11 April, 14 (and note), 21.

Altmark, S.S., Introduction (note).

Altona, S.S., sunk, Narvik, 10 April, 13 (note).

Amazon, H.M.S., Destroyer, 38.

Amazone, French Submarine, 20.

Ammunition, Anti-aircraft, heavy expenditure, 12, 26, 32 (note), 37, 42 ; shortage, 37 (note) ; Bombardment, 23 ; German destroyers run short, Narvik, 18 (notes) ; Norwegian stocks at Molde, 31.

Angle, H.M.S., A/S Trawler at Namsos, 27.

Ankenes, Ofot Fjord, 45 ; occupied by Allies, 47 ; S.W. Borderers leave, 53 55; 57 ; stiff fighting, 58.

Annesley, Captain J. C., D.S.O., R.N., Commanding Officer H.M.S. *Enterprise*, takes convoy to Bodo, remarks on value of A.A. ships' armament, 52.

Antares, S.S., sunk by submarine, 21 (note).

Antelope, H.M.S., Destroyer, 62 (note).

Anti-aircraft cruisers, general employment, 26 ; 37.

Anti-aircraft fire, insufficient to stem attacks, 42.

Anti-submarine trawlers, inshore operations, 27, App. A (1).

Anti-submarine patrols, German, 1.

Antiope, French submarine, 20.

Anton Schmitt, German destroyer, 1 ; sunk, Narvik, 13 (and note).

Appeasement, Policy of, Introduction.

Arab, H.M.S., A/S Trawler, at Namsos, 27.

Arandora Star, S.S., 62.

Arbroath, S.S., A.S.I.S., 62.

Ardent, H.M.S., Destroyer, 19 (note), 62 ; sunk while escorting *Glorious*, 63.

Arendal, 1 ; occupied by Germans, 9.

Arethusa, H.M.S., Cruiser, 4 (and note), 8 ; 12 ; 21 ; 24 ; 31 ; lands troops Aandalsnes, 37, and stores, 38 (and note) ; at evacuation of Aandalsnes, 42.

Ark Royal, H.M.S., Aircraft Carrier, Flag V.A. (A), 21, 23 ; operations, 25, 41, 52, 53 ; Supports Bjerkvik landing, 55 (and note), 56 ; at withdrawal from Narvik, 61, 62 ; 63 ; 65 ; movements and F.A.A. attack, Trondheim, 13 June, 66.

Army Operations, General situation, 15 April, 21 (and note) ; *Allied*, Namsos area, 31, 32, 34, 35 ; Aandalsnes area, 37, 39 ; withdrawal from Central Norway, 40, 41, 42, 43 ; Narvik area, 45, 55, withdrawal, 62 ; Bodo area, 47, 49, 51, 52, withdrawal, 60.

German, initial landings, 11 ; Oslo troops join Trondheim force, 39 ; Bodo area, 50, 51, 53 ; Narvik area, 55, 58.

Arrow, H.M.S., Destroyer, Operation Sickle, 37 ; rammed by German trawler, 38 ; at Bodo evacuation, 60 (note).

Ashanti, H.M.S., Destroyer, 24, 33, 62 (note).

Askim, Commodore, Royal Norwegian Navy, S.N.O., Narvik, 9 April, 9 (note).

Assault Landings, at Bjerkvik, 55 ; at Narvik, 57, 58.

Aston Villa, H.M.S., A/S Trawler, at Namsos, 27.

Atherstone, H.M.S., Destroyer, 62 (note).

Atlantis, Hospital Ship, attacked by aircraft, Harstad, 54 ; intercepted by *Hipper*, 63 ; informs *Valiant* of sinking of *Orama*, 68, 69.

Atljarl, S.S., Norwegian, rams *Unity*, 29.

Auchinleck, Lieutenant-General Claud J. E., C.B., C.S.I., D.S.O., O.B.E., 30 (note) ; relieves Major-General Mackesy, 52, 55 (and note) ; remarks on Mo–Mosjoen operations, 53 ; witnesses Bjerkvik landing, 55 ; 56 ; 57 ; at capture of Narvik and remarks, 58, 59 ; remarks on Bodo evacuation, 60 (note) ; 61 ; 62 ; extracts from despatch, App. G.

Auckland, H.M.S., Sloop. Operation Primrose, 21 ; at Namsos, 26, 34 ; lands French troops, Namsos, 35 ; at Aandalsnes, 36, 42.

Audet, General, commands French troops, Namsos, 33 ; at evacuation of Namsos, 43.

Auphan, Captain, French Navy, 23.

Aurora, H.M.S., Cruiser, 3, 8 ; rescues *Gurkha*'s survivors, 12 ; hoists Flag of Admiral of the Fleet Lord Cork, and sails for Narvik area, 17 (and notes), 19 (and note) ; arrives Vaags Fjord, 21, 41 (and note), 45 ; bombards Narvik, 46 ; in Ofot Fjord, 47 ; damaged by air attack, and at Bjerkvik landing, 55 ; 57.

Aylmer, Captain E. A., D.S.C., R.N., S.N.O., Aandalsnes, and remarks in German air attacks, 37.

B

Bahia Castillo, S.S., damaged by *Narwhal*, 29.

Ballangen, Ofot Fjord, German destroyers at, 13 ; S.W. Borderers land, 45, 46 ; 47 ; advanced anchorage, 54 ; German parachutists land, 7 June, 62.

Baltic, Introduction, 68.

Bangsund, *Glasgow*'s party lands, 31 ; 32.

Bardufoss, Norwegian airfield, 54 (and note) ; unfit for use, 56 ; fogbound, Narvik landings, 58 ; 61 ; R.A.F. leaves, 62.

Barenfels, S.S., German store ship, 1 (note) ; sunk, air attack, Bergen, 21.

Barham, H.M.S., Battleship, Landing party from, 21, 22, 36.

Bases, destruction of Allied, Norway, 40 ; development of Harstad, 54.

Basilisk, H.M.S., Destroyer, at Bjerkvik landing, 55.

Batory, M.V., Polish, joins Convoy NP1, 17, 19 (note) ; evacuation Narvik area, 62, 69.

Batteries, No A/A at Narvik, 17.

Beagle, H.M.S., Destroyer, at capture of Narvik, 57, 58.

Bedouin, H.M.S., Destroyer, 4 (note), 7, 11, 14 ; at second battle of Narvik, 18 ; 62 (note).

Beisfjord, Ofot Fjord, German positions bombarded, 47 ; 55 ; Poles reach head of, 58.

Bergen, Introduction ; 1, 2, 3, 4, 6, 8 ; occupied by Germans, 9 ; attack by Admiral Layton ordered and cancelled, 9 April, 12 (and note) ; *Königsberg* sunk by F.A.A., 12 (and note) ; U-boat disposition off, 20 ; 21, 22, 25, 71, 72.

Bernd von Arnim, German destroyer, 1 ; engages *Glowworm*, 5 ; engaged by *Norge*, 9 ; damaged, 13 (and note) ; sunk, second battle of Narvik, 13 (and note).

Berney-Ficklin, Major-General H. P. M., M.C., 23.

Berwick, H.M.S., 8-in. cruiser, 3, 8, 12, 15, 19, 21 ; embarks marines for Iceland, 24 ; 25 ; 47.

Bethouart, General, joins Lord Cork, 47 ; lands at Bjerkvik, 55, 57 ; at capture of Narvik, 58 ; 59 ; 62.

Bickford, Captain J. G., D.S.C., R.N., Captain (D), 20 ; H.M.S. *Esk*, 2, 3 ; patrols Vest Fjord, 9 April, 11 ; 14.

Biggs, Commander H. W., R.N., Commanding Officer H.M.S. *Hero*, at second battle of Narvik, 18.

Binney, Vice-Admiral Sir T. Hugh, K.C.B., D.S.O., Vice-Admiral Orkneys and Shetlands, remarks on F.A.A. attack on *Königsberg*, 12 (note).

Birmingham, H.M.S., Cruiser, 3, 4, 5 ; fails to join Admiral Whitworth, 7 ; escorts convoy NP1, 17, 19 (and note), 21 ; 24 ; operations off Little Fisher Bank, 28 ; covers Operation Maurice, 32 ; escorts *Ville d'Alger*, 35 ; sinks German minelaying trawler, 38 ; at evacuation of Aandalsnes, 42.

Bismarck, German battleship. 66 (note), 69 (and note).

Bison, French destroyer, at evacuation of Namsos, bombed and sunk, 43.

Bittern, H.M.S., Sloop, Operation Primrose, 21 ; bombed and sunk, Namsos, 25, 27, 43 ; at Aandalsnes, 36, 37.

Bjerkvik, Ofot Fjord, 47, 51, 52 ; Allied landing, 12/13 May, 55 ; 56.

Blackheath, S.S., 62.

Black Swan, H.M.S., Sloop, Operation Primrose, 21 ; damaged at Aandalsnes, 26 ; at Aandalsnes, 36, 37 ; bombed and returns to United Kingdom, 42 (and note).

Blake, Vice-Admiral Sir Geoffrey, K.C.B., 23.

Blücher, German 8-in. cruiser, Introduction, 1 ; reported at sea, 8 ; damaged and sunk, Oslo Fjord, 9.

Blyskawica, O.R.P., Destroyer, 4 (note).

Bockenheim, S.S., sunk, Narvik, 10 April, 13 (note).

Bodo, suspected German landing, 14 ; Scots Guards land, 47 ; object of operations, 48 ; first landings, 49 ; 50 ; reinforcements, 52 ; 53 ; 54 (note), 55 ; decision to withdraw, 59 ; withdrawal, 60 ; 61.

Bogen, Ofot Fjord, Irish Guards land, 45, 46 ; advanced anchorage, 54 ; 55.

Bombardment, 23 ; Stavanger airfield by *Suffolk*, 28 (and note) ; 41 ; Narvik, 24 April, 46 (and note) ; in Ofot Fjord, 47 ; Hemnes (Bodo) area, 51, 52 ; at Bjerkvik landing, 55 ; at capture of Narvik, 57, 58.

Bombers, bombing, see Air Attacks.

Bonte, Commodore, German S.O. Destroyers, Narvik group, 1 ; arrives Narvik, 9 ; dispositions, and killed, first battle of Narvik, 13, 21 ; misled by U-boat report, 71 ; 72 ; 73.

Borgund, S.S., Norwegian, picks up *Glorious* and *Acasta* survivors, 63.

Boyle, Commander R. C., R.N., Commanding Officer H.M.S. *Grenade*, gallant assistance to *Bison*, 43 (and note).

Bradman, H.M.S., A/S Trawler, lost by air attack, 39.

Brazen, H.M.S., Destroyer, 4 (note), 19 (note), 21 (note) ; with *Fearless*, sinks *U.49*, 45.

Bredsdorff, Captain, Royal Norwegian Navy, S.N.O., Tromsö, 19.

Bremen, S.S., German liner, 35 (note).

Bremse, German gunnery training ship, 1 ; damaged at Bergen, 9 ; supplements coast defences, 12.

British Lady, S.S., Oiler, 14 ; arrives Skjel Fjord, 12 April, 17 (note).

Brummer, German gunnery training ship, sunk by *Sterlet*, 29.

Bruno Heinemann, German Destroyer, 1, 15.

Bulldog, H.M.S., Destroyer, tows torpedoed *Kelly*, 28.

Burch, Captain A. R., R.M., commands *Furious* striking force, second battle of Narvik, 18.

Buenos Aires, S.S., sunk by *Narwhal*, 29.

Burza, O.R.P., Destroyer, 4 (note).

C

Cadart, Rear-Admiral, conducts French landing, Namsos, 33 ; at evacuation Namsos, 43.

Cairo, H.M.S., A.A. Cruiser, escorts convoy NP1, 17 (and note), 19 (and note), 21 ; at Operation Maurice, 32 ; leads French convoy in to Namsos, 33 ; 53 ; 55 ; 56 (note) ; Flag, Lord Cork, at capture of Narvik, 57, 58 (and note) ; damaged and proceeds to United Kingdom, 61.

Calcutta, H.M.S., A.A. Cruiser, 4 ; at Aandalsnes and Namsos, 25, 33 ; escorts *Ville d'Alger*, 35 ; at evacuation of Aandalsnes, 42 ; 43 ; sinks transport, Hemnes, and escorts *Penelope* to United Kingdom, 51.

Campbell, H.M.S., Destroyer, lands reinforcements, Aandalsnes, 38.

Carlisle, H.M.S., A.A. Cruiser, Flag, Rear-Admiral Vivian, 24 ; at Aandalsnes and Namsos 26 ; lands troops, Aandalsnes, 37 ; at evacuation of Namsos, 43 (and note).

Carriers, see Aircraft Carriers.

Carter, Able Seaman C., sole survivor of *Acasta*, 63 (note).

Carton de Wiart, Major-General A., V.C., C.B., C.M.G., D.S.O., commands at Namsos, 19 ; arrives Namsos, 21, 31 ; 22 ; 23 ; 30 (note) ; 32 ; report on Namsos, 21 April, 34, 35 (and note) ; 37 ; 40 ; at evacuation of Namsos, 43 ; 49.

Casualties, in *Afridi*, 43 ; *Glorious*, *Acasta*, *Ardent*, 64 (and note), 73 (and note) ; German at first battle of Narvik, 13 (and note).

Cedar Bank, M.V., sunk by U-boat, 20, 38.

Chamberlain, Rt. Hon. Neville, P.C., M.P., Prime Minister, 72 (note).

Chances of war, 71.

Chrobry, M.V., joins convoy NP1, 17 ; diverted to Namsos, 19 (and note), 32 ; bombed and sunk on passage to Bodo, 52, 53, 56 ; 69 ; 73 (note).

Churchill, Rt. Hon. Winston S., C.H., P.C., M.P., 1st Lord of the Admiralty, Introduction ; message to C.-in-C., H.F., on withdrawal from Central Norway, 40 ; 68 ; Reference, to published works, Introduction (and notes), 12 (note), 22 (note), 23 (and note), 68, 72 (note).

Clarke, Rear-Admiral M. L., D.S.C., Rear-Admiral, 2nd in command 18th C.S., hoists Flag in *Sheffield*, 42 (and note) ; remarks on Narvik landing, 58.

Clouston, Commander J. C., R.N., Commanding Officer H.M.S. *Isis*, reconnoitres Trondheim, 11 April, 15.

Clyde, H.M.S., S/M, 20 ; reports *Gneisenau* and *Hipper*, 10 June, 66.

Coast defences, Norway, lack of warning, 6; damage *Königsberg* and *Bremse* (Bergen), sinks *Blücher* (Oslo Fjord), 9; 12; as reported at Narvik, 13; at Trondheim reconnoitred by *Isis*, 15; Narvik, 18; proposed defences, Harstad area, 54.

Codrington, H.M.S., Destroyer, 4 (note), 12, 19 (note); hoists Lord Cork's Flag, reconnoitres Narvik, 47.

Command, system of Naval, 12 (note), 68.

Commanders-in-Chief,
    Allied Home Fleet, *see* Forbes.
            Rosyth, *see* Ramsey.
            The Nore, *see* Plunkett-Ernle-Erle-Drax.
            Expeditionary Force, Central Norway, *see* Massy.
            French Navy, *see* Darlan.
            French Army, *see* Gamelin.
            Norwegian Army, *see* Ruge.
    German Navy, *see* Raeder.
            Fleet, *see* Marschall.
            Occupation Forces, *see* Falkenhorst.

Commanding Officers, H.M. Ships, *see* App. A.

Commandos (Independent Companies), land in Bodo area, 49; morale, 51.

Congreve, Commander Sir Geoffrey, Bt., R.N., Commanding Officer S.S. *Ranen*, 60; destroys oil tanks, Svolvaer, 62.

Convoys, general remarks, 24; return from Central Norway, 41; HN25, 4 (and note), 12; ON25, 4 (and note); NP1, sails for Norway, 11 April, 17 (and note), 19; arrives, 32, 45; Norwegian troop convoy covered, 19; French convoy arrives Namsos, 33, 35; 38; withdrawal from Central Norway, 41, 42, 43; withdrawal from Northern Norway, 61, 62, 63, 65; 66; German, attacked by submarines, 20, 29.

Cork and Orrery, Admiral of the Fleet the Earl of, G.C.B., G.C.V.O., hoists Flag in *Aurora*, 17 (and note), 18, 19 (and note); meets General Mackesy, 21; 24; 25; arrives Vaags Fjord, naval and army instructions at variance, appointed Supreme Commander, Rupert, 45; directs bombardment of Narvik, 46; reconnoitres and bombards in Ofot Fjord, 47; 49 (and note); reinforces Bodo area, 50; attempts to support Colonel Gubbins, 51; 52; 53; 54 (and note); at Bjerkvik landings, 55; final preparations, plan and capture of Narvik, 56, 57, 58; ordered to withdraw from Norway, 59; 60; plans withdrawal, 61; hauls down Flag, 62; 63; 68; 72.

Cornwall, H.M.S., 8-in. cruiser, decision *re* wireless silence, 69 (note).

Co-operation, 72.

Cossack, H.M.S., Destroyer, *Altmark* incident, Introduction (note), 4 (note), 12 (note); damaged at second battle of Narvik, 18 (and note).

Coventry, H.M.S., A.A. Cruiser, 53, 55; at capture of Narvik, 57, 58; Flag, Rear-Admiral Vivian, evacuation Northern Norway, 62.

Couch, S.S., 62.

Cover, Heavy ship, Plan R4, 2; Convoy HN25, 12; Norwegian troop convoy, 19; convoys evacuating Northern Norway, 61.

Coxwold, S.S., 62.

Creasy, Captain G. E., M.V.O., R.N., Captain (D) 1, H.M.S. *Codrington*, 47.

Cromarty Firth, S.S., 62.

Cruisers, role in Plan R4, 2; operations, 10–14 April, 19.

Crutchley, Captain V. A. C., V.C., D.S.C., R.N., Commanding Officer H.M.S. *Warspite*, at second battle of Narvik, 18 (note).

Cumberland, H.M.S., 8-in. cruiser, decision *re* wireless silence, 69 (note).

Cumming, Lieutenant-Commander, D.S.C., R.N. (retd.), British Vice-Consul, Tromsö, 19 (and note).

Cunningham, Vice-Admiral J. H. D., C.B., M.V.O., Vice-Admiral 1st C.S., 3; movements, 8 April, 8; joins C.-in-C., 9 April, 12; searches Inner Lead, 15, 16; visits Tromsö and Kirkenes, 19, 21; responsible for evacuation of Namsos, 41; plan, decision to evacuate in one night, and evacuation, 43 (and note); 47; 59; embarks King of Norway for passage to United Kingdom, 62 (and note); passes intercepted signal from *Glorious* to C.-in-C., 65; decision to break wireless silence, 69.

Curacoa, H.M.S., A.A. Cruiser, damaged at Aandalsnes, 26; lands troops, Aandalsnes, 37.

Curityba, S.S., 21 (note).

Curlew, H.M.S., A.A. Cruiser, 25; at Operation Maurice, 32; 33; sunk by air attack, 56, 57.

Cyphers, breaking of, 69.

D

Damage, to *Hipper (Glowworm)*, 5 ; to *Königsberg* and *Bremse*, 9 ; *Gneisenau (Renown)*, 10 ; to Germans and British, first battle of Narvik, 13 (and notes) ; to *Lützow (Spearfish)*, 16 ; to *Punjabi, Cossack, Eskimo,* second battle of Narvik, 18 ; to *Furious*, 25 ; to *Curacoa, Black Swan, Pelican, Bittern*, 26 ; to *Suffolk, Kelly*, 28 ; to *Seal*, 29 ; *Emile Bertin*, 33 ; *Curacoa*, 37 ; *Aurora*, 55 ; *Cairo*, 58 ; *Oleander*, 62 ; to *Scharnhorst (Acasta)*, 64.

Darlan, Admiral, C.-in-C., French Navy, 23.

Delight, H.M.S., Destroyer, at evacuation, Aandalsnes, 42 (note) ; Narvik, 62.

Demolitions, at Narvik, 62 (and note).

Denny, Captain M. M., R.N., N.O.I.C., Molde, 36 (and note), 37, 38, 41 ; at evacuation, Aandalsnes, 42.

Derrien, Admiral, Flag in *Emile Bertin*, joins Admiral Cunningham, 8, and C.-in-C., 12 ; 33 ; 43.

De Salis, Captain A. F., R.N., Captain (D) 8, H.M.S. *Faulknor*, reconnoitres Rombaks Fjord, 45 ; commands detached squadron, Ofot Fjord, 46.

Destroyers, number available, Home Fleet, 4 ; shortage of, 19 (note), 23, 24, 25 (note), 49, 65 ; land troops, Namsos, 32 ; Harstad, 54 ; evacuation of Bodo, 60 (and note), and Northern Norway, 62.

Devonshire, H.M.S., 8-in. Cruiser, Flag, Vice-Admiral J. H. Cunningham, 3, 12 ; 15 ; 19 ; 21 ; at evacuation, Namsos, 43 ; 47 ; takes King of Norway to United Kingdom, 62 ; intercepts signal from *Glorious*, 65, 69.

Diana, H.M.S., Destroyer, at evacuation, Aandalsnes, 42 (and note), Narvik, 62 (note).

Diesen, Admiral N., Royal Norwegian Navy, 42, 59.

Diether von Roeder, German destroyer, 1 ; severely damaged, 13 (and note) ; sunk, second battle of Narvik, 18.

Dietl, German General, commanding Narvik detachment, 1, 9, 55, 58, 60.

Dispositions, C.-in-C., H.F., night 8/9 April, 8 ; Vest Fjord area, 9 April, 11 ; German destroyers at Narvik, 13 ; initial submarine dispositions, Allied and German, 20 ; German U-boat disposition captured, 45 ; Apps. C (1)–(4).

Dittmarschen, S.S., German store ship, 63.

Dive bombing, *Königsberg* sunk by, 12 (and note) ; F.A.A. successes, 25 ; German sinks *Chrobry*, 53.

Diversion, by German battle cruisers during landings, 1, 71.

Doenitz, Admiral, Flag Officer, U-boats, remarks on German torpedoes, 20.

Dombaas, railway junction, Oslo–Trondheim, 21, 36, 37, 39.

Dormer, Sir Cecil, K.C.M.G., H.B.M. Minister, Norway, informs King of Norway of decision to evacuate, 59.

Duchess of Athol, S.S., 23.

Duchess of York, S.S., 62.

Duck, Operation, bombardment of Stavanger airfield, 19, 28.

Dunkirk, evacuation of B.E.F., 61 (and note).

Durnford, Captain J. W., R.N., Commanding Officer H.M.S. *Suffolk*, lands force at Faeroes, and intercepts tanker *Skagerrak*, 19 ; carries out Operation Duck, 28.

E

E-boats, damage *Kelly*, 28.

Echo, H.M.S., Destroyer, 53 (note) ; at Bodo evacuation, 60 (note).

Eclipse, H.M.S., Destroyer, damaged by air attack, 11 April, 15 ; 16.

Economy of Force, 72.

Edds, Captain W. F., R.M., commands landing party, Operation Henry, 31.

Edward-Collins, Vice-Admiral Sir George F., K.C.V.O., C.B., Vice-Admiral, 2nd C.S., 2, 4 (note) ; movements, 7/8 April, 12 (and note) ; ordered to embark troops, 19 ; 21 ; 24 ; 32 ; conducts landing, Aandalsnes, 37, 38 ; conducts first part of evacuation, Aandalsnes, 41, 42.

Effingham, H.M.S., Cruiser, placed under Lord Cork, 17 (note), 19 (note) ; 33 ; covers landing, Aandalsnes, 37 ; hoists Lord Cork's Flag, bombards Narvik, 46 ; bombards in Ofot Fjord, 47 ; at landing at Bjerkvik, 55 ; runs aground, total loss, 53 ; 60.

Egersund, 8 (note).

Eidsvold, H. Nor. M.S., Coast defence vessel, treacherously sunk by Germans, Narvik, 9 (and note) ; 13.

El d'Jezair, S.S., French transport, at Namsos, 33, 43.

Electra, H.M.S., Destroyer, 4 (note), 19, 46 (note), 47.

El Kantara, S.S., French transport, at Namsos, 33, 43.

El Mansour, S.S., French transport, at Namsos, 33, 43.

Emden, German cruiser, 1, 8, 24 (note).

Emile Bertin, attached Home Fleet, 4 (and note) ; 8 ; 12 ; bombed and damaged off Namsos, 33 (and note).

Empire, S.S., 23.

Empress of Australia, S.S., sails in convoy NP1, 17 ; 19 ; 32.

Encounter, H.M.S., Destroyer, 14 (note), 17 (note).

Enemy reports, delay, air contact, 7 April, 4 (and note) ; F.A.A. and Submarine reports, 8 April, 8 ; forces reported in Aalesund area, 19, 31 ; *Glorious* report, 8 June, 65 ; *Clyde* reports *Gneisenau* and *Hipper*, 10 June, 66.

Enterprise, H.M.S., Cruiser, placed under Lord Cork, 17 (note) ; 19 (note) ; bombards Narvik, 46 ; transports Scots Guards to Mo area, 51 ; 52 ; 55 (note) ; 57.

Erich Giese, German destroyer, 1 ; at first battle of Narvik, 13 (and note) ; sunk, second battle of Narvik, 18.

Erich Koellner, German destroyer, 1 ; at first battle of Narvik, 13 (and note) ; sunk, Djupvik Bay, second battle of Narvik, 18.

Erichson, General, commanding 1st Division, Norwegian Army, 21 (note).

Escapade, H.M.S., Destroyer, 4 (note), 19.

Escort, H.M.S., Destroyer, tows damaged *Eclipse* to Lerwick, 15.

Esk, H.M.S., minelaying destroyer, 3 (note), 18 (note).

Eskimo, H.M.S., Destroyer, 4 (note), 7, 11 ; tows *Penelope* to Skjel Fjord, 14 (and note) ; at second battle of Narvik, attacks U-boat, torpedoes *Künne*, damaged by torpedo, 18 ; 58.

Europa, German S.S., liner, 35 (note).

Evacuations, Central Norway, 35, 41, 42, 43 ; Mosjoen, 51 ; Bodo area, 60 ; Northern Norway, 59. 61.

Evans, Admiral Sir Edward R. G. R., K.C.B., 2 ; hoists Flag in *Aurora*, 3 ; hauls down Flag, but remains in *Aurora*, 8 (note) ; special mission to Sweden and Norway, 17 (note).

F

Faeroes, landing in, conducted by *Suffolk*, 19 ; 64.

Falkenhorst, General von, German C.-in-C., Norway operations, 1.

Fame, H.M.S., Destroyer, 47 ; at Bjerkvik landing, 55 ; and capture of Narvik, 57, 58.

Faulknor, H.M.S., Destroyer, reconnoitres Rombaks Fjord, 45.

Fearless, H.M.S., Destroyer, 3 (note), 19 (note), 21 (note), 24, 25 (note) ; with *Brazen* sinks *U.49*, Vaags Fjord, 45.

Fejeosen Fjord, Northern entrance to Bergen, patrols, 12.

Fell, Acting-Commander W. R., R.N., runs ' Gubbins ' Flotilla, 53 ; at withdrawal from Bodo, 60.

Fighter protection, 25, 28 ; withdrawal, Aandalsnes, 42 ; Bodo and Narvik areas, 52, 54, 55, 56 ; Bodo evacuation, 60 ; evacuation, Northern Norway, 61, 62.

Finland, Russian invasion, Introduction.

Firedrake, H.M.S., Destroyer, at capture of Narvik, 57, 58 ; at Bodo evacuation, 60 (note).

Flag Officers, *see* App. A.

Flamingo, H.M.S., Sloop, Operation Primrose, 21, 36 ; 26 ; at Aandalsnes, 37.

Fleet Air Arm, General employment, 25 ; commendation by 1st Lord, 40 ; *Carrier borne*, 15, 17, 18, 25, 54, 55, 61, 66 ; *ship borne*, 8 (and note), 18 (and note) ; *shore-based*, 9 (note), 12 (and note), 25.

Fleetwood, H.M.S., Sloop, at Aandalsnes, 26, 42 ; transports troops to Bodo, 52.

Fleischer, General, Norwegian G.O.C., Tromsö area, 45 ; on importance of Bodo, 52 ; 58.

Florida, S.S., sunk by Submarine, 21 (note).

Flyingdale, S.S., guide of convoy HN25, 4 (note).

Follow up, German arrangements, 1 (and notes), 21.

Forbes, Admiral of the Fleet Sir Charles M., G.C.B., D.S.O., Commander-in-Chief, Home Fleet, Introduction (note), 2 ; sends Vice-Admiral Whitworth to cover Vest Fjord minelayers, 3 ; proceeds to sea, 7 April, 4 (and note), 5 (note) ; receives delayed report of *Rio de Janeiro*, 6 ; sends reinforcements to Admiral Whitworth, 7 ; surprise at abandonment of Plan R4, movements, 8 April, appreciation and dispositions, dispositions annulled by Admiralty, 8 ; orders to Captain Warburton-Lee, 9 April, 11 ; movements, 9–10 April, proposes to attack enemy in Bergen, general ideas consequent on air attack on Fleet, 12 ; covers *Furious* air attack, Bergen, and then proceeds to northward, 15 ; arrives Lofoten area, 17 ; plans attack on enemy at Narvik, returns to Scapa, 18, 21 ; 19, 22 ; views on attack on Trondheim, 23 ; proposals for employment of fleet, 24 ; remarks on employment of A.A. cruisers, sloops, A/S trawlers, 26, 27, 37 (and note) ; 28 ; measures to assist *Suffolk* and remarks, 28 (and note) ; 31 ; 33 ; 40 ; arrangements for evacuation, Central Norway, 41 ; 42 (and note), 43 ; suggests landing Bodo area, 48 ; covering forces for withdrawal from Northern Norway, 61 ; dispositions on report of German battlecruisers, 9 June, 65 ; promoted Admiral of the Fleet and operations, 9–15 June, 66 (and note) ; remarks on intelligence and reconnaissance, 4 (note), 15, 65 (note) ; general remarks on campaign, 67 ; relations with Admiralty, 68 ; 69.

Foresight, H.M.S., Destroyer, 24 (note), 28.

Forestern, H.M.S., Destroyer, at second battle of Narvik, 18 ; 61 (note).

Fortune, H.M.S., Destroyer, 24 (and note).

Foudroyant, French Destroyer, in Bodo area, 52.

Foxhound, H.M.S., Destroyer, at second battle of Narvik, 18(and note) ; 46 (note) ; 61 (note).

Francklin, Lieutenant M. B. P., R.N., commands landing flotilla, Narvik, 58.

Franconia, S.S., 24 (note), 62.

Fraser, Brigadier Hon. W., D.S.O., M.C., placed in command, Bodo area, but invalided, 52 (and note).

French, Troops for Plan R4, 2 ; destroyers arrive Scapa, 4 ; views on Operation Hammer, 23 ; destroyers sweep Skagerrak, 28 ; landings, Namsos, 33, 35 ; withdrawal from Namsos, 43 ; Chasseurs Alpins, Rupert, 44, 47 ; land Mosjoen, 49 ; Foreign Legion landing, Bjerkvik, 52, 55 ; at capture of Narvik, 57, 58, 59 ; withdrawal from Northern Norway, 62.

Friedenau, S.S., sunk by Submarine, 21 (note).

Friedrich Eckholdt, German destroyer, 1, 15.

Frielinghaus, S.S., sunk, Narvik, 10 April, 13 (note).

Furious, H.M.S., Aircraft Carrier, 2 (note), 8 (and note), 12 ; joins C.-in-C., H.F., 12 ; F.A.A. attack Trondheim, 15 ; 16 ; F.A.A. attack Narvik, 12 April, 17 (and note), 13 April, 18 ; 21 ; 23 ; operations and damage, near miss, 25 ; 46 ; 47 ; transports R.A.F. fighters to Narvik area, 56.

Fury, H.M.S., Destroyer, 24 (note), 25 (note), 28.

G

Galatea, H.M.S., Cruiser, 4 (and note), 8, 12, 21, 24, 31 ; lands troops Aandalsnes, 37 ; reinforcements, 38 ; at evacuation Aandalsnes, 42.

Gallant, H.M.S., Destroyer, 28.

Galster, German destroyer, 63.

Gamelin, General, 34.

Gaul, H.M.S., A/S Trawler, at Namsos, 27.

George VI, H.M. The King, 5 (note), 13 (note), 27 (note), 66 (note).

Georgic, S.S., 62.

Georg Thiele, German destroyer, 1 ; damaged, first battle of Narvik, 13 (and note) ; torpedoes *Eskimo* and destroyed, second battle of Narvik, 18.

German Group Command, West, instructions to naval forces, 10 April, 16 ; disapproves Admiral Marschall's change of plan, 8 June, 63.

German Naval War Staff, concern over *Rio de Janeiro*, 6 (note) ; on loss of destroyers, Narvik, 21 (and note) ; on frontal attack, Trondheim, 23 ; on situation, Allied troops, Aandalsnes, 39 ; 42 (note) ; dissatisfaction with Admiral Marschall, 66 (note), 68.

' Gladiator,' Lake, *see* Lesjaskog.

Glasfurd, Commander C. E., R.N., Commanding Officer, H.M.S. *Acasta*, gallant attack on *Scharnhorst*, 63.
Glasgow, H.M.S., Cruiser, 3, 8 ; movements, slightly damaged, 9–10th April, 12 ; operations off Aalesund, 19 ; Operation Henry, 19, 31 ; 21 ; embarks marines for Iceland, 24 ; 33 ; lands reinforcements, Aandalsnes, 38 ; embarks King Haakon, Molde, 41, 42.
Glorious, H.M.S., Aircraft Carrier, leaves Gibraltar, 21 ; 23 ; operations, 25 ; 39 ; transports R.A.F. fighters to Narvik area, 56 (and note) ; at withdrawal from Northern Norway, 61, 62 ; sunk by *Scharnhorst* and *Gneisenau*, 63 ; 65 ; 66 (note) ; 68 ; 69 ; 73 (note).
Glowworm, H.M.S., Destroyer, 3 ; engaged and sunk by *Hipper*, 8 April, 5 (and note) ; 7 ; 8 ; 71.
Gneisenau, German battlecruiser, Flag, Vice-Admiral Lütjens, 1 ; reported movements, 4 (and note), 8 ; engagement with *Renown*, 10 ; movements, 10–12 April, 16 ; Operation Juno, 63 ; with *Scharnhorst* sinks *Glorious*, 64 ; 65 ; abortive sweep, 66.
Goering, Reichs Marshal Hermann, cancels minelaying operations, 1 (note).
Graf Spee, German pocket battleship, 69 (note).
Green Howards, 1st, Aandalsnes area, 38.
Greif, German torpedo boat, 1.
Grenade, H.M.S., Destroyer, 4 (note), 14 (note), 17 (note) ; at evacuation, Namsos, assists bombed *Bison*, 43 (and note).
Greyhound, H.M.S., Destroyer, 3 (note), 5, 11, 14.
Griffin, H.M.S., Destroyer, 4 (note), 19 (note), 21 (note) ; reinforcements to Aandalsnes, captures German armed trawler, 38 ; at evacuation, Namsos, 43 (and note).
Grom, O.R.P., Destroyer, 4 (note) ; bombed and sunk, 55.
Groundings, *Penelope*, 14 ; *Cossack*, 18 ; *Highlander*, 32 ; *Wanderer*, 42 ; *Effingham*, *Matabele*, 53.
Gubbins, Brigadier C. McV., D.S.O., Senior Officer Bodo–Mosjoen forces, 49 ; withdraws from Mosjoen, 50 ; takes passage to Bodo, 51 ; 52 ; 59 ; withdrawal from Bodo area, 60.
'Gubbins' Flotilla, 53, 60.
Gunnery, A.A., in fjords, 37.
Gurkha, H.M.S., Destroyer, 4 (note) ; bombed and sunk, 9 April, 12.

H

Haakon VII, H.M. The King of Norway, escapes first German onslaught, 9; 17 (note), 21; leaves Molde in *Glasgow*, 41, 59 ; leaves Tromsö in *Devonshire* for United Kingdom, 62 ; 65 ; 69 ; 73.
Hamilton, Captain L. H. K., D.S.O., R.N., Commanding Officer, H.M.S. *Aurora*, commands detached squadron, Ofot Fjord, 46, 55.
Hammond, H.M.S., A/S Trawler, lost by air attack, 39.
Hans Lüdeman, German destroyer, 1 ; engages *Glowworm*, 5 ; damaged, first battle of Narvik, 13 (and note) ; captured, subsequently sunk, second battle of Narvik, 18.
Hardy, H.M.S., Flotilla Leader, 3 (note), 11 ; at first battle of Narvik, damaged and beached, 13 (and note).
Harmattan, S.S., 62.
Harstad, Allied base, Narvik area, 25, 30 ; arrival of Rupert force, 45 ; development of base, 54 ; 60 ; evacuation, 62 ; 63 ; 70 ; 72.
Hasty, H.M.S., Destroyer, 24 (note), 25 (note) ; at evacuation, Namsos, 43 (and note).
Hatston, F.A.A. base, Orkneys, 12, 25.
Haugesund, Swordfish lay mines off, 25.
Havant, H.M.S., Destroyer, at Faeroes landing, 19.
Havelock, H.M.S., Destroyer, at Bjervik landing, 55 ; at capture of Narvik, 57, 58 ; at Bodo evacuation, 60 (note).
Havock, H.M.S., Destroyer, 3 (note), 11 ; at first battle of Narvik, sinks *Rauenfels*, 13 ; 18 (note), 24 (note), 28, 46 (note).
Hein Hoyer, S.S., sunk, Narvik, 10 April, 13 (note).
Henry, Operation, preliminary landing, Namsos, 22, 30, 31.
Hereward, H.M.S., Destroyer, 24 (note), 25 (note), 28.
Hemnes, German landing, 51 ; bombarded, 52.

Herjangs Fjord (Ofot Fjord), German destroyers at, 13 ; 18 ; enemy positions engaged, 46 ; 55 ; 57.
Hermann Künne, German destroyer, 1 ; damaged, first battle of Narvik, 13 (and note) ; beached and torpedoed, second battle of Narvik, 18 (and note).
Hero, H.M.S., Destroyer, 3, 24 (note), 46 (note).
Hesperus, H.M.S., Destroyer, at Faeroes landing, 19 ; transports troops to Bodo area, 52
Hewitt, Commander J. G., R.N., Commanding Officer H.M.S. *Auckland*, 36.
Heye, Captain, Commanding Officer *Hipper*, 1.
Highlander, H.M.S., Destroyer, escorts NP1, 19 (and note) ; grounds off Lillesjona, 32, 62 (note).
Hipper, German 8-in. cruiser, 1, 4 (note) ; sinks *Glowworm*, 5 ; reported on misleading course, 8 April, 8 ; 10 ; narrowly misses Home Fleet, 15 ; joins Admiral Lütjens, 16 ; Operation Juno, sinks *Orama*, 63 ; 66 ; 71.
Hitler, Adolf, German Führer, decides to invade Norway, Introduction, 35 (note).
Hogg, Brigadier D. McA., Commander Army Base Staff, Aandalsnes, 42.
Holland, Rear-Admiral L. E., C.B., 21, 23.
Home Fleet, nominal list, with C.O.s, App. A ; dispositions, 4–7 April, 2, 3 ; operations, invasion period, 4, 7, 8, 10, 11, 12, 14, 15, 17, 18, 19, 21 ; general employment, April–June, 24 ; operations, 9–15 June, 65, 66 ; system of command, 68.
Hood, H.M.S., Battlecruiser, landing party drawn from, 21, 22, 36.
Horton, Vice-Admiral Sir Max, K.C.B., D.S.O., F.O. Submarines, instructions to submarines, 20.
Hostile, H.M.S., Destroyer, 3 (note), 11 (and note) ; at first battle of Narvik, 13 ; 14 ; 18 (note) ; 24 (note) ; 28 ; 46 (note).
Hotblack, Major-General F. E., D.S.O., M.C., 23.
Hotspur, H.M.S., Destroyer, 3 (note) ; damaged, first battle of Narvik, 13 ; proceeds to Skjel Fjord, 14.
Hunter, H.M.S., Destroyer, 3 (note) ; 11 ; sunk, first battle of Narvik, 13.
Hussars, 3rd, 53.
Hyperion, H.M.S., Destroyer, 3, 15, 24 (note), 25 (note), 28.

I

Icarus, H.M.S., Minelaying Destroyer, 3 (note), 11 ; captures *Alster*, 14 (and note) ; at second battle of Narvik, 18 ; minelaying, Trondheim Lead, 24 ; lands reinforcements, Aandalsnes, 38.
Iceland, 7 ; landing of Royal Marines, 24 ; report of German landing, 61.
Ilex, H.M.S., Destroyer, 3 (note) ; reconnoitres Trondheim, 11 April, 15, 19 (and note), 24 (note).
Imogen, H.M.S., Destroyer, 3 (note), 15, 19 (and note).
Imperial, H.M.S., Destroyer, 24 (note) ; at evacuation of Namsos, 43 (and note).
Impulsive, H.M.S., Minelaying Destroyer, 3 (note), 11 ; minelaying, Trondheim Lead, 24 ; lands reinforcements, Aandalsnes, 38.
Independent Companies, *see* Commandos.
Inglefield, H.M.S., Destroyer, 3 (note), 15, 19 (and note) ; at evacuation, Aandalsnes, 42 (note).
Intelligence, pointing to German invasion of Norway, unfortunate assessment, 4 (and note) ; obtained from Tranoy, 11 ; position of German main units uncertain, 24 ; collected by *Penelope*, 48 (note) ; 65 (note) ; Admiralty's responsibility, 68.
International Law, Introduction ; restrictions on Allied Submarines, 20 (note).
Invasion of Norway and Denmark, German plan and naval organisation, 1 ; troops embarked, 3 ; 8 ; initial landings, 9 ; general situation, 13 April, 21.
Invergordon, Primrose force stormbound at, 21, 36.
Irish Guards, 1st, arrive Narvik area, 45 ; bombed in *Chrobry*, 53 ; Bodo withdrawal, 60.
Iron ore, Scandinavian traffic with Germany, Introduction (and note).
Isis, H.M.S., Destroyer, 3 (note) ; reconnoitres Trondheim, 11 April, 15, 19 (and note).
Ivanhoe, H.M.S., Minelaying Destroyer, 3 (note), 11, 18 (notes) ; minelaying, Trondheim Lead, 24 ; lands reinforcements, Aandalsnes, 38.

J

Jackal, H.M.S., Destroyer, 38, 41 ; evacuates Colonel Gubbins from Sandnesjoen, 51.

Janus, H.M.S., Destroyer, 4 (note), 24 (note), 28 ; operation off Little Fisher Bank, 28 ; takes party to Mosjoen, 43, 49.

Jan Wellem, S.S., German tanker, 1 (note) ; survives first battle of Narvik, 13 ; 21.

Jardine, H.M.S., A/S Trawler, lost by air attack, 39.

Javelin, H.M.S., Destroyer, 4 (note), 38, 41 ; escorts troops from Sandnesjoen to Bodo, 51.

Jonia, S.S., sunk by submarine, 21 (note).

Juniper, H.M.S., A/S Trawler, sunk by surface craft, 63, 65.

Juno, H.M.S., Destroyer, 4 (note), 24 (note), 25 (note), 28.

Juno, Operation, German attack on Harstad area, 63.

Jupiter, H.M.S., Destroyer, 4 (note).

K

Kaholm, torpedo battery, Oslo Fjord, sinks *Blücher*, 9.

Kandahar, H.M.S., Destroyer, 24 (note) ; engages M.T.B.s, 28.

Karl Peters, German depot ship, 1 ; supplements Bergen defences, 12.

Karlsrühe, German cruiser, 1 ; torpedoed and sunk by *Truant*, 12, 20.

Kashmir, H.M.S., Destroyer, 4 (note) ; collision with *Kelvin*, 12 (note).

Kattegat, German command of sea, 1 (and note) ; 8 ; Submarine operations in, 20 ; to be mined, 24 ; *Seal* captured in, 29.

Kattegat, M.V., German tanker, 1 (note) ; sunk by Norwegians, 14 (note), 19 (note), 21.

Kelly, H.M.S., Destroyer, 24 (note) ; torpedoed by M.T.B. and towed to Tyne, 28 ; at evacuation, Namsos, 43.

Kelvin, H.M.S., Destroyer, 4 (note) ; collision with *Kashmir*, 12 (note) ; 61 (note).

Khartoum, H.M.S., Destroyer, 24 (note).

Kimberley, H.M.S., Destroyer, 4 (note), 7, 11, 14 ; at second battle of Narvik, 18 (and notes) ; 24 (note) ; 28.

King-Harman, Commander, R.N. (Retd.), Commanding Officer *Teviot Bank*, 2.

Kings Own Yorkshire Light Infantry (1/4), at Namsos, 32 ; 38.

Kingston, H.M.S., Destroyer, 24 (note).

Kipling, H.M.S., Destroyer, 28.

Kirkenes, Introduction, 14 (note), 19 (and note), 23.

Knowling, Lieutenant-Commander R. G. K., R.N., Commanding Officer, H.M.S. *Kimberley*, at second battle of Narvik, 18.

Köln, German cruiser, 1 ; leaves Bergen, 12 ;] 24 (note).

Kondor, German torpedo boat, 1.

Kongsmoen, 26 (note), 48.

Königsberg, German cruiser, 1 ; damaged, Bergen, 9 (and note) ; sunk by F.A.A., 12 (and note) ; 25.

Kors Fjord, Southern entrance to Bergen, patrols, 12.

Kristiansund (South), 1 ; *Rio de Janeiro* sunk off, 6, 8 (and note) ; occupied by Germans, 9.

Kummetz, Rear-Admiral commanding Oslo Force, 1 ; Flag in *Blücher*, 9 April, 9.

Kvarven, Coast defence battery, Bergen, damages *Königsberg*, 9 (note).

L

Lambert, Lieutenant-Colonel H. R., D.S.C., R.M., commands Fortress Unit, Harstad, 54.

Lancastria, S.S., 24 (note), 62.

Larvik (West of entrance to Oslo Fjord), 72 (note).

Larwood, H.M.S., A/S Trawler, lost by air attack, 39.

Layman, Commander H. F. H., R.N., Commanding Officer, H.M.S. *Hotspur*, S.O., 2nd D.F., after first battle of Narvik, 14.

Layton, Vice-Admiral Geoffrey, C.B., D.S.O., Vice-Admiral, 18th C.S., 2 ; covers convoy ON25, 7 April, 4 ; joins C.-in-C., 9 April, ordered to attack Bergen, 12 ; 13 ; escorts convoy NP1, 17, 19 (and note) ; 21 ; 24 ; covers damaged *Kelly*, 28–31 ; conducts landing at Namsos, 32 ; covers French convoy, 33 ; 35 ; reinforcements to Molde, 38 ; conducts final evacuation, Aandalsnes area, 41, 42.

Lean, Commander J. I., R.N., Commanding Officer, H.M.S. *Punjabi*, at second battle of Narvik, 18.

Lees, Captain D. M., R.N., Commanding Officer, H.M.S. *Calcutta*, 43.

Leicesters (1/5), at Aandalsnes, 37.

Le Luc, Admiral, 23.

L'Indomptable, French contre-torpilleur, sweep in Skagerrak, 28.

Le Malin, French contre-torpilleur, sweep in Skagerrak, 28.

Leopard, German torpedo boat, 1.

Lesjaskog Lake (' Gladiator ' Lake), R.A.F. Squadron land on, but destroyed, 25 ; 36 ; 39.

Le Triomphant, French contre-torpilleur, sweep in Skagerrak, 28.

Levante, M.V., German store ship, 1 (note) ; reaches Trondheim, 21.

Lillehammer, on Oslo–Trondheim railway, 21 ; Norwegian G.H.Q., 36 ; 37 ; 39.

Lillesjona, Admiral Layton's convoy ordered to, 31 ; 45.

Lincolns (4th), land Namsos area, 32.

Lody, German destroyer, 63.

Losses, naval, *Warships*, Allied and German, *see* App. H ; *Transports, tankers, merchant ships*, Allied, 20, 53, 62, 63, 64 ; German, 1, 6, 13 (note), 19 (and note), 20, 21 (and note), 29.

Luchs, German torpedo boat, 1.

Lucy, Lieutenant W. P., R.N., F.A.A., attack on *Königsberg*, 12.

Lûlea, Gulf of Bothnia, Introduction (and note).

Lumley, Major H., R.M., in command, Aalesund party, 36.

Lützow, German pocket battleship, 1, 8 ; with Oslo Force, 9 April, 9 ; leaves Oslo and torpedoed by *Spearfish*, 16, 20 (and note).

Lyster, Rear-Admiral A. L. St. G., C.V.O., D.S.O., Flag Officer, Harstad, 54.

M

Mackesy, Major-General P. J., C.B., D.S.O., M.C., commanding land forces, Rupert, 17 ; 18 ; 30 (note) ; meets Lord Cork, 21 ; conflicting instructions, 45 (and note) ; at bombardment of Narvik, 46 (and note) ; relieved by General Auchinleck, 52 ; 68 ; 72.

Maillé Brézé, French destroyer, joins Admiral Cunningham, 8.

Main, S.S., German store ship, 1 (note) ; sunk by Norwegians, Haugesund, 8 April, 21.

Manchester, H.M.S., Cruiser, Flag, Vice-Admiral Layton, 4, 8 ; movements, 9–10 April, 12 ; escorts convoy NP1, 17, 19 (and note), 21 ; 24 ; covers damaged *Kelly*, 28 ; and Operation Maurice, 32, 33 ; takes reinforcements to Molde, 38 ; at evacuation of Aandalsnes, 42.

Maori, H.M.S., Destroyer, at evacuation of Namsos, 43 (and note), 61 (note).

Margot, S.S., takes stores to Bodo area, 52.

Marines, *see* Royal Marines.

Martha Hendrik Fisser, S.S., sunk, Narvik, 10 April, 13 (note).

Marschall, Admiral, C.-in-C., Afloat, German Fleet, 1 (note) ; in command Operation Juno, decides to attack convoys, 63 (and note) ; 65 ; conduct not approved and relieved, 66 (and note) ; relations with Naval Staff Ashore, 68.

Mashobra, S.S., M.N.B.D.O. ship, arrives Harstad, 54 ; sunk, 62.

Mashona, H.M.S., Destroyer, 4 (note), 19, 31 (note) ; lands troops, Namsos, 32, 33 ; at evacuation, Aandalsnes, 42 ; 62 (note).

Massy, Lieutenant-General H. R. S., D.S.O., M.C., Commander-in-Chief, Central Norway, 30 (note).

Matabele, H.M.S., Destroyer, 4 (note), 19, 31 (and note) ; lands troops, Namsos, 32 ; escorts *Royal Ulsterman*, 49 ; damaged by grounding, 53 (and note).

Maud, Lieutenant-Commander C. D., R.N., Commanding Officer, H.M.S. *Icarus*, at second battle of Narvik, 18.

Maund, Captain L. E. H., R.N., Chief of Staff to Lord Cork, 45.

Mauranger Fjord (near Bergen), *Köln* anchors in, 12.

'Maurice', Operation, main landing at Namsos, 19; 22, 30, 31, 32 ; withdrawal, 43.

McCoy, Commander J. A., R.N., Commanding Officer, H.M.S. *Bedouin*, at second battle of Narvik, 18 (note).

Micklethwait, Commander St. J. A., D.S.O., R.N., Commanding Officer, H.M.S. *Eskimo*, at second battle of Narvik, 18.

Milan, French destroyer, 55.

Milch, Colonel-General, commands German Air Forces, Norway, 21 (note).

Minelaying: *Allied*—Decision to mine off Norway, Introduction ; positions of minefields, 2 ; final Cabinet decision, 3 ; mines laid, Vest Fjord, 5 ; Trondheim Lead, 24 ; by Swordfish aircraft, 25 ; submarines, 29 ; proposals for Harstad defences, 54.

    German, 1 (and note) ; by aircraft, Tjelsundet, 54.

Mo, 47 ; object of operations, 48 ; first landings, 49 ; 50 ; reinforcements delayed by air attack, 51 ; 53 ; withdrawal from, 60.

M.N.B.D.O., arrival at Harstad, 54.

Mohawk, H.M.S., Destroyer, 4 (note), 19, 24 (and note), 28, 31 (note), 38 ; escorts *Royal Ulsterman*, 49

Molde, 24 ; ammunition depot, 31 ; base established, Aandalsnes area, 36; reinforcements and enemy bombing, 38 ; King of Norway leaves, 41 ; evacuation, 42 ; 48.

Monarch of Bermuda, S.S., sails in convoy NP1, 17, 19 (note) ; at evacuation, Narvik, 62.

Monark, S.S., sunk by *Severn*, 29.

Montcalm, French cruiser, relieves *Emile Bertin*, 33 (note) ; at evacuation, Namsos, 43.

Moore, Group Captain M., O.B.E., R.A.F., 62.

Morale, effect on German, second battle of Narvik, 18 ; in A/S Trawlers, 27 ; at evacuation, Aandalsnes, 42 ; 72.

Morgan, Brigadier H. de R., 19, 22, 36 ; conducts first flight landing, Aandalsnes, 37 ; 39.

Mosjoen, 26 (note), 47 ; object of operations, 48 ; first landings, 49 ; 50 ; evacuation, 51 ; 52 ; 53.

Mountbatten, Captain the Lord Louis, G.C.V.O., Captain (D) 5, H.M.S. *Kelly*, engages M.T.B.s, gets damaged *Kelly* to Tyne, 28 ; at evacuation, Namsos, 43.

Möwe, German torpedo boat, 1.

Murmansk, 1, 7, 21.

N

Namsos, Introduction ; reported clear of Germans, 19 ; 21 ; Allied landings planned, 22 ; 23 ; 24 ; 25 ; 26 ; 30 ; facilities poor, 31 ; landings, 31, 32 ; French landing, final reinforcements, 33, 34 ; enemy air attacks, 32, 33, 34 ; decision to withdraw, 40 ; withdrawal, 43 ; 44 ; 48 ; 51 ; 52 ; 69 ; 70.

Napier, Commander T. M., R.N., Commanding Officer, H.M.S. *Jackal*, remarks on Colonel Gubbins' troops, 51.

Narvik, winter shipment of iron ore, Introduction; 1 ; 2 ; 3 ; 7 ; 8 ; occupied by Germans, 9 ; 11 ; 12 ; first battle of, 13 ; 14 ; 15 ; German destroyers detained at, 16 ; *Furious* F.A.A. attack, 17 ; second battle of, 18 ; 19 ; U-boat disposition off, 20 ; 21 ; Allied expedition "Rupert" planned, 22 ; 23 ; 30 ; 44 ; 45 ; bombarded, 46 (and note); 47 ; 48 ; 54 ; 55 ; preparations and final plan of assault, 56, 57 ; captured by Allies, 58 ; 59 ; demolitions at and withdrawal, 62 (and note) ; 63 ; 66 (note) ; 71 ; 72.

Narwhal, H.M.S., Submarine, minelaying operations, sinks *Buenos Aires*, 29.

Nelson, H.M.S., Battleship, *Renown* mistaken for, 10 (note) ; landing party drawn from, 21, 22, 36.

Neuenfels, M.V., beached, Narvik, 10 April, 13 (note).

Newcastle, H.M.S., Cruiser, 61 ; covers Rear-Admiral Vivian's convoy, 65.

Nicholson, Captain R. S. G., D.S.O., D.S.C., R.N., Captain (D) 6, H.M.S. *Somali*, at Namsos, 19, 21 ; Operation "Henry", meets General Carton de Wiart, 31 ; report on Namsos, 32 ; 52.

Nordkap, H. Nor. M.S., Gunboat, sinks tanker *Kattegat*, 19.

Norfolk, H.M.S., 8-in. Cruiser, 28 (note).

Norge, H. Nor. M.S., Coast defence vessel, engages Germans at Narvik and sunk, 9 (and note) ; 13.

Northern Foam, H.M.S., Trawler, at Faeroes landing, 19.

Northern Gem, H.M.S., Trawler, 62.

Northern Sky, H.M.S., Trawler, at Faeroes landing, 19.

Norwegians, Introduction ; military forces not mobilised, 9 ; 19 (and note) ; situation, 15 April, 21 (and note) ; in Central Norway, 36, 37, 39 ; in Northern Norway, 47 ; 52 ; at capture of Narvik, 57, 58 ; 59.

Nubian, H.M.S., Destroyer, 24 (and note) ; lands troops, Namsos, 32, 33 ; air attacks, 34 ; at evacuation, Namsos, 43 (and note).

Nürnberg, German cruiser, reported at sea, 4.

Nyakoa, S.S., A.S.I.S., 62.

O

Ofot Fjord, 13 ; suspected minefield, 14 ; 18 ; 21 (note) ; operations, 16–26 April, 46 ; 51 ; operations in, 55 ; final withdrawal, 62, 63.

Oil Pioneer, S.S., Tanker, 62 ; sunk by *Hipper*, 63, 65.

Olav Tryggvason, H. Nor. M.S., Minelayer, engages *Albatros* and German minesweepers, 9 April, 9.

Oleander, R.F.A., Tanker, sunk, Harstad area, 62.

Oligarch, S.S., 62.

Orama, S.S., sunk by *Hipper*, 63, 65.

Orion, S.S., 19, 21, 23, 31, 37.

Ormonde, S.S., 62.

Orneset, Rombaks Fjord, landing at, 57.

Oronsay, S.S., 23 ; at evacuation, Narvik, 62.

Orphée, French Submarine, attacks U-boat, 29.

Orzel, O.R.P., Submarine, sinks *Rio de Janeiro*, 6, 20 (and note).

Oscarsborg, Coast defence battery, Oslo Fjord, engages *Blücher*, 9.

Oslo, 1, 8 ; occupied by Germans, 9 ; German advance from, 21 ; railway communication, Aandalsnes, 36.

Oydejord, Rombaks Fjord, 45 ; occupied by French, 55 ; 58.

P

Paget, Major-General B. C. T., D.S.O., M.C., 30 (note) ; takes command, Operation ' Sickle, Aandalsnes area, 38 ; 39 ; 40 ; 42.

Partridge, Captain R. T., R.M., F.A.A., attack on *Königsberg*, 12.

Patrols, withdrawn from Vest Fjord, minefield, 8, 9 ; off Vest Fjord, 11, 14 ; off Bergen, 9/10 April, 12.

Paul Jacobi, German destroyer, 1, 15.

Pegram, Captain F. H., R.N., Commanding Officer, H.M.S. *Glasgow*, S.O., southern patrol, Bergen, 9/10 April, 12 ; commands force off Namsos, Operation ' Henry,' 19, 31 ; operations, 17–20 April, 33.

Pelican, H.M.S., Sloop, damaged off Aandalsnes, 26, 38.

Penelope, H.M.S., Cruiser, 3, 4 ; detached to *Glowworm's* assistance, 5 (note) ; reinforces Admiral Whitworth, 7 ; 11 ; movements, Vest Fjord, area, 10–12 April, and strikes rock off Bodo, 14 ; 18 (note), 45 ; 48 (and note) ; leaves Skjel Fjord for United Kingdom, 51 ; 54 ; 55 (note).

Peters, Lieutenant-Commander G. H., R.N., Commanding Officer, H.M.S. *Foxhound*, at second battle of Narvik, 18.

Phillips, Acting Vice-Admiral Sir Tom, K.C.B., D.C.N.S., 44.

Phillips, Brigadier C. G., D.S.O., M.C., Namsos area, 32, 34, 35.

Pinkney, Captain J. S., Master S.S. *Flyingdale*, 4 (note).

Plan R4, proposed countermeasures to German aggression in Norway, 2 ; troops embark, 3 ; plan abandoned, 8 (and note), 22 ; 70 ; 72.

Plunket-Ernle-Erle-Drax, Admiral the Hon. Sir Reginald, K.C.B., D.S.O., C.-in-C., The Nore, 24.

Poland, Captain A. L., D.S.C., R.N., Commanding Officer, H.M.S. *Black Swan*, S.N.O., 'Primrose,' passage and landing, Aandalsnes, 36 ; 37 ; 42.

Policy, Allied, towards Norway, Introduction ; after invasion, 22.

Polish Forces, Submarine *Orzel* sinks *Rio de Janeiro*, 6 ; destroyers, 4 (and note), 12 ; *Grom* sunk, 55. Army, 47, 55 ; at capture of Narvik, 57, 58.

Porpoise, H.M.S., Submarine, minelaying, 29.

Posidonia, S.S., German tanker, sunk by *Trident*, 20 (and note).

Pound, Admiral of the Fleet Sir Dudley P., G.C.B., 1st Sea Lord, 23 ; message to C.-in-C., H.F., 37 (note); 68.

Press, report of German landing, Narvik, 11.

'Primrose,' Operation, preliminary landing, Aandalsnes, 22 ; 30 ; passage and landing, 36.

Prince of Wales, H.M.S., Battleship, 20 (note).

Principles of War, 72.

Protector, H.M.S., Netlayer, joins convoy NP1, 17 (and note) ; arrival Vaags Fjord, 45 ; 54 ; at Bjerkvik landing, 55.

Punjabi, H.M.S., Destroyer, 4 (note), 7, 11 ; damaged, second battle of Narvik, 18 (and note).

Q

Quisling, Major V., Norwegian traitor, contact with Berlin, Introduction, 9 (note) ; failure to form Government, 21 ; 72 (note).

R

Radar, in its infancy, Introduction.

Raeder, Grand Admiral, C.-in-C., German Navy, suggests occupation of Norway, Introduction ; directive for operations, 1 (and note), 6 ; assessment of risks, 71.

Ramsey, Vice-Admiral C. G., C.B., C.-in-C., Rosyth, 4.

Ranen, S.S., decoy ship, harasses enemy, Bodo area, 60 ; destroys oil tanks, Svolvaer, 62.

Rauenfels, S.S., German store ship, 1 (note) ; sunk by *Havock*, 13 ; 18 ; 21.

Ravenhill, Commander R. W., R.N., Commanding Officer, H.M.S. *Nubian*, remarks on enemy bombing, Namsos, 34 ; 43.

Rawlings, Captain H. B., O.B.E., R.N., Commanding Officer, H.M.S. *Valiant*, 61.

Reconnaissance, *Isis* and *Ilex*, Trondheim, 15 ; failure to locate *Scharnhorst* and *Gneisenau*, 9–12 April, 15 ; Lord Cork, Narvik, 46, 47. Air reconnaissance, *see* Air.

Reina del Pacifico, M.V., sails in convoy NP1, 17, 19 (note).

Reinforcements, reports of German, Narvik, 11 April, 14 ; Allied to Namsos, 33, 35, Aandalsnes, 38 (and note), Mo and Bodo, 52.

Renown, H.M.S., Battlecruiser, Flag, Vice-Admiral Whitworth, 2, 3, 4 ; patrols off Vest Fjord, 5, 7 ; 8 ; action against German battlecruisers, 10 ; operations, 10–12 April, 14 ; 17 ; Admiral Whitworth shifts Flag, 18 ; 21 ; 23 (and note) ; to Rosyth for repairs, 24 ; 28 ; to Iceland coast, 61 ; covering operations, Admiral Vivian's convoys, 65, 66.

Repulse, H.M.S., Battlecruiser, 2, 4 ; detached to *Glowworm's* assistance, 5 (note), 7, 8 ; joins Admiral Whitworth, 11 ; operations, 10–12 April, 14 ; detached to cover convoy NP1, 17, 20 (note), 23, 24, 28, 41 ; to Iceland coast, 61 ; covering operations, Admiral Vivian's convoy, 65, 66.

Resolution, H.M.S., Battleship, 23 (note) ; relieves *Warspite*, Narvik area, 24, 47 (and note) ; 41 ; bombards in Ofot Fjord, 47 ; at Bjerkvik landing, 55.

Reykjavik, Iceland, occupied by Royal Marines, 24.

Rieve, Captain, Commanding Officer, *Karlsrühe*, 1.

Rio de Janeiro, S.S., disguised German transport, sunk by *Orzel*, 8 April, 6 (and note) ; 8 ; 21 (note) ; 71.

Risks, 71.

Rodney, H.M.S., Battleship, Flag, C.-in-C., H.F., 2, 4, 8 ; struck by bomb, 9 April, 12 ; 17 ; 18 ; 20 (note) ; 21 ; 23 ; 24 ; 41 ; 65 ; 66.

Rombaks Fjord, surviving German destroyers destroyed, 13 April, 18 ; 21 (note), 45 ; 55 ; 56 ; French advance up, 58.

Romsdals Fjord, importance of, 31, 36.

Roope, Lieutenant-Commander G. B., R.N., Commanding Officer, H.M.S. *Glowworm*, drowned, posthumously awarded V.C., 5 (and note).

Rosyth, striking force at, 2 ; Plan R4 troops embark, 3 ; 4 ; 8 ; 17 ; 24.

Royal Air Force, report and attack German heavy ships, 7 April, 4 ; attack on Bergen, 9 April, 12 ; fighters land on 'Gladiator' Lake, and destroyed, 25, 39, at Harstad, 54, at Bardufoss, 56, cover evacuation, Northern Norway, 61, leave Bardufoss, land on *Glorious*, 62, attack battlecruisers, Trondheim, 66.

Royal Marines, Occupy Thorshavn, Faeroes, 19, Reykjavik, Iceland, 24 (and note) ; Operation Henry, 31 ; Operations Primrose and Sickle, 36 ; with M.N.B.D.O., Harstad, 54.

Royal Scotsman, S.S., lands troops, Bodo, 49.

Royal Ulsterman, S.S., lands troops, Mosjoen area, 49 ; evacuation, Northern Norway, 62.

Rubis, French submarine, minelaying, 29.

Ruge, General, C.-in-C., Norwegian Army, 21, 42 ; on importance of Bodo, 52 ; 59.

'Rupert', Operation, for re-capture of Narvik, 19, 22, 30 ; inception, 44 ; arrival at Harstad, Lord Cork and General Mackesy, with conflicting instructions, 45 ; Lord Cork appointed Supreme Commander, 45 ; operations, 46-58 ; withdrawal, 59-62 ; arrival in United Kingdom, 65.

Russia, attack on Finland, Introduction ; attitude to Norway uncertain, 19 (note).

S

St. Magnus, S.S., takes reinforcements to Aandalsnes, 38.

St. Sunniva, S.S., takes reinforcements to Aandalsnes, 38.

Sandnesjoen, Colonel Gubbins evacuated from, 51.

Sao Paulo, S.S., German store ship, 1 (note) ; mined and sunk, 21.

Scandinavia, importance of, Introduction.

Scapa Flow, Orkneys, Home Fleet base, 2 ; 3 ; 4 ; 7 ; air raid, 12 ; 16 ; 19 ; air defence, 25 ; 28 ; 64 ; 66.

Scharnhorst, German battlecruiser, 1 ; reported movements, 4 (and note), 8 ; engagement with *Renown*, 10 ; movements, 10-12 April, 16 ; Flag, Admiral Marschall, Operation Juno, 63 ; sinks *Glorious*, torpedoed by *Acasta*, 64 ; 65 ; bombed in Trondheim, no damage, 66.

Schlesvig-Holstein, old German battleship, 1.

Schmundt, Rear-Admiral, F.O. German scouting forces, 1 ; return passage from Bergen, 12.

Schoemann, German destroyer, 63.

Scots Guards (1st), arrive Narvik area, 45 ; Bodo area, 47, 49, 51, 52 ; withdrawal, 60.

Seal, H.M.S., Submarine, reports enemy in Skagerrak, 9 April, 8 ; 20 ; marks position, bombardment Stavanger airfield, 28 ; damaged and captured by Germans, 29.

Sealion, H.M.S., Submarine, 20 ; attacks transports, 29.

Sea Wolf, H.M.S., Submarine, damages ships in convoy, 29.

Seeadler, German Submarine, 1.

Severn, H.M.S., Submarine, 20 ; sinks S.S. *Monark*, 29.

Shark, H.M.S., Submarine, 20.

Sheffield, H.M.S., Cruiser, 4 (and note), 8 ; movements, 9-10 April, 12 ; operations off Aalesund, 19 ; Operation Henry, 19, 31 ; 21 ; 24 ; 25 ; covers damaged *Kelly*, 28 ; 33 ; takes reinforcements to Molde, 38 ; 41 ; at evacuation, Aandalsnes, 42.

Sherbrooke, Commander R. St. V., R.N., Commanding Officer, H.M.S. *Cossack*, at second battle of Narvik, 18.

Sherwood Foresters (8th), in Aandalsnes area, 37.

'Sickle' Operation, main landings, Aandalsnes, 22 ; 30 ; landing and enemy bombing, 37 ; reinforcements, 38 ; withdrawal, 39, 40, 41, 42.

Sikh, H.M.S., Destroyer, 4 (note), 19, 24, 31 (and note) ; lands troops, Namsos, 32 ; 38 ; at evacuation, Aandalsnes, 42.

Silhouettes, similarity of German, 10 (note), App. D.

Simpson, Lieutenant-Colonel H. W., R.M., commands Primrose landing party, 36 ; wounded and evacuated, 42.

Skaanland, Harstad area, airfield under construction, 54 (and note) ; unfit for use, 56.

Skagerrak, German command of sea, 1 (and note), 40 ; *Orzel* torpedoes *Rio de Janeiro*, 6 ; 8 ; 20 ; French destroyer sweep, 28 ; 29.

Skagerrak, M.V., German tanker, 1 (note), 4 (note) ; scuttled to avoid capture, 19, 21.

Skjel Fjord, Lofoten Islands, advanced fuelling and repair base, 14, 18, 19, 51, 53 54.

Skomvaer, S.W. Lofotens, Vice-Admiral Whitworth's movements off, 7 ; engagement, 10 ; 14 ; 18 ; 19.

Sleipner, H. Nor. M.S., Torpedo boat, sinks supply ship, 21 (and note).

Sloops, general employment, 25 ; strain on personnel, 34 ; 37.

Smoke screen, *Glowworm* rams *Hipper*, 5 ; *Acasta* attacks *Scharnhorst* through, 64.

Snapper, H.M.S., Submarine, 20 ; sinks two A/S trawlers, 29.

Sobieski, S.S., 23, 62.

Solfolla, Installations attacked by F.A.A., 25 ; destroyed by *Ranen*, 62 (and note).

Somali, H.M.S., Destroyer, 4 (note), 19, 21, 24, 31 (and note) ; attacked by bombers, Namsos, 32 (and note) ; at evacuation, Aandalsnes, 42 ; damaged, Bodo area, and returns to United Kingdom, 52 ; at Bjerkvik landing, 55.

Sonsbukten, Oslo Fjord, German landing, 9.

Southampton, H.M.S., Cruiser, 4, 8 ; slight damage, air attack, 12 ; embarks General Mackesy, 17, 19 (and note) ; arrives Vaags Fjord, 21, 45 ; 41 ; at evacuation, Aandalsnes, 42 ; 47 ; at capture of Narvik, 57, 58 ; 65.

South Wales Borderers (2nd), Narvik area, 45 ; 46 ; 47 ; to Bodo area, 53.

Spearfish, H.M.S., Submarine, torpedoes *Lützow*, 11 April, 16, 20 (and note) ; sinks Danish fishing vessels, 29.

Stadtlandet, proposed minefield off, 2, 3 ; minelaying cancelled, 4 ; Captain Pegram's force arrives off, 19.

Stannard, Lieutenant R. B., R.N.R., Commanding Officer, H.M.S. *Arab*, awarded V.C., Namsos, 27 (and note).

Stavanger, Introduction, 1, 2, 3, 8 (and note) ; occupied by Germans, 9 ; 12 ; 25 ; airfield bombarded, 28.

Steinbrink, German destroyer, 63.

Stenkjaer, North-east of Trondheim, 22 ; occupied by Brigadier Phillips' troops, 34 ; German landing, 35.

Sterlet, H.M.S., Submarine, sinks *Brummer*, later sunk by A/S craft.

Stevens, Captain E. B. K., D.S.C., R.N., Captain (D) 9, H.M.S. *Havelock*, remarks on covering fire, 58.

Stork, H.M.S., Sloop, escorts *Chrobry*, 53 ; at capture of Narvik, 57, 58 ; 62.

Sturges, Colonel R. G., R.M., commands Marines, Iceland, 24 (and note).

Submarines, *Allied*, Initial dispositions, 20 ; operations, 20, 29.

German, see U-boats.

Suffolk, H.M.S., 8-in. Cruiser, lands force at Faeroes, intercepts tanker *Skagerrak*, 19 ; 21, 23 ; 24 ; bombards Stavanger airfield, serious damage by air attacks, 28.

Sundlo, Major, O.C. in Narvik, Norwegian traitor, 9 (note).

Sunfish, H.M.S., Submarine, reports *Blücher*, 8 April, 8 ; sinks four enemy merchant ships, 20.

Surprise, German plan based on, 1 ; achieved, 9, 72.

Survivors, *Glowworm*, 5 ; *Glorious, Ardent, Acasta*, 64.

Sussex, H.M.S., 8-in. Cruiser, 61 ; covers Admiral Vivian's convoy, 65.

Svalbard II, S.S., Norwegian, picks up survivors from *Glorious*, 64.

Sydney-Turner, Lieutenant-Commander, R.N., F.A.A., air attack, Narvik, 17.

T

Tactical Loading, of expeditionary forces, overlooked, 37 ; remarks by Commanding Officer, *Arethusa*, and Admiral Edward-Collins, 38 ; 45 ; 70.

Taku, H.M.S., Submarine, attacks on merchant shipping, 29.

Tancock, Lieutenant-Commander E. B., D.S.C., R.N., Commanding Officer, H.M.S. *Forester*, at second battle of Narvik, 18.

Tank-Nielsen, Admiral, R. Nor. N., stresses importance of Romsdals Fjord, 31, 36.

Tanks, at Bjerkvik landing, 55 (and note); at capture of Narvik, 57, 58.
Tarpon, H.M.S., Submarine, sunk by A/S craft, 20.
Tartar, H.M.S., Destroyer, 4 (note); escorts convoy HN25, 12; 24; at evacuation, Molde, 42; 62 (note).
Tartu, French destroyer, joins Admiral Cunningham, 8.
Tennholm Fjord, German tanker *Kattegat* sunk in, 14 (and note).
Terboven, Reich Commissioner, Norway, 21.
Tetrarch, H.M.S., Submarine, attacks transport, 29.
Teviot Bank, H.M.S., Minelayer, 2; leaves Scapa, 3: recalled, 4; 8.
Theodor Riedel, German destroyer, 1, 15.
Theseus, S.S., 62.
Thiele, Captain, Commanding Officer, *Lützow*, takes over command, Oslo Force, 9.
Thistle, H.M.S., Submarine, sunk by *U.4*, 20.
Tjelsundet, passage Vaags Fjord to Vest Fjord, 13, 14, 53; Allied Naval base sited in, 54; *Curlew* sunk, 56; 62.
Todd, Captain P., R.N., Captain (D) 3, H.M.S. *Inglefield*, escorts *Teviot Bank*, 3.
Torpedoes, inefficiency of German, 20 (and note).
Tothill, Commander J. A. W., R.N., Commanding Officer, H.M.S. *Janus*, remarks on Mosjoen, 49.
Transports, German, reported at Bodo, 11 April, 14; German losses, 21 (and note); Allied withdrawal from Northern Norway, 61, 62.
Triad, H.M.S., Submarine, attacks convoy, 29.
Trident, H.M.S., Submarine, sinks tanker *Posidonia*, 20 (and note).
Triton, H.M.S., Submarine, attacks *Gneisenau* off Skaw, 8 April, 8 (and note); attacks convoy, 20.
Tromsö, 15; Vice-Admiral Cunningham visits, 19; 32; *Furious* damaged, 47; A/A artillery allocation, 54; 59; King of Norway leaves, 62.
Trondheim, Introduction, 1, 2, 3; occupied by Germans, 9; 12; reconnoitred by *Isis*, 15; 16; U-boat disposition off, 20; question of frontal attack, 21, 22, 23; importance to Germans, 21; 30; 32; 33; 44; *Hipper* detached to, 63; R.A.F. attack on ships, 11 June, 66, 71, 72.
Troubridge, Captain T. H., R.N., Commanding Officer, H.M.S. *Furious*, remarks on F.A.A. pilots, 15; 18.
Truant, H.M.S., Submarine, torpedoes and sinks *Karlsrühe*, 12, 20.
Tsingtau, German depot ship, 1.

U

U-boats, 12, 18; dispositions, 20; take supplies to Trondheim, 21 (and note); 28. *U.4* sinks *Thistle*, 20; *U.22* lost in North Sea, 29 (note); *U.49* sunk in Vaags Fjord, 45 (and note), 54; *U.51* reports Captain Warburton-Lee, Vest Fjord, 13 (note); *U.64* sunk by *Warspite*'s aircraft, 18, 54.
Ulster Monarch, S.S., at evacuation, Aandalsnes, 42; 62.
Ulster Prince, S.S., at evacuation, Molde, 42; lands troops, Mosjoen area, 49; 62.
Unity, H.M.S., Submarine, 20, rammed and sunk, 29.
Urundi, S.S., German store ship, runs aground, 21 (note).

V

Vaags Fjord, examined by *Berwick*, 19; 21; arrival, 'Rupert' and *U.49* sunk, 45; 47; proposed German attack, Operation Juno, 63.
Vaernes, airfield near Trondheim, 23; bombed by F.A.A., 25; and R.A.F., 66.
Valiant, H.M.S., Battleship, 2, 4, 8, 12; covers convoy NP1, 17, 19, 32; 20 (note); arrives Vaags Fjord, 21, 45; 23 (and note); 24; 25; 41; 61; covers Lord Cork's convoys, 65; 69.
Vandyck, S.S., Sunk, air attack, evacuation of Northern Norway, 62 (and note), 65.
Vanoc, H.M.S., Destroyer, escorts convoy NP1, 19 (and note); 32; at Bodo evacuation, 60 (note).

Vansittart, H.M.S., Destroyer, lands reinforcements, Aandalsnes, 38.

Vefsen Fjord, 48, 51, 52.

Verdalsoren, north-east of Trondheim, occupied by Brigadier Phillips' troops, 34 ; shelled by German destroyer, 35.

Vest Fjord, mines laid, 5, 7 ; 10 ; patrol off, 11 ; operations, 14 ; 16 ; 45 ; 47 ; dive bombers attack *Chrobry*, 53 ; 72.

Veteran, H.M.S., Destroyer, Appendix C (3).

Vian, Captain Philip L., D.S.O., R.N., Captain (D) 4, H.M.S. *Afridi*, Introduction (note) ; at evacuation, Namsos, 43 ; independent action against *Bismarck*, 69.

Victoria Cross, bestowed on Lieutenant-Commander Roope, 5 (note) ; Captain Warburton-Lee, 13 (note) ; Lieutenant Stannard, 27 (note).

Ville d'Alger, S.S., French transport, lands troops, Namsos, 35.

Ville d'Oran, S.S., French transport, lands troops, Namsos, 33.

Vindictive, H.M.S., Repair ship, joins convoy NP1, 17 (note), 19 ; arrival at Vaags Fjord, 45 ; 46 ; at Bjerkvik landing, 55 ; transports troops, Bodo to United Kingdom, 60 ; 61 ; 62.

Viscount, H.M.S., Destroyer, 62 (note).

Visibility, of Vest Fjord, 8 April, 7 ; German landing, Narvik, 9 ; *Renown's* engagement, 9 April, 10 ; at first battle of Narvik, 13 ; return passage, German battlecruisers, 16 ; *Furious* F.A.A. attack, Narvik, 17 ; and second battle of Narvik, 18 ; evacuation, Namsos, 43 ; at bombardment, Narvik, 46 ; 52 ; at Bjerkvik landing, 55 ; at sinking of *Glorious*, 64.

Vivian, Rear-Admiral J. G. P., Rear-Admiral, A.A. Cruisers, 26 ; S.N.O. Aandalsnes, 37 ; at evacuation, Namsos, 43 (and note) ; commands Ofot Fjord detached squadron, 55 ; in general charge of embarkation, evacuation Northern Norway, 62 ; 65.

W

Walker, H.M.S., Destroyer, at evacuation, Aandalsnes, 42 ; at capture of Narvik, 57, 58.

Wanderer, H.M.S., Destroyer, at evacuation, Aandalsnes, 42.

Warburton-Lee, Captain B. A. W., R.N., Captain (D) 2, H.M.S. *Hardy*, 3 ; attack at Narvik, preliminary movements, 11 ; 12 ; defeats Commodore Bonte's force, killed and posthumously awarded V.C., 13 (and note) ; 71 ; 73.

War Office, 41.

War Pindari, R.F.A., Tanker, sent to Lillesjona and Tromsö, 32.

Warspite, H.M.S., Battleship, 8 ; joins C.-in-C., H.F., 12 ; 17 ; hoists Vice-Admiral Whitworth's Flag, second battle of Narvik, 18 ; 21 ; 23 (note) ; transferred to Mediterranean, 24 ; 45 ; bombards Narvik, 46 ; leaves Narvik area, 47 ; 71.

Weather, *Glowworm* misses *Renown*, 3 ; off Vest Fjord, 8–9 April, 7 ; *Renown's* engagement, 9 April, 10 ; off Bergen, 9 April, 12 ; first battle of Narvik, 13 ; return passage, German battlecruisers, 16 ; *Furious* F.A.A. attack, Narvik, 17 ; 28 ; Primrose passage, 21, 36 ; withdrawal, Namsos, 43 ; Narvik area, 45, 46, 47 ; at Bjerkvik landing, 55 ; final evacuation, 62 ; at sinking of *Glorious*, 64 ; 66.

Wells, Vice-Admiral L. V., C.B., D.S.O., Vice-Admiral (A), Flag in *Glorious*, leaves Gibraltar, 21   conducts Operation 'DX', 25 ; 39 ; part in evacuation, 41 ; 43 ; 55 ; 61 ; 65 ; 66.

' Weserübung ' Operation, German invasion, Norway and Denmark, Introduction.

Westcott, H.M.S., Destroyer, at evacuation, Aandalsnes, 42.

Whirlwind, H.M.S., Destroyer, escorts convoy NP1, 19 (and note) ; 32.

Whitworth, Vice-Admiral W. J., C.B., D.S.O., Vice-Admiral, Battle Cruiser Squadron, Flag in *Renown*, to support Vest Fjord minelayers, 3 ; arrives off Vest Fjord, 5 ; movements and appreciation, 7 ; engages German battlecruisers, 10 ; movements and dispositions, 9 April, 11 ; instructions to *Penelope*, requests clarification of Admiralty policy, movements and intentions, 10–12 April, 14 ; movements and junction with C.-in-C., 12 April, 15 ; 17 ; shifts Flag to *Warspite*, wins second battle of Narvik, 18 ; 21 ; 32 ; 44 ; leaves Narvik area, 47 ; to Iceland coast, 61 ; 70 ; 73.

Wigbert, S.S., sunk by submarine, 21.

Wilhelm Heidkamp, German destroyer, 1 ; sunk, first battle of Narvik, 13 (and note).

Wireless silence, Admiral Lütjens' precautions, 16 ; importance of 68, 69 (and note).

Wireless telegraphy, conditions in Northern Norway difficult, 45.

Witch, H.M.S., Destroyer, lands reinforcements, Aandalsnes, **38**.
Witherington, H.M.S., Destroyer, 38, 62 (note).
Wolf, German torpedo boat, 1.
Wolfgang Zenker, German destroyer, 1 ; at first battle of Narvik, 13 (and note) ; **sunk,** second battle of Narvik, 18.
Wolverine, H.M.S., Destroyer, rescues survivors from *Chrobry,* 53 ; 62 (note).
Wren, H.M.S., Destroyer, at Bjerkvik landing, **55**.

Y

Yates, Captain G. D., R.N., Commanding Officer, H.M.S. *Penelope,* operations at Vest Fjord, 10–12 April, exchange of signals with Admiralty, 14 ; collects intelligence, 48 (note).
Yermont, S.S., 62.
York, H.M.S., 8-in. Cruiser, 3, 8, 12 ; escorts damaged *Eclipse,* 15 ; 16 ; 33 ; covers landing Aandalsnes, **37** ; takes reinforcements to Aandalsnes, **38** ; at evacuation, Namsos, 43.
York and Lancasters (1st), employed in Namsos area, 32.

Z

Zone time, Minus 1 (B.S.T.) used throughout.
Zulu, H.M.S., Destroyer, 4 (note), 12 (note) ; reconnoitres Rombaks Fjord, 45 ; bombards Narvik, 46 ; sinks transport and stores, Hemnes, 51 ; 61 (note).

CONFIDENTIAL

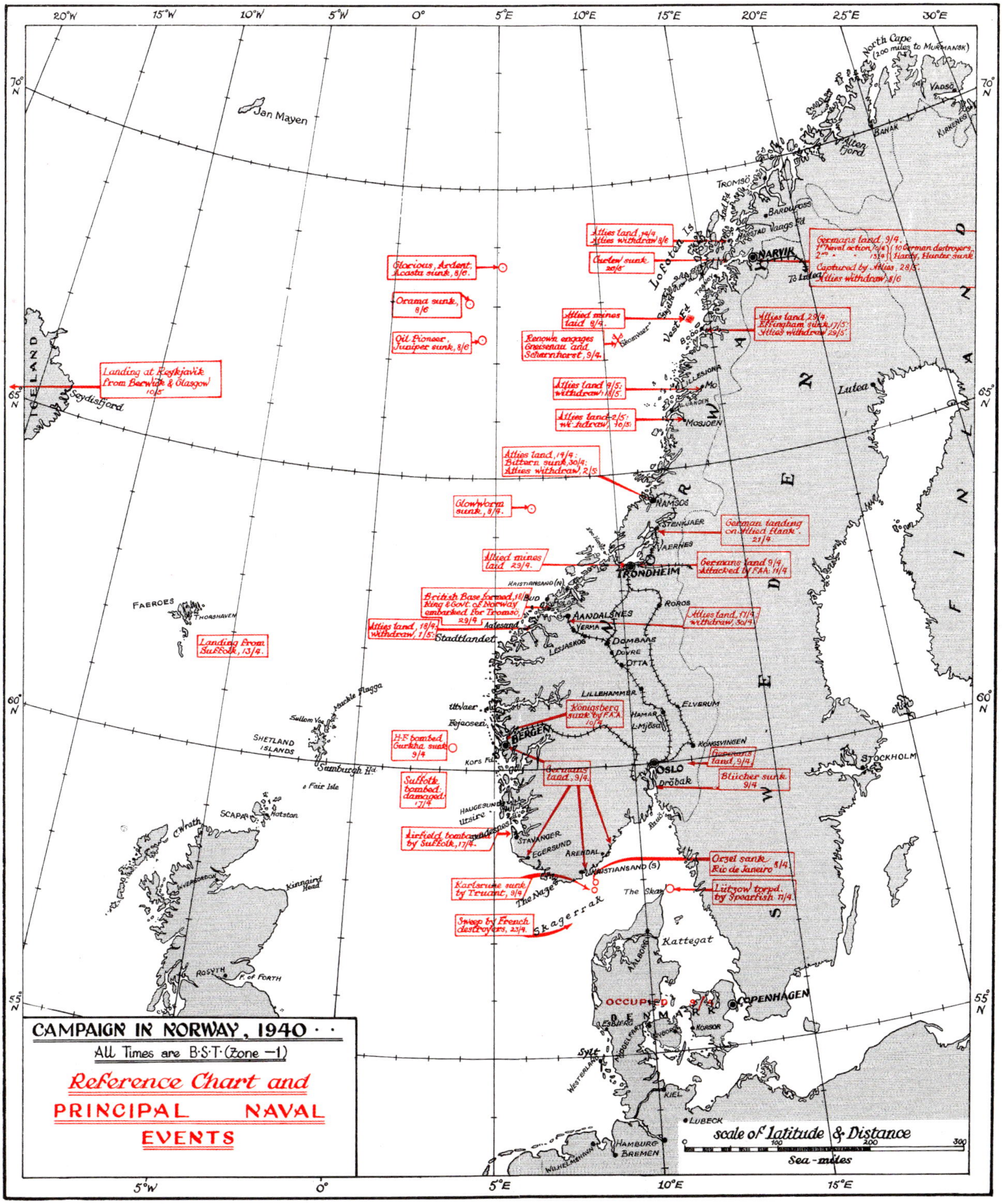
CAMPAIGN IN NORWAY, 1940
All Times are B·S·T·(Zone −1)
Reference Chart and
PRINCIPAL NAVAL EVENTS
Landing at Reykjavik from Berwick & Glasgow 10/5
Glorious, Ardent, Acasta sunk, 8/6.
Orama sunk, 8/6
Oil Pioneer, Juniper sunk, 8/6
Renown engages Gneisenau and Scharnhorst, 9/4.
Allied mines laid 8/4.
Allies land 14/4 Allies withdraw 8/6
Curlew sunk 26/5
Germans land, 9/4.
1st Naval action 10/4 (10 German destroyers
2nd " " 13/4 Hardy, Hunter sunk
Captured by Allies 28/5.
Allies withdraw 8/6
Allies land 29/4. Effingham sunk 17/5. Allies withdraw 29/5.
Allies land 4/5 withdraw 18/5.
Allies land 2/5 withdraw 10/5.
Allies land 14/4. Bittern sunk 30/4. Allies withdraw 2/5.
Glowworm sunk, 8/4.
German landing on Allied flank. 21/4
Allied mines laid 29/4.
Germans land 9/4. Attacked by F.A.A. 11/4.
British Base formed 18/4. King & Govt. of Norway embarked for Tromsö 29/4
Allies land 18/4. withdraw 1/5.
Allies land 17/4 withdraw 30/4.
Landing from Suffolk 13/4.
Königsberg sunk by F.A.A. 10/4
H.F. bombed Gurkha sunk 9/4
Suffolk bombed damaged 17/4
Germans land 9/4
Germans land 9/4.
Blücher sunk 9/4
Airfield bombarded by Suffolk, 17/4.
Orzel sank Rio de Janeiro 8/4.
Karlsruhe sunk by Truant, 9/4
Lützow torpd. by Spearfish 11/4.
Sweep by French destroyers, 23/4.
OCCUPIED 9/4
North Cape (200 miles to Murmansk)
Jan Mayen
ICELAND
Seydisfjord
FAEROES
THORSHAVEM
SHETLAND ISLANDS
Sumburgh Hd.
Fair Isle
SCAPA
C. Wrath
Kinnaird Head
ROSYTH
F. of FORTH
NORWAY
SWEDEN
FINLAND
DENMARK
TROMSÖ
BARDUFOSS
NARVIK
Lofoten Is.
Vest Fd.
Bodö
Mo
MOSJOEN
NAMSOS
STEINKJAER
VAERNES
TRONDHEIM
KRISTIANSAND (N)
AANDALSNES
Aalesund
Stadtlandet
DOMBAAS
OTTA
LILLEHAMMER
ELVERUM
HAMAR
BERGEN
OSLO
Dröbak
KONGSVINGER
STOCKHOLM
Lulea
STAVANGER
EGERSUND
ARENDAL
KRISTIANSAND (S)
The Naze
Skagerrak
The Skaw
Kattegat
AALBORG
COPENHAGEN
ESBJERG
KORSOR
Sylt
KIEL
LUBECK
HAMBURG
BREMEN
WILHELMSHAVEN
VADSÖ
KIRKENES
BANAK
Alten Fjord
Scale of Latitude & Distance
0 100 200 300
Sea-miles
20°W 15°W 10°W 5°W 0° 5°E 10°E 15°E 20°E 25°E 30°E
70°N 65°N 60°N 55°N

PLAN 2

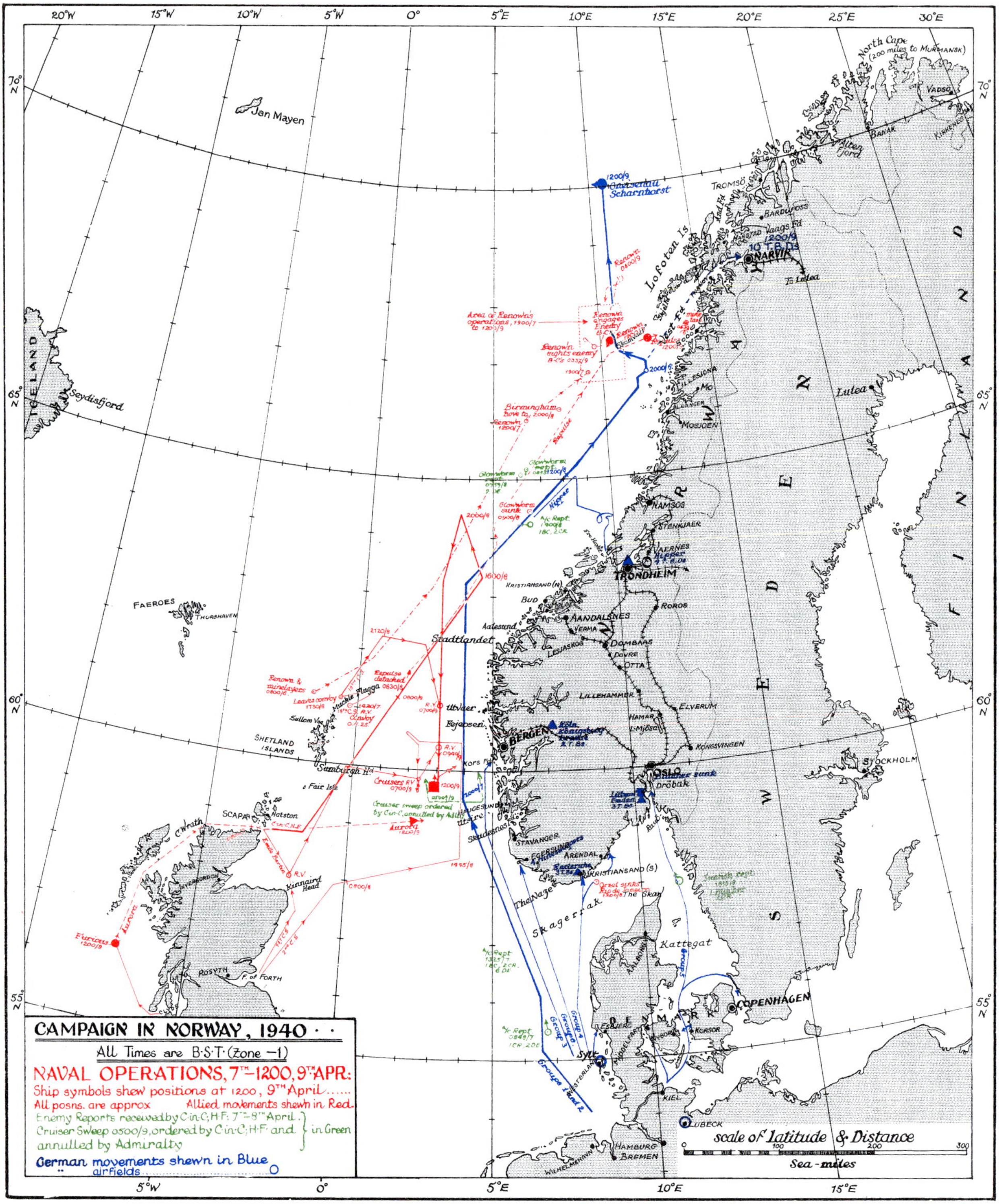
CAMPAIGN IN NORWAY, 1940
All Times are B·S·T·(Zone −1)
NAVAL OPERATIONS, 7TH–1200, 9TH APR:
Ship symbols shew positions at 1200, 9TH April
All posns. are approx
Allied movements shewn in Red.
Enemy Reports received by C-in-C; H·F; 7TH–8TH April.
Cruiser Sweep 0500/9, ordered by C-in-C; H·F and annulled by Admiralty
in Green
German movements shewn in Blue
airfields
scale of Latitude & Distance
Sea-miles
Jan Mayen
ICELAND
Seydisfjord
FAEROES
THORSHAVEN
SHETLAND ISLANDS
Sullom Voe
Sumburgh Hd.
Fair Isle
SCAPA
C. Wrath
INVERGORDON
Kinnaird Head
ROSYTH
F. of FORTH
Stadtlandet
BERGEN
STAVANGER
KRISTIANSAND (S)
ARENDAL
OSLO
Dröbak
TRONDHEIM
NAMSOS
MOSJOEN
NARVIK
TROMSÖ
BARDUFOSS
Lofoten Is
North Cape
VADSÖ
BANAK
KIRKENES
Alten fjord
Vest Fd
Skagerrak
Kattegat
The Naze
The Skaw
COPENHAGEN
KIEL
LUBECK
HAMBURG
BREMEN
WILHELMSHAVEN
Sylt
S W E D E N
F I N L A N D
N O R W A Y
D E N M A R K
STOCKHOLM
Lulea
Gneisenau
Scharnhorst
Renown
Repulse
Glowworm sunk
Hipper
Birmingham
Furious 1200/9
Aurora
Cruisers R.V.
10 T.B.Ds
Groups 1 and 2
Group 3
Group 4
Group 5

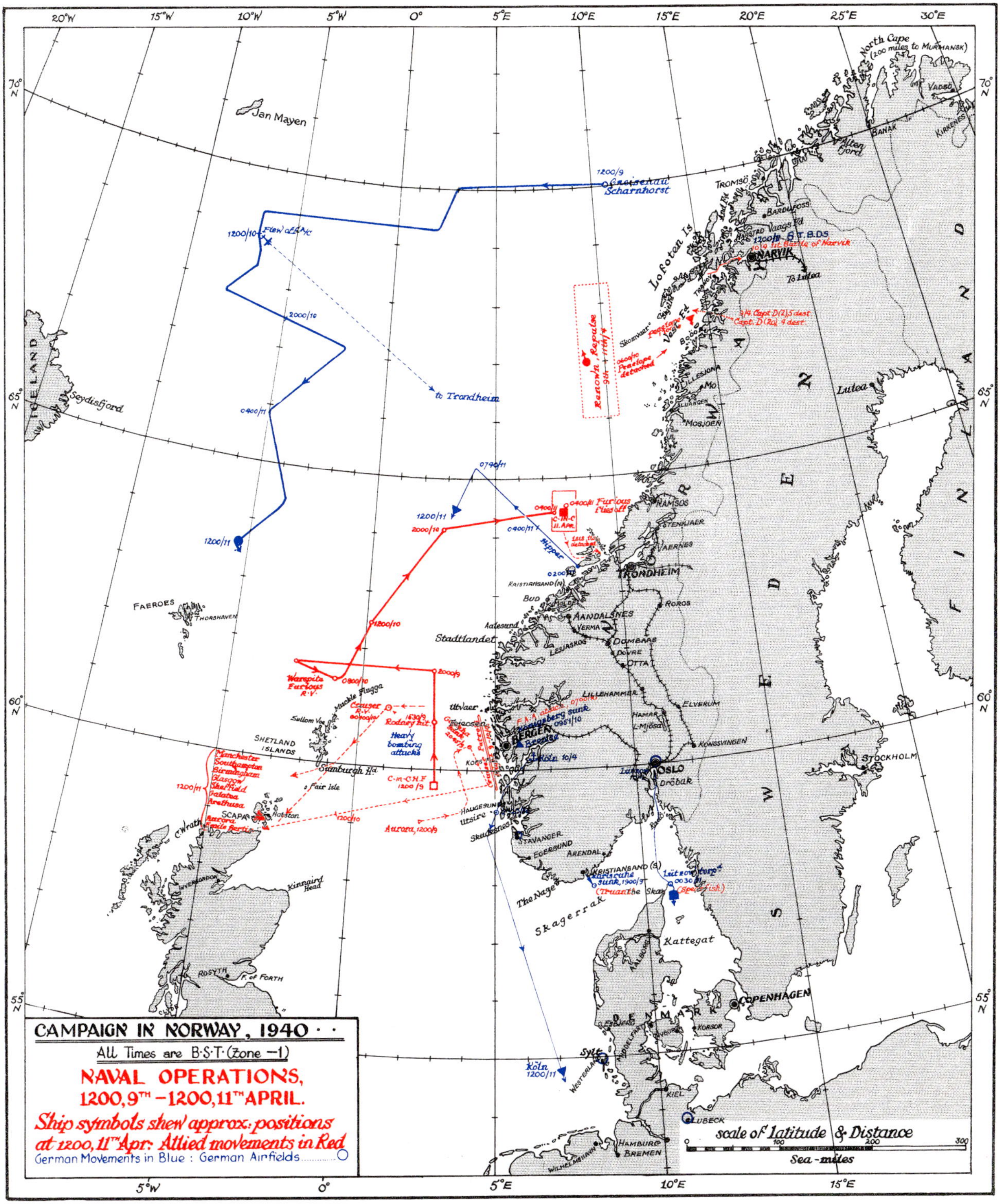

C.B.H. 20101 - Wt. 17299 - Dd. PK. 4005 - 500 - 6/51

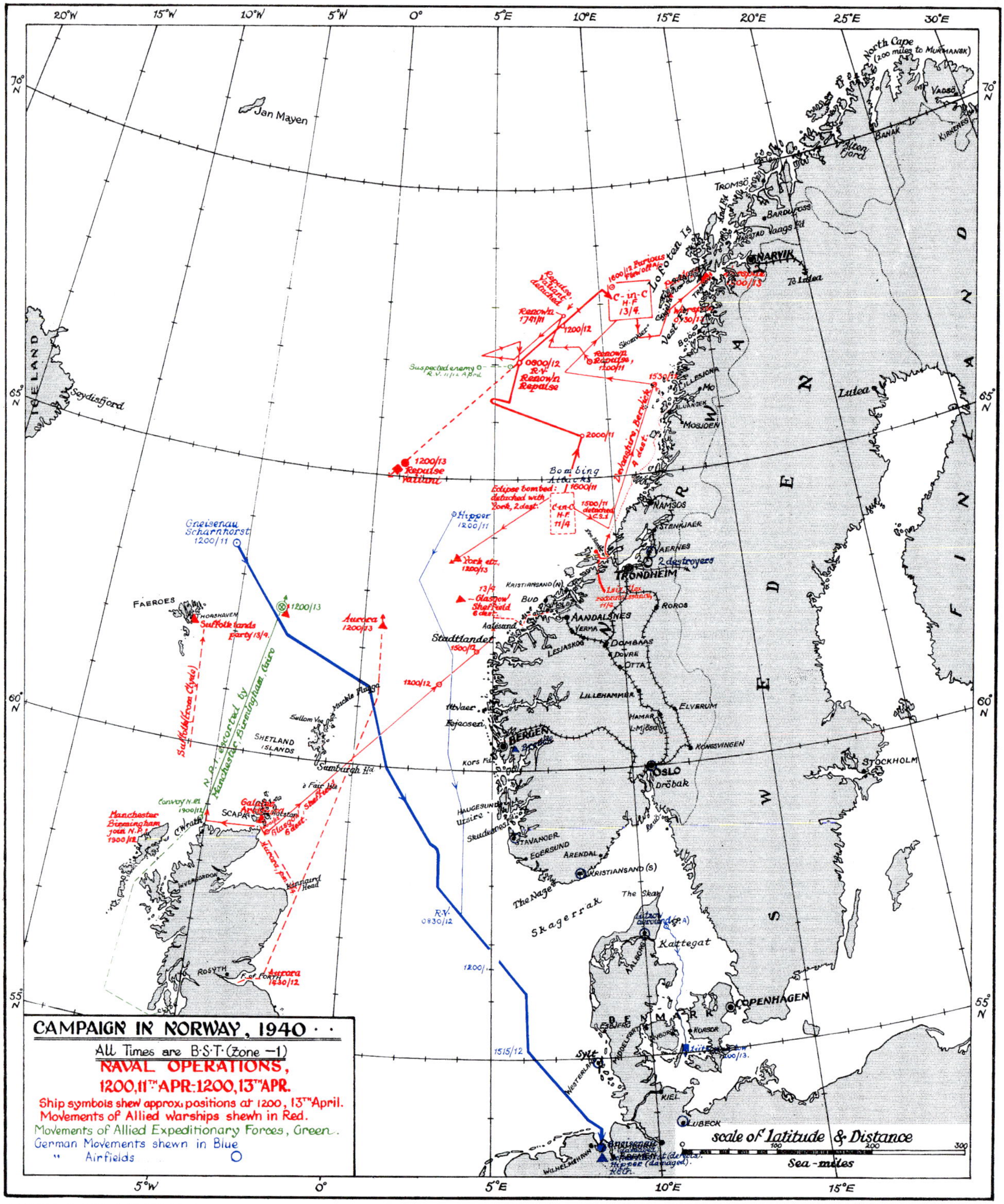

C.B.H. 20101 - Wt. 17299 - Dd. PK.4005-500 - 6/51

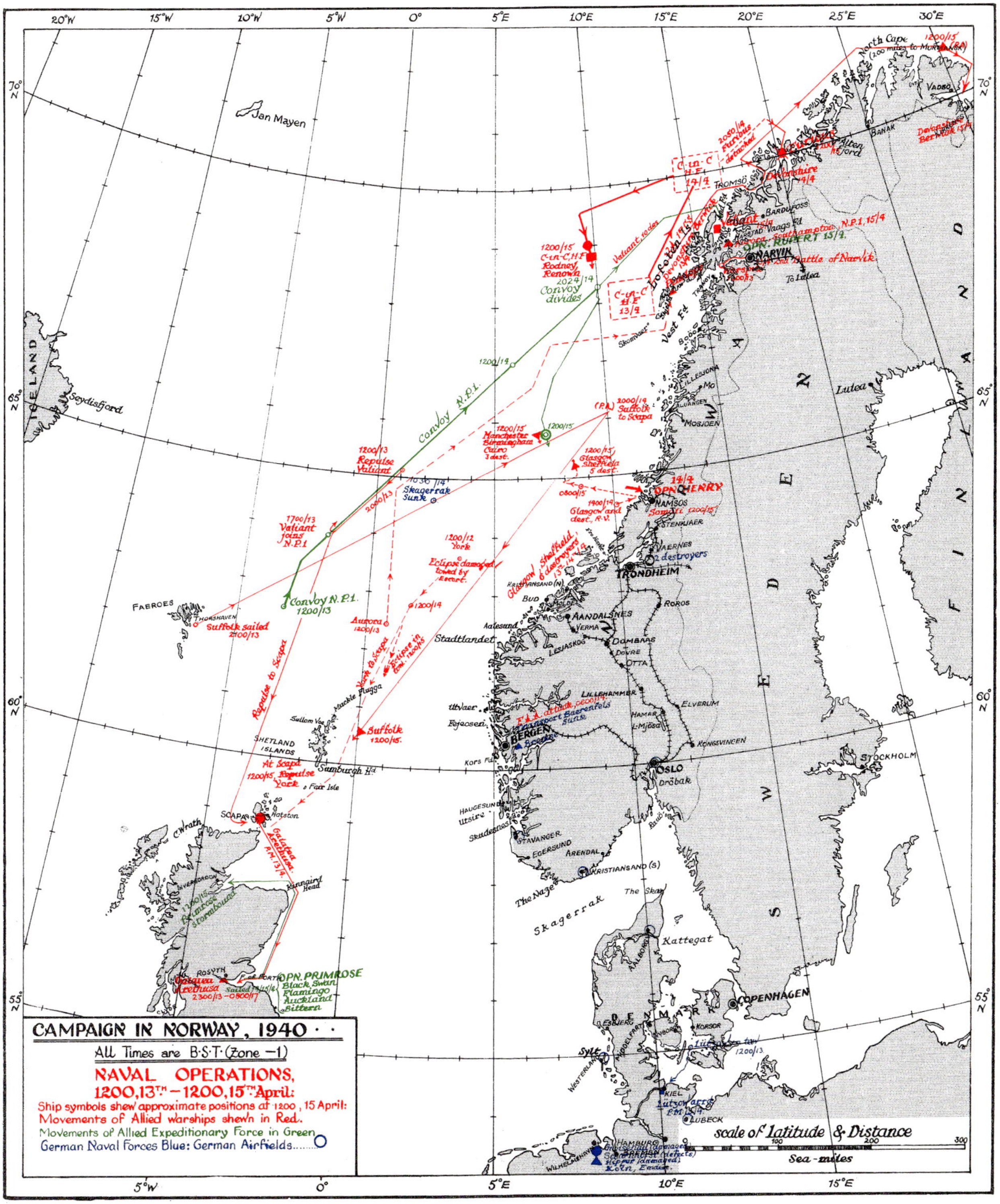

C.B.H. 20101 - Wt. 17299 - Dd. PK.4005 - 500 - 6/51

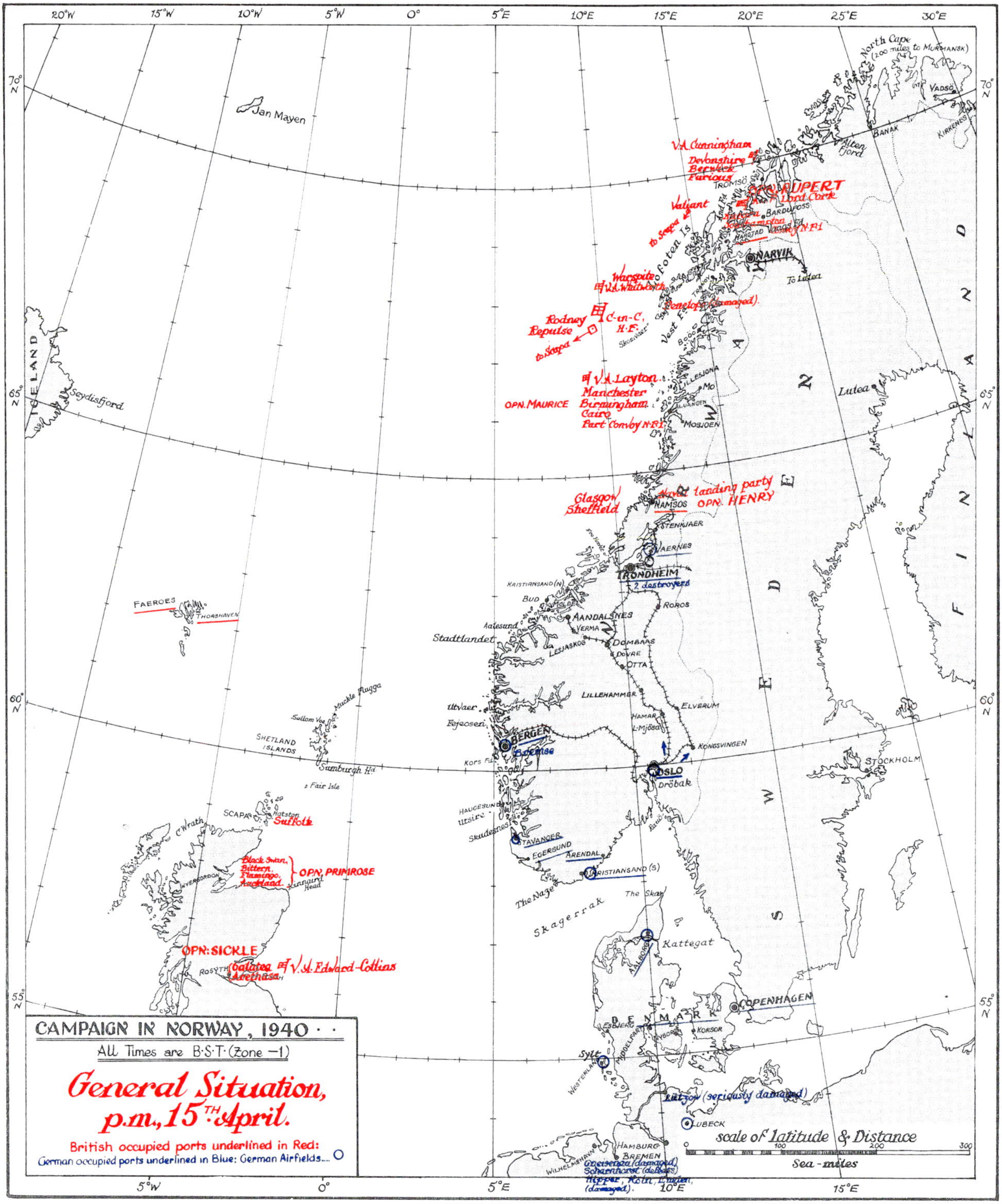

C.B.H. 20101 - Wt. 17299 - Dd. PK 4005-500 - 6/51

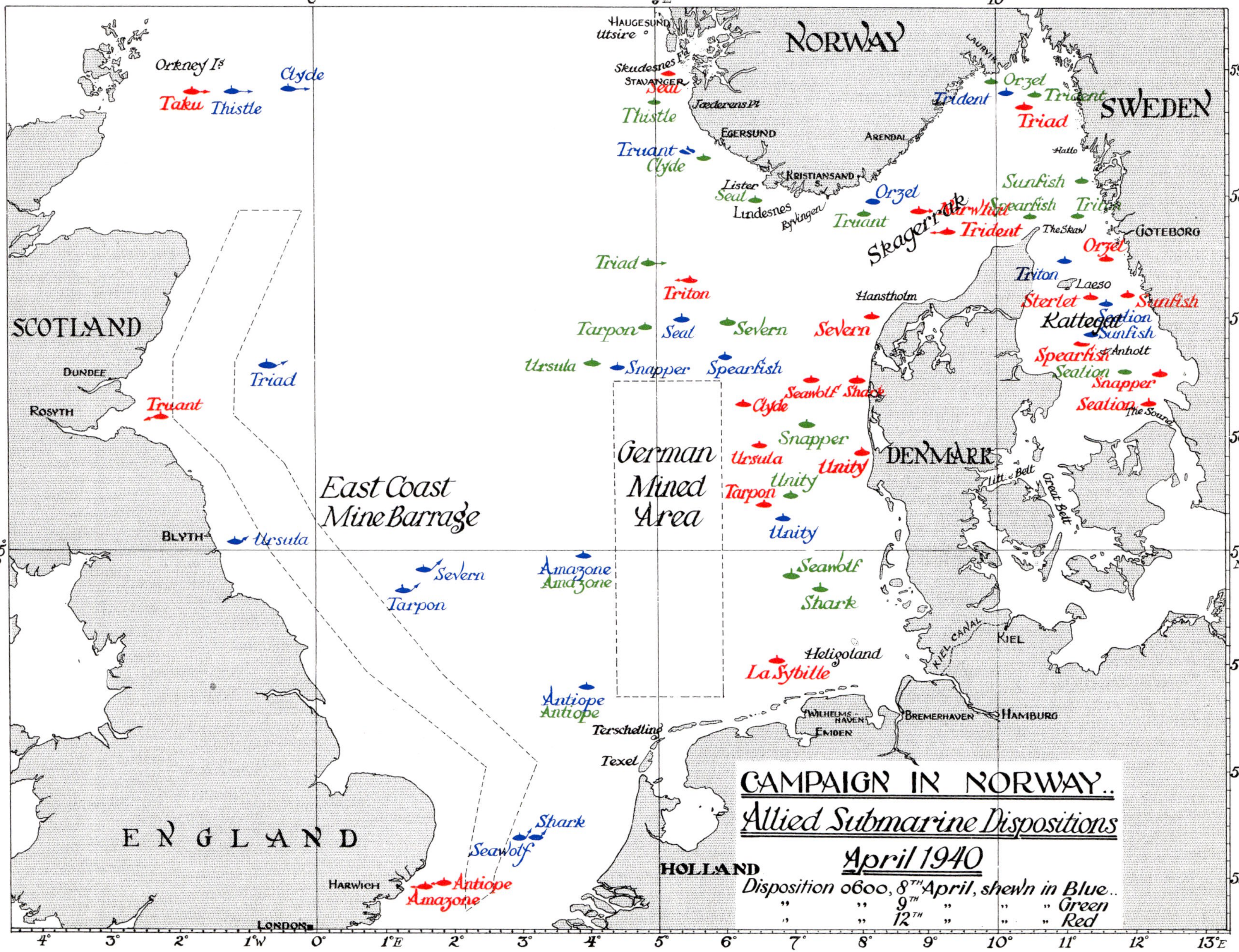

CAMPAIGN IN NORWAY..
Allied Submarine Dispositions
April 1940
Disposition 0600, 8TH April, shewn in Blue..
" " 9TH " " " Green
" " 12TH " " " Red
NORWAY
SWEDEN
DENMARK
SCOTLAND
ENGLAND
HOLLAND
Skagerrak
Kattegat
German Mined Area
East Coast Mine Barrage
Orkney Is
Haugesund
Utsire
Skudesnes Fd
Stavanger
Jæderens Pt
Egersund
Arendal
Kristiansand S.
Lister
Lindesnes
Ryvingen
Laurvik
Hatto
The Skaw
Goteborg
Laeso
Anholt
The Sound
Hanstholm
Little Belt
Great Belt
Kiel
Kiel Canal
Heligoland
Hamburg
Bremerhaven
Wilhelmshaven
Emden
Terschelling
Texel
Dundee
Rosyth
Blyth
Harwich
London
Taku
Thistle
Clyde
Seal
Truant
Triad
Orzel
Trident
Sunfish
Spearfish
Triton
Narwhal
Tarpon
Severn
Ursula
Snapper
Sterlet
Sealion
Seawolf
Shark
Unity
La Sybille
Amazone
Antiope
59°
58°
57°
56°
55° N
54°
53°
52°
4°
3°
2°
1° W
0°
1° E
5°
6°
7°
8°
9°
10°
11°
12°
13° E

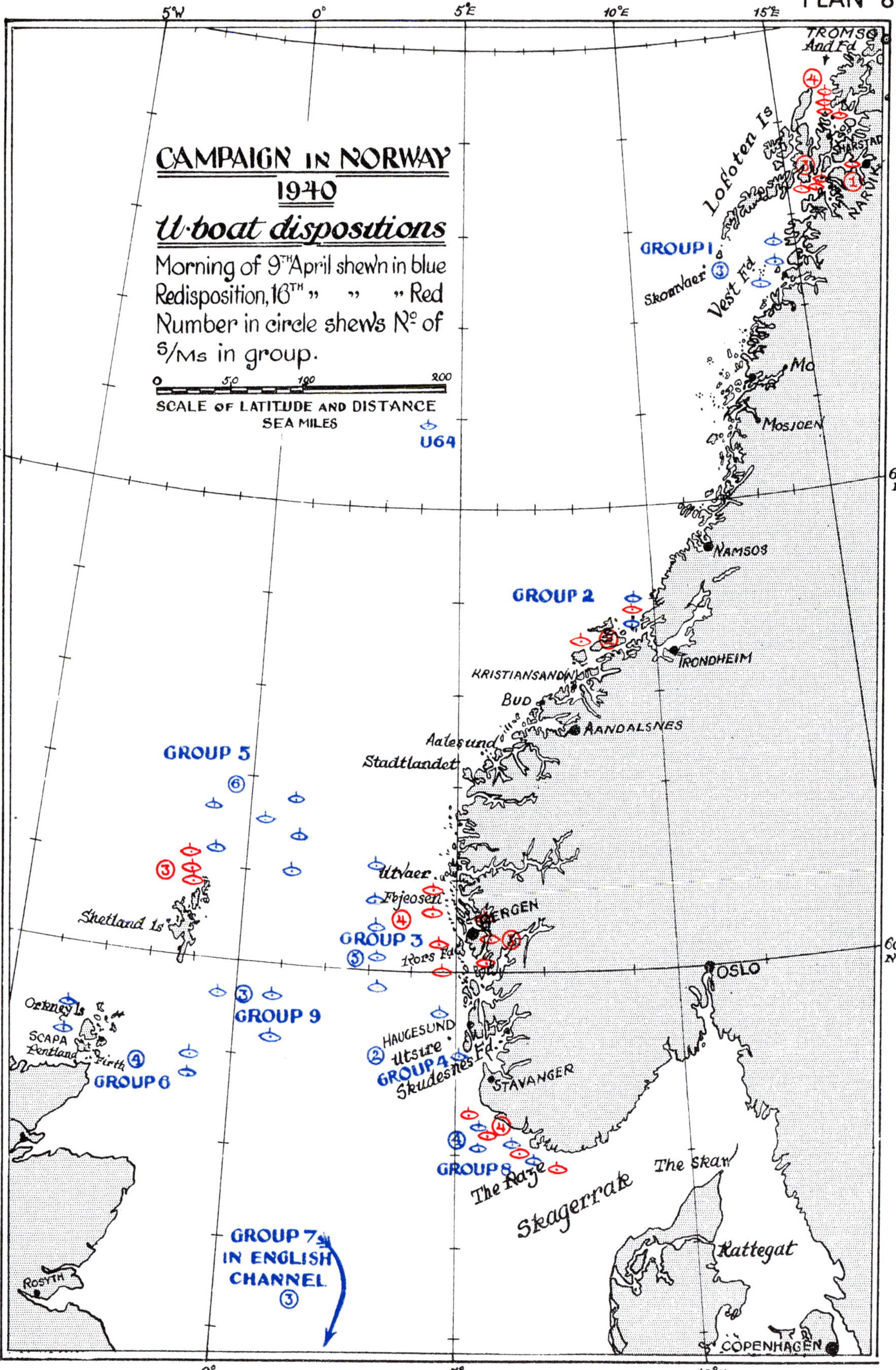
CAMPAIGN IN NORWAY
1940
U-boat dispositions
Morning of 9TH April shewn in blue
Redisposition, 16TH " " " Red
Number in circle shews No. of S/Ms in group.
0 50 100 200
SCALE OF LATITUDE AND DISTANCE
SEA MILES
5°W
0°
5°E
10°E
15°E
65° N
60° N
TROMSO
And Fd
Lofoten Is
HARSTAD
NARVIK
GROUP 1
Skomvaer
Vest Fd
Mo
MOSJOEN
U64
NAMSOS
GROUP 2
TRONDHEIM
KRISTIANSAND
BUD
AANDALSNES
Aalesund
Stadtlandet
GROUP 5
Utvaer
Fejeosen
BERGEN
Shetland Is
GROUP 3
Kors Fd
OSLO
GROUP 9
Orkney Is
SCAPA
Pentland Firth
GROUP 6
HAUGESUND
Utsire
GROUP 4
Skudesnes Fd
STAVANGER
GROUP 8
The Naze
The Skaw
Skagerrak
Kattegat
GROUP 7
IN ENGLISH
CHANNEL
ROSYTH
COPENHAGEN

C.B.H.20101

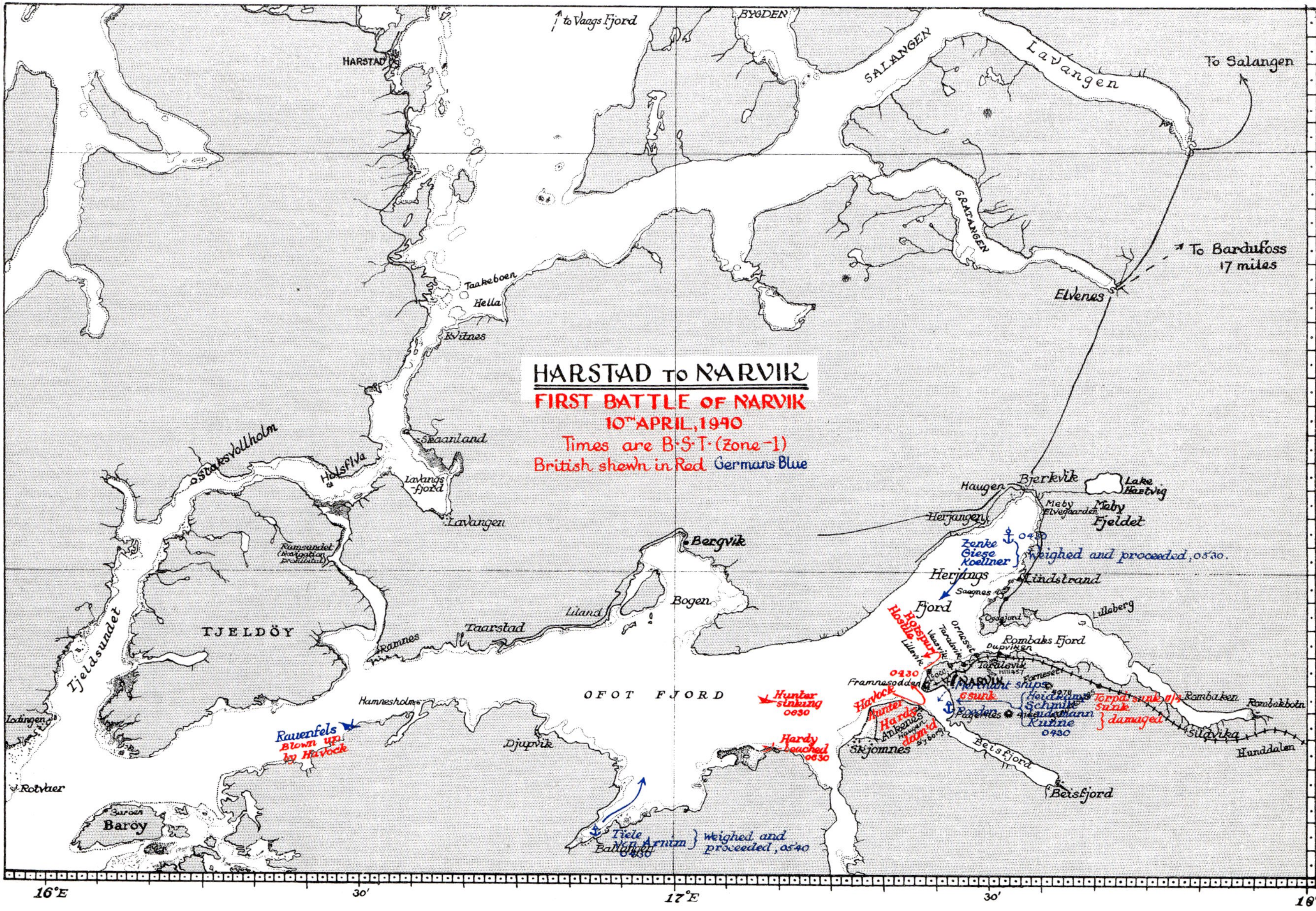
HARSTAD TO NARVIK
FIRST BATTLE OF NARVIK
10TH APRIL, 1940
Times are B.S.T. (Zone -1)
British shewn in Red Germans Blue
to Vaags Fjord
HARSTAD
BYGDEN
SALANGEN
Lavangen
To Salangen
GRATANGEN
To Bardufoss 17 miles
Elvenes
Taakeboen
Hella
Kvitnes
Saanland
Lavangs -fjord
Lavangen
Staksvollholm
Holsflva
Ramsundet
TJELDÖY
Tjeldsundet
Lodingen
Rotvaer
Baröy
Ramnes
Taarstad
Liland
Bogen
Bergvik
Hamnesholm
OFOT FJORD
Djupvik
Rauenfels
Blown up by Havock
Tiele
Von Arnim
weighed and proceeded, 0540
Hunter sinking 0630
Hardy beached 0630
Haugen
Bjerkvik
Lake Hastvig
Herjangen
Meby
Fjeldet
Zenke
Giese
Koellner
weighed and proceeded, 0530.
Herjangs
Lindstrand
Fjord
Saegnes
Lilleberg
Hotspur
Hostile
Lillevik
Ornes
Rombaks Fjord
Dupvikan
Taralsvik
Framnesodden
0430
NARVIK
Havock
Hunter
Hardy
damaged
Ankenes
Skjomnes
Beisfjord
Roeder
Kunne
0430
damaged
Rombaken
Rombakbotn
Sildvika
Hunddalen
68°50′ N
68°45′ N
68°30′ N
68°19′ N
16°E
30′
17°E
30′
18°E

PLAN 10

HARSTAD TO NARVIK
ILLUSTRATING
SECOND BATTLE OF
NARVIK
13TH APRIL, 1940.
Times are B.S.T. (Zone -1)
British shown in Red.
Track of H.M.S. Warspite ———
Positions where Germans were sunk ⚓

PLAN 11

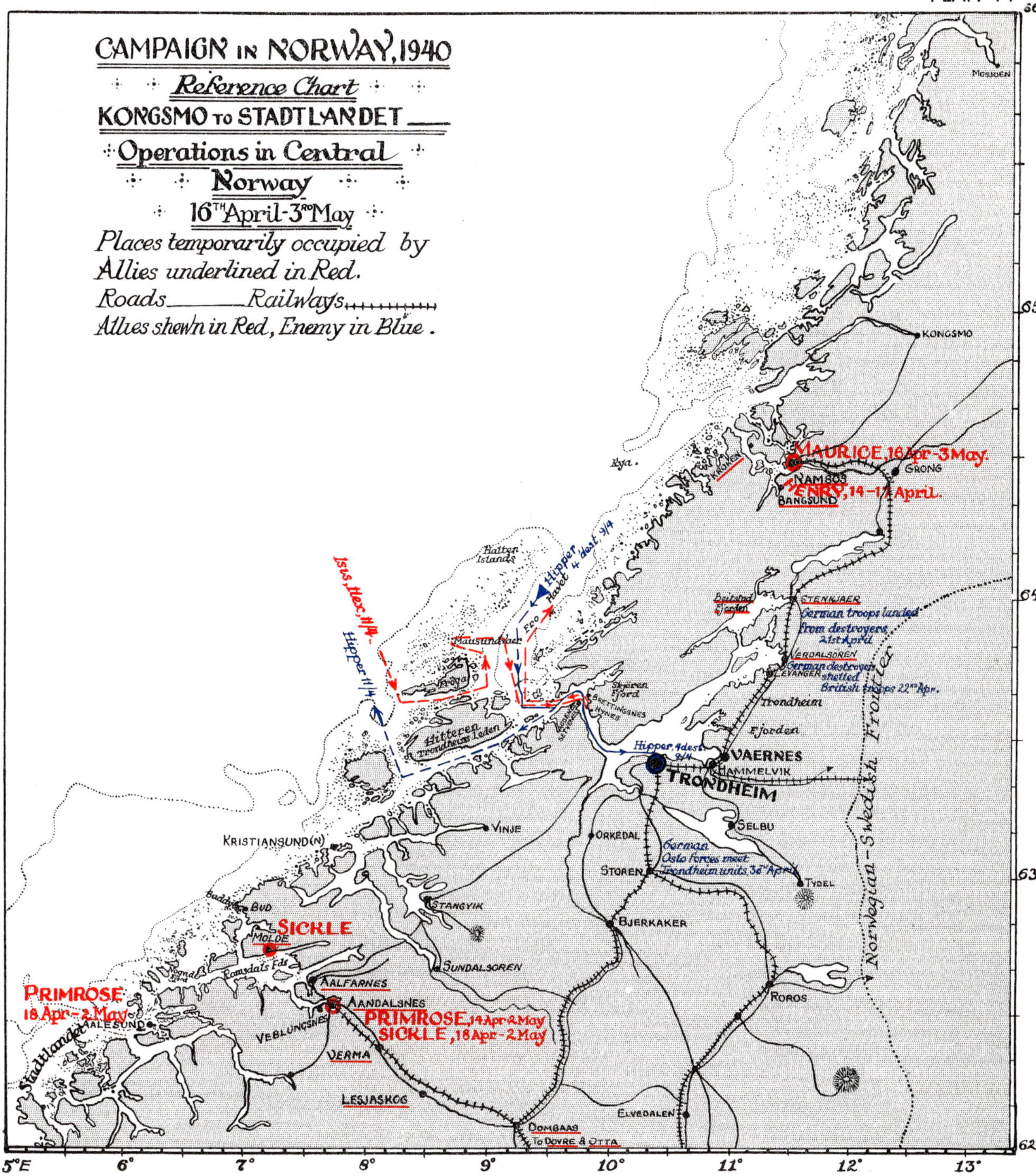

CAMPAIGN IN NORWAY, 1940
Reference Chart
KONGSMO TO STADTLANDET
Operations in Central Norway
16TH April-3RD May
Places temporarily occupied by Allies underlined in Red.
Roads ——— Railways
Allies shewn in Red, Enemy in Blue.
MOSJOEN
KONGSMO
MAURICE, 16 Apr-3 May.
GRONG
NAMSOS
HENRY, 14-17 April.
BANGSUND
Halten Islands
Hipper 11/4
Hipper Havet 4 dest. 9/4
Mausundvaer
Frøya
Hitteren
Trondheim Leden
Skjøren Fjord
BRETTINGSNES
HYNES
STENKJAER
German troops landed from destroyers, 21st April
VERDALSØREN
German destroyers shelled British troops 22nd Apr.
LEVANGER
Trondheim Fjorden
Hipper, 4 dest. 9/4
VAERNES
HAMMELVIK
TRONDHEIM
SELBU
VINJE
KRISTIANSUND (N)
ORKEDAL
German Oslo forces meet Trondheim units, 30th April
STØREN
TYDEL
BUD
STANGVIK
SICKLE
MOLDE
BJERKAKER
Romsdals Fd
SUNDALSØREN
Norwegian-Swedish Frontier
AALFARNES
PRIMROSE 18 Apr-2 May
AANDALSNES
RØROS
AALESUND
PRIMROSE, 14 Apr-2 May
SICKLE, 18 Apr-2 May
VEBLUNGSNES
VERMA
Stadtlandet
LESJASKOG
ELVEDALEN
DOMBAAS
To DOVRE & OTTA
66°
65°
64°
63°
62°
5°E
6°
7°
8°
9°
10°
11°
12°
13°

CAMPAIGN IN NORWAY, 1940.
Reference Chart
TROMSÖ TO MOSJOEN
Operations in Northern
Norway
14TH April–8th June

PLAN 13

CAMPAIGN IN
NORWAY
Reference chart
OSLO FJORD

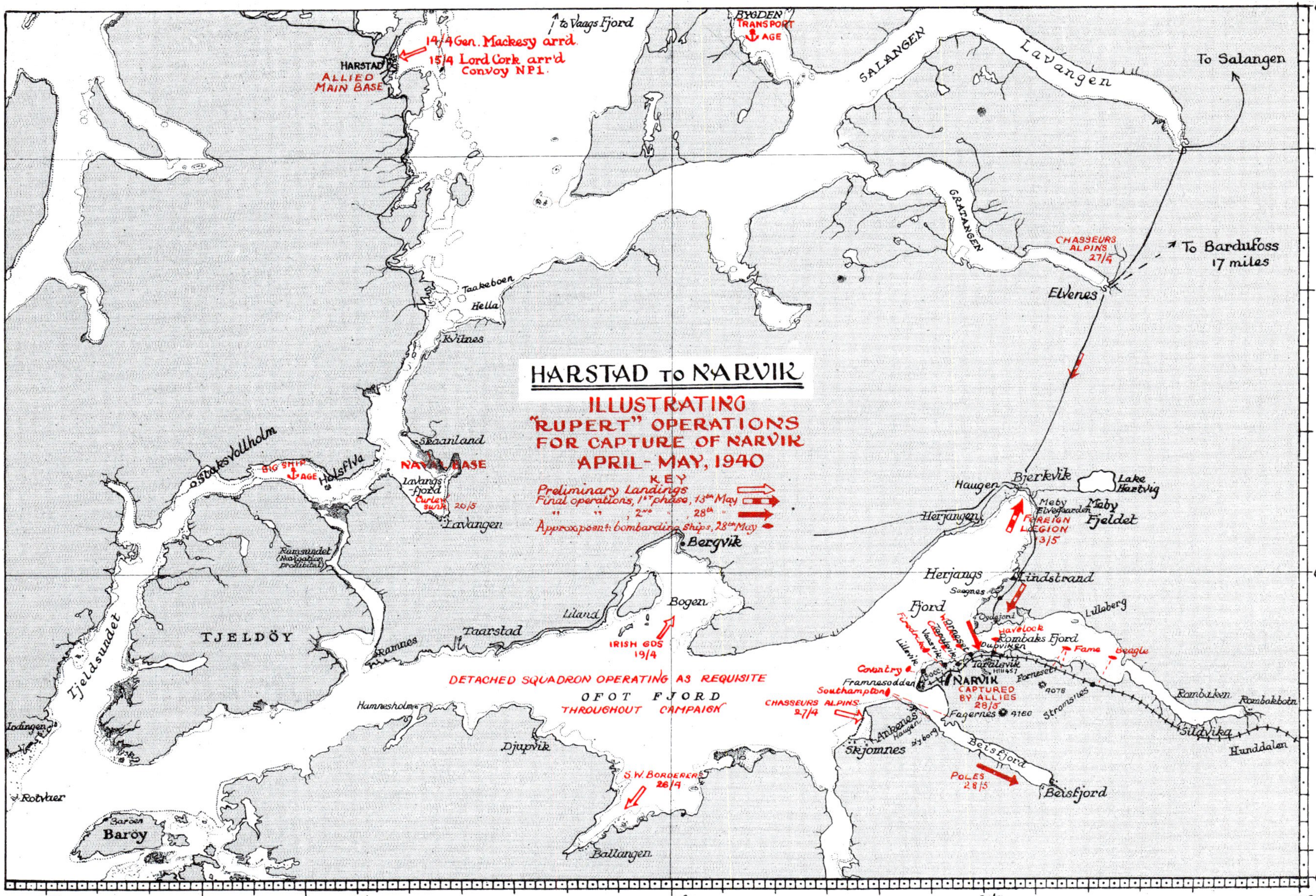
HARSTAD to NARVIK
ILLUSTRATING
"RUPERT" OPERATIONS
FOR CAPTURE OF NARVIK
APRIL-MAY, 1940
KEY
Preliminary Landings
Final operations, 1st phase, 13th May
" " , 2nd " , 28th "
Approx. posn. bombarding ships, 28th May
14/4 Gen. Mackesy arr'd.
15/4 Lord Cork arr'd
Convoy NP1.
HARSTAD
ALLIED MAIN BASE
to Vaags Fjord
BYGDEN
TRANSPORT AGE
SALANGEN
Lavangen
To Salangen
GRATANGEN
CHASSEURS ALPINS 27/4
To Bardufoss 17 miles
Elvenes
Taakeboen
Hella
Kvitnes
Skaanland
NAVAL BASE
Lavangs-fjord
Curlew sunk 20/5
Lavangen
Staksvollholm
BIG SHIP AGE
Holsflva
Ramsundet (Navigation prohibited)
TJELDÖY
Tjeldsundet
Lodingen
Rotvaer
Baröen
Baröy
Bergvik
Bogen
Liland
Taarstad
Rannes
IRISH GDS 19/4
DETACHED SQUADRON OPERATING AS REQUISITE
OFOT FJORD
THROUGHOUT CAMPAIGN
Hamnesholm
Djupvik
S.W. BORDERERS 28/4
Ballangen
Haugen
Bjerkvik
Lake Hartvig
Meby
Elvegaarden
Meby Fjeldet
FOREIGN LEGION 13/5
Herjangen
Herjangs
Fjord
Lindstrand
Lillebérg
Havelock
Rombaks Fjord
Fame
Beagle
Coventry
Framnesodden
NARVIK
CAPTURED BY ALLIES 28/5
Southampton
CHASSEURS ALPINS 27/4
Ankenes
Skjomnes
Fagernes
Beisfjord
POLES 28/5
Lillevik
Taraldsvik
Forneset
Stromsnes
Rombaken
Rombakbotn
Sildvika
Hunddalen
16°E
30'
17°E
30'
18°E
68°50' N
68°45' N
68°30' N
68°19' N

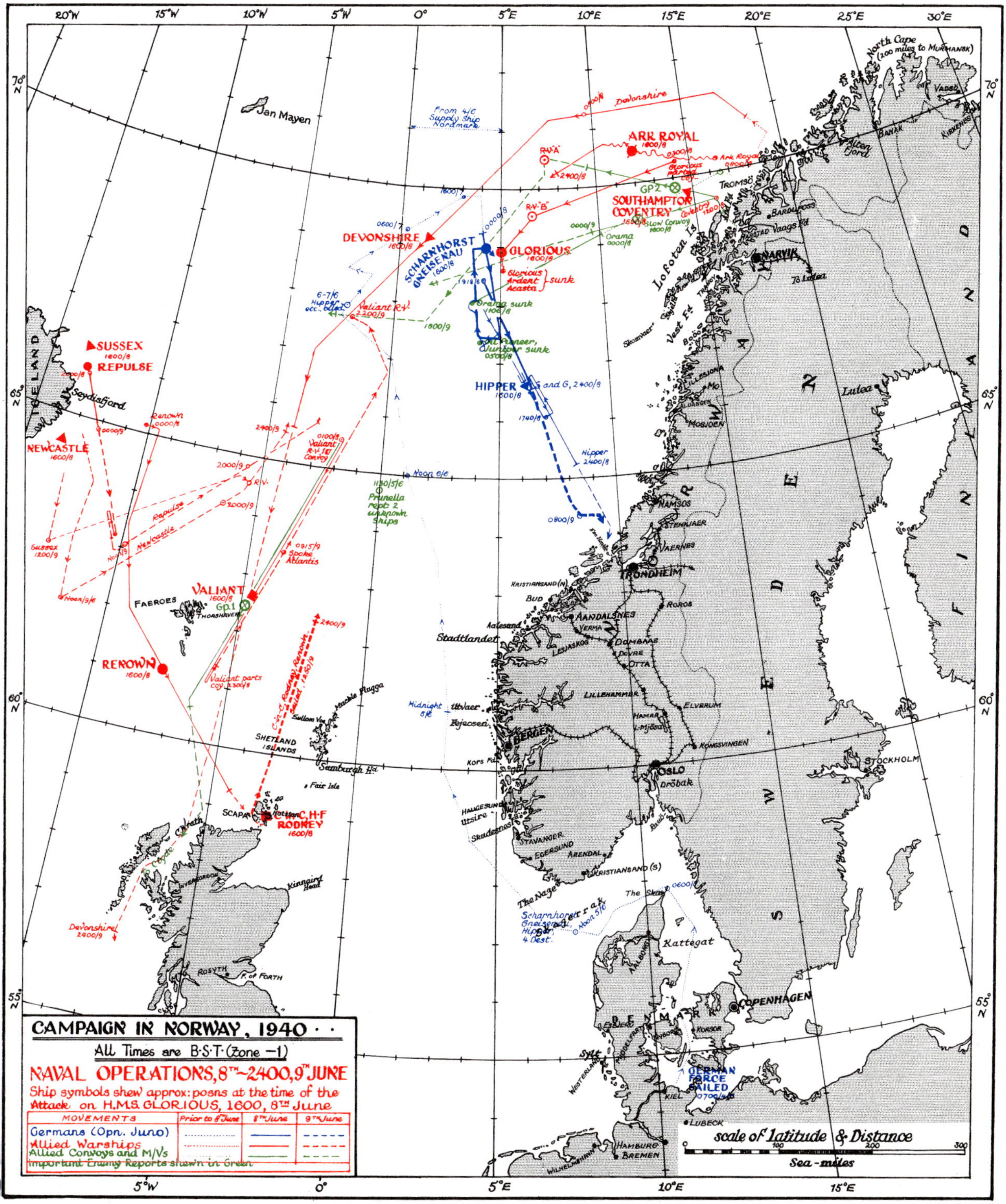
CAMPAIGN IN NORWAY, 1940
All Times are B·S·T·(Zone –1)
NAVAL OPERATIONS, 8TH–2400, 9TH JUNE
Ship symbols shew approx: posns at the time of the Attack on H.M.S. GLORIOUS, 1600, 8TH June
MOVEMENTS
Prior to 8th June
8TH June
9TH June
Germans (Opn. Juno)
Allied Warships
Allied Convoys and M/Vs
Important Enemy Reports shewn in Green
scale of Latitude & Distance
Sea-miles
Jan Mayen
From 4/6 Supply Ship Nordmark
Devonshire
ARK ROYAL 1600/8
Ark Royal
R.V. 'A'
R.V. 'B'
GP 2
SOUTHAMPTON
COVENTRY
Slow Convoy 1600/8
Orama 0000/8
DEVONSHIRE 1600/8
SCHARNHORST GNEISENAU 1600/8
GLORIOUS 1600/8
Glorious Ardent Acasta } sunk
Orama sunk
Oil Pioneer, Juniper sunk
Valiant R.V.
HIPPER 1600/8
and G, 2400/8
Hipper 2400/8
SUSSEX 1600/8
REPULSE
Seydisfjord
ICELAND
Renown 0000/8
NEWCASTLE 1600/8
Repulse
Newcastle
Sussex 1200/9
Noon 8/6
Prunella rept. 2 unknown Ships
VALIANT 1600/8
Gp.1
FAEROES
THORSHAVEN
RENOWN 1600/8
Valiant parts coy
SHETLAND ISLANDS
Sumburgh Hd.
Fair Isle
SCAPA
C.-in-C. H.F RODNEY 1600/8
Kinnaird Head
Cape Wrath
ROSYTH
F. of FORTH
Devonshire 2400/9
North Cape (200 miles to Murmansk)
VADSØ
BANAK
KIRKENES
Alten Fjord
TROMSÖ
BARDUFOSS
NARVIK
To Lulea
Lofoten Is.
Vest Fd.
Bodö
Mo
MOSJÖEN
NAMSOS
STEINKJAER
TRONDHEIM
KRISTIANSAND (N)
BUD
AANDALSNES
RÖROS
Stadtlandet
DOMBAAS
OTTA
LILLEHAMMER
HAMAR
ELVERUM
BERGEN
KONGSVINGEN
OSLO
Dröbak
STOCKHOLM
Utsire
Skudesnes
STAVANGER
EGERSUND
ARENDAL
KRISTIANSAND (S)
The Naze
The Skaw
Kattegat
COPENHAGEN
KORSÖR
GERMAN FORCE SAILED 0700/4/6
KIEL
LUBECK
HAMBURG
BREMEN
WILHELMSHAVN
Lulea
NORWAY
SWEDEN
FINLAND
DENMARK

PLAN 16

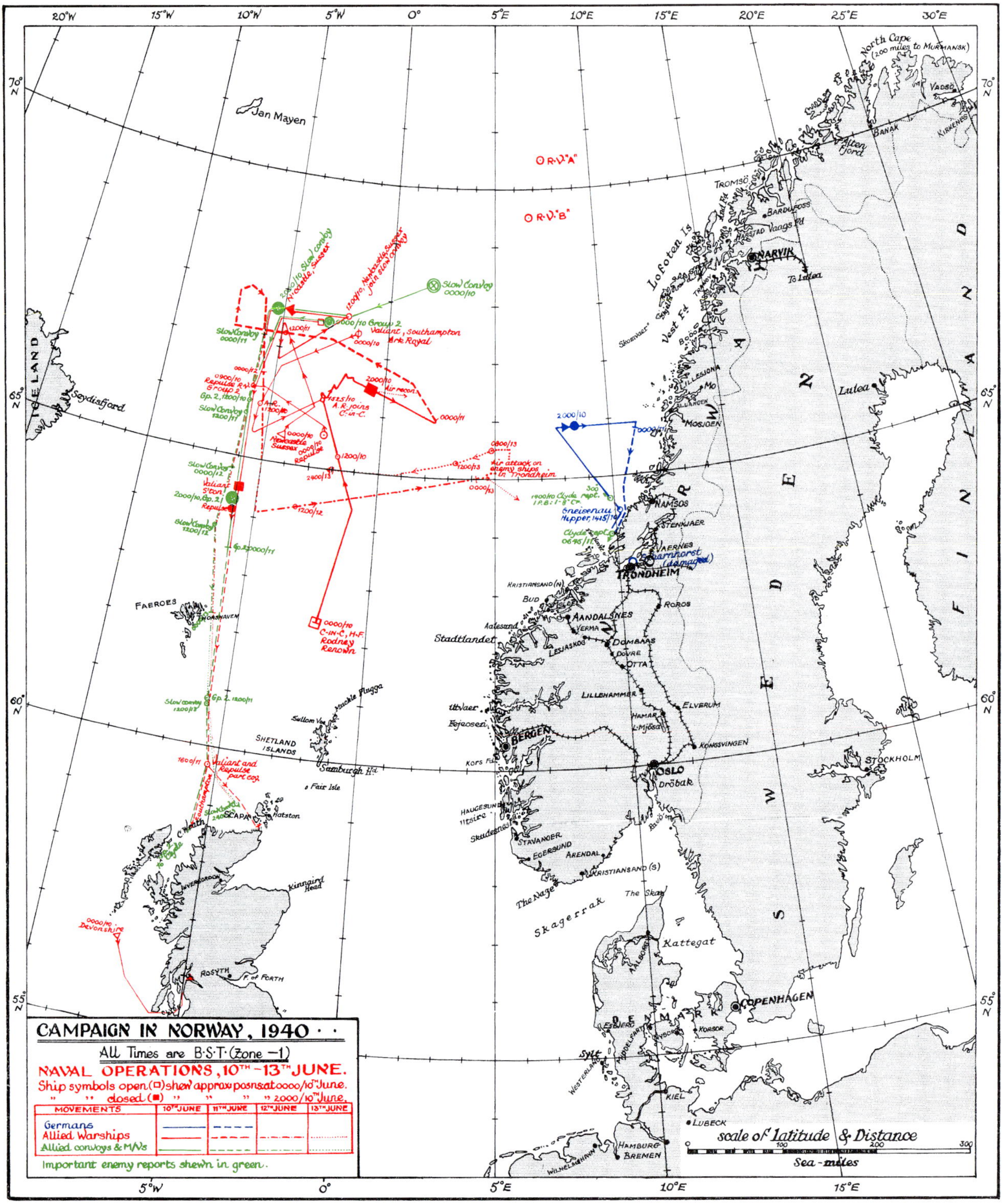

C.B.H. 20101 - Wt. 17299 - Dd. PK. 4005 - 500 - 6/51